To my Mother, Sarah,
in Memory of my Father, Ernest
and to my Wife, Shirley

Contents

Preface

This book is a framework for the study of economic analysis in the context of the open economy of Ireland. The broad objectives are, first, to outline, in a concise but intelligible manner, the method and content of introductory economic analysis of an open economy and second, where appropriate, to indicate the relevance of that analytical structure to the Irish economy in particular. For maximum effectiveness the book should be complemented by lectures and by further reading, but above all, the reader should not attempt to go through this book in the fashion of a novel. *With pencil and paper, he should test his comprehension of each chapter before proceeding to those which follow.* It cannot be emphasised too strongly that a long analytical argument can be understood on a first reading only when it is very elementary indeed, relative to the reader's knowledge of the material. As L. J. Savage wrote in his *Foundations of Statistics:* 'If one wants only to get the gist of it, he may read such material only once; but otherwise he may expect to read it at least once again. Serious reading [of analytical subjects] is best done sitting bolt upright on a hard chair at a desk. Pencil and paper are nearly indispensable; for there are always figures to be sketched and steps in the argument to be verified.' Fuzzy thinking and vague impressions, generated by a desire to read through the text as rapidly as possible, will get the reader nowhere.

This is not just another book on introductory economics:

(i) All of the established texts known to me assume that the economy can, for most purposes, be assumed closed. It is true that those texts do consider some aspects of openness; but these are generally in the nature of afterthoughts. In an extremely large number of respects the analytical framework of established introductory texts yields conclusions which are *fundamentally erroneous* when applied to a highly open economy, such as Ireland. The present text appears to be unique in its emphasis on openness. If we do wish to analyse an open economy we should assume an open economy, not a closed one; otherwise we shall be seriously deceiving ourselves and our audience.

(ii) Hitherto there have been no texts suited to third level education, which blend a moderate amount of economic theory with the institutional environment of the Irish economy. Thus the present text includes a good deal of Irish institutional detail.

(iii) A third respect in which this book differs from other introductory texts on economic analysis is that it is assumed that not many of the readers are very far below average intelligence, and that readers are willing to concentrate and persevere. Thus redundant examples are hopefully few. I have tried to avoid repetition and to provide a concise rather than a long-winded exposition.

It is not assumed that the reader has any prior knowledge of economic analysis. Almost all the material in the text is drawn from lectures in introductory economics given by me at Cornell University, the University of California at Berkeley and the University of New Hampshire in the USA, and at UCC and UCD in Ireland. The pattern set is therefore that of a general course in economics suited to first year university students. I have also experimented with most of this material in lectures delivered to businessmen and academic audiences outside universities.

Appropriately adapted, the text provides suitable preparation for economics examinations other than those at the end of first year at university (for example, the examinations at the National Institute for Higher Education and at the colleges of technology, as well as those of the Institute of Bankers in Ireland and the accountancy bodies). It is hoped that the text will also be of value to the general reader who wishes to make sensible judgments concerning the open economy in which he lives. I would greatly appreciate receipt of readers' suggestions in regard to how the text might be improved. I can assure those who contact me that all communications shall be acknowledged in writing.

Almost the entire manuscript was prepared and completed in the 1978/79 academic year when I was on leave from UCD, at Cornell University. The facilities provided by Cornell were superb.

I owe great debts to a large number of economists who read parts of the manuscript and made constructive comments. In particular, I would like to mention Patrick T. Geary and Moore McDowell at UCD, and Mark Gertler at Cornell. At the risk of causing offence by omission, I would like to acknowledge the receipt of other written comments and suggestions from James Meenan, John Murphy, Louis Smith, John Sheehan and Seamus Sheehy (all of UCD); Liam Ebrill (Cornell); Padraig McGowan (Central Bank of Ireland); Rory O'Donnell (University of Cambridge); Bob Puth (University of New Hampshire) and Brendan Walsh (ESRI).

For providing oral comments or information on particular issues I would like to thank Seamus Heslin and Patrick Lynch (UCD), John

Walsh (Restrictive Practices Commission) and John McKeon and Padraic White of the IDA; however, I must add that Patrick Lynch was of invaluable assistance in a large number of other respects also. Not all of the advice received was accepted by me; so I alone am responsible for remaining errors. Finally, I would like to mention that my greatest debt of all is to Mrs Pat Paucke, my secretary at Cornell, who typed two versions of the manuscript at great speed, cheerfully and expertly.

Desmond A. G. Norton
Ithaca, New York
24 June 1979

Postscript: I wish to express my gratitude to Alex Miller of the IMI for his competent editorial work and for his professional handling of publication arrangements. I also wish to thank my printers, Mount Salus Press Ltd. for an excellent job on their part. In particular I would like to mention Mannix Cullinan, Edward Finn, Kevin McFeely and Michael Norris. Any errors remaining from the proof stage are mine alone.

PART ONE

THE SCOPE AND METHOD OF ECONOMICS

CHAPTER 1

The Scope of Economics

Economic problems affect the daily lives of everyone. Economics (sometimes called Political Economy) encompasses an extremely broad range of questions, including the following:

(i) Why in recent years has the per capita real income of Irish citizens — the purchasing power of the average citizen's money income — been higher than ever before? What can be done to increase the rate of growth of output and employment in Ireland?

(ii) Why did Ireland experience high inflation in the 1970s? Was it due to aggressive bargaining by trade unions? Could inflation have been reduced substantially by action on the part of the monetary authorities, or by some appropriate fiscal policies — public policies concerning government revenues and expenditures? Or did we inevitably experience roughly the same rate of inflation as the UK by virtue of the sterling link — the fixed exchange rate which our governments maintained between the Irish pound and the UK currency unit?

(iii) To what extent can government create employment in the economy by increasing the National Debt — by financing government expenditures by borrowing?

(iv) Suppose that the government's current budget is initially balanced (i.e., its current expenditures are matched by an equal sum in tax and other current receipts), that it increases its current expenditures and also raises tax rates so as to maintain a balanced budget. Would output and employment in the economy tend to increase, or would the two policy changes tend to offset each other in their effects on output and employment?

(v) In what manner must firms allocate resources if they are to maximise profits obtainable from the employment of those resources? And how must a household allocate its expenditures between different goods if it is to maximise the satisfaction obtainable from its money income?

(vi) In what sense, if any, do monopolistic market structures involve waste of the economy's resources? What are the effects of public policy towards monopoly?

3

(vii) Suppose a per unit tax is imposed on transactions (purchases or sales) in a competitive market. What are the effects? In what sense is it irrelevant whether the tax is administratively levied on sellers or buyers?

(viii) What effect would an increase in the demand for housing have on house rentals and on the incomes of landowners, construction workers and others? Would it be possible for the authorities (central government, urban corporations or county councils) to tax the resulting increase in the incomes of landowners without affecting their incentives concerning how they wish to utilise their land?

(ix) Suppose that all income earners in the economy attempted to save 50 per cent of their incomes. Would aggregate savings increase? Or would aggregate income fall, possibly leading to a lower *level* of national savings than initially?

These questions are quite typical of those analysed in economics. Very frequently the answers which on first sight appear to be 'obviously' correct turn out to be fundamentally erroneous when subjected to economic analysis. Note that the words 'should' or 'ought' appear nowhere in the questions: as is emphasised below, economics describes rather than prescribes. It examines the implications of pursuing objectives but is not concerned with whether the objectives are good or bad, desirable or not.

Economics Defined: Ends and Means

Due perhaps to the wide range of questions encompassed by economics and due to the rapid evolution of the discipline, economists themselves have not always agreed on a concise definition of the subject. The great economist Alfred Marshall (1842-1924) defined economics as 'a study of mankind in the ordinary business of life; it examines that part of individual and social actions which is most closely connected with the attainment and with the use of the material requisites of well-being. Thus it is on the one side a study of wealth; and on the other, and more important side, a part of the study of man'.[1] This definition is very broad indeed — so much so that it fails to pinpoint the central characteristics of *the* economic problem. In at least one respect it is typical of definitions in the English language economics literature until the early decades of this century. These tended to regard economics as the study of the causes of wealth or of economic welfare, with the latter defined as 'that part of social welfare that can be brought directly or indirectly into relation with the measuring rod of money'.[2] Thus what many regard as the first truly influential book on economics, written by the Scotsman Adam Smith and published in 1776, bore the title *An Inquiry into the Nature and Causes of the Wealth of Nations.* In the century following Smith's work economists tended to define their discipline as the study of the nature, production and distribution of wealth. But as the nineteenth century approached its close the emphasis shifted from wealth to welfare. These traditions in the perceived scope of economics reached their culmination in Pigou's *Wealth and Welfare* and in the same author's subsequent book *The Economics of Welfare* (final edition, 1932).

In 1932 Lionel Robbins suggested a concise definition which is acceptable in spirit to the majority of economists. What Robbins sought was an analytical rather than a classificatory definition. By this is meant a definition which would not focus on certain facts or actions or causes, which would be termed 'economic', as distinct from others which would be deemed 'non-economic'; rather, what Robbins sought was a definition which would pinpoint what the truly economic *aspect* of human behaviour is. By the standards of this requirement classificatory definitions, such as those which regard economics as the study of the causes of wealth or economic welfare, are rejected. A central objection to such definitions is that even if there were a precise concept 'economic welfare' there would still remain the *economic* problem of how time, effort and other resources must rationally be *allocated* to the pursuit of 'economic' and 'non-economic' activities. Furthermore, classificatory definitions which regard economics as the study of the causes of wealth or of economic welfare subsume the study of technology as part of economics — but few if any of us would agree with that.

Robbins's definition is that, 'Economics is the science which studies human behaviour as a relationship between ends and scarce means which have alternative uses'.[3]

Some clarification is appropriate. The *ends* (objectives, desires or goals) of individuals, governments and other groups, are many, and are normally capable of being ranked in order of priority. However, few if any decision-makers can attain all their objectives. (If they could they would have no further wants; for example they would desire neither more income nor more leisure.) The key constraint on our ability to attain all our ends is the fact that the *means* at our disposal are scarce. These means may be factors of production — land, labour, capital equipment and enterprise — and/or what are generally termed policy instruments, for example (in the case of government), tax rates, the exchange rate for the currency, administrative orders of various kinds, etc. Apart from being limited, the means usually have *alternative uses*. Thus the use of a means to pursue one objective generally implies that the means cannot at the same time be used to pursue other objectives. For example, a government's decision to change the tax system to foster economic growth may imply that it must forgo its use to promote what it regards as an equitable distribution of disposable income among individuals. Or if a person decides to allocate more of his time to the pursuit of income (via labour) he must normally forgo leisure. Similarly if at a given level of technical knowledge the nation wishes to produce more defence goods it must normally utilise its labour and other resources more fully (thereby forgoing leisure) *or* it must forgo the production of those non-defence goods which it could have produced had it not decided to divert resources (away from leisure and the production of non-defence goods) towards expansion of defence. Hence every decision involving time and scarce means for the pursuit of one end involves the relinquishment of their use for the pursuit of another: it has an economic aspect.

Thus given that he has decided on a set of objectives and ranked them in order of priority, the economic problem of any decision-maker is how to allocate rationally the means available to him among competing uses. Note that if the means were not scarce — if, for example, they were unlimited — an economic problem might not arise and there might be no need for the study of economics. For if all objectives could be attained simultaneously we would indeed be in Utopia. The *choice* of means in the pursuit of ends, necessitated by the *scarcity* of means, is that *aspect* of human behaviour which is the core subject-matter of economics. Because the means are scarce the rational decision-maker seeks to make a sensible choice in the utilisation of those means in the pursuit of his objectives. If he is rational, that is, he *economises*.

What, then, are the boundaries of the subject-matter of economics? In the words of Robbins, the analytical conception of economics we have adopted

> does not attempt to pick out certain *kinds* of behaviour, but focuses attention on a particular *aspect* of behaviour, the form imposed by the influence of scarcity. It follows from this, therefore, that in so far as it presents this aspect, any kind of human behaviour falls within the scope of economic

generalisations. We do not say that the production of potatoes is economic activity and the production of philosophy is not. We say rather that, in so far as either kind of activity involves the relinquishment of other desired alternatives, it has an economic aspect. There are no limitations on the subject-matter of Economic Science save this.[4]

The Robbins definition clarifies the distinction between economics and technology. The confusion which once existed on this point (for example, by defining economics as the study of the causes of wealth or of economic welfare) 'derived from the fact that both economics and technology were concerned with the phenomenon of production, and it was not always possible to distinguish in what way one was concerned and in what way the other'.[5] The distinction lies in the fact that technology is concerned with the feasibility of means for attaining certain ends, leaving entirely out of consideration both the degree of scarcity of means and the order of priority of the ends. Economics, on the other hand, accepting what technology has to contribute, evaluates the means according to their scarcity and the order of priority of the ends.

Notions of benefit and cost are implicit in Robbins's definition. As economists we do not attach any moral content to those words. In economic analysis the benefit of any decision in regard to the use of means is the contribution it makes to the attainment of specified objectives. The economic costs (termed *opportunity costs*) of utilising means in any particular manner are the alternatives forgone by so doing. A decision to utilise means in the pursuit of a particular objective usually implies forgoing the use of those means towards the attainment of other objectives. The notion 'opportunity cost' is perhaps best understood with the aid of an example. To keep analysis simple we consider a case in which choice is being made between the production of only two goods.

Every nation has to make choices between production of goods for consumption by individuals and production of goods for defence. Given the factors of production available to the economy in any year, the more defence goods it is decided to produce, the smaller the potential output of consumers' goods. If the amount of labour-time and of the other factors of production is fixed, the nature of the choice between defence and consumption is as depicted in Figure 1. The quantities of defence goods and of consumers' goods are measured along the vertical and horizontal axes, respectively.

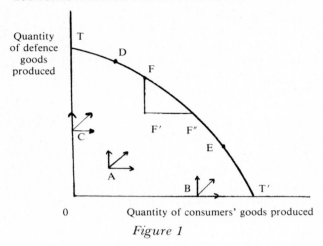

Figure 1

Any point in the diagram represents a certain output of both goods. If the economy's resources were unlimited, it could produce as many of each as might be desired. However, the fixity of available resources implies certain *trade-offs* between production of one good and the other; the more of one produced the less the potential output of the other. Given its resource endowments the downward-sloping curve TT' — called a *production possibility curve* — separates those combinations of goods which it can and cannot produce. If it allocated all its factors of production — all available land, labour, capital equipment and enterprise — to defence, it could produce OT of such goods; if, on the other hand, it allocated all its resources to production of consumers' goods, it could produce OT' of those goods. The production possibility curve represents the *maximum* amount of one good which the economy could produce if it has been decided to produce any particular amount of the other good. The key feature of the curve is that it slopes down from left to right. As we have depicted it, the curve is also concave (bow shaped), but we shall defer consideration of that property until Chapter 26. The downward slope reflects the fact that the more of one good the economy produces, the less of the other it can produce if it is fully utilising its resources. Production levels above and to the right of TT' are unattainable. Combinations below TT' (such as points A, B or C) are attainable, but inefficient. They are inefficient because (as the arrows indicate) more of one good could be produced with the given resources without necessitating a reduction in the amount produced of the other good.

But production levels along TT′ are both attainable and *efficient* in the sense that along TT′ it would be impossible to increase production of one good without (via reallocation of factors of production) reducing the quantity produced of the other. Given the government's preferences between defence and consumption, its central economic problem is to decide on how to allocate resources so that production will take place at the government's preferred point on TT′. (If the government behaves rationally, and if its choice is between consumption and defence only, it *must* seek to guide production to somewhere on TT′. Why?) If defence is paramount in its priorities, it may select a point such as D; if it attaches greater weight to consumption, it may seek to guide the economy to a point like E.

The slope of the production possibility curve — sometimes called a transformation curve because it indicates the extent to which one good can indirectly be transformed into another via reallocation of factors of production — indicates the economic or opportunity cost of one good in terms of the other. Suppose, for example, that the economy is producing on TT′ at point F. Then if the community wishes to have F′F″ more consumer goods, it must forgo the production of FF′ defence goods. This reflects the fact that since the means are scarce and have alternative uses, a decision to have more consumption goods implies a cost in terms of output of defence goods forgone. So there really is no free lunch: if the nation wants more of one good, given its leisure time and factor endowments, it must forgo production of other goods.

We can summarise as follows: Economics is the study of the relationship between human objectives and the scarce means, which normally have alternative uses, by which individuals and groups attempt to attain those objectives. It is the scarcity of means, which implies that not all objectives can be attained simultaneously, that gives rise to economic problems. The key aspects of the discipline are *scarcity* of means and the resulting necessity of *choice* in the allocation of those means among competing ends. The ends or objectives are many. But the scarcity of means which have alternative uses implies that the greater the extent to which one set of objectives is attained, the less is the potential attainment of others — there are *trade-offs* among the ends. That is because means must be diverted from the pursuit (or potential pursuit) of one set of objectives towards the pursuit of others. The ultimate economic costs, the opportunity costs, of pursuing any one set of objectives are the most beneficial alternatives forgone by utilising means in the pursuit of that set of objectives. Thus economics investigates the implications for use of scarce means of pursuing actual or hypothetical ends; the effects, on the attainment of ends, of using particular sets of possible means; changes in the effectiveness of means (such changes may occur due to changes outside the economic system itself, but the latter changes are beyond the scope of the economic analysis of a particular economic system); and the trade-offs between actual or hypothetical ends.

Some comment on the meaning of *rationality* in economics is appropriate. In economics we accept the objectives of decision-makers as *given*; the economist as economist does not state what the objectives ought to be for behaviour to be rational. In economics the word rational pertains to the manner in which means are used in the pursuit of objectives. A particular utilisation of means is deemed rational in a specific context only if the means are utilised in such a manner as to make the greatest possible contribution to the decision-maker's objectives.

It is recognised that Robbins's definition of economics is rather abstract. However, the nine questions posed at the beginning of this chapter do fall within its scope. The reader is urged to refer back to confirm this claim. Each of the questions is concerned with actual or possible objectives of individuals or groups. And the answer to each inevitably involves consideration of, or implications for, means, as follows:

(i') The objective in question (i) can be construed as being high growth in national output and employment. The means by which these can be pursued pertain, *inter alia,* to (*a*) the structure and size of the nation's physical capital stock (reflecting decisions in the past to incur costs by refraining from consumption) and (*b*) public policy concerning government revenues (tax rates etc.) and expenditures (their levels and structures).

(ii') A low rate of inflation may be the principal objective in question (ii). As will be indicated later, the means by which this could be attained involve considerations of exchange rate and monetary policies.

(iii') The objective here is employment; the principal means, government expenditure financed by borrowing. Note that the size of the National Debt might itself be an objective as well as a means for affecting employment. Contrary to what is sometimes assumed, this kind of situation is *not* inconsistent with Robbins's definition of economics. If employment is positively related to (i.e., moves in the same direction as) government expenditure financed by borrowing, and if government wishes to maximise employment while simultaneously keeping borrowing as low as possible, then its central problem of choice is in deciding the extent to which it will increase borrowing to increase employment. Its task, that is, is to find the appropriate trade-off between borrowing and the creation of employment.

(iv') The question posed concerns the effects of manipulating means on possible ends, the two mentioned ends being national output and employment.

(v') The concern here is allocation of means — factors of production or bundles of consumer goods — among competing uses in order to pursue the two clearly stated objectives efficiently.

(vi') The objectives are not explicitly stated. However, it can be shown that, depending on the objectives set for the operation of the economy as a whole, profit maximising monopolists *may* misallocate the nation's resources (its ultimate means, the factors of production) in the sense that these resources might not be allocated in the most rational way from the standpoint of society's objectives.

(vii') An increase in government revenue may be the immediate objective here, the tax rate being a means. However, governments generally have objectives other than raising revenue. They will accordingly wish to know the several effects of the tax — its impact on resource allocation in the economy, how it affects standards of living of different social classes, etc. The extent to which imposition of the tax interferes with the attainment of other objectives is the ultimate economic cost of raising revenue via the tax.

(viii') If, for reasons unrelated to the prices of housing, consumers come to desire more housing than previously, then either their incomes or their objectives (or both) have changed. Housing prices are likely to rise in consequence. It is also likely that increased housing demand would bid up the prices of scarce means — for example, land prices/rents and the wages of construction workers — reflecting their increased scarcity relative to demand. If factor prices have changed, the pattern of income distribution has almost surely changed. Governments may have certain objectives concerning that, and may accordingly seek to devise means (such as lump-sum taxes) to affect income distribution without significantly affecting the supply of factors of production such as land.

(ix') Individuals saving, say, 10 per cent of their incomes may wish to save more. Their means may be longer hours of work, or simply decisions to refrain from consuming 50 per cent of their incomes. It will be shown later that their objective of increased savings may be frustrated: one person's consumption expenditure is another's income, so if all individuals refrain from consuming, aggregate expenditure and income are likely to fall. It is therefore possible that aggregate savings will fall rather than rise.

The Neutrality of Economics

Having established a working definition of economics, we examine its implications. The principal one from the standpoint of scientific method is that economics is a positive rather than a normative science (if, indeed, there can be such a thing as a normative *science*); it is concerned with what is or could be rather than what ought to be. Normative disciplines (such as ethics or aesthetics) are concerned with what ought to be. Economics is entirely neutral between ends. There is nothing in economic analysis which indicates that certain ends are good or bad. For economics simply highlights implications (for means) of pursuing whatever ends may be chosen. Note that the use of the adjectives 'economic' and 'uneconomic' to describe particular policies can be misleading. For the criterion of economy following from Robbins's definition is the pursuit of specific objectives with least disposal of means. It does, therefore, make sense to say of a certain policy that it is uneconomical (economical) if, in order to achieve certain ends, it uses more (no more) scarce means than are necessary. But it may not be intelligible to use these adjectives to describe the ends themselves. For 'there are no economic ends. There are only economical and uneconomical ways of achieving given ends'.[6]

The Irish economist J.E. Cairnes (1824-75) of TCD, Queens College Galway (subsequently UCG) and University College London, was one of the first to forcefully emphasise the neutrality of economics. It is worthwhile quoting him in some detail:

> Political Economy stands apart from all particular systems of social or industrial experience. It has nothing to do with laissez-faire [i.e., unregulated private enterprise economies in which government plays little role] any more than with communism . . . It pronounces no judgement on the worthiness or desirableness of the ends aimed at in such systems . . . [Economics is to be regarded] as standing neutral between competing social schemes; neutral, as the science of Mechanics stands neutral between competing plans of railway construction, in which expense, for instance, as well as mechanical efficiency, is to be considered . . .

It is sometimes supposed that because Political Economy comprises in its expositions theories of wages, profits, and rent, the science is *therefore* committed to the approval of our present mode of industrial life, under which three distinct classes, labourers, capitalists and landlords, receive remuneration in those forms. Under this impression, some social reformers, whose ideal of industrial life involves a modification of our existing system, have thought themselves called upon to denounce and deride economic science . . . But this is a complete mistake. Economic science has no more connection with our present industrial system than the science of mechanics has with our present system of railways. Our existing railway lines have been laid down according to the best extant mechanical knowledge; but we do not think it necessary on this account, as a preliminary to improving our railways, to denounce mechanical science. If wages, profits, and rent find a place in economic theories, this is simply because these *are* the forms [under which distribution occurs] as society is now constituted. They are phenomena which need to be explained. But it comes equally within the province of the economist to exhibit the working of any proposed modification of the system.[7]

Economics and Public Policy

The fact that economics is a neutral science — that it is concerned with the relationship between ends and means rather than with the ends *per se* — may suggest that economics is irrelevant to policy. Such a conclusion — with which we certainly do not agree — might be inferred from Nassau Senior (1790-1864) who wrote that the conclusions of the economist, 'whatever be their generality and their truth, do not authorise him in adding a single syllable of advice . . . The business of a Political Economist is neither to recommend nor to dissuade, but to state general principles'.[8] We note, however, that Senior himself was not an economist who hesitated from advising policy-makers.

When an economist suggests that a certain objective ought to be pursued he is making a *value-judgment* — he is expressing opinions concerning what ought to be reflecting his own personal values — rather than making a conclusion within the confines of economics. In this context it is necessary to distinguish between economist *qua* economist and economist *qua* ordinary mortal. It is not the job of the economist *qua* economist to pronounce on the desirability of pursuing certain objectives; as an economist he is interested in ends only in so far as they have implications for rational disposal of means. But an economist is as much a human as is a physicist, a labourer or an artist. As ordinary humans, economists often make pronouncements concerning the ends which they believe ought to be pursued. But strictly speaking in doing so they are acting in their capacity as ordinary citizens rather than as economists. For there are no economic ends; there are only economic and uneconomic ways of pursuing given ends.

In the context of policy, economics consists of propositions of the form 'if you want to attain those objectives efficiently, then you must do this'; 'if that is your objective, then the manner in which you propose to go about it is not rational' or 'is inconsistent with the pursuit of it'; 'if you do that, the effects will be as follows'. But granted that the role of economist *qua* economist is not to state what policy-makers ought to do — for views on such matters are left to the priest, the politician, the businessman and the voter amongst others — he is concerned with the implications of what policy-makers want to do and with the effects of what they actually do. So we cannot conclude that economics has no vital role to play in the formation of policy. In practice economists make important contributions to the world around us, by advising decision-makers on how to pursue their chosen objectives (such as a high level of employment, more profits, economic growth, a target rate of inflation) in an efficient manner; by analysing the existing trade-offs between different objectives and indicating how, if possible, they might be improved; by estimating the effects of manipulating policy instruments in various ways (their analyses may then be guides in the formulation of new policies); by estimating the impact of changes in the environment — such as changes in technology, an 'oil crisis', economic recovery abroad, etc. — on the effectiveness of actual or potential means; by forecasting what would happen if there were no changes in policy (thereby possibly highlighting, but not prescribing, the need for changes in the instruments of policy); by educating the public — the voters — so that they may assess public and private policies more intelligently.

The role of the economist in policy formation is very much similar to that of analysts in other sciences, nuclear physicists or missiles experts, for example. Thus suppose that the Prime Minister of country Aggress wishes to exterminate the population of another nation, Unfortuna. Since he is unlikely to be an expert in missiles he will probably benefit from the advice of nuclear physicists and missiles experts in deciding on the design of a feasible offensive strategy. But this does *not* imply that the nuclear physicists or the missiles experts are in agreement with the policy-maker's objective of extermination. For apart from being professional scientists they are also human beings who have their personal views concerning what ought to be done. But as scientists they can advise by making statements of the form: 'if you want to do that, then the means which we suggest are consistent with the pursuit or attainment of your objective'. A rational choice of offensive strategy would then be one which the missiles experts deem technically feasible and which is efficient (in the economist's sense).

The policy significance of economics should be reasonably clear. As Robbins indicated, its significance 'consists in just this, that, when we are faced with a choice among ultimates, it enables us to choose with full awareness of the implications of what we are choosing . . . It makes it possible for us to select a system of ends which are mutually consistent with each other'.[9]

If economics be such an objective science, 'unadulterated' by ethics and politics, why, it may reasonably be asked, do economists so frequently disagree? One reason is that each economist, like everyone else, has his personal views on what is good or bad, desirable or undesirable. If two economists disagree in regard to ends, the resolution to their conflict is not to be found in economics — for there are no economic ends. Under such circumstances they would be disagreeing, *not* as economists, but as ordinary mortals. But if they disagree on means of pursuing the same ends, then the resolution to their disagreement can hopefully be found in economic analysis.

Objectives change over time. The environment in which we make decisions changes from instant to instant. Governments come and go. Individuals are being born at this moment while others are dying. Thus in what pertains to economics, the problems of decision-makers are not all resolved in some eternal cookbook of economic recipes. In this context, John Maynard Keynes (1883-1946) wisely wrote that economics 'does not furnish a body of settled conclusions immediately applicable to policy. It is a method rather than a doctrine, an apparatus of the mind, a technique of thinking, which helps its possessor to draw correct conclusions'[10] (in regard to efficient means, and effects, of pursing various objectives).

Although economics is neutral between ends, there can be no doubt that the impact of economists on the world around us has been enormous. Keynes may not have been exaggerating greatly when in his

General Theory of Employment, Interest and Money — a book which helped transform the lives of millions — he wrote that

> the ideas of economists and political philosophers, both when they are right and when they are wrong, are more powerful than is commonly understood.
>
> Indeed the world is ruled by little else. Practical men, who believe themselves to be quite exempt from any intellectual influences, are usually the slaves of some defunct economist. Madmen in authority, who hear voices in the air, are distilling their frenzy from some academic scribbler of a few years back. I am sure that the power of vested interests is vastly exaggerated compared with the gradual encroachment of ideas. Not, indeed, immediately, but after a certain interval; for in the field of economic and political philosophy there are not many who are influenced by new theories after they are twenty-five or thirty years of age, so that the ideas which civil servants and politicians and even agitators apply to current events are not likely to be the newest. But, soon or late, it is ideas, not vested interests, which are dangerous for good or evil.[11]

The thoughts expressed in this passage are surely good reasons for studying economics with a fresh, open mind. But to escape from the incarceration of established modes of thought may not be easy, and is likely to require concentration and perseverance on the part of the reader.

Suggested Reading

Cairnes, J.E., *The Character and Logical Method of Political Economy,* 2nd edn, London 1875, Lecture 1.

Gray, Alexander, *The Development of Economic Doctrine,* London 1931.

Myrdal, Gunnar, *The Political Element in the Development of Economic Theory,* translated from the German by Paul Streeten, London 1953, esp. Prefaces and Chapter 1.

Napoleoni, Claudio, *Economic Thought of the Twentieth Century,* ed. A. Cigno, New York 1973, esp. Chapter 2.

Pigou, A.C., *The Economics of Welfare,* 4th edn, London 1932, Chapter 1.

Robbins, Lionel, *An Essay on the Nature and Significance of Economic Science,* 2nd edn, London 1935, Chapters 1, 2, 6.

Streeten, Paul, editor's Introduction to Gunnar Myrdal, *Value in Social Theory,* New York 1958.

FOOTNOTES

1. Alfred Marshall, *Principles of Economics,* 8th edn, London: Macmillan 1920, 1.
2. A.C. Pigou, *The Economics of Welfare,* 4th edn, London: Macmillan 1932, 11.
3. Lionel Robbins, *An Essay on the Nature and Significance of Economic Science,* 2nd edn, London: Macmillan 1935, 16.
4. Robbins, 16-17.
5. Claudio Napoleoni, *Economic Thought of the Twentieth Century,* ed., A. Cigno, New York: Wiley 1973, 35.
6. Robbins, 145.
7. J.E. Cairnes, *The Character and Logical Method of Political Economy,* 2nd edn, London: Macmillan 1875, 20-22.
8. Nassau Senior, *An Outline of the Science of Political Economy* (first published in 1836), New York: Augustus Kelley 1965, 3.
9. Robbins, 152.
10. J.M. Keynes in his (the editor's) Introduction to the Cambridge Economic Handbooks series of monographs.
11. J.M. Keynes, *The General Theory of Employment, Interest and Money,* London: Macmillan 1936, 383-4.

CHAPTER 2

The Method of Economics

It was stated in Chapter 1 that economics is a science. In this context we note that in recent decades there have been tendencies in popular usage to regard subjects described as scientific with acclaim; conversely, some people use the adjective 'unscientific' to denote 'sloppy'. However, when in this book we refer to economics as a science we purport merely to describe rather than to praise implicitly or to impute some judgment of value.

Science and Generalisation

The central characteristic of science is the establishment of generalisations in regard to the relationship between categories of phenomena. Thus, if from some corpus of positive analysis one can conclude 'if this, then that', one has a scientific theory, hypothesis or law. The importance of scientific theories is that they may enable the analyst to make predictions about the world around us, and prediction is sought because it may permit control over phenomena. If scientific investigation predicts that 'if you do A, then x will result, whereas if you do B, then y will follow', decision-makers may be able to control x or y or both. The relationship between scientific generalisations, prediction and control has been outlined by Stigler as follows:

> That control requires prediction is self-evident, for unless one knows what 'causes' a particular phenomenon, one cannot effect or prevent its occurrence. Prediction, however, requires a knowledge of *general* relationships. No matter how detailed our study of a particular phenomenon (say the price of wheat in March 1874) may be, we would never [on the basis of those raw facts alone] be able to predict the movement of the price of wheat in similar circumstances, because the 'similar' circumstances would differ in literally an unlimited number of respects. It is for this reason that general laws are sought between classes of phenomena.[1]

18

In similar vein the French mathematician Poincaré (1854-1912), referring to the science of experimental physics, wrote that a good experiment 'is that which teaches us something more than an isolated fact. It is that which enables us to predict, and to generalise. Without generalisation, prediction is impossible. The circumstances under which one has operated will never again be reproduced simultaneously. The fact observed will never be repeated . . . To predict . . . we must generalise'.[2]

We have referred to scientific theories, hypotheses and laws as though the words were interchangeable. In this book we adopt the practice of Stigler:

> It was once popular to call a *relationship* a *hypothesis* if it had not been tested, a *theory* if there were some evidence to support it, and a *law* if it were certain. This order contains a grain of truth, but it is essentially naive and mistaken (witness the fact that no sensible hypothesis can be made about a subject matter of which one is completely ignorant, and no scientific 'law' is ever certain). Historical accident plays a large part in such matters (Boyle's 'law' of gases is only an approximation), and everyday usage has corrupted any possible distinction (why is relativity a theory and 'supply and demand' a law?).[3]

Pure and Applied Science

When a researcher sets out on a scientific investigation, the objective of his inquiry may be light-bearing or fruit-bearing — knowledge for its own sake or knowledge which increases understanding of the world around us and which may enable decision-makers to change that world. The two aspects may be present in varying degrees in different sciences. Some sciences purport to be primarily of the pure or light-bearing variety; others are mainly applied or fruit-bearing. At one side of the spectrum stand formal logic and pure mathematics; towards the other side, experimental physics, chemistry, and the biological and social sciences. In the case of light-bearing investigations the generalisations made purport to be logical implications of various assumptions, *whether or not such assumptions correspond to the world which was, which is, or which is likely to be.* The test of validity of such generalisations in pure science is to be found in logical consistency in determining whether the implications follow from the assumptions. Observed facts are irrelevant to pure science.

The distinction between pure and applied science is apparent in the following passage from the philosopher-mathematician Bertrand Russell:

> Pure mathematics has no concern with the question whether the axioms and propositions of Euclid hold of actual space or not: this is a question for applied mathematics, to be decided, so far as any decision is possible, by experiment and observation. What pure mathematics asserts is merely that the Euclidean propositions follow from the Euclidean axioms, i.e., it asserts an implication: any space which has such and such properties has also such and such other properties . . . All propositions as to what actually exists, like the space we live in, belong to experimental or empirical [i.e., applied] science.[4]

The distinction drawn by Russell is applicable in principle to the field of economic investigation. As Pigou noted:

> It is open to us to construct an economic science either of the pure type represented by pure mathematics or of the realistic type represented by experimental physics. Pure economics . . . would study . . . groups of persons actuated by any set of motives x. Under it . . . would be included at once an Adam-Smithian political economy, in which x is given the value of the motives assigned to the economic man — or to the normal man — and a non-Adam-Smithian political economy . . . under which x consists of love of work and hatred of earnings . . . For pure economics both these political economies would be equally true . . . Contrasted with this pure science stands realistic economics, the interest of which is concentrated upon the world known in experience.[5]

Economics is essentially an applied science. Indeed the potential for empirical description and operational application characterises all the social sciences — those sciences which are concerned with human behaviour. Pigou, very much a pragmatic humanitarian in the tradition of Marshall, expressed his own motivation in studying economics by noting that 'it is not wonder, but rather the social enthusiasm which revolts from the sordidness of mean streets and the joylessness of withered lives, that is the beginning of economic science'.[6]

Given that economics is an applied science it is not *only* concerned with the logical implications of assumptions — though such implications are certainly relevant. Logical consistency alone is not a sufficient test of an economic theory. Nor is economics confined to observation alone: infinite narration of facts does not enable us to derive scientific generalisations about the world around us. In order to explain what was, what is, or what plausibly might be, we need *theory* to relate *classes of facts* — to explain the relationship between some classes of facts and others. Thus in applied science the facts are not simply brought together; they are 'compelled by thought to speak'. Or, as Poincaré wrote of the applied science of experimental physics,

> science is built up of facts as a house is built of stones; but an accumulation of facts is no more a science than a heap of stones is a house . . . Detached facts cannot therefore satisfy us . . . By generalisation, every observed fact enables us to predict a large number of others . . . [Generalisation or theory] should always be as soon as possible submitted to verification . . . If it cannot stand this test, it must be abandoned.[7]

Similarly, quoting Pigou once more, every applied science

> through examination and cross-examination of the particular facts which it is able to ascertain, seeks to discover the general laws of whose operation these particular facts are instances. The motions of the heavenly bodies are exhibited in the light of the laws of Newton; the breeding of the blue Andalusian fowl in the light of that of Mendel. These laws . . . are *generalisations.*[8]

The above passages from Pigou and Poincaré can be summarised and linked together: All we observe are events or facts. *Any* proposed explanation of facts is a theory. Theories in applied science purport to explain why certain events occur; they purport to consist of the implications of one class of facts on another class of facts. They are therefore generalisations: rather than reporting that events A and B were observed simultaneously or sequentially, theory attempts to explain the manner in which events of category A are linked to events of category B. Some theories in applied science may be little more than assertions of causation (in contrast to normative, prescriptive assertions), but they may, on the other hand, be the logical implications of one set of apparent facts (the assumptions) for another class of apparent facts (the implications or conclusions). But logical consistency is no guarantee that theories in applied science are valid; since they purport to offer generalised explanations of facts, they must be substantively consistent with those facts. If in applied science a theory is significantly inconsistent with observed facts, then that theory is deemed invalid. Note that this is in contrast to pure science, where logical rigour is all that matters. Thus, although theory is a vital aspect of applied science — for it attempts to explain why the facts are as they are, were the way they were, or how certain facts would be affected if other facts were to change or to be changed — it is not the only aspect; the second, complementary aspect is in appeal to the facts to ascertain whether those facts are consistent with the theory. (This is also in contrast to normative statements, which are themselves often described as theories or laws, but which cannot be refuted by appeal to facts alone.) If in applied science facts are significantly inconsistent with a theory (leading to rejection of that theory), it will be the endeavour of scientists to find a better theory — one which is logically consistent and which is not refuted by facts.

It follows that statements of the form 'that explanation is fine in theory but not in practice' are misleading. For *any* proposed explanation of practice is a theory. If we do not agree with a theory because it is inconsistent with facts it is up to us to construct a better theory. But to reject theory *per se,* while hoping to understand facts, is absurd. If we want to understand reality the choice is not between theory and observation, but between theories which are broadly consistent with facts and theories which are significantly inconsistent with facts. In discussing theory in the remainder of this chapter we confine ourselves to applied, positive science.

Economic Theory, Abstraction and Generalisation

A well-specified economic theory has three aspects:
  (i) A set of definitions indicating the meaning of technical terms.
(ii) Assumptions concerning the general circumstances under which the theory purports to apply.
(iii) Conclusions purporting to describe aspects of the world which was, is, or could plausibly be, and which purport to follow logically from the assumptions in (ii).
  The following is an example of an economic theory:
  If:
(i) A firm seeks maximum attainable profits.
    (ii) Its average costs are constant.
    (iii) There is at least one level of output at which it can make some profit.

(iv) It can vary output by small amounts.

Then:

The firm will produce an output at which marginal cost (the change in total cost due to small variation in output) equals marginal revenue (the change in total revenue due to small variation in output).

The definitions (often excluded because they are presumed known), the assumptions and the conclusion are clear in the statement of this theory. Note that the theory does not pertain to a single, isolated firm: provided assumptions (i) to (iv) are satisfied, *it purports to predict what any firm will produce; the conclusion is a generalisation.* The assumptions may be true — in accordance with observation — or totally false or partially true. The conclusion is *formally* (though not necessarily empirically or factually) valid only if it follows logically from the assumptions.

In assessing the usefulness of a theory we note, first, that the assumptions may be true but the conclusions logically false. If the errors in logic are serious the theory may be useless. Second, even though the assumptions may be in some respects unrealistic the theory may nevertheless be a useful approximation to, or simplification (abstraction) of, reality. The theories outlined in this book — and probably in any book on applied science — fall into that category. Nevertheless, useful conclusions concerning reality may be drawn from the simplifying assumptions. The purpose of simplification or abstraction is merely to make analysis tractable in an otherwise unmanageably complex and/or partially unknown environment. Thus Stigler notes that

> reality is too complex ever to be described fully . . . In order to reduce any problem to manageable proportions, we must . . . concentrate our investigation on *important* and *relevant* factors — and this is nothing more or less than abstraction. As a corollary, no scientific law will ever fully describe reality; no theory of rent will ever predict the 196th word in the lease or the disposition of the farmer's second cousin on rainy days . . .[9]

All applied scientific theories simplify or abstract from reality in specifying their assumptions. What we consider a good theory abstracts in a significantly useful way; a poor theory, even if it is logically consistent, does not.

Theory Versus Tautology

We have seen that theories are typically propositions of the form, 'if this, then that'. But not all propositions of that form are theories. Propositions which are true *by definition* are not theories; they are *tautologies* or *identities.* Suppose for example that Y is national income, that C is annual consumption expenditure in the economy and that investigation leads us to believe that the relationship between C and Y is represented by the equation

$$(1) \quad C = 0 \cdot 75Y$$

Equation (1) is a theory. It states the hypothesis that if national income is at any particular level (in, say, £ million), then consumption expenditure must be three-quarters that level (in £ million), and that if national income changes by any amount, then consumption expenditure must change by three-quarters that amount. Note that (1) *may or may not be true, and if it is true, it is not true by definition.* Two sets of remarks are appropriate in this context:

First, an alternative theory might be that the relationship between C and Y is represented by the equation

$$(2) \quad C = 0 \cdot 5Y$$

which states that if Y is at any particular level, then consumption expenditure must be one half that level. This too is a theory which may or may not be true — it surely is not true if (1) is true, and if it is true, it is not true by definition.

Second, the propositions represented by (1) and (2) purport to hold, not for all conceivable values of C and Y, but only for those subsets of values of C and Y which satisfy the equations. For example, equation (1) is not satisfied by the values Y = 1, C = 97. But consider the following proposition:

If we denote $(u + w)^2$ by

$$(3) \quad z = (u + w)^2, \text{ then}$$

$$(4) \quad z = u^2 + 2uw + w^2$$

This (if, then) proposition is true but it is not a theory. It is a *tautology* or truism; the second equation is merely a *repetition* of the first. The *identity*

$$(5) \quad (u + w)^2 \equiv u^2 + 2uw + v^2$$

could not be refuted by any conceivable state of the universe; it could not be refuted by any choice of pair of values for u and w. (We use three bars in (5) to denote 'identically equal to' rather than the customary two bars to denote 'equal to' as in normal equations representing hypotheses.) Identities, such as (5), imply no testable hypotheses.

Tautologies can tell us nothing about the causes of phenomena. Defining a cow as x and stating that x is a cow tells us nothing about cows. Nor can the statement that if £x million of wheat was purchased then £x million of wheat was sold tell us anything substantive about reality; it is true by definition of the two-sided character of purchase and sale. Thus not all 'if this, then that' propositions are theories; some are tautologies and as such of little interest in scientific research.

Science is not concerned with defining terms so that propositions are true by definition. Thus commenting on meaningful theorems — what we call theories — in the applied science of economics, the Nobel prize-winning American economist, Paul Samuelson, has written as follows:

> By a meaningful theorem I mean simply a hypothesis about empirical data which could conceivably be refuted, if only under ideal conditions. A meaningful theorem may be false. It may be valid but of trivial importance. Its validity may be indeterminate, and practically difficult if not impossible to determine. Thus, with existing data it may be impossible to check on the hypothesis that the demand for salt is of elasticity $-1 \cdot 0$. But it is meaningful because under ideal circumstances an experiment could be devised whereby one could hope to refute the hypothesis. The statement that if demand were inelastic, an increase in price will raise total revenue is not a meaningful theorem in this sense. It implies no hypothesis . . . and is true simply by definition.[10]

The theories of economics are meaningful in Samuelson's sense: since they are not statements which are true by definition they can in principle be tested, and rejected if false.

Experiment, Ceteris Paribus and Statistics

In natural sciences such as chemistry, the scientist, having posed a theory, is often able to generate observations by means of *controlled experiments* to provide evidence for or against the theory. Suppose, for example, that a theory states that some variable, z, depends in some specific manner on another variable, x. In a controlled experiment (perhaps a laboratory experiment) it is attempted to hold constant all variables apart from x which are believed to influence z, to vary x, and to observe the resulting variation in z, in order to test the hypothesis that z depends on x in the manner claimed in the theory. In a controlled experiment the researcher varies whatever independent variables he wishes, controlling at constant levels yet other independent variables, and observes the consequences for the dependent variable (or dependent variables). However, such methods of testing theories are possible in social sciences to a much more limited extent than in the natural sciences.

Suppose we want to set up a controlled experiment to test the theory that at times of economy-wide depression, increases in government expenditure financed by printing money will increase national output and employment. It is unlikely that it will be possible to conduct the experiment, because national output and employment depend on other variables apart from government expenditure financed by printing money, and *it will surely be impossible to hold constant,* during the experiment of varying government expenditure, *all the other causal factors* which influence output and employment. Even a dictator like George Orwell's *Big Brother* could not keep the age structure of the population constant during the experiment. Nor could he maintain constant weather and harvest conditions, or prevent fluctuations in income abroad which affect the demand for the home country's exports. Apart from government expenditure financed by printing money, these are all factors, uncontrollable or imperfectly controllable, which influence variation in output and employment. It would therefore be virtually inconceivable to test the hypothesis posed by means of *controlled* experimentation, as in the natural sciences. The main reason, then, why economists are not normally able to test their theories by means of controlled experiments is that most of the variables of interest to economists are influenced by a very large number of factors, many of which vary simultaneously and often in opposite directions, and which are *beyond the full control* of any individual.

We have seen that economic theories simplify reality. In order to make analysis tractable economic theories are generally conditional propositions of the form 'other things being equal (or, using the Latin, *ceteris paribus*) if x becomes such-and-such, then z will be affected in such-and-such a manner', or 'other things being equal, if you want z to be as you say, you must manipulate x in this manner'. Even if the qualification 'other things being equal' is not stated, it is usually implied in the specification of economic theories. By 'other things being equal' the economist means (taking the example at hand) 'if all factors apart from x which influence z remain constant'. The economist does not necessarily believe that these 'other things' can really be held constant as x varies; if he did he might advocate controlled experiments to test theories. But the effects on z of variation in these 'other things' can also be theorised, with appropriate *ceteris paribus* qualifications applied to those theories also. If, as is likely, a given dependent variable depends on many independent variables, the approach of a large part of economic analysis is the construction of theories concerning the effects of variation in each of those independent variables *in isolation* (i.e., other things being equal, or holding constant in one's reasoning all other causal factors). Then combining aspects of each of these theories makes it possible to predict the consequences of simultaneous changes in many independent variables.

If many explanatory factors underlying the phenomena of economic analysis are varying simultaneously, often in opposite directions, and if these explanatory variables cannot be held constant, so that *controlled* experiments are largely out of the question, how can we 'appeal to facts' to test a theory? The answer is: (i) Millions of *uncontrolled* experiments are taking place every year. Returning to our previous example, we do observe fluctuations in national output and employment simultaneously with variations in government expenditure, in agricultural output, in exports, demographic changes, and so on. (ii) We can apply *the methods of statistical inference* (which we do not discuss in any detail here) to test whether observed facts are consistent with theory. If observed facts are significantly inconsistent with our simplified theories we reject them and seek better ones.

Thus economics is *both logically deductive* and *empirical* in method. Economic theory starts with certain assumptions and, by a process of logical deduction, draws conclusions or generalisations which purport to explain central features of the world around us. In highlighting the implications of his assumptions, logical deduction enables the economist to make *predictions* about the future, contingent on the assumptions which he postulates for the future. The empirical aspect consists in application of the methods of statistical inference in testing the correspondence of theory with observation. The role of statistical methods is at least twofold: (i) As already mentioned, they are used to test theories against empirical data. (ii) We frequently assume in our theories that one thing is related to another in some very general way; if a sufficient number of observations on our variables is available, statistical methods can be used to improve our estimate of the quantitative manner in which one variable depends on another, or to suggest that one variable might depend on another in some manner which we had not thought of.

On one hand, then, statistical analysis is used to test theories; but statistical analysis of the data may *suggest* new theories to the analyst. Theories which originate from analysis of, or even casual observation of, empirical data are sometimes called *inductive* hypotheses in contrast to *deductive* hypotheses. However, the distinction is nebulous. Most theories in economics proceed by logical deduction from various assumptions. But they also have their inductive element: economists and others tend to theorise because they have some familiarity with the world around them, and wonder how that world can be explained or changed. That being the case, their theories are not only deductive, but also inductive. Thus the Nobel prize-winning Swedish economist, Gunnar Myrdal, has written that

> there is an inescapable *a priori* element in all scientific work. Questions must be asked before answers can be given. The questions are an expression of our interest in the world, they are at bottom valuations. Valuations are thus necessarily involved already at the stage when we observe facts and carry on theoretical analysis, and not only at the stage when we draw political inferences from facts and valuations.[11]

These considerations in no way detract from the neutrality of economics. A person may study economics in order to make the world what he regards a better place; this is an expression of values. But in analysing the implications for scarce means of pursuing that objective (given some criterion of 'good' and 'better') the economist is acting as a positive scientist, not as a moralist.

A theory may be deemed significantly false, and hence rejected, if: (i) There are important logical discrepancies between its assumptions and conclusions. (Not all economists appear to agree with us on this point.) (ii) There are important empirical discrepancies between its assumptions or conclusions and observable facts. What matters from the standpoint of operational validity of a theory is whether it simplifies in a useful way. But can we prove that a theory — an economic theory or a theory in some other applied science — about the world around us is true? The answer is no; we may say no more than that it is broadly consistent or inconsistent with facts in two billion controlled experiments or in two billion statistical studies. But we cannot prove that it will hold true in the next controlled experiment or in the next observation, although we can regard it as extremely probable. It is possible, indeed, that two alternative theories explain the facts equally well. Under such circumstances the criterion normally used by scientists in choosing between the theories is analytical simplicity; by this criterion that explanation which requires fewer assumptions, and is therefore the more general, is the preferred theory.

The Master Economist

Around the middle of the nineteenth century the economist-philosopher J.S. Mill wrote that a man is unlikely to be a good economist if he is nothing else. We are inclined to agree (though note that this implies a value-judgment on our part). To be a good economist one must be able to conceptualise in an empirically relevant way. Useful inductive hypotheses may be suggested by appreciation of the evolutionary forces underlying economic activity. Thus socio-historical intuition can be an asset to the economist. But he must also be able to conceptualise abstractly and think logically; indeed it may be nigh impossible to draw logically firm conclusions from the assumptions of many theories unless the theories are specified as formal (mathematical) propositions. And, finally, an economist must be down-to-earth when it comes to testing theories using the methods of statistical inference; but creativity and versatility in that direction also presume some mathematical abilities.

J.M. Keynes regarded his lecturer Alfred Marshall as perhaps the greatest of economists. There are millions of people who know a little economics and tens of thousands who describe themselves as economists, but few truly great economists. Why? We do not necessarily agree with *all* the views expressed, but perhaps the following passage from Keynes's essay on Alfred Marshall offers some insights:

> The study of economics does not seem to require any specialised gifts of an unusually high order . . . Yet good, or even competent, economists are the rarest of birds. An easy subject, at which very few excel! The paradox finds its explanation, perhaps, in that the master-economist must possess a rare *combination* of gifts. He must reach a high standard in several different directions and must combine talents not often found together. He must be mathematician, historian, statesman, philosopher — in some degree. He must understand symbols and speak in words. He must contemplate the particular in terms of the general, and touch abstract and concrete in the same flight of thought. He must study the present in the light of the past for the purposes of the future. No part of man's nature or his institutions must lie entirely

outside his regard. He must be purposeful and disinterested in a simultaneous mood; as aloof and incorruptible as an artist, yet sometimes as near the earth as a politician. Much, but not all, of this many-sidedness Marshall possessed.[12]

Suggested Reading

Poincaré, Henri, *Science and Hypothesis,* reproduction of the first English translation, New York 1952.

Samuelson, P.A. *Foundations of Economic Analysis,* Cambridge, Mass. 1947, Chapter 1.

Stigler, George, *The Theory of Price,* New York 1946, Chapter 1.

APPENDIX TO CHAPTER 2

Functions, Graphs and Slope

Here we review some simple technical concepts which should already be familiar. These are the *only* prior mathematical notions required for understanding the entire text.

Functions
We all recognise that consumption expenditure depends on income, and that the quantity produced of a good depends on the amounts of inputs to the production of that good. Instead of saying that consumption expenditure depends on income we might alternatively say that consumption is a function of income. When we say that y is a function of x, what we mean is that y depends on x in some particular way, and we denote this as $y = f(x)$, which we read as 'y is a function of x' or 'y depends on x'. (The mathematician would be more restrictive in defining function.) When we write $y = f(x)$ we are *not* saying that y equals f multiplied by x; the letter f (or any other letter unlikely to cause confusion) is used merely as shorthand to denote that the value of y depends on x.

Dependent and Independent Variables
In the above example, x (the variable on the right-hand side) is called the independent variable, while y (the variable on the left-hand side), is called the dependent variable. In that equation only one variable is postulated as independent — y depends on x and on x alone.

Functions of Many Independent Variables

We could likewise discuss functions of many independent variables. $Q = f(x_1, x_2, \ldots, x_n)$ is an example. Q might be the number of motor cars (a particular model) produced per month. The variables x_1, x_2, x_3, $\ldots$, x_n might then be the amounts used of various inputs, n in number, per month. The variable x_1 might be the amount of engine assembly capacity used, x_2 might represent the amount of metal stamping capacity employed, and so on.

Equations

An equation tells us *how* variables are related. We read $y = f(x)$ as y depends on x. If we were told that $y = 7 + 2x$ we would know not just that y depends on x, but the precise manner in which y depends on x. If, for example (in the last equation), $x = 1$, then $y = 9$; if $x = 10$, then $y = 27$; if x increases by unity from 6 to 7, then y increases by two from 19 to 21, and so on. Equations normally enable us to calculate the values of dependent variables corresponding to any values of independent variables.

Variables and Parameters

Inspect the equation $y = 7 + 2x$. The x and the y are called variables, since they can take on different values in a single equation. The 7 and 2 are called parametric constants or, simply, parameters. A parameter is a symbol or number which remains constant in a given equation; if a parameter changes, the equation changes.

Standard Form of Linear Equations in Two Variables

A linear equation is one in which all variables are raised to the power of unity, and in which there are no products or quotients of variables. (Thus $y = ax^2 + bx$ or $z = 7uv$ are not linear.) The standard form of linear equations in two variables is $y = a + bx$, where x and y are variables, a and b being parameters. Note the standard mathematical convention of using letters at the end of the alphabet to represent variables, and those at the beginning to represent parameters, or constants. If an equation can be written in the standard linear form, the parameters provide us, on sight, some information about the graph of the equation.

The Rectangular Coordinate System

A graph is a pictorial representation of one or more equations. One method of constructing graphs of equations in two variables is to use the rectangular coordinate system, depicted in Figure 2. The two axes,

X and Y, intersect at right angles at a point 0 (where x = 0 and y = 0). In mathematical convention the horizontal axis is assigned to the independent variable and the vertical axis to the dependent variable. (Note that this convention is not always abided by in economic applications.) The intersection of the X and the Y axes yields four quadrants. Any real number can be represented as a point on a line. The values of both x and y are positive inside quadrant I. Inside quadrant II, x is negative and y is positive. Both x and y are negative inside quadrant III, while inside quadrant IV, x is positive and y is negative. Along the axes themselves, at least one variable has a value of zero. For example, the point labelled A has the values x = 0 and y = 1; that labelled B has the values x = 2, y = 1; and that labelled C corresponds to x = −3, y = 1. Quadrant I is the most relevant to economic analysis, since economists seldom deal with negative quantities.

Return to the equation y = 7 + 2x. It is a simple matter to calculate that

If x =	0	1	2	3	4	5	6
Then y =	7	9	11	13	15	17	19

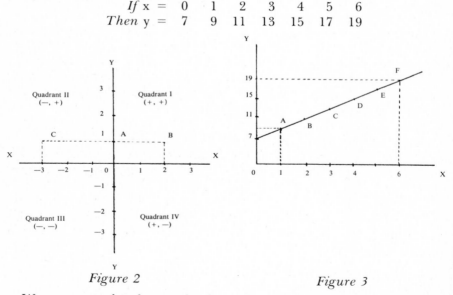

Figure 2   Figure 3

We can now plot the graph of y = 7 + 2x (concentrating on only positive values of the variables). Taking various values of x and plotting the corresponding values of y in the X-Y plane, quadrant I, we get a set of points like A, B, C, D, E and F in Figure 3. If we join these points we get a smooth locus which is the graph of the equation as x varies from 0 to 6. The value of the dependent variable if the independent were zero is called the intercept; in the present example, it is $+7$.

The Slope of a Line

The slope of any line (or curve) is the rate of change in the dependent variable with respect to a small change in the independent variable. It shows by how much the dependent variable will change if the independent variable changes by a small amount.

We saw, in the case of the equation $y = 7 + 2x$, that every time x increased by one unit, y increased by two units. Hence the slope, $\Delta y/\Delta x$ (read change in y with respect to change in x) is 2. (Note that we can speak interchangeably of the slope of an equation in two variables and the slope of the graph of that equation.) Note also that the slope of a straight line (a linear equation) is constant, and that this slope is given by the coefficient of (i.e., the parameter before) the independent variable. Thus the slope of the standard linear equation in two variables, $y = a + bx$, is b; the dependent variable y changes by b units for every unit change in the independent variable x.

Suppose that $x = 3$ in Figure 3 and ask the question: if x changes by a small amount — say by one unit — from $x = 3$ to $x = 4$, by how much will y change? We can read from our graph that if $\Delta x = +1$, then $\Delta y = +2$. Hence the slope of the line between C and D — and, indeed, between any two points — is $\Delta y/\Delta x = 2$. This is exactly the value of the coefficient of x in the equation $y = 7 + 2x$.

But consider the equation $y = 7 - 2x$. The reader should recognise that, unlike the preceding example, the graph of this equation will slope down from left to right. He should also recognise that its slope is -2, reflecting the fact that a unit change in x brings about a change of two units, in the opposite direction, in y.

It should now be obvious that we can tell the properties of the graph of any linear equation in two variables, $y = a + bx$, on sight, merely by inspecting the parameters of the equation. Thus the intercept is a and the slope is b.

Linear Equations, More Than Two Variables

A linear equation in more than two variables is of the form $y = a + b_1x_1 + b_2x_2 + \ldots + b_nx_n$ where y is the dependent variable, $x_1, \ldots, x_n$ are independent variables, and a, $b_1, \ldots, b_n$ are parameters. The main point to note is that the coefficient of any of the x's, say x_i, shows the amount by which y changes if x_i changes by one unit (assuming all the other x's are given).

Non-linear Equations: The Slope of a Curve
Not all equations are of the simple linear forms discussed above. If an equation in two variables cannot be reduced to the form $y = a + bx$, it is non-linear. Its graph is not a straight line. The slope of a curve — the graph of a non-linear equation — can change in both value and sign from one point to another. We defined slope as the rate of change in a dependent variable with respect to a small change in an independent variable. Alternatively we can say that the slope of a curve at a point is the slope of the straight line tangent to the curve at that point. Thus we could measure the slope of the curve in Figure 4 below at, say, point A, by measuring $\Delta y/\Delta x$ along the tangent locus $A'A'$.

Convexity and Concavity

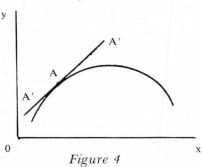

Figure 4

Consider a curve $y = f(x)$. This function is strictly convex if its slope continues to increase as x increases; if, on the other hand, the slope always decreases as x increases, the function is strictly concave. The curve in Figure 4 is strictly concave. However, if that curve were inverted (so it would be U-shaped) it would be strictly convex.

Inequalities: Notation

     $A > B$ means A is greater than B.
     $A \geqslant B$ means A is greater than or equal to B.
     $A < B$ means A is less than B.
     $A \leqslant B$ means A is less than or equal to B.

FOOTNOTES

1. George Stigler, *The Theory of Price*, New York: Macmillan 1946, 3-4.
2. Henri Poincaré, *Science and Hypothesis*, reproduction of the first English translation, New York: Dover 1952, 141-2.
3. Stigler, 4, footnote.
4. Bertrand Russell, *Principles of Mathematics*, 2nd edn, New York: Norton 1937, 5.
5. A.C. Pigou, *The Economics of Welfare*, 4th edn, London: Macmillan 1932, 6.
6. *Ibid.*, 5.
7. Poincaré, 141, 143-4, 150.
8. Pigou, 7.
9. Stigler, 9.
10. Paul Samuelson, *Foundations of Economic Analysis*, Cambridge, Mass.: Harvard University Press 1947, 4.
11. Gunnar Myrdal, *The Political Element in the Development of Economic Theory*, translated from the German by Paul Streeten, London: Routledge and Kegan Paul 1953, vii.
12. J.M. Keynes, *Essays in Biography*, London: Macmillan 1933, 170-1.

PART TWO

THE ELEMENTS OF SUPPLY AND DEMAND

CHAPTER 3

Introductory

There are two principal branches of economic analysis. *Macroeconomics* is concerned with aggregates rather than the individual elements which make up those aggregates. In *microeconomics* we focus on individual markets and deal with questions of the form: What inputs, and how much of each input, will a firm operating in particular product and factor markets hire if its objective is to maximise profits? What would be the effects of a tax per unit on a good? What determines the price and quantity traded of a particular commodity? In macroeconomics we analyse questions such as: What determines the overall rate of inflation, the level of national output and the rate of economic growth? What can government do to avert large-scale unemployment? Suppose that the Irish monetary authorities attempted to generate a large increase in the money supply. Under what circumstances could that be done, independently of what might be happening in the rest of the world? How would the national economy be affected?

An understanding of macroeconomics requires prior comprehension of some of its microeconomic foundations. This should come as no surprise, given that macro or aggregative variables are made up of micro components. Microeconomic theory tends to be quite abstract; macroeconomics, while also necessarily abstract, is more public-policy oriented. Before we involve ourselves in macroeconomic theory we should acquire some expertise in the elementary (microeconomic) analysis of individual markets.

The Allocation Problem

What goods shall be produced and in what quantities? *How,* or by what technique, shall they be produced? *For whom* shall goods be produced? (i.e., by what rules, of deservedness and the like, shall production be distributed among individuals in society?) These questions constitute the allocation problem of every economy. The problem might, in principle, be solved by centralised planning without use of prices. A central planning bureau could make orders concerning the amounts to be produced of each good, as well as directions in regard to choice of technique. It could distribute the goods in accordance with the government's ethical priorities. However, a private enterprise economy relies on a mechanism of markets and prices to solve its allocation problem. In that system prices serve as *signals* which allocate flows of resources into different productive activities and flows of products among consumers.

The questions *what* goods and how much of those goods shall be produced, as well as *how* goods shall be produced, are solved in an efficient manner in the ideal decentralised market economy. We shall elaborate on the matter of efficiency in Part Five. The system is decentralised because, in its pure form, there is no controlling body coordinating activities in various markets. The market mechanism may also determine the pattern of income distribution — the question of *who gets goods* — but to say that it does so in a desirable or undesirable manner is a normative judgment, and as such requires more than economic analysis. The way in which the market mechanism solves the allocation problem is roughly as follows:

If consumers come to desire more of a particular good than previously, the price of that good will be bid upwards. This acts as a signal for firms to expand production. In a competitive economy firms tend to produce only those goods which yield profit; furthermore, they expand output of any good up to a point at which they would be adding more to their total costs than to their total revenues if they were to expand output further. Only then can they be maximising profits. In this manner supply and demand determine the quantities of *what* shall be produced. *How* goods shall be produced — the choice of technology — is determined by supply and demand in the markets for the factors of production. Firms demand factors to gain profit from the production which the hire of those factors generates. The assumed increase in demand for a particular good, which increased its price, leads to an increase in demand by firms for certain factors. The resulting increase in factor prices acts as a signal inducing resource-owners (labour, landowners and the owners of capital equipment) to supply more factors to the industry in question. Given these market-determined factor prices, firms, in maximising profits, choose those mixes of factors which minimise costs; this determines *how* goods shall be produced. For example, if the price of labour is cheap relative to the price of capital equipment, firms tend to opt for labour-intensive techniques (i.e., methods of production involving high ratios of labour to capital equipment). Finally, the factor prices determined by supply and demand are the incomes of the factors of production. These accrue to households who indicate their 'votes' for different goods by the pattern of their demands. Thus the very process of factor pricing determines *for whom* goods are produced. It follows that the configuration of prices emerging from the operation of markets is not independent of the pattern of income distribution. In a market economy some individuals earn very high incomes because they have skills very scarce in relation to the demand for them. Because of the high incomes thereby earned they bid up the prices of Queen Anne furniture and choice residential lots in scenic locations. If all incomes were equal, the prices of such goods would not be bid up so high; but nor would other goods be low in price. The manner in which the pattern of income distribution emerging from the factor market of a decentralised market economy determines what goods are produced has been described as an 'undemocratic' voting system in which some individuals (those on high incomes) have more votes than others. We mention in passing that even some opponents of private enterprise (opponents mainly because of the manner in which the pattern of income distribution is determined in such a system) have been so impressed by the efficiency of the ways in which decentralised markets handle the questions *what* and *how,* that they have advocated the adoption of those features in the economic systems which they have proposed as alternatives.[1]

The mechanism of decentralised markets which solves the allocation problem is not one of chaos; it does operate in a systematic way despite the absence of conscious coordination. It has in fact been argued that resource allocation via free markets is efficient *because* of the absence of State intervention and control. That was the view of Adam Smith, who in 1776 wrote that

> it is not from the benevolence of the butcher, the brewer or the baker that we expect our dinner, but from their regard to their own interest . . . Every individual intends only his own gain, and he is in this led by an invisible hand to promote an end which was no part of his intention. By pursuing his own interest he frequently promotes that of society more effectually than when he really intends to promote it.[2]

The belief that each individual, in pursuing his own interests in a competitive economy, was also pursuing the interests of society as a whole by way of 'an invisible hand', led Smith to oppose almost every kind of interference with the operation of free competitive markets, whether by government, by trade unions or in the form of conspiracies in constraint of free trade by employers.

Although the market mechanism does have several attractive features, these should not be exaggerated. First, the market mechanism may determine the pattern of income distribution, which may be inegalitarian; depending on one's social philosophy, this may be deemed undesirable. Second, not all markets are freely competitive. There may be monopoly in both the product and factor markets, and these may interfere with the efficient functioning of the system. If wages are flexible in an upward direction but inflexible downwards (due, for example, to trade union activity), large-scale unemployment may result. More efficient operation of the economy may then require appropriate intervention by the public authorities. Third, unregulated firms, in maximising profits, may impose costs on third parties, as with pollution, for example. Fourth, it may be felt that it is necessary that government provide goods in the public interest which profit-maximising firms would not have incentive to provide. In the century following the publication of *The Wealth of Nations,* British governments tended to apply Smith's *laissez-faire* philosophy (a political philosophy advocating non-intervention by government in the economy). One has only to read Cecil Woodham-Smith's classic, *The Great Hunger: Ireland 1845-9,* for details of how that government, by refusing to intervene in economic activity until it was largely too late, failed to prevent the starvation of millions of Irish people in the 1840s. Finally, although it may be granted that a free market economy would tend to be highly efficient if it were stable, it may be argued that such a system would be prone to oscillations in output and employment, or that it would take a long time to attain efficiency at what we shall call equilibrium. Perhaps central planning or simply pragmatic intervention could bring the economy to an efficient equilibrium more rapidly.

Economic Goods, Productive Activities and the Market

In this book when we refer to *goods* we mean *physical goods as well as services* (such as restaurant facilities, legal advice or banking services). However, lest the reader forget our meaning we shall sometimes refer explicitly to 'goods and services'. Goods which command a price, or exchange value, are called *economic goods* in distinction to free goods, such as fresh air is or once was, which do not command a price. In order to possess exchange value a good must be subjectively *useful* (it must give satisfaction or utility to consumers) and *scarce*. It is only because economic goods are of subjective use that they are demanded. They cannot be produced in unlimited quantities because resources are limited. The opportunity costs of scarce goods are positive; to provide more of them resources have to be induced away from other uses, including leisure. Utility and scarcity find their explicit expression in the demands of buyers and the supplies of sellers. By their interaction, supply and demand determine market price, or exchange value.

In modern economics *any* activity which creates economic goods is regarded as *productive,* simply because it leads to satisfaction of human wants. That is the case whether the end product of the activity is a physical good or a service. In this respect modern economics is at variance with Adam Smith and other early economists who regarded activities the end product of which was a service, as unproductive.

The concept *'market'* is not amenable to a simple operational definition. In his *Principles of Economics* (8th edition, 1920) Alfred Marshall took eight pages to discuss the term, and since then a large number of refinements have been added. Any place in which buyers and sellers communicate to trade is a market. But the word 'place' should not be interpreted too narrowly. We think of a market as a medium of communication between buyers and sellers rather than as a well-defined geographic location. The foreign exchange market is not well-defined geographically, but in that market there is constant communication between buyers and sellers by means of batteries of telephones and telexes. The only essential requirement for market is that buyers and sellers can communicate — regardless of how — to carry out trading.

FOOTNOTES

1. See for example the papers of Lange and Taylor in B. Lippincott (ed.), *On The Economic Theory of Socialism,* Minneapolis: University of Minnesota Press 1938.
2. Adam Smith, *The Wealth of Nations,* Indianapolis: Bobbs-Merrill abridged edn, 14-15, 166. We have skipped several of Smith's clauses in the second sentence quoted.

CHAPTER 4

Supply and Demand in Perfectly Competitive Markets

As a starting point in the analysis of the allocation process, we outline in this chapter the determination of price and output in a perfectly competitive market. We complete the discussion of the allocation process only after we return to microeconomics in Part Five.

The market for a particular good is perfectly competitive if the following conditions are satisfied:

(i) There must be *a very large number of both buyers and sellers* so that no single trader can influence price. No single buyer could bargain down the established market price in his own favour. He accepts price as given, a datum beyond his control. If any seller tried to raise price above the established level he would find no willing purchasers. These conditions assume that traders have perfect knowledge about conditions in the market. In a perfectly competitive market each trader is accordingly a *price-taker*.

(ii) The *product* traded must be *homogeneous,* or *identical*, in the minds of buyers. Competitive advertising, trade marks and brand names are therefore ruled out — for their purpose is to differentiate, in buyers' minds, one firm's product from that of a competitor. The homogeneity requirement, along with that of perfect knowledge ensures that buyers will not purchase from firms charging higher prices than others.[1]

(iii) There must be no *collusion or conspiracy* anywhere in the market; nor must there be *institutional restrictions* (for example, government rationing or maximum price orders) on supplies, demands or prices. The first condition implies that no group of traders organise together to influence price. The second condition (no institutional restrictions) ensures that all potential traders are free to enter the market and that prices are free to move as they will if conditions underlying supply or demand change.

It should be obvious from these conditions that few if any markets are fully perfectly competitive. We shall of course analyse other market structures later on. But as indicated in Chapter 2, all theory abstracts, and a good theory abstracts in a useful way. Actual markets often approximate the requirements of perfect competition. Government intervention aside, Irish agriculture is in large measure perfectly competitive. The individual potato grower does not perceptibly affect price by deciding to sow a few acres under potatoes. His supply is negligible compared to total market supplies of potatoes; it is like a grain in the bucket. Nor does he collude with other farmers to restrict supplies, or attempt to promote his product over that of other growers by competitive advertising. Furthermore, because it is subject to brisk competition from firms in other EEC countries, it is useful for *some* purposes to analyse the market conditions of much of Irish manufacturing industry as closely approximating perfect competition. That may be true even if each of the Irish firms in an industry is one of only a few *producers* (as distinct from sellers) in the domestic economy. If domestic firms in an industry are producing products which are very close substitutes for each other as well as for those of competitors located in other EEC countries, the individual Irish producer can have little impact on price. Even if the Irish producers colluded to restrict their outputs, and to raise their prices significantly above those of other EEC producers, they would face the constraints imposed by external competition; they could not, therefore, effectively collude to raise prices significantly above those of close substitutes in the form of competing imports. Nor would UK or continental consumers be willing to buy Irish manufactures at significantly higher prices than those charged by UK or continental firms for similar goods.

Some markets diverge from perfect competition largely because of government intervention. To analyse the effects of such public policies it is then appropriate to start assuming perfect competition, and to superimpose the public policies on that analytic framework. That is what we shall do in Chapter 6, where we consider some applications of supply and demand analysis. Useful theories abstract in a useful way; they explain and predict central features of reality. It is our belief that the applications in Chapter 6 and subsequently will satisfy those criteria.

In the analysis of price determination which follows, it is assumed that the good under discussion is sold under conditions approximating perfect competition. We emphasise that the analysis is offered as an explanation of price determination *only* in markets approximating perfect competition; for other types of market structure, such as monopoly, the analysis can be significantly misleading.

Market Demand

Throughout this book we assume that consumers seek to maximise the utility (subjective satisfaction) obtainable by allocating their expenditures among goods. Unless indicated to the contrary, we assume that their tastes among goods are constant.

A *market demand curve* shows the various alternative quantities of a good which consumers would attempt to buy per period of time at various alternative prices of that good, *other things being equal.* To clarify 'other things being equal' we consider the concept of general demand function, implicit in our definition of demand curve. Suppose that many kinds of goods, say n different types of goods, are available and consider any one of them, say the nth. Upon what things does the quantity demanded of good n depend? To answer we introduce a general demand function

$$(1) \quad q_d^n = f(p^1, p^2, \ldots, p^{n-1}, p^n, y, \text{pop}, \text{dist}, g)$$

This demand function states that quantity demanded of good n (q_d^n) *depends on:* the price of good n itself (p^n); the prices of all other goods ($p^1, p^2, \ldots, p^{n-1}$); total *money* income (y); the number of consumers (pop); the distribution of income (dist) and possibly on a variable (g) representing government interference in the market.

We assume here that there is no government interference; so $g = 0$. Quantity demanded of good n also depends on the tastes of consumers, but tastes are not included as an explicit independent variable in the demand function; rather, tastes determine the *functional form* of (1) — they determine the *manner* in which quantity demanded depends on the variables on the right-hand side.

We agree that quantity demanded of good n — say apples — depends on the price of apples (p^n). We expect that if all variables on which the demand for apples depends — other than the price of apples — remain constant, then the lower the price of apples, the more apples will consumers wish to buy. Apart from the good's own price, p^n, the demand for good n, apples, depends on the prices of all other goods, $p^1, p^2, \ldots, p^{n-1}$. That is so for *two* reasons:

(i) Suppose p^1 is the price of pears. Then, given $p^2, p^3, \ldots, p^n$, the lower p^1 happens to be, the smaller will desired purchases of apples be. That is because apples and pears are *substitutes*.

(ii) Consideration of substitute goods (and their opposites, complements[2]) aside, the demand for any good depends on the prices of all other goods which consumers buy. To see this we simplify and suppose that there are only three goods entering consumers' expenditure plans, their prices being p^1, p^2 and p^3. Then the demand function for good 3 would be of the form: $q_d^3 = f(p^1, p^2, p^3, y, \ldots)$. Substitutability (and complementarity) aside, q_d^3 depends on (for example) the price of good 2, p^2, because if the price of good 2 increased, while the prices of all other goods and consumers' *money* incomes stayed fixed, consumers would experience a decline in general purchasing power — they could buy fewer goods with their fixed money incomes. Although they would experience no changes in their money incomes, their *real* incomes — the general purchasing power of their money incomes — would have fallen, and this could affect their demands for *all* goods.

Hence, returning to the general demand function (1) above, we can state that q_d^n depends on p^1, p^2, . . ., p^n [1] because (i) good n is likely to have substitutes (and complements) and (ii), given their money incomes, the size of consumers' *real* incomes depends on the prices of all goods.

To explain why q_d^n depends on the remaining variables is a more simple task. If total money income (y) or the number of consumers (pop) change, one would expect changes in the amount of any good demanded. Furthermore, as was mentioned in Chapter 3, one would expect the pattern of demand among goods to be sensitive to the pattern of income distribution between households (dist). Finally, the demand for a good may depend on government interference (g). For example, suppose that a tax per unit is imposed on transactions in good n, and that it is administratively levied on buyers. Then the demand for good n would depend on p^n (the price offered to sellers) *plus* the tax per unit.

A demand function represents the amount of a good consumers would desire to buy *per period of time* if prices, money income, etc., were at various alternative levels. Thus the dependent variable is a *flow* over time rather than a *stock* at a point in time; it is so much per day, per month, or over some other specific time period. We are now ready to move from the demand function (1) to a simple demand curve and to explain what we mean by 'other things being equal'.

Reflect on the general demand function for good n, (1) above. If tastes and all variables inside parentheses on the right of (1) stay constant, except for p^n, there would be a stable relationship between q_d^n and p^n, and we could write

$$(1') \qquad q_d^n = f(p^n)$$

This function states that quantity demanded of good n depends in some particular manner on the price of good n, so long as all *other things* upon which q_d^n depends *remain constant*. Alternatively, $(1')$ states that *other things being equal,* quantity demanded of good n depends in some particular manner on the price of good n. We assume as before that q_d^n is the demand for apples and that p^n is the price of apples. Now suppose that *using techniques of statistical inference* an economist correctly estimates that the relationship between quantity demanded of apples and their price (given tastes and specific levels of all other variables in the general demand function) is as in Table 1.

Table 1
A Schedule of the Demand for Apples (Bushels per week)

Price (£)	18	15	9	6	3
Quantity Demanded (Bu.)	250	500	1000	1250	1500

The dependence of q_d^n on p^n is represented in graphical form in Figure 5 below. Along the vertical axis we measure p^n. Quantity demanded is measured along the horizontal axis. We plot the demand schedule from Table 1 as a set of points. If we join these points we get the continuous *demand curve* DD.

Demand curves generally slope downwards implying that more of a good will usually be bought at low than at high prices. In Figure 5 the demand curve DD traces the dependence of the demand for apples (q_d^n) on the price of apples (p^n). For any particular price of apples a specific quantity of apples would be demanded — but *only on the assumption that tastes, p^1, p^2, . . ., p^{n-1}, y, pop, dist and g remain constant* as p^n varies. Hence we can say that *other things being equal,* if the price of apples falls from £12 to £6 per bushel, quantity demanded will increase from 750 to 1250 bushels per week.

Consider what would happen if some of the things which were regarded as constant in constructing DD were to change. Suppose that tastes changed in favour of apples. Instead of demanding 750 bushels a week at a price of £12 consumers might now want to buy 1250 bushels. Similarly, they might now seek to buy 1750 instead of 1250 bushels at a price of £6 per bushel. The change in tastes would have led to an *outward shift* in the demand curve from DD to D'D' in Figure 5. Other reasons why, at any particular price of apples, consumers might wish to buy more apples include an increase in the price of a substitute good (pears, for example), growth of money incomes, change in the distribution of income in favour of vegetarians, etc.

The demand curve for good n (apples) could shift to the left as, for example, from DD to D"D" in Figure 5. This might happen if tastes moved against the good, if money incomes fell, if several of p^1, p^2, . . ., p^{n-1} increased, thereby reducing the purchasing power of consumers, or if the price of a close substitute for good n decreased. The shift to the left of the demand curve from DD to D"D" would reflect the fact that at any particular price of good n, consumers are now willing to buy a smaller quantity of good n than previously.

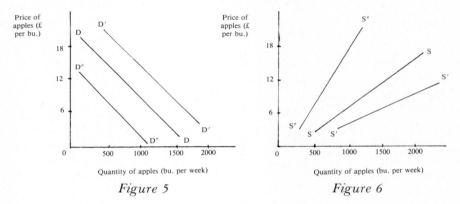

Figure 5   *Figure 6*

Market Supply

It is only for markets which approximate perfect competition that the supply and demand analysis of this chapter is valid. As will be demonstrated much later, that is mainly because a well-defined supply curve does not generally exist in other market structures.

A *market supply curve* shows the alternative quantities of a good producers will supply *per period of time* at various alternative prices of that good, *other things being equal.* We assume throughout that the objective of firms is to maximise profits, and that they act accordingly. Also, unless stated to the contrary, we assume that the state of technical knowledge is given, and that the situation in regard to the availability of various factors of production to firms stays constant in whatever time period is under analysis. These considerations influence the functional form of the general supply function

$$(2) \qquad q_s^n = F(p^1, p^2, \ldots, p^{n-1}, p^n, w^1, \ldots, w^m, g)$$

which states that quantity of good n supplied (q_s^n) per period depends on the prices of all goods (p^1, . . ., p^n), n in number, on the prices of all resources (w^1, . . ., w^m), m in number and possibly on government interference (for example, by taxes on suppliers) in the market. We continue to assume no such interference; so $g = 0$.

Quantity supplied of a good depends on the good's price; we expect producers to increase supply of a good if its price increases. It also depends on the prices of other goods. Suppose, for example, that a farmer's land is equally suitable for oats and barley. Given the price of oats, he would not grow oats rather than barley unless the price of barley were below a certain level. Quantity supplied also depends on the prices of resources which could be used as inputs, since these help determine production costs. And as already stated, our assumptions concerning the goals of producers, the state of technology and the availability of factors, influence the functional form of (2); they influence the *precise manner* in which q_s^n depends on the variables on the right hand side of (2).

If all variables affecting quantity supplied of good n, except for p^n, remain constant, we have a stable relationship between q_s^n and p^n, and can write the simple supply function

$$(2')   q_s^n = F(p^n),$$

which states that *other things being equal* quantity supplied of good n (apples) per period depends in a particular way on that good's price. Suppose that an economist, on the basis of statistical analysis of market data, correctly estimates that the relationship between quantity supplied of apples and their price (given technology and constancy of all other independent variables) is as in Table 2.

Table 2
A Schedule for the Supply of Apples (Bushels per week)

Price (£)	3	6	9	12	15	18
Quantity Supplied (Bu.)	550	850	1150	1450	1750	2050

The dependence of q_s^n on p^n in Table 2 is more clearly seen graphically, by the supply curve SS in Figure 6. *Supply curves generally slope upwards implying that other things being equal, in order to give producers an incentive to expand production price must rise.* But apart from the good's own price, if any of the conditions underlying the supply of good n change, the supply curve will shift. If, for example, technical change brings improved methods of production and lower unit costs, or if input prices fall, then the supply curve will shift to the right, from SS to, say, S'S', reflecting the fact that at any particular price of apples, producers are now willing to supply more than before. If changes in the reverse directions take place, the supply curve will shift to the left, perhaps to S"S". Thus the only independent variable which changes in moving along any particular supply curve is the good's own price; if technology or any *other* independent variable change, the supply curve shifts. Some general comments are in order at this stage.

First, the demand and supply curves DD and SS in Figures 5 and 6 are straight lines. That is only because the numbers in Tables 1 and 2, to which these curves correspond, *happen* to imply linear demand and supply curves.

Second, in the exposition above we assumed that good n was apples; it could in fact have been *any* good which is traded in markets approximating perfect competition.

Third, in the analysis which follows we focus on what we shall call the equilibrium price and quantity traded in a single market, on the assumption, except where otherwise indicated, that all 'other things' remain 'equal' (i.e., that all factors underlying the demand and supply of the good under consideration, except the good's own price, remain constant). Since we shall be dealing with a specific good there can be no confusion concerning the price and quantity to which we refer; so we can dispense with superscripts above variables and denote the price of the good under analysis by p and its quantity by q (with subscripts below those variables representing different levels of p and q).

Price Determination by Supply and Demand

Quantity traded and price are in *equilibrium* if, given all things discussed earlier governing supply and demand, there is no tendency for price or quantity to change. By equilibrium we mean a position of rest, a situation in which there is no tendency toward change, a balance between opposing forces. An equilibrium may be stable or unstable. It is *stable* if, when any deviation from equilibrium takes place, forces come into operation to re-establish the equilibrium. It is *unstable* if a deviation from equilibrium generates forces which operate in a cumulative manner to drive the system away from equilibrium. Thus an egg standing unobstructed at the side of a smooth table is in unstable equilibrium. But as we shall see, most of the equilibria studied in this text are plausibly stable: if the phenomena under study are not in a position of rest, they tend to converge toward such a position unless they are continuously prevented from doing so due to outside shocks. Unless we indicate to the contrary, given that they are likely to be stable, we will refer to the equilibrium price and quantity traded as that price and quantity traded which tends to prevail, and towards which market forces converge. To see how the equilibrium price and quantity traded are determined in a perfectly competitive market we simply enter the supply and demand curves on the same diagram, as in Figure 7.

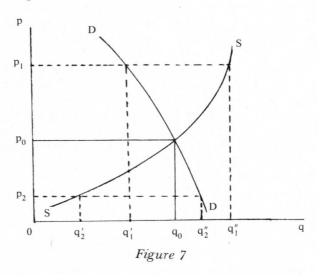

Figure 7

The curve DD in Figure 7 relates quantity demanded of a good per period of time to its price, when tastes, the prices of all other goods, per capita money incomes, etc., are given. The curve SS relates quantity supplied of the good (over the same time period) to its price, given all other conditions underlying supply. Equilibrium price and quantity traded are determined by the intersection of the supply and demand curves; this occurs at p_0 and q_0. They are equilibrium values because once p and q have attained those levels, they will remain unchanged unless some disturbance (a change in the things we are assuming constant underlying either curve) causes one or both of the curves to shift. The equilibrium at p_0 and q_0 is likely to be stable; other things remaining constant, if these variables are at any other levels, they tend to converge towards their equilibrium values.

To see why equilibrium price and quantity traded are those

corresponding to the intersection of the supply and demand curves, and why that equilibrium is likely to be stable, consider the kinds of pressures which would prevail if price were at any level other than p_0. If price were above p_0, say p_1, suppliers would attempt to sell q_1'' units but buyers would be willing to take only q_1' units. Quantity supplied would exceed quantity demanded — there would be an excess supply — to the extent of $(q_1'' - q_1')$ units.

To avoid such undesired stock accumulation, suppliers are likely to reduce prices. As competition among sellers forces prices down, quantity supplied decreases and quantity demanded increases. The excess supply disappears only when price has fallen to p_0. Symmetrical reasoning would apply if price were below p_0. If price were p_2, quantity demanded would be q_2'' and quantity supplied would be q_2'; there would be an excess demand of $(q_2'' - q_2')$ units per period, and the ensuing competition among buyers would drive price towards p_0. As price rises quantity demanded decreases while quantity supplied increases. The excess demand disappears only when price has been bid up to p_0 per unit.

Only at p_0 is there neither excess demand nor excess supply. Thus price and quantity traded remain constant only when they have attained the levels corresponding to the intersection of the supply and demand curves. No other price or quantity traded could be maintained for long. Hence p_0 and q_0 represent a stable market equilibrium. So long as the conditions underlying supply and demand remain constant, that price and quantity combination will continue to prevail.

Consider next what would happen if either of the curves shift (due to changes in the conditions underlying the supply or demand curves). The supply curve might shift to the right due to some technical development leading to lower unit costs. At any particular price producers are now willing to supply more than previously. The supply curve therefore shifts to the right from SS to S'S' in Figure 8, leading to reduction from p_0 to p_3 in equilibrium price and increase from q_0 to q_3 in equilibrium quantity. Note that the equilibrium price could also fall due to a shift of the demand curve. Suppose that the conditions underlying the supply curve remain constant but that there is a movement in tastes away from the good. The demand curve then shifts to the left from DD to D'D' in Figure 9. Equilibrium price falls from p_0 to p_4 and equilibrium quantity declines from q_0 to q_4. We should now be crystal clear on the question of how supply and demand determine equilibrium price and quantity traded in a perfectly competitive market, and on how changes in either (or both) of those curves cause a rise, a fall or no change in equilibrium price and quantity.

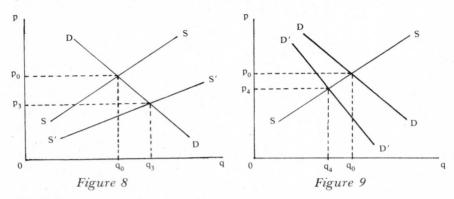

Figure 8   Figure 9

'Change in Demand' and 'Change in Quantity Demanded'

It is important to distinguish between a change (increase or decrease) in demand and a change in quantity demanded. A *change in demand* reflects a change in the conditions underlying a demand curve. It is represented by a *shift* of the demand curve, due to the fact that at least one of the determinants of demand, other than a good's own price, has changed. A *change in quantity demanded* is represented by a *movement along* a demand curve. In Figure 8 there is a change (an increase) in quantity demanded (a movement along a demand curve); in Figure 9 there is a change (a decrease) in demand (a shift of a demand curve).

The distinction between change in supply and change in quantity supplied is similar. A *change in supply* reflects change in the conditions underlying the supply of a good (other than variation in the good's own price). It is represented by a *shift* of the supply curve. A *change in quantity supplied* is represented by a *movement along* a supply curve. In Figure 8 there is a change (an increase) in supply. In Figure 9 there is a change (a decrease) in quantity supplied.

FOOTNOTES

1. Pressed to its extreme, this assumption implies zero transport costs; strictly speaking, two physically identical products are not homogeneous if costs must be incurred in bringing them to the same place.
2. We postpone discussion of complementary goods until Chapter 5.

Elasticities of Supply and Demand

Firms are interested in the effects of changes in price on their receipts from sales. To know how much they can raise in tax revenue, governments must estimate the response in quantity demanded of various goods to changes in their prices entailed by taxation. In long-term economic planning, change in the demand for various goods as income increases over time, has to be considered. In the formation of a price support policy for agricultural products, government wants to know the response in quantity supplied of such goods to changes in their prices. If estimates of the relevant elasticities are available, positive answers can be given to such questions.

An elasticity of demand (or supply) is a measure of the degree of responsiveness in the demand for (or in the supply of) a good to changes in the value of some independent variable. *Price elasticity of demand* is a measure of the response in quantity demanded of a good to changes in the good's own price. *Income elasticity of demand* is a measure of response in the demand for a good to changes in money income. *Cross elasticity of demand* is a measure of the response in the demand for a good to changes in the price of some other good. *Elasticity of supply* is a measure of the response in quantity of a good supplied to changes in its price.

Price Elasticity of Demand

Subject to a qualification stated in the next paragraph, we use the symbols E_d to denote price elasticity of demand. If, in absolute value, the proportionate change in quantity demanded of a good exceeds a proportionate change in its price, the demand for that good is *elastic*. If the absolute value of the proportionate change in quantity demanded of a good is less than the proportionate change in price the demand for the good is *inelastic*. If the absolute value of the proportionate change in quantity demanded equals the proportionate change in price, demand is of *unit elasticity*.

We can measure E_d by the formula E_d = (proportionate change in quantity demanded)/(proportionate change in price). Thus

$$(1) \qquad E_d = (\Delta q/q)/(\Delta p/p) = (\Delta q/\Delta p)(p/q)$$

An important convention should be noted. Since price and quantity are almost always inversely related (if price rises, quantity demanded falls) $\Delta q/\Delta p$ is normally negative. But p and q are positive. Therefore E_d is usually negative. However, Alfred Marshall laid down the convention of treating price elasticity of demand as a non-negative number. We shall accordingly measure price elasticity of demand by the absolute (i.e., non-negative) value of E_d, written $|E_d|$.

Another point liable to cause confusion in using measure (1) to calculate elasticity is best seen by taking an example. If price falls from £8 to £6 in Figure 10 below, leading to an increase in quantity demanded from 200 to 400 units per period of time, what is the numerical value of elasticity within the relevant range of price variation? Use the formula $E_d = (\Delta q/\Delta p)(p/q)$. The interpretation of Δq and Δp is straightforward: $\Delta q = 200$ and $\Delta p = -2$. So $\Delta q/\Delta p = -100$. But what about the measure of p and q in our formula? Does p refer to the first price ($p_1 = 8$) or the second price ($p_2 = 6$), or does it refer to some price between p_1 and p_2? Similarly, does q refer to q_1 (200 units) or q_2 (400 units) or to some quantity between q_1 and q_2? To resolve the ambiguity in the quotient p/q, the convention is to let p = p_3, the price *half-way* between the first and second prices. In like manner let q = q_3, the quantity half-way between the first and second quantities. Hence we have, for the numerical example at hand, p/q = p_3/q_3 = 7/300. Thus E_d = $(-100)(7)/(300)$ = $-2\cdot3$, and adopting the convention of expressing elasticity as a non-negative number, $|E_d|$ = $|-2\cdot3|$ = $2\cdot3$. Interpreted in this way, formula (1) is identical to

$$(2) \qquad E_d = \frac{\Delta q}{\Delta p} \cdot \frac{\frac{1}{2}(p_1 + p_2)}{\frac{1}{2}(q_1 + q_2)} = \frac{\Delta q}{\Delta p} \cdot \frac{(p_1 + p_2)}{(q_1 + q_2)}$$

where p_1 and q_1 represent the initial price and quantity demanded, p_2 and q_2 are the new price and quantity demanded, and Δp and Δq are the changes in price and quantity demanded.

Note that if the demand curve were the dotted non-linear locus D′D′ in Figure 10, the estimate of elasticity given by formula (2), when price falls from £8 to £6, would be exactly as we have calculated above. Thus the measure makes a linear estimate of elasticity between two points. If the demand curve is non-linear, formula (2) in effect assumes that the curve is linear over the range of price variation under study.

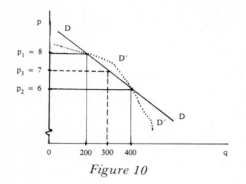

Figure 10

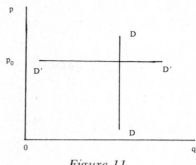

Figure 11

$|E_d|$ can have any value between zero and infinity, but there are five general possibilities:

(i) If $|E_d|$ <1, demand is *inelastic*. Quantity demanded is not particularly responsive to changes in price. If price changes by a given proportion, quantity demanded will change by a smaller proportion. If, for example, a 10 per cent change in price led to a 5 per cent change in quantity demanded, demand would be inelastic in the range of price variation in question.

(ii) If $|E_d|$>1, demand is *elastic*. Quantity demanded is quite responsive to changes in price.

(iii) If $|E_d|$ = 1, demand is of *unit elasticity*. A proportionate change in price would lead to an equiproportionate change in quantity demanded.

There are two limiting cases in the value of $|E_d|$:

(iv) If $|E_d|$ = 0, demand is *perfectly inelastic*. A change in price would lead to no change in quantity demanded. If a demand curve were perfectly inelastic for *all* ranges of price variation, it would look like DD in Figure 11.

(v) If $|E_d|$ is infinite, demand is *infinitely elastic*. If a demand curve were infinitely elastic throughout its length it would look like D'D' in Figure 11. If price were increased to the slightest extent conceivable above p_0 in the diagram, quantity demanded would be zero.

It is emphasised that the term price elasticity of demand refers to the response in quantity demanded in a neighbourhood of a specific point on a demand curve. Price elasticity varies along most demand curves; only in special cases is it constant. At high prices demand is normally elastic. At low prices it is likely to be inelastic. The reader should never — except in the two limiting cases (iv) and (v) — simply look at the steepness of a demand curve and on that basis alone declare the curve to be elastic or inelastic. Consider, for example, the straight line demand curve in Figure 12.

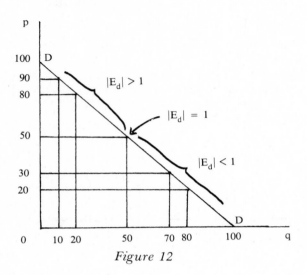

Figure 12

Because slope in this diagram is constant, $\Delta q / \Delta p$ is constant. At very low quantities p/q is very high. Thus $|E_d|$ is high; demand is elastic. At very low prices p/q is very low; demand is inelastic. Elasticity decreases as we move down a linear demand curve. It can be shown that elasticity equals unity half-way down a linear demand curve, and that it is elastic to the left, inelastic to the right, of the half-way point.

Price Elasticity of Demand and Changes in Total Revenue

Consider now the relationship between price elasticity of demand and changes in total revenue (TR). Total revenue from sales of a good is simply price multiplied by the amount sold, pq. There are three general cases:

(i) If $|E_d| < 1$ (inelastic demand) a rise in price increases TR and a fall in price reduces TR. The relationship between inelastic demand and changes in TR can be seen in Figure 12. We know that demand is inelastic in the price range (0, 50), i.e., to the right of the half-way point of this straight line demand curve. When p = 20, TR = (20)(80) = 1600. If price is raised to p = 30, TR = (30)(70) = 2100, an increase in TR. The converse would hold if price were reduced from p = 20 to p = 10.

(ii) If $|E_d| > 1$ (elastic demand) a rise in price implies a fall in TR and a fall in price implies a rise in TR. The relationship between elastic demand and changes in TR can be seen in Figure 12. We know that demand is elastic in the price range (50, 100). When p = 80, TR = (80)(20) = 1600. If price is raised to p = 90, TR = (90)(10) = 900, a fall in TR. The converse holds if price is reduced from p = 80 to p = 70.

(iii) If $|E_d| = 1$ over some range of price variation, TR will be constant over that range of price variation. (Elasticity is unity only at a single point in Figure 12, but approximately unity throughout a small neighbourhood around that point.) If a demand curve were of unit elasticity throughout, pq = TR would stay constant for any paired p and q.

We can summarise the three cases as follows:

If $|E_d| < 1$: As p↑, TR↑; As p↓, TR↓.
$|E_d| > 1$: As p↑, TR↓; As p↓, TR↑.
$|E_d| = 1$: As p↑ or ↓, no change in TR.

Determinants of Price Elasticity of Demand

The most important factor governing price elasticity of demand is the extent to which a good has *close substitutes*. The more substitutes there are, the more elastic will demand for the good tend to be, given the prices of those substitute goods. As successive Ministers for Finance have long recognised, the demand for cigarettes, which for many people have no close substitutes, is quite inelastic — that is why they have been such reliable targets of annual taxation. The demand for a particular brand of cigarettes, by contrast, is very elastic; if only one brand were raised in price by a significant amount, smokers would consume considerably less of it, and more of other brands. It should be clear that if consumers regard some good as essential, then that good does not have close substitutes. As a group, food products are biological essentials. Essentials tend to be price inelastic; if the price of food fell by 50 per cent, Europeans would not consume as much as 50 per cent more food. The low price elasticity of demand of many agricultural products is important, and merits further consideration in Chapter 7.

Another factor governing price elasticity of demand involves consideration of goods which are *the opposite of substitutes — complementary goods*. When a good is purchased to be used jointly with a more expensive product, the demand for that good tends to be price *inelastic*. Two or more goods are in *joint demand* if they are all necessary for the satisfaction of a given want. Examples are automobiles and driving licences; golf clubs and golf balls; pipes and pipe tobacco. Goods which are jointly demanded are called complementary goods, in distinction to substitute goods. If the price of driving licences were doubled, it is unlikely that the percentage decrease in purchases of licences would be significant. For law-abiding people, licences are necessary to drive a car. However, a 100 per cent increase in the price of driving licences represents, on average, only a small rise in the annual cost of running a car. Therefore driving licences, the cheaper of two complementary or jointly demanded goods, are price inelastic in demand.

Income Elasticity of Demand

Income elasticity of demand, a measure of the response in the demand for a good to changes in money income, other things being equal, is measured as

$$(3) \quad E_y = \frac{\text{Proportionate change in demand}}{\text{Proportionate change in income}} = (\Delta q/q)/(\Delta y/y) = (\Delta q/\Delta y)/(y/q)$$

where y denotes the average of the initial and new income levels, q denotes the average of the initial and new quantities of a particular good demanded and Δq and Δy are the changes in the demand for that good and in money income.

For any particular good, E_y can be greater than, equal to or less than zero. If $E_y < 0$ for some good, then the demand for that good falls *in absolute terms* as money income increases, and increases as money income falls. Such goods are called *inferior goods*. If $E_y = 0$ for some good, then a proportionate change in money income leads to no change in the demand for that good. If for some good $E_y > 0$, then a change in money income leads to a change *in the same direction* in the demand for the good. Goods for which $E_y > 0$ are called *normal goods*.

Among the positive values of income elasticity, $E_y = 1$ is a dividing line. If for some good $E_y = 1$, then a proportionate change in money income leads to an equiproportionate change (in the same direction) in purchases of the good. If $E_y < 1$ for a good, then the proportion of income spent on the good falls as income rises. (Under such circumstances the absolute amount spent on the good increases so long as E_y is positive.) If $E_y > 1$ for some good, the proportion of income spent on that good increases as income increases. (In this case sales of the good increase both absolutely and relatively as income increases.) Goods for which $0 < E_y < 1$ are called *necessities;* those for which $E_y > 1$ are termed *luxuries.* Goods for which income elasticity is close to zero are said to be *income inelastic.* Others, which have a higher (positive) income elasticity, so that purchases are significantly responsive to changes in income, are *income elastic.* Thus the demand for basic foods like cereals is income inelastic in developed economies; in very poor countries, however, it is income elastic.

Whether a good or a group of goods is high or low in income elasticity of demand is a matter of great importance. In developed economies, on average, aggregate income has tended to double every twenty to thirty years. The demand for various goods has therefore increased. But the demand for some goods has increased proportionally more than others. For example, the demand for food products as a group has increased proportionally much more slowly than the demand for manufactured goods such as automobiles and household durables in Western Europe over the last thirty years. Partly because of the differing income elasticities of demand for different groups of goods, there are substantial changes in the structure of national output as an economy develops towards high levels of per capita income: although the outputs of all three sectors (agriculture, industry, services) tend to increase in absolute terms, agricultural output tends to decline relative to the output of the industrial and services sectors. Because of differing income elasticities of demand for output (but also because the rate of increase in output per man has been more rapid in agriculture than in the two other sectors), the distribution of employment between sectors of the economy tends to change as the process of economic evolution unfolds.

Cross Elasticity of Demand

The cross elasticity of demand between two goods, A and B, measures the degree of responsiveness in the demand for A to changes in the price of good B, other things being equal. It is measured as

$$(4) \quad E_{ab} = \frac{\text{Proportionate change in purchases of A}}{\text{Proportionate change in price of B}}$$

$$= \quad (\Delta q^a / q^a) / (\Delta p^b / p^b) = (\Delta q^a / \Delta p^b)(p^b / q^a)$$

where, on the assumption that the change in the price of good B is small, p^b represents the price half-way between the first and second prices of B, and q^a denotes the quantity half-way between the first and second quantities of A.

The measure E_{ab} can take on any value between minus infinity and plus infinity. A widely used definition of substitute and complementary goods is that two goods A and B are substitutes if $E_{ab} > 0$; they are complements if $E_{ab} < 0$. For example, margarine (good A) and butter (good B) are substitutes. Their cross elasticity of demand is positive; if p^b increases ($\Delta p^b > 0$), q^a will also increase as some consumers substitute margarine for butter. Pipes (good A) and pipe tobacco (good B) are complements. Their cross elasticity of demand is negative because if p^b increases ($\Delta p^b > 0$), q^a will decrease ($\Delta q^a < 0$), as some consumers curtail their purchases of both pipes and tobacco.

Elasticity of Supply

Elasticity of supply is calculated as

(5) $E_s = \dfrac{\text{Proportionate change in quantity supplied}}{\text{Proportionate change in price}}$

$$= \frac{\Delta q}{\Delta p} \cdot \frac{(p_1 + p_2)}{(q_1 + q_2)}$$

where the variables are measured as in equation (2) for price elasticity of demand, except that q now represents quantity supplied rather than quantity demanded.

Because supply curves usually slope upwards like SS in Figure 13 below, E_s is normally positive. If $E_s < 1$ over a specific range of price variation, supply is *inelastic*. Note, however, that E_s normally varies from the neighbourhood of one point to that of another along a supply curve.

If $E_s = \infty$, supply is infinitely elastic. If supply were infinitely elastic throughout the length of a supply curve its graph would look like $S'S'$ in Figure 13. If $E_s = 0$ for a specific range of price variation, supply is of zero elasticity. If a supply curve were of zero elasticity throughout its length, its graph would look like $S''S''$ in Figure 13.

The possibility that E_s may be negative is often misunderstood. If $E_s < 0$, a reduction in price would be associated with an increase in quantity supplied. We will investigate this possibility in Part Five in the context of industry equilibrium in perfectly competitive product markets.

In the previous chapter we pointed out that supply curves pertain to flows of a good over time. Time periods may be long or short. Thus two crucial determinants of the elasticity of supply of a good are:

(i) The length of the time period under consideration. If an unanticipated increase in demand causes price suddenly to increase, producers will not be able to adjust outputs instantaneously. As time elapses they can respond to the higher price and increase their outputs by hiring more labour and buying more raw materials to use as inputs. Quantity supplied will then be more responsive to changes in price. As time further elapses firms already in the industry can add to their plant and equipment and new firms can establish themselves in the industry. Thus the longer the time period under consideration, the more elastic supply is likely to be.

(ii) Other determinants of elasticity of supply of a particular good are the elasticities of supply of the various inputs used in its production. If the inputs are elastic in supply, the final product will tend to be elastic in supply. The converse will tend to prevail if the inputs are inelastic in supply.

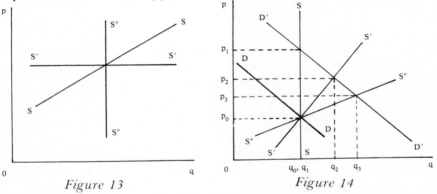

Figure 13   Figure 14

Momentary, Short-run and Long-run Equilibrium

Since time is a crucial factor in determining elasticity of supply, an increase in the demand for a good will generally lead to different increases in price, depending on whether the time period under consideration is long or short. There is, of course, an infinity of time periods. But to make analysis tractable, we follow Marshall's analytic framework by distinguishing equilibria in the context of three conceptual time periods, momentary equilibrium (associated with what is perhaps best called the *very short run*), short-run equilibrium (associated with Marshall's *short run*) and long-run equilibrium (associated with Marshall's *long run*).[1]

Suppose that starting at a full equilibrium which has long prevailed there is a permanent increase in demand for some good which cannot be stored, fresh fish, for example. The very short run is so short a period that firms can vary none of the variables which influence supply; supplies have already gone to market or are on their way to market, and will fetch whatever price, whether it be high or low, which equates the momentarily fixed supply of fish with the increased demand.

The initial situation is at (p_0, q_0) in Figure 14. The increase in demand is represented by an upward shift in the demand curve from DD to D'D'. Since supplies are momentarily fixed along SS, the new *momentary equilibrium* price is p_1. This high price is likely to be one at which suppliers earn large windfall profits. The high price acts as a signal for suppliers to expand supplies. The short run is defined as a period of time in which producers may vary their employment of certain factors, perhaps labour and raw materials, but are constrained by the fixed availability of certain other factors, such as plant and equipment. The former group of factors are called *variable factors*; the latter (i.e., whatever inputs are fixed in the time period in question) are *fixed factors.* Returning to our example of fish, the fishing industry in the short run is constrained by a given number of fishing boats, nets, etc.; however, if price has increased, the supply of fish can be increased by working longer hours, hiring more fishermen, etc., thereby utilising the existing number of boats more intensively. The relevant supply curve would then be S'S' in Figure 14, and the *short run equilibrium* price would be p_2.

In the long run the fishing industry could add to its capacity by waiting for the construction of new boats and by varying other factors which were fixed in the short-run. Thus supply would be more responsive to change in price than in the short-run — the long-run supply curve would be like, say, S"S" in Figure 14, and p_3 would be the *long-run* equilibrium price.

The long-run supply curve is likely to slope upwards, reflecting the fact that the fishing industry (in the present example) must bid up prices of some inputs to attract them away from other industries. Note that after the shift in demand from DD to D'D', the long-run equilibrium price is lower, and quantity supplied is higher, than in the short-run, and the short-run equilibrium price is lower, and quantity supplied is higher, than in the very short run. This reflects the fact that elasticity of supply is generally higher the longer the time period under consideration.

FOOTNOTE
1. Alfred Marshall, *Principles of Economics,* 8th edn, London: Macmillan 1920, Book V, Chapter 5.

CHAPTER 6

General Applications of Supply and Demand Analysis

Government intervention and legal restrictions are among the reasons why markets diverge from perfect competition. That is not to say that all government intervention in markets, or all legal restrictions on their operation, are inconsistent with perfect competition. But when they do involve significant departures from such assumptions in markets which would otherwise approximate perfect competition, the effects of public policies are best analysed by starting with the assumption of perfect competition and imposing the public policies on that analytic framework. That is what we do in this chapter. We assume that, apart from the effects of government intervention, the markets under analysis approximate the relevant assumptions of perfect competition. We assume that, if unregulated, the markets have unique and stable equilibria, and that if they are not in equilibrium they rapidly converge towards equilibrium.

The examples which follow in this and in the next two chapters indicate how supply and demand analysis is applied to situations in the world around us. Examples other than those discussed in the text are abundant. The reader may wish to devise his own applications.

Taxes on Transactions

Governments raise revenue by taxes on sale of goods. What are the effects of such taxes? Does the burden fall on the seller, or does he mainly pass the tax on in the form of higher prices? How much may government expect to raise in revenue from a tax on a good? Would it make any difference if the buyer rather than the seller were administratively liable for its payment? Suppose we are dealing with a per unit tax on a good, and that it is the *suppliers* who must pay the government so many pounds or pence per unit sold. If, as we assume, the good in question is traded in markets approximating in relevant ways the assumptions of perfect competition, it is easy to give definite answers to these questions.

Suppose that initially there is no government interference in the market and that next a tax of £t per unit sold is imposed on suppliers of a good. In Figure 15, SS is the pre-tax supply curve; equilibrium price and quantity are p_0 and q_0 respectively. The introduction of a per unit tax on sellers causes no change in the demand curve, for none of the factors underlying the demand curve have changed. But because the sellers are liable for payment of the tax (the variable g in the general supply function (2) of Chapter 4 has changed) the supply curve shifts upwards by the full amount of the tax per unit to, say $S'S'$. The vertical distance between SS and $S'S'$ is exactly £t, the amount of the tax per unit. For example, before the tax producers were willing to supply, say q_1 units, at a price p_1. After the tax they would be willing to supply that same quantity only if they receive the same *net* receipts per unit as before; they would therefore be willing to supply q_1 units at the price $(p_1 + t) = p_2$ pounds. Similarly, after the tax they would be willing to supply q_2 units at the old supply price for that quantity plus the tax, i.e., at $(p_3 + t) = p_4$ pounds.

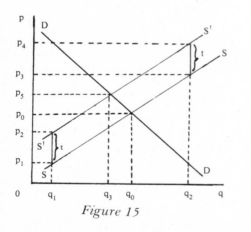

Figure 15

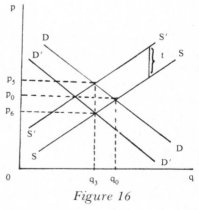

Figure 16

Figure 15 has become a little clogged, so we reproduce those supply and demand curves in Figure 16, where it is clear that the tax per unit sold causes the equilibrium price to increase from p_0 to p_5, and the equilibrium quantity to decrease from q_0 to q_3. Thus the theory predicts that a per unit tax on a good traded in a market, approximating in relevant respects the assumptions of perfect competition, will increase the equilibrium price paid by consumers and decrease the equilibrium quantity traded. In the context of our discussion on methodology in Chapter 2, this is a meaningful theory. As such, it is not true by definition; its empirical validity could in principle be tested, and rejected if substantively inconsistent with facts.

It may be worthwhile to point out that our conclusion concerning the effects of a per unit tax would be valid even if sellers were exempt from payment of tax, but if a tax of £t per unit were imposed, administratively payable by *buyers*. The reader should be able to show that in this case it is the demand curve which would shift to the left — to D'D' in Figure 16. The locus SS would remain the supply curve, but the new demand curve would be a vertical distance of £t below the pre-tax demand curve DD. The equilibrium after-tax quantity is again q_3, and the equilibrium *effective* price paid by buyers (though not that posted by sellers) is again $p_5 = (p_6 + t)$. In both cases the after-tax effective price paid by buyers has increased to p_5 and the after-tax net price received by sellers has decreased to p_6. Conclusions like these hold whether or not the supply and demand curves are linear. However, in reality it is sellers who are usually liable for payment of a per unit tax, because there are usually fewer sellers of a good than there are buyers, and it is easier, from an administrative standpoint, to collect tax revenue from the fewer sellers. We will therefore assume that per unit taxes are administratively payable by suppliers. Before proceeding to the relevance of elasticities we note in passing that a per unit subsidy is the exact opposite, and has the opposite effects, of a per unit tax. We leave it to the reader to analyse the effects of a per unit subsidy.

The Relevance of Elasticities

Our central conclusion is that so long as supply curves slope upwards and demand curves slope downwards, a per unit tax will increase the effective price paid by consumers (though not the net price received by sellers) and will reduce quantity traded.

However, we have not investigated the determinants of *the extent* to which such a tax may lead to higher prices paid by buyers, or lower net (after-tax) prices received by sellers. Thus we have not examined what determines the extent to which a per unit tax on suppliers is 'passed on' in the form of higher prices. These questions are intimately related to (price) elasticities of supply and demand.

Assume, starting from an equilibrium price-quantity combination, that a per unit tax of £t is imposed on the suppliers of a good. The curves SS in Figures 17a, 17b and 17c indicate some possible supply curves at the pre-tax equilibrium, (p_0, q_0). The demand curve DD is unaffected by the tax. In regard to supply, we warned earlier of the dangers of merely looking at the slope of a supply (or demand) curve and on that basis alone drawing conclusions in regard to price elasticity. However, in the neighbourhood of a *given* price-quantity combination (such as p_0 and q_0 in Figures 17a, 17b and 17c) we can legitimately conclude that the less steep the slope of a supply curve, the greater its price elasticity. Thus in the neighbourhood of the point (p_0, q_0) in the three diagrams, SS is infinitely elastic in Figure 17a; in 17b it is moderately elastic; in 17c it is inelastic. The loci S'S' (which lie a vertical distance of £t above the pre-tax supply curves SS) represent the after-tax supply curves in the three cases depicted.

It can be seen that the price paid by consumers increases by the full amount of the tax when supply is infinitely elastic (Figure 17a); in 17b, where supply is moderately elastic, price increases by about 50 per cent of the tax, and in 17c, where supply is inelastic, price increases by a small percentage of the tax. Hence although, as assumed, suppliers are administratively responsible for payment of the tax, the *incidence* or *burden* of the tax (by which we mean the question of who *ultimately* pays the tax, by having to offer a higher price for goods bought, or by having to accept a lower after-tax price for goods sold) may fall mainly on buyers or sellers, or on both more or less equally, depending on elasticity of supply (and, as we shall soon see, on elasticity of demand also). In the case of infinitely elastic supply, producers fully 'pass on' the tax by charging consumers a higher price. In the opposite case, where supply is of zero elasticity, the tax leads to no change in price to consumers; in that case the entire burden of the tax falls on suppliers, who must accept an after-tax net price equal to the original price minus the per unit tax.

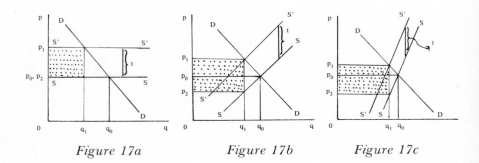

Figure 17a   *Figure 17b*   *Figure 17c*

Price elasticity of demand is also of relevance. Figures 18a, 18b and 18c illustrate three possible demand curves leading to the same pre-tax price-quantity combination, (p_0, q_0). The initial pre-tax supply curve SS is the same in each case. The demand curve in Figure 18a is perfectly inelastic, and the per unit tax of £t, which causes the supply curve to shift upwards by a vertical distance of £t, to $S'S'$, is fully passed on in the form of higher prices paid by consumers; in 18b demand is more elastic, and price rises by less than the tax; in 18c, where demand is infinitely elastic, the tax leads to no change in price paid by consumers.

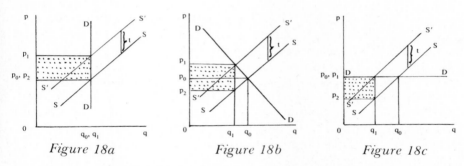

Figure 18a   *Figure 18b*   *Figure 18c*

We can generalise the results obtained for three different ranges of price elasticity of demand by stating the general proposition that the less elastic the demand curve in the neighbourhood of the pre-tax equilibrium price, the larger the increase in price charged to consumers entailed by a per unit tax (and the smaller the reduction in net after-tax price received by suppliers); on the other hand, the higher the price elasticity of demand, the lower the increase in prices charged consumers after the tax (and the more the burden of the tax falls on suppliers).

We have not yet indicated what the net after-tax equilibrium prices received by suppliers actually are in the various cases considered. The net after-tax equilibrium price received by suppliers is the equilibrium price charged to consumers after the imposition of the tax minus the tax per unit. For example, in Figures 18a, 18b and 18c it is p_2.

We conclude this discussion by stating that *given a particular initial supply curve,* a per unit tax levied on suppliers will raise price paid by consumers most, and reduce purchases least, the lower is price elasticity of demand. *Given a particular initial demand curve,* the price paid by consumers, as well as purchases, will change least, and net after-tax price received by suppliers will fall most, the less elastic the supply curve. The tax tends to be passed on to consumers when the demand curve is very inelastic, but its burden tends to fall on suppliers when the supply curve is very inelastic. The reader may need pencil and paper to satisfy himself — and he should satisfy himself — that these assertions are correct.

Per Unit Taxes and Government Tax Revenue

If government imposes a per unit tax of £t on sales of a good, the increase in tax revenue will be the tax rate multiplied by the number of units sold after the imposition of the tax. Thus revenue raised by taxing a good may be high or low depending on the good's price elasticities of demand and supply. In Figure 17a to 18c, the pre-tax equilibrium prices and quantities are p_0 and q_0 respectively. The after-tax equilibrium prices and quantities are p_1 and q_1. In each case the net after-tax equilibrium price received by sellers is p_1 minus the tax per unit. The tax per unit is the height of the dotted rectangles; thus in each case the net after-tax price received by sellers is p_2. In each case total revenue raised from taxation of the good is given by the area of the dotted rectangle. It can be seen from the diagrams that tax revenue is high or low depending on the elasticities of supply and demand. There are two extreme cases, depicted in Figures 19 and 20, in which the introduction of a per unit tax on suppliers would cause no change in the equilibrium quantity bought.

The pre-tax equilibrium price-quantity combination is the same in Figures 19 and 20. In Figure 19, where demand may be of *any* elasticity other than zero (so it may be infinitely elastic like DD, or less elastic like D'D'), supply is of zero elasticity. Under such circumstances a per unit tax would not affect the supply curve; all it can affect is the after-tax net price received by suppliers; which, in this example, falls to p_2, the dotted rectangle being the government's total receipts from the tax. In Figure 20, where the pre-tax supply curve, such as SS *or* S"S", may be of any elasticity other than zero in the neighbourhood of the initial price, the demand curve is of zero elasticity, and the tax (represented by the shift to S'S' or S'"S'" in the supply curve) again causes no change in quantity purchased. If the per unit tax has been the same in each diagram, the government's total receipts from the tax are the same in either case. Since we do not wish to be drawn into mathematical analysis, we simply report that the closer actual markets approximate the circumstances of Figures 19 and 20 in the neighbourhood of the initial price-quantity combination, the larger a government's receipts from a per unit tax of a given size.

Finally, without making specific reference to elasticity of supply, we can state the generalisation that the more inelastic the demand curve in the neighbourhood of the pre-tax equilibrium price, the larger the increase in government revenue from a per unit tax.

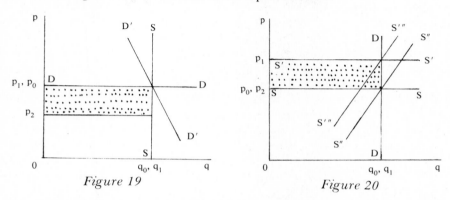

Figure 19   Figure 20

Price Elasticities of Tradeable Goods and Tax Revenue in Small Open Economies

An open economy is one which, among other things, depends heavily on foreign trade, and which has relatively free mobility of goods (exports and imports) across its national frontiers. If an economy were fully open there would be no tariffs or quantity quotas restricting the movement of goods across its frontiers. We regard an open economy as small if its output of tradeable goods is only a small proportion of the total output of similar tradeable goods in the countries with which it has relatively free mobility of goods. We can regard tradeable goods as those for which transportation costs are not prohibitive, and which are not impeded, on that count, from entering international trade. The Republic of Ireland is a small, open economy within the European Economic Community (EEC). Because EEC countries do not maintain tariffs and quotas against each other, and because Ireland's output and consumption of tradeables is only a small proportion of EEC output and consumption of tradeables, Ireland, in so far as tradeable goods are concerned, is in many respects close to being a perfectly competitive supplier and demander within the whole EEC market, as is suggested by popular reference to the EEC as The Common Market. These considerations have important implications for elasticities of supply and demand for tradeable goods in Ireland.

Consider first supply. The supply of a good to an individual in a market approximating perfect competition is infinitely elastic, or at least very elastic. That is because he can purchase in effect any quantity of the good at the going market price; he does not bid up price against himself by increasing his purchases, simply because those purchases are a negligibly small fraction of total purchases of that good in the market. For tradeable goods — the output of manufacturing industry and of the agricultural sector — Ireland is in a situation similar to such an individual buyer in a perfectly competitive market, except that now the market of relevance is the Common Market. Since there is freedom of movement of goods within the EEC, and since Irish buyers are only a small fraction of all buyers in the EEC, Irish buyers are, as a group, closely akin to price-takers: abstracting from taxation, so long as they pay roughly the going market prices for tradeable goods in the EEC as a whole, they can buy in effect any quantities of those goods without bidding up prices against themselves. Thus, ignoring very short periods of purely localised shortages, the supply curve of a tradeable good to the Irish market is infinitely elastic (like SS in Figure 21) or very elastic (like S'S'in Figure 21). If, then, government imposes a per unit tax on supplies to Irish buyers (regardless of whether supply is domestically produced or produced in other EEC countries) the supply curve will shift upwards by the amount of the tax to S"S" or S"'S"' in Figure 21.

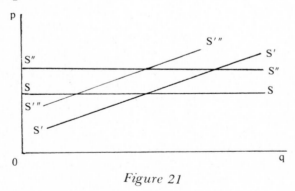

Figure 21

The demand curve of relevance to the pricing of tradeable goods in the Irish economy reflects both domestic demand and export demand. If there were perfect information among buyers in the EEC market; if transport costs were zero; if the product under analysis and available to Irish consumers were identical to other goods available to all EEC consumers; and if there were no taxes on goods, the demand curve would, in effect, be infinitely elastic at the prevailing common EEC market price. If, for example, Irish producers as a group conspired to raise their price for the tradeable good under analysis above the level prevailing in other EEC countries, they would lose all their sales. For then Irish consumers would import the good from abroad, and if there were originally any exports of the good from Ireland, those would fall to zero. Conversely, if Irish producers were to charge a lower price than the equilibrium price in the rest of the EEC, Europeans would switch their purchases towards Irish sellers, thereby bidding upwards the Irish price toward that prevailing in the rest of the EEC.

However, the existence of inertia and imperfect information among buyers, and the fact that transportation costs are positive, implies that the demand curve of relevance to the pricing of a tradeable good in Ireland is not quite infinitely elastic. In the case of manufactures, another reason why the demand for Irish goods is not generally infinitely elastic is the fact that many manufactured goods are not (in buyers' minds) identical substitutes for those produced in other EEC countries; they may differ in design, packaging or brand names and in the effectiveness of advertising outlays. All of these considerations imply that the demand curves of relevance to the pricing of tradeable goods in Ireland are not generally infinitely elastic. Our central conclusions at this stage are:

(i) Very short periods of localised shortages aside, supply curves of manufactured goods to the Irish economy are likely to be very elastic in the neighbourhood of equilibrium prices.

(ii) Demand curves may range from very high to low elasticity in the neighbourhood of equilibrium prices. They are more elastic than they would be if Ireland were a closed economy with little market dependence on the rest of the EEC.

(iii) Consideration (i) implies that if a per unit tax is imposed on tradeable goods to the Irish economy, price is likely to increase by close to the full amount of the tax.

What we have said above applies to tradeable goods only. But not all goods and services are tradeable; one does not go to Liverpool to get a haircut, or import a house (and the site upon which it is built) from Germany. Considerations of international trade are of less immediate relevance to the pricing of such goods and services. The supply curves for non-tradeables are therefore likely to be less elastic than in the case of tradeable goods. Hence, for any given value of price elasticity of demand in the neighbourhood of a pre-tax equilibrium, the imposition of a per unit tax would tend to raise equilibrium price by a smaller percentage of the tax than in the case of tradeables. Correspondingly, the burden of a per unit tax falls mainly on buyers in the case of tradeables; for non-tradeables it falls more heavily on suppliers.

Direct Price Controls

Governments often invoke legislation enabling them to control the prices which may legally be charged for various commodities, both final goods as well as factors of production. In Ireland, minimum agricultural wages have for several decades been fixed in accordance with legislation of 1936 and subsequently. During, and for a short period after, World War II, industrial wages were regulated by Emergency Powers Orders, the general effect of which was to prohibit increases above 'standard rates' in operation in April 1942.[1] In more recent years maximum prices which could legally be charged for various consumer goods have been subject to control. We will refer to such maximum permissible prices as *price ceilings.*

As examples of government interference in the market, price controls differ very substantively from per unit taxes. A per unit tax on the sale of a good usually shifts the supply curve; the equilibrium price and quantity traded are still determined by supply and demand. However, a price ceiling, if it has any effect at all (i.e., if the maximum permissible price is less than the equilibrium price) is likely to prevent a market from attaining equilibrium.

Suppose that the supply and demand curves for a good are as in Figure 22 below. The equilibrium price and quantity are p_0 and q_0 respectively. Suppose that government imposes an Order to the effect that p_1 is the maximum price which may legally be charged; note that this is less than the equilibrium price. At this ceiling price, buyers wish to purchase q'_1, but suppliers are willing to provide only q_1; there is an excess in quantity demanded over quantity supplied. Under these circumstances there is no way of knowing which potential buyers will obtain what quantities of the good. All we can say for sure is that if the law is rigidly enforced there will be unsatisfied potential buyers who are willing to pay the price asked for by sellers, who in turn are not willing to supply the quantity demanded at the ceiling price. Early morning queues may develop, with sales on a 'first come, first served' basis, leaving many at the end of the line, unable to buy because supplies have been exhausted by the time they register their desire to buy. Or suppliers may simply confine sales to 'regular' customers. However, it may be impossible to enforce the law rigidly. If that is the case it is likely that at least some transactions will take place at prices in excess of the ceiling, in 'black markets'. If enforcement of the law is lax, suppliers may sell at prices between the ceiling and the equilibrium levels, but so long as actual prices are less than the equilibrium level there will be some unsatisfied demanders. There is of course the possibility that the ceiling price is rigidly enforced on the original suppliers, but not on secondary transactions in the good. Thus secondary markets may emerge, with middlemen buying the total supply, q_1, from the original suppliers at the ceiling price, but selling at prices, or at a single price, as high as p_2 in Figure 22. In this case the intent of the price ceiling is totally frustrated: as compared to the initial unregulated market situation, quantity traded is reduced from q_0 to q_1, while price charged is increased from p_0 up to p_2.

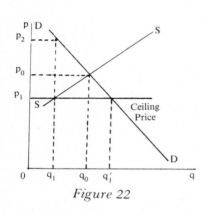

Figure 22

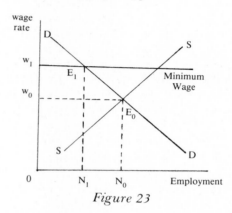

Figure 23

It has already been remarked that if an effective price ceiling is imposed there is no way of knowing which consumers will obtain what quantities of the good. Government may therefore seek to allocate the good in accordance with its own preferences (rather than the preferences of suppliers and demanders). It may try to do so by issuing ration coupons sufficient for the purchase of the quantity q_1 (the amount which suppliers offer at the ceiling price) in Figure 22. It may issue ration coupons on the basis of household size, for example. But we can be practically certain that a market for ration coupons would emerge, largely reflecting the fact that the preferences of individuals are not identical. The emergence of prices for ration coupons would mean that some individuals would be paying effective prices for the rationed good above the ceiling price. The effective price paid by a buyer for any particular unit of the good would then be the ceiling price, p_1, plus the price, if any, paid for a ration coupon enabling the consumer to buy that unit of the good. Thus, if a price ceiling is imposed it is likely that 'black markets' and effective prices above the ceiling level will emerge whether or not the good is rationed.

Minimum Prices

A law controlling the minimum or *floor price* at which a good or factor may be bought or hired can have no substantive effect if that floor is below the equilibrium price. Common kinds of floor prices which come to mind are those on factors of production such as labour. Since these are normally designed to raise prices above their equilibrium market levels, thereby reducing the amount of such factors hired, these conrols may harm many of those they are designed to help.

Suppose that the market for unskilled agricultural labour, for example, is initially free from government intervention, and that it approximates the assumptions of perfect competition in relevant ways. Figure 23 shows the initial market situation. The price of labour services, in hours, is the wage rate. It is assumed in the diagram that the lower the wage rate, the higher the demand for, and the lower the supply of, labour hours. The equilibrium wage and employment levels are given by the coordinates of point E_0. If the minimum wage is as in the diagram, the resulting wage and employment levels will be represented by the coordinates of point E_1. Those workers who remain employed will have obtained a higher wage, but others will be made unemployed.

In the above example we assumed that the wage floor was imposed by law. However, it could have been introduced by trade union organisation in a labour market which was previously unorganised. Under such circumstances the effect of trade union bargaining for a wage w_1 would be to increase the wage (from w_0), but at a cost of reducing employment from N_0 to N_1 in the diagram (where N denotes the number of hours worked).

Price Control, Allocation and Equity

We observed in Chapter 3 that, although one might not like the resulting pattern of income distribution, reliance on market forces in the ideal market economy would tend to solve the economy's allocation problem in an efficient manner. We have seen in the present chapter that government interference with supply and demand may introduce inefficiencies. Thus price ceilings may cause production of goods to be contracted and may make their allocation among consumers *a priori* indeterminate. Price floors may cause unemployment, which is clearly inefficient. Why, then, do governments introduce price control? In wartime, government seeks to control the allocation of an economy's resources toward the war effort; it seeks to encourage the release of resources away from production of consumer goods not considered essential towards production of defence goods. Price control combined with rationing may be appropriate under such circumstances. In peacetime, governments implement price control under the declared objective of curbing inflation, and on grounds of what they consider equity. But attempts to curb inflation by price control in an open economy like Ireland are likely to meet little success; if the reader finds this mysterious, he will be enlightened when we get to macro-economics. It might appear then that, wartime aside, the main arguments for price ceilings and floors involve considerations of equity. Consider these briefly.

Government may place a legal floor on the price of labour services in order to raise the wages of those who remain employed. But it may then find (given its objectives of 'fairness' in income distribution) that it must use the tax system to finance income maintenance ('dole') payments to those made unemployed by the imposition of the price floor. Given its objectives, it may be more rational for government to place more reliance on the market mechanism by abstaining from such direct interference with the forces of supply and demand, by using the tax system to assist mobility of labour to more high-paying jobs and to finance retraining of workers in low-paying jobs for employment elsewhere in the economy, where rates of pay are higher. This would represent improvement in efficiency of resource allocation, for total production in the economy would then increase, while at the same time the pattern of income distribution could be improved by mildly influencing the market mechanism in the manner suggested, rather than blocking it via wage controls.

Government may try to control the price of a final product because it believes that excess profits are being reaped. Such controls may lead to 'black markets' with large profits being pocketed by middlemen, a class not normally held in esteem by government or the public. We saw that allocation of goods among consumers may be *a priori* indeterminate if a price ceiling is enforced; of all the consumers who are prepared to buy a reduced supply of a good at a ceiling price, the good may be sold to those who desire it least rather than most. If the objective of price control is the prevention of excess profits, that objective can usually be pursued more efficiently by means of the tax system.

We repeat that price controls, by affecting supply of goods and employment of factors, frequently harm those they are intended to benefit. For example, France had virtually no residential construction between 1914 and 1948, partly due to rent control, and the same kind of interference with the market mechanism led to decay (failure to repair and maintain) and ultimate abandonment by owners of apartment dwellings in New York City in the 1960s and in Rome in the 1970s. Unless politicians and civil servants have competent economic expertise to assess proposed measures of price control, their actions may involve serious misallocations of resources. We therefore do not advocate price controls as general policy measures unless their implications are competently analysed, and unless the principal alternative means of promoting the objectives motivating proposed price controls are competently assessed. If change in the pattern of income distribution is an important objective, this is normally more efficiently attained by manipulating the tax system and by further means other than blocking the operation of markets. Finally, to think that one can substantively, or for long, control the rate of inflation by means of ceilings on prices legally charged in a highly open economy like Ireland is to indulge in fantasy.

FOOTNOTE

1. James Meenan, *The Irish Economy Since 1922*, Liverpool: Liverpool University Press 1970, 68-9.

CHAPTER 7

Supply and Demand Applied to Agriculture

Until recent decades agriculture was the major source of employment in Ireland. However, as in other economies as they developed, the percentage of the labour force engaged in agriculture has long been declining. In the 1920s over 50 per cent of our labour force was in agriculture; today the figure is about 20 per cent. Government interference aside, there have been a number of reasons for this long-term outflow of labour from agriculture. On the side of supply, (i) technical progress has been greatly reducing the number of people required to produce any given amount of food, and (ii) for several decades after the State was established, Ireland had an excess supply of labour in agriculture, in the sense that, given the state of technology, any particular level of output could have been produced by an amount of labour smaller than was actually engaged; this meant that per capita incomes in Irish agriculture were lower than they would otherwise have been. On the marketing side, the demand for food products *as a group* in developed countries is income inelastic, though in this context Ireland is fortunate in an important respect: as incomes increase people tend to consume more meat, instead of bread and potatoes, and Ireland is very well endowed for beef production. However, beef production has been land-intensive rather than labour-intensive. Despite its declining farm population, Ireland is still far more dependent on agriculture than any other EEC country. In 1975 the percentages of the working population engaged in agriculture were as in Table 3.

Important aspects of the experience of agriculture in developed economies over the last century are summarised by Figure 24. With little government intervention in the market at the beginning of the century, the initial equilibrium is at point E. Improved production methods have shifted the supply curve to the right. Growth in population and in per capita income have also shifted the demand curve to the right, but because of *low income and price elasticities* of demand for most food products, this, in free markets, leads to

Table 3
Percentages of Working Population Engaged in Agriculture, 1975

Germany	7.3	Luxembourg	6.2
France	11.3	United Kingdom	2.7
Italy	15.8	Ireland	24.3
Netherlands	6.6	Denmark	9.8
Belgium	3.6		

Source: Directorate General for Press and Information, *The Common Agricultural Policy,* Brussels: Commission of the European Communities 1977. 3.

downward pressure on agricultural prices relative to those of goods and services in general. In the absence of government intervention to support agricultural prices, the resulting equilibrium for recent years would be at a point like E′ in Figure 24; agricultural incomes would accordingly lag behind incomes in the industrial and services sectors. For these and other reasons governments have intervened in agricultural markets. Agricultural prices and incomes are therefore probably higher than they would be if their determination were left to the free play of markets alone.

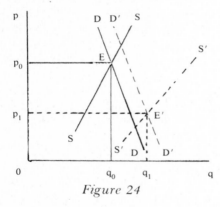

Figure 24

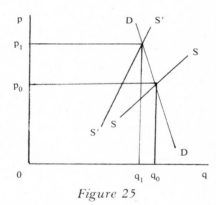

Figure 25

Government Intervention in Agricultural Markets

Governments intervene in agriculture for many reasons. However, it appears that the primary motive has been the belief that agricultural markets, if left to themselves, would result in levels of income among the rural population which would be socially unacceptable. Government may seek to affect farm prices and/or farm incomes by influencing the supply of, and/or the demand for, agricultural goods, by standing willing to buy from farmers at a fixed price — a guaranteed price — or by outright cash payments to farmers. These actions are not necessarily mutually exclusive. It may also assist farmers by means of tariffs and export subsidies; however, we defer consideration of the latter two measures until the next chapter.

Crop Limitation Programmes and Similar Schemes

In the USA, government has paid farmers (i) for leaving land idle and (ii) for not surpassing maximum quotas on production of particular crops. Consider the effects of such crop limitation programmes, *assuming that the market in question is isolated from international trade*. The initial supply curve slopes upwards, as in Figure 25. The demand curve slopes steeply downwards, reflecting the fact that in developed countries the quantity of food demanded does not vary much as the price of food varies. Application of a crop limitation plan causes the supply curve to pivot to the left, from SS to $S'S'$. Equilibrium price rises from p_0 to p_1 and equilibrium quantity falls from q_0 to q_1. Consideration of cash grants to farmers (for their cooperation in the limitation plan) aside, this market reaction may or may not raise farm incomes; it will do so if, in the neighbourhood of the equilibrium prices, the demand for the product is price inelastic. This is the case in Figure 25, as is clear from the fact that the area of the rectangle p_1q_1 exceeds that of p_0q_0. If, in the neighbourhood of the initial equilibrium, the demand for a farm product is price inelastic, any government policy which reduces supply would tend to increase total farm receipts. Even without government cash payments to farmers for their cooperation, there would be a second reason why farm incomes would tend to increase: since output would have fallen, so too would costs.

A few remarks are appropriate. First, the above results would not necessarily hold if the demand curve were price elastic: with elastic demand, reduction in the supply of some good by farmers as a group would reduce their total receipts from sales, but incomes would increase if total costs fell more than total revenues. Second, even if the overall demand for a product were price inelastic, if only *an individual farmer* reduced his supplies while all others maintained them at their previous levels, that farmer's sales receipts would fall. That is because the demand curve for the output of an individual farmer in a very competitive market is, in effect, *infinitely elastic*: his supply of any particular good is such a small part of total supply of that good that he is a price-taker; he can sell as much as he likes at the ruling price. Thus our main conclusion is that if the market demand for a product is price inelastic, then adoption of a crop limitation programme by farmers *as a group* would increase total sales receipts of farmers.

Whether those crop limitation programmes which raise farm incomes are desirable or not is a question of ethics; as economists we merely indicate that crop limitation programmes, whether or not they raise farm incomes, do raise agricultural prices, and on that count involve reduction in real incomes of the non-farm population. They involve misallocation of resources: either a resource (land) is left producing nothing or it is allocated to uses in which it is less productive than it would be if the free play of market forces were operating. Crop limitation programmes may drive the economy into operation below its production possibility frontier; if they do so they are certainly inefficient. These considerations suggest that if maximisation of national output, subject to the maintenance of farm incomes, are objectives of policy, then the latter goal might be pursued more rationally by means other than crop limitation programmes.

With foreign trade, crop limitation programmes may be sensible policy instruments depending on whether the country or group of countries applying such programmes are price-takers on international markets, and if they do influence price (i.e., if they are price-makers), depending on whether world demand for the product is price elastic. Furthermore, whether crop limitation programmes are sensible policy instruments may depend on whose standpoint we adopt — that of countries applying them or that of the world as a whole.

Consider the case of Ireland. Beef is Ireland's most important export, and virtually all of it goes to the EEC. It is a close approximation to say that beef prices are determined by EEC regulations. Thus, Ireland is effectively a price-taker in beef; we can sell as much as we wish without affecting the obtainable price to a significant degree. Limitation of our beef production would not make sense. Even if beef prices were not determined by EEC regulations, we would have no incentive to limit our beef production under conditions of free trade, because we would remain a relatively marginal supplier of beef to international markets.

Consider next a country (group of countries) which accounts (account) for a high proportion of world production of a particular crop. Coffee, the bulk of which originates in Latin America, is a case in point. World price elasticity of demand for coffee is estimated[1] as being about 0.25; it is inelastic. Hence if coffee producers *as a group* could agree to reduce coffee output, their receipts from coffee sales would increase. However, it does *not* follow, if an *individual* small country producing coffee were to reduce its coffee production, that it would increase its receipts. For example, Haiti and Honduras each account for less than 1 per cent of total world coffee production. Because they are marginal suppliers to the world economy they are effectively price-takers — the demand for their coffee is, in effect, infinitely elastic. If such countries reduced their output, that would bring about little change in total world output of coffee or in its price; the receipts of such countries would fall. Brazil, on the other hand, is by far the most important coffee producer, accounting for about one third of world exports of the crop. With a world price elasticity of demand of about 0.25, 'Brazil thus is the sole country that can increase its export receipts by restricting its exports. This explains why 80% of world stocks [of coffee] in the years of oversupply in the early sixties were accumulated by Brazil'.[2]

Similar observations apply to a wide range of primary (i.e., agricultural and natural resource) products originating in the developing countries: if *as a group* they contracted their output of primary products for which world demand is price inelastic, their total foreign exchange earnings, and hence their real incomes, would increase. However, even if a single country or a group of countries gain from restricting output of a product price inelastic in demand, such policies misallocate resources in the world economy. We saw that a crop limitation programme in a closed economy involves misallocation of resources; the world as a whole is a closed economy. Thus it would potentially be in the interests of *all* nations if the developed countries compensated the developing countries whose (group) exports are price inelastic in demand, for *not* colluding to restrict such exports.

Guaranteed Minimum Prices

In most developed economies government seeks to support farm incomes by providing minimum price guarantees for certain agricultural products. The manner in which such a programme is usually implemented is roughly as follows:

Suppose government guarantees a price floor of p_1 in Figure 26. Assume for simplicity that the country does not engage in international trade in the good the price of which is guaranteed. If the price which would emerge from the free play of domestic market forces is higher than p_1, say p_2 (in which case the supply curve is $S'S'$), government will not intervene. But suppose that the equilibrium price in the absence of government intervention turns out to be less than p_1, say p_0

in the diagram (the supply curve is then SS). Government may add to market demand by buying the excess in quantity supplied over quantity demanded at the guaranteed price; in Figure 26 it would have to buy AB per period in order to support the price at p_1. Quantity demanded would then be q_1 (demanded by consumers) plus $q_3 - q_1$ (bought by government). This would equal quantity supplied, q_3, at the guaranteed floor price, p_1.

What will government do with its purchases? So long as p_1 is the guaranteed price and so long as the supply and demand curves remain at SS and DD, it cannot release its purchases to be sold on the free market; if it did so, the equilibrium price would fall below p_1. Its purchases will, therefore, go into storage; will be given away to the poor or offered at special low prices to the poor (those who cannot afford to pay a price as high as p_1) or will be destroyed. (If there is foreign trade, government might subsidise exports of the good or might donate it to poor countries.)

Who pays for the higher prices received by farmers? By and large it is the taxpaying consumers, who are paying government to finance its purchases of the excess supply at the guaranteed price. (This cost is represented by the rectangle q_1q_3BA in Figure 26.) In the absence of government intervention price would be p_0; after intervention it is higher, p_1. So consumers must pay both more in taxes as well as higher prices for what they buy. The farming community is made better off: its receipts in the absence of intervention would be p_0q_0; after intervention it receives p_1q_3.

What is the effect on the allocation of resources? More agricultural goods are being produced than the free play of market forces would warrant. This implies that actual or potential production of other goods must be reduced. The price support programme does not necessarily drive the economy below its production possibility frontier, but if the economy does remain on that locus, it will be producing goods in the wrong proportions; it will be producing too many agricultural goods and too few non-agricultural goods relative to the wants of consumers as represented by the prices they would be willing to pay in a free market.

Price Stabilisation in a Static Framework

Transactions by government in agricultural markets — what we call *intervention transactions* — do not necessarily have higher prices as their central objective. Stabilisation of agricultural prices, which might

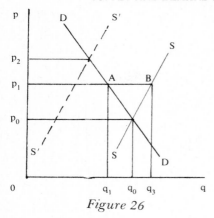

Figure 26

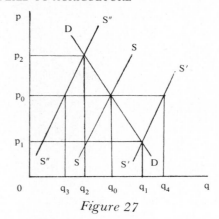

Figure 27

fluctuate severely in the absence of intervention, may be an objective. Weather conditions may, in a free market, cause agricultural prices to fluctuate, increasing uncertainty for producers and thereby impeding investment planning in agriculture. Government intervention to peg agricultural prices may then be desirable. How this may be done is indicated in Figure 27. In what follows in this section we assume that, apart from the effects of unexpected weather conditions,[3] output plans of producers are fulfilled in the year in which those plans are made. We also assume that the economy does not engage in international trade in the good under analysis.

Suppose policy seeks to stabilise price at p_0 in Figure 27. Given the demand curve DD, government intervention is not needed (in, say, years of average harvests) when SS is the supply curve. In years of good harvests the supply curve will have shifted to the right to, say, $S'S'$. Government can then buy q_1-q_0 to peg price at p_0. Such purchases could be allocated to the intervention agency's (the government's) *buffer stock.* In years of poor harvests the supply curve will have shifted to the left to, say, $S''S''$; without intervention, price would rise to p_2. However, government could maintain price at p_0 by drawing on its buffer stock, selling q_0-q_3. Supply (q_3 from current production plus q_0-q_3 from buffer stocks) would then equal demand at price p_0. Thus accumulation and decumulation of buffer stocks can avert fluctuations in price. But if price stabilisation is the dominant objective, and if government does not wish to destroy some of its intervention purchases or to let them rot, etc., the price chosen as the goal of stabilisation policy will have to be such that cumulative intervention purchases approximate cumulative intervention sales. Otherwise, if the target price is too high, the intervention agency will be left with inventories increasing over time, part of which may have to be destroyed; if the target price is too low, it will be drawing on its buffer stock more than it is replenishing that stock. In the latter case, and (as we assume) in the absence of imports of the good, intervention would ultimately be unable to peg price in the manner indicated, because it would use up all the buffer stock from which it had been selling. These considerations indicate that if government wishes to peg farm prices and if it also wishes to use the level at which prices are pegged to raise average year-to-year farm incomes above what they would be in a free market, then it will have to take into intervention, at times of good harvests, more than it cumulatively sells from intervention when harvests are poor; it may, then, have to allow some of its purchases to rot, or wilfully destroy them.

Supply and Demand: Elements of Dynamics

Even if weather conditions stayed constant from one year to the next, product stocks would be highest just after harvest or at times of peak production — the early summer for milk, the autumn for beef and cereals. For these reasons government might intervene to even out supplies via accumulation and decumulation of buffer stocks. However, there are further reasons why government might seek to peg prices. These are related to the probability that many unregulated agricultural markets would be more unstable than the above considerations suggest. To highlight such potential instability we assume, until further notice, no government manipulation of supply or demand, perfect competition and no international trade in the good under analysis, and turn to elementary dynamics.

Statics and Dynamics
It takes time before production can be increased. The lag between a change in the desire to expand production and the change in production is called the *supply lag*. We have virtually ignored supply lags, though in discussing elasticity of supply at the end of Chapter 5 we hinted towards the lagged response of supply to changes in price. Nevertheless, the method of analysis used up to now has been static in a fundamental sense.

Consider, for example, the analysis of a per unit tax in Chapter 6. We saw that if the tax were administratively payable by sellers, then the supply curve would shift upwards by the full amount of the tax, leading to various *predictions* which pertained to comparison of the initial equilibrium and the new after-tax equilibrium. The method of analysis used up to now is called *comparative static equilibrium analysis* or *comparative statics*. That method is essentially along the following lines:

Starting from an equilibrium, some disturbance causes departure from equilibrium; *on the assumption that a new equilibrium will be reached,* the new equilibrium is characterised as such-and-such; comparison is then made between the initial equilibrium and the new equilibrium, which is assumed to be attainable. Thus, although the method of comparative statics is very useful, it is deficient in two respects. First, it cannot tell us what happens out of equilibrium. Second, although an equilibrium may exist, the behaviour of a system out of equilibrium may be such that equilibrium is never reached. If an initial equilibrium is disturbed and if the behaviour of the system out of equilibrium is *such that the new equilibrium is never reached,* then the *predictions* yielded by the comparative static method will almost certainly be wrong. To avoid the two deficiencies of the comparative static method we need dynamic analysis, which is the study of behaviour of systems (e.g., whole economies or individual markets) in disequilibrium situations.

An Example of Dynamics: The Cobweb

To get some feeling for dynamic analysis, consider the so-called cobweb model. We assume that there is no attempt to stabilise the market and that producers do not carry forward inventories from one period to the next, or if they do so, they are either constant or negligible.

In earlier analyses of supply we assumed that apart from the effects of unexpected weather conditions, the output plans of producers are always fulfilled *in* the period in which those plans are made. Thus we assumed that other things being equal, quantity supplied in any time period was related in some particular manner to the good's own price in the *same* time period, i.e., that $q_t^s = F(p_t)$, where we add the subscript t to denote a particular time period.

To make the analysis dynamic we now assume that the output plans of producers are always fulfilled *one time period after those plans are formed.* Thus, as before, we assume that, other things being equal, planned supply of a good depends on the good's current price; however, we now alter our previous assumptions by postulating that those planned supplies are not converted into actual supplies until one time period later. The amount actually supplied in any period then depends on price in the *previous* period: $q_t^s = F(p_{t-1})$. If that is the case, the amount supplied in the current period is independent of the current period's price (which determines quantity supplied in the next period). Supply lags of the kind just mentioned are typical of agricultural products for which there is a single crop annually. Thus we assume that producers look at this year's harvest price in deciding how much to plant this year for next year's crop season; hence next year's supply depends on this year's price, and this year's supply depends on last year's price. We continue to assume that quantity demanded in any period depends on price in the same period. The demand and supply functions are then as follows

(1) $q_t^d = f(p_t)$

(2) $q_t^s = F(p_{t-1})$

where t denotes time (in, say, years). Equation (1) states that quantity demanded in year t — say the current year — depends on price in the same year. Equation (2) states that quantity supplied in year t (this year) depends on price in the previous year (last year). These supply and demand functions can be represented graphically as SS and DD in a diagram like Figure 28.

Suppose that p and q are initially at equilibrium levels, (p_e, q_e) in Figure 28. Suppose next there is an increase in demand, so that the demand curve shifts upwards to D'D', and examine how the system reacts over time. It does not immediately attain the new equilibrium (p_e', q_e'); rather, its motion is as depicted by the arrows in the diagram. With $q = q_e$, the increase in demand first bids price upwards to p_1.

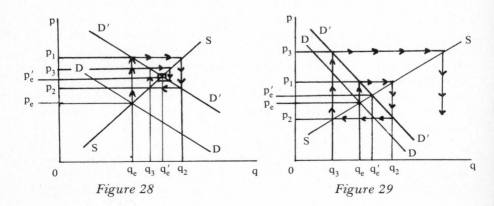

Figure 28   Figure 29

At $p = p_1$ suppliers plan to produce q_2. However, because of the lag in supplies, q_2 appears on the market only one period later; price then goes to p_2. That price calls forth a quantity supplied equal to q_3 after yet another period, which means that price goes to p_3 in that period. Thus we see that in this case the dynamics of the system are such that, starting from an equilibrium (p_e, q_e), the time path is (p_1, q_e), (p_2, q_2), (p_3, q_3) and so on as indicated by the arrows, oscillating but converging over time towards the new equilibrium ($p_{e'}$, $q_{e'}$).

In the example just considered the oscillations became smaller as time elapsed and the system approached its new equilibrium. However, the way in which the system oscillates depends on the slopes of the two curves, SS and D'D'. In the case just considered the slope of the supply curve exceeded the absolute value of the slope of the new demand curve. But consider Figure 29, where the slope of the supply curve is less than the absolute value of the slope of the new demand curve.

The analysis in Figure 29 is formally similar to that in Figure 28. The initial equilibrium is at (p_e, q_e); after the change in demand it is ($p_{e'}$, $q_{e'}$). However, the trouble here is that *the new equilibrium will never be reached.* The system will oscillate as before, but now the oscillations, instead of getting smaller, will become larger over time, and the system will explode away from the new equilibrium. Thus starting from the initial equilibrium (p_e, q_e) in the diagram, the reader should verify that the time path of the system after the increase in demand is (p_1, q_e), (p_2, q_2), (p_3, q_3), etc. Note that, since the new equilibrium is never reached, the method of comparative statics, in focusing on equilibrium positions, would give wrong predictions; it would predict that if there were an increase in demand, then price and quantity traded would tend to increase, and this would be more or less the end of the story. Thus predictions obtained via the comparative statics method may be empirically correct if equilibrium is stable (as in Figure 28) but are likely to be erroneous if equilibrium is unstable (as in Figure 29).

We have considered two cases of the cobweb model. In the first the system oscillated over time toward a new equilibrium; the model was stable. In the second, the model was unstable. We saw that the manner in which the system oscillated depended on the absolute values of the slopes of the supply and demand curves in the neighbourhood of the new equilibrium. Thus the system converges to equilibrium if the slope of the supply curve exceeds the absolute value of the slope of the demand curve, but if the inequality is in the opposite direction, then the system is explosive or divergent. There is of course a third possibility in this simple model — that in which the absolute values of the slopes of the supply and demand curves are equal. It is left to the reader to verify that, after a change in demand, in this case the system will oscillate in an orbit around (p_e', q_e'), without ever approaching equilibrium; however, the cycles are of constant amplitude, so the system does not explode away from equilibrium.

Government Intervention Once Again

We have shown that the free play of a perfectly competitive market may generate instability. Thus, starting from an equilibrium in an individual competitive market, and on the assumption of a single-period lag in supply, disturbance to that equilibrium may lead to a situation in which price and output spiral explosively away from equilibrium, fluctuate indefinitely in an orbit around equilibrium, or approach equilibrium only via a process of convergent oscillations. These considerations provide an *a priori* argument in favour of government interference — by intervention purchases or sales to stabilise prices and output.

Suppose that the situation is initially as at (p_e, q_e) in Figures 28 and 29. If there were an increase in demand, price would rise to p_1 in the absence of intervention, initiating a process of oscillation. However, if government maintains buffer stocks of the commodity and is willing to intervene in the market, the new equilibrium at (p_e', q_e') can be attained in a single step. All government needs to do is to promptly sell (q_e'-q_e) from its buffer stock after demand has increased. Total supply would then be q_e'; q_e from current production and (q_e'-q_e) from intervention sales. The market price is then p_e' — the new equilibrium price. Observing this price, producers plan to supply q_e'; this quantity will arrive on the market in the next period. In that subsequent period the market will be in equilibrium at (p_e', q_e') *without* any further need for government intervention. Similar reasoning applies in reverse — if there is a *decrease* in demand, *starting* at (p_e', q_e') in the diagrams: in that event oscillations can be prevented, and the new equilibrium can be reached in a single step, if government *buys* (q_e'-q_e) promptly after the decrease in demand.

Some general observations are appropriate at this stage:

(i) In our illustrations of the cobweb we assumed that quantity supplied in any period depended on price in the previous period — there was a single-period supply lag. In reality quantity supplied might depend on prices in several earlier time periods.

(ii) Suppose in the neighbourhood of an equilibrium that the cobweb cycles are explosive. In real-world economies there must be some limits to such oscillations. A more complete dynamic theory would incorporate upper and lower bounds on the amplitude of oscillation.

(iii) Whether the supply lag is single-period or multi-period, the present introduction to dynamic analysis should make us wary of the method of comparative statics. First, starting from an initial equilibrium, disturbance to that equilibrium in a model with lags will drive the system to a new equilibrium — if the system is stable — only over time. Second, even though a new equilibrium may exist, the dynamics may be such that it is never approached. In the latter case predictions made using the methods of comparative statics may be not only facile, but outright erroneous. But, with this warning in mind, we shall continue (as before) to adopt the method of comparative statics throughout this text. Thus *we shall make the implicit assumption that the markets under analysis are dynamically stable,* and we shall be focusing on equilibrium solutions.

FOOTNOTES

1. Jos de Vries, *Structure and Prospects of the World Coffee Economy,* Washington, D.C.: International Bank for Reconstruction and Development, Working Paper No. 208, 1975, 13, from which this paragraph is drawn.
2. Jos de Vries, 13. A 3 per cent cut-back in Brazilian coffee production represents a reduction in world production of about 1 per cent. With price elasticity of demand at about $0 \cdot 25$, this would raise the world price of coffee by about 4 per cent. Thus if Brazil were to contract its coffee output by about 3 per cent, with no change in the output of other producers, Brazilian receipts would increase by about 1 per cent, while the receipts of the other producers as a group would increase by about 4 per cent.
3. Returning to the general supply function (2) of Chapter 4, the effect of weather on supply would be captured by 'technology' in determining the functional form of (2).

CHAPTER 8

Agriculture and the European Economic Community

The European Economic Community (EEC) was established by the Treaty of Rome, signed in 1957 by West Germany, France, Italy, The Netherlands, Belgium and Luxembourg. It was extended at the beginning of 1973 with the accession of Denmark, Ireland and the UK. Its primary function has been the creation of a framework for free trade between member countries.

Progress toward the creation of a common market in industrial goods was made at an early stage by phased reduction and removal of tariffs and quotas between members. But a common market in farm goods presented more complex problems. Prior to their entry to the EEC, all member countries had pursued policies involving regulation of agriculture, one of the objectives being maintenance of farm incomes at levels generally higher than would have prevailed under the free play of market forces alone. Given the determination of member countries to maintain support for agricultural incomes after entry to the EEC, development toward free trade in farm products within the EEC had to be accompanied by a common approach to farm policy. Thus, the EEC's Common Agricultural Policy (CAP) was developed. It sought to create an environment of free competition between farmers in member countries, to replace the price and income support policies of individual governments by a single system of agricultural price and income supports and to provide help on a Community scale for the modernisation of European agriculture. The financial costs of the common arrangements were to be borne by the Community as a whole.

The CAP has two main aspects, market policy and structural policy. Structural policy is concerned with matters such as the size of farms and the age-structure of the farming community. The objectives of market policy are to allow farm goods to move freely within the EEC while maintaining prices in neighbourhoods of specified target levels.

Farm prices are maintained in neighbourhoods of common target levels by intervention purchases by national authorities (on behalf of the Community) at times when supplies within the EEC are abundant, and by sales from intervention when supplies are low and prices would otherwise be high; by subsidisation of exports of surplus production; by special import levies (over and above the EEC's Common External Tariff) to prevent outside competition from driving prices within the EEC below what are deemed reasonable levels, and by other means.

Agricultural Structure and Structural Policy[1]

In 1958 about 19 million people in the nine countries today comprising the EEC were employed in agriculture. The figure is now about 8 million, or about 8 per cent of the work force. The decline in numbers in agriculture has meant that average farm size has increased. In the EEC as a whole it is now about 42 acres, varying from an average of 17·3 acres in Italy to 153 acres in the UK; Ireland is above average at about 55 acres. Amalgamations — many of them encouraged by EEC policy — continue to increase farm size.

In 1975 it was estimated that more than 25 per cent of those working in EEC agriculture were over fifty-five years old, but at the same time only 14 per cent of the EEC's total working population were more than fifty-five years of age. The predominance of older people on farms was most marked in Ireland (36 per cent of the agricultural labour force aged over fifty-five, 19 per cent in the case of industry and services combined.)

Although the bulk of the EEC's expenditure under the CAP is devoted to price support, programmes have been implemented under *structural policy* to modernise farming and to increase the size of farms, making them more viable for full-time farmers. For the most part these programmes are joint schemes, under which the EEC makes a financial commitment to measures undertaken in member countries.

The *modernisation aid* scheme is designed mainly for farms generating low incomes per person employed, which through a six-year development plan (approved by the relevant authorities at the national level) can achieve incomes favourably comparable with non-farming incomes. Farmers assisted under this scheme — called development farmers — have prior call on land released under the agricultural retirement scheme (outlined below) and can receive aid in the form of a capital grant toward investment under the development plan.

The *retirement scheme* provides for an annual payment to farmers aged between fifty-five and sixty-five who give up farming; alternatively, eligible persons may be paid a lump sum. The land released when an applicant opts for the retirement scheme must be rented out for at least twelve years or sold to a development farmer or withdrawn from agricultural use (subject to the qualification that it may be allocated to forestry).

For approved measures under the modernisation and retirement schemes, Community aid from its farm fund (discussed below) is at a basic rate of 25 per cent, the balance being paid by the member government. However, in those countries (Ireland and Italy) where the percentage of the working population engaged in farming exceeds the EEC average and where per capita incomes are below the EEC average, the Community's financial contribution to the retirement scheme is considerably more.

Structural policies affect supply and incomes mainly in the long run. By making farming more efficient they increase supplies, and at given prices (determined as outlined below) for the output they thereby generate higher incomes for those remaining in agriculture.

Market Policy

In designing the CAP it was seen that if trade in agricultural products were to flow freely between member countries, the first priority would have to be amalgamation of the various government support prices to common levels. The key sector was cereals, a basic raw material for much of livestock production. It was felt that trade in livestock products could not be freed from restrictions while such a dominant element of production costs in most regions varied between member countries.

Cereals

Although details differ from commodity to commodity, the characteristic features of market policy are those devised for cereals, the first products to come under the CAP. In mid-1967 common official prices for cereals were introduced, allowing grains to flow between the original six members of the EEC unimpeded by levies or duties. *Target prices,* which are described by the EEC as prices which it is hoped producers will receive, are set each year for the main types of cereal traded in the wholesale market. All other cereal prices are linked to the target price. Closely allied to the target price is the *threshold price* for imported grain. It is calculated so that the threshold price plus transport costs at least equal the target price. Each day *variable import levies* are calculated, making up the difference between the lowest offers available on world markets and the threshold price. The variable import levies are payable on each consignment shipped into the EEC from non-member countries, so Community producers need not fear undercutting by imports at very low prices. Thus:

(1) Threshold price + transport cost ⩾ target price.
(2) World price + import levy = threshold price.

Import levies are used to control EEC market prices only so long as imports are coming in and there is no internal surplus. As is indicated from (2) above, potential imports will not come in if (due to abundant domestic production) EEC market prices are less than threshold prices. Intervention purchases become necessary when, at the target prices, home production significantly exceeds market demand. (If the contrary prevails, sales are likely to be made from stocks stored in intervention.) The *intervention price* for any commodity under the CAP is the price at which national intervention agencies (on behalf of the Community) are obliged to buy commodities offered to them; they are therefore guaranteed prices. The intervention price for each cereal runs parallel to the target price, being pitched slightly below it. Obviously farmers will sell into intervention only if they are unable to obtain a better price on the free market. Thus, the intervention prices are designed to be the ultimate floors on the prices received by farmers. The intervention agencies either store their purchases or export them (probably at a loss).

There are also arrangements for subsidies on exports by private traders to make up the difference between lower world prices and EEC official prices when the EEC itself is in surplus. But when world cereal prices are higher than EEC prices, levies may be imposed on EEC exports.

Dairy Products

For dairy products the arrangements are in many respects similar to those for cereals. The emphasis is on milk products. There are, accordingly, threshold prices, variable import levies and intervention purchases of butter and skim milk.

Partly due to the Community's price support policies, the EEC's dairy farmers have been producing more milk since the late 1960s than has been consumed directly or processed for domestic consumption. Mountains of butter and skim milk have been accumulating in intervention. Export subsidies have been made to facilitate sales on world markets and grants have been made available to encourage use of skim milk for animal feed. However, in 1977 the Community agreed on a programme for the dairy sector designed to boost demand and reduce output. The measures introduced included a levy on production known as the *co-responsibility levy,* assistance to producers to leave dairying, consumer subsidies on butter and subsidies for school milk.

Beef and Veal

The so-called *guide prices* fixed each year for beef and veal are target prices which act as trigger mechanisms for import control and intervention activity within the EEC. The intervention arrangements provide an outlet at a guaranteed price — in 1977, 90 per cent of the guide price — when market prices become unattractive to producers. Beef and live cattle imported to the EEC have to carry customs duties at fixed rates under the Common External Tariff, though they can be temporarily suspended or reduced. The import levies, on the other hand, are variable, as previously explained in discussing cereals.

Import levies on beef and cattle are set each week, comprising the difference between the price at which consignments are imported (including duties under the Common External Tariff) and the guide price, but the proportion of the levy payable by the importer depends on the state of the home market. This is assessed on the basis of representative market prices, usually known as reference prices, which are calculated in each member country and are then brought together as a composite or Community reference price. If the Community reference price is well above the guide price, no import levy is payable by the importer.

Other Commodities

Most of the other major products produced by EEC agriculture have regulations more or less similar in effect to those outlined above. However, although about 96 per cent of EEC farm production is covered by the CAP there are important sectors not as yet included — potatoes, mutton, lamb and wool, for which member governments may apply their own policies for managing the market.

Analysis of Market Policy

It has been seen that the central features of the system by which the EEC pegs prices in the neighbourhood of target levels are:

(i) Purchases and sales of intervention agencies so as to stabilise domestic supplies coming to market. The reader should be able to analyse these operations along the lines of Figure 27 in Chapter 7.

(ii) Variation of import levies so that (a) EEC farmers may be exposed to import competition if domestic market prices would otherwise rise significantly above their target levels, and so that (b) imports will not drive domestic farm prices downwards if those prices are already below their target levels.

For analysis of these controls over flows from the rest of the world into the EEC, we focus on Figures 30 and 31 below.

Case (a): If EEC agriculture were fully insulated from outside, the Community's market supply and demand curves for some food product x would be like SS and DD in Figure 30 where, without intervention, the equilibrium price is p_0. Suppose that the target price is p_T. The equilibrium price could be pegged at p_T by selling AB per period from intervention agencies' buffer stocks (assuming stocks sufficiently large). But suppose intervention sales are zero, and that the 'world' price (the price at which x can be obtained from abroad, exclusive of both duties under the Common External Tariff and the variable import levies of the EEC) is less than p_T, say p_W. For simplicity ignore transportation charges. Suppose also that AB in Figure 30 — the excess of EEC demand over domestically-produced supply at the target price — is small relative to 'world' production of x. If combined import duties and levies are adjusted to a level L so that $p_T = p_W + L$, foreigners will be willing to supply the good to the EEC at the EEC's target price, p_T. The relevant supply curve would then look like SAS' in Figure 30. The equilibrium EEC price would then be p_T, the target price, and q_1 would be the equilibrium quantity traded. Of that quantity, q'_1 would be from domestic production and q_1-q'_1 would be imported. (If EEC imports of x were large relative to world production of x, EEC demand would bid p_W upwards, so that given L, the AS' part of SAS' would begin to slope upwards.)

The policies just outlined could not operate if the 'world' price (p'_W in Figure 30) exceeded the initial EEC market price, p_0; imports would then need to be subsidised before they would flow in. Without such subsidies the EEC's intervention agencies would have to sell q_1-q'_1 per period in order to peg price at its target level, p_T. But if those agencies exhaust their buffer stocks the equilibrium price could not be prevented from moving upwards towards p_0. A situation like this occurred in the case of beef in 1973, when beef supplies were low throughout the world.

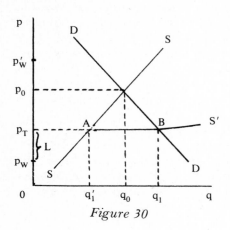

Figure 30

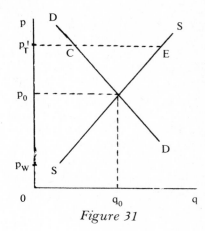

Figure 31

Case (b): Suppose, as before, that the EEC supply and demand curves for farm good x, with EEC agriculture insulated from abroad, are as in Figure 31. With no intervention the equilibrium price would be p_0. Suppose that p_T' is the target price, while p_w is the 'world' price. If imports were allowed in freely, the equilibrium price would be driven toward p_w in Figure 31. To keep such imports out, the variable import levies will be adjusted so that import duties plus import levies, per unit of x, are slightly higher than p_T'-p_w. Price would then be pegged at p_T' if intervention agencies bought CE per period.

On Some Effects of the CAP

In the early years of the CAP it was assumed that the EEC would be, for an indefinite future, a deficit area in basic agricultural products. This assumption no longer applies. The EEC has tended to produce surpluses of soft wheat, sugar and pork, and there have been mountains of surplus dairy products. An effect of *structural policy* has been to *shift supply curves to the right. Market policy,* in seeking to stabilise prices at levels generally higher than would prevail in its absence, has led to *movements upwards along supply curves,* so that supplies have increased on that count also. There have, then, been two reasons — one mainly short-run, the other mainly long-run in character — why the CAP has led to increased supplies from EEC agriculture. Especially in those countries where farm incomes were very low prior to their entry to the EEC, the higher farm production, given the EEC's price supports, has led to significant improvements in rural living standards.

In the years before her entry to the EEC in January 1973, the levels of agricultural support prices maintained in Ireland had been generally lower than those obtained by Community farmers. Although our entry to the EEC coincided with a period of exceptionally high beef prices throughout the world, it also represented a transition to a market of higher food prices in general, purely short-term factors aside. This transition, along with continued outward mobility from Irish agriculture, has helped narrow the differential between urban and rural living standards. Professor Seamus Sheehy of UCD has compared[2] per capita incomes net of income tax of family farm workers and industrial workers in Ireland in 1970-78: he found that although the incomes of family farm workers were generally below those of industrial workers before 1972, family farm workers obtained the higher after-tax incomes in each of the years 1975-78. Although little meaning is attached to comparison of the absolute incomes of the two groups, there can be little doubt that this relative improvement of farmers was largely due to the CAP.

Financing the CAP: The Farm Fund

Support buying by intervention agencies and subsidies on farm exports require financing. This is administered by the *Guarantee Section* of the Community's farm fund. The *Guidance Section* administers expenditures by the Community under structural policy. Of the two divisions of the farm fund, the Guarantee Section is by far the larger, accounting for about 65 per cent of the Community's total (farm and non-farm) budget — not surprising given the extent of intervention buying and export subsidisation in which the Community has had to engage.

The CAP has been financed by a variety of formulae. Until 1971 the bulk of the requisite funds were contributed to the Community by national exchequers, under various criteria. But in 1971 a programme was initiated for giving the Community its own independent resources, or *'resources propres'* ('own resources'). The system of 'own resources' is designed to finance *all* the Community's expenditures (not just those under the CAP) and it thus replaces previous systems under which separate arrangements were made to finance different aspects of Community policy. The 'own resources' are almost entirely made up of:

(i) Levies on trade in agricultural products with non-member countries.

(ii) All customs duties raised from Community imports on the basis of the rates of duty fixed in the Common External Tariff.

(iii) A proportion of the Value Added Tax receipts of member governments, that proportion being a maximum of 1 per cent.

Member governments collect the levies and customs duties on behalf of the Community and pay them into an EEC Commission account. Some 10 per cent of the levies and duties are refunded to member governments to cover collection costs.

Currency Chaos and the Green Currencies

The exchange rate between a currency and an ordinary good is the number of units of currency which must be paid to receive one unit of that good; it is the price of the good; currency is simply a numeraire or measuring-rod in terms of which prices, or exchange rates, are expressed. In like manner we define the exchange rate between two currencies, A and B, as the number of units of A which must be paid to obtain one unit of B; it is the price of B in terms of A. Exchange rates between currencies are *fixed* if the number of units of any one of the currencies required to obtain any other remains unchanged. If the number of units of currency A required to obtain one unit of currency B increases — if the price of B in terms of A increases — we say that A has *devalued* or *depreciated* (in terms of B) or that B has *appreciated* or *revalued* (in terms of A). Thus a devaluation of the domestic currency is an increase in the price of foreign currency.

The official prices of the EEC's CAP system (e.g., target prices and intervention prices) are fixed, not in national currency units, but in notional EEC accounting units, called *units of account*.

The official farm support prices denominated in units of account are converted into official farm support prices expressed in terms of national currencies by applying special exchange rates, popularly called *green exchange rates,* to the official prices denominated in units of account. The adjective 'green' — green denoting farm products — is used because application of those exchange rates to official prices expressed in units of account determines official prices in terms of national currencies. Thus the green exchange rate between the unit of account and a national currency expresses the value of that currency in terms of units of account. Since there are nine countries in the EEC, there are nine green exchange rates. These green exchange rates are determined at the discretion of the Community on behalf of all member countries; however, the rates applied are to some extent the outcome of bargaining between member governments and the Community. In this context a *green* national *currency* unit is the value of a particular national currency in terms of units of account. Thus there is a green Irish pound, a green French franc, etc.

By way of example, for the purpose of calculating official agricultural support prices in Ireland in terms of Irish currency in December 1977, the Irish (green) pound was valued at approximately 1·35 units of account. This meant that if the Community's official support price for some commodity included under the CAP was 1·35 units of account, then the support price of that commodity in Ireland would be one Irish pound. At the same time (in December 1977) the UK's green pound was valued at approximately 1·7 units of account. This meant that the levels of support prices in the UK, expressed in pounds, were lower than in the Republic. The fact that the green exchange rates have not been kept in line with the exchange rates between the currencies of member countries has caused problems for the Community.

The CAP was initially devised on the assumption that the exchange rates between member countries of the EEC would remain fixed. The following three sets of propositions are particularly relevant in understanding the system.

Proposition (I):

If exchange rates between national currencies remain constant, fixing agricultural support prices in terms of units of account and converting such prices into the several national currencies at (green) exchange rates *reflecting the exchange rates between those national currencies* would yield the same official agricultural support prices throughout the Community, regardless of the national currency in which those prices in different countries were compared. Thus a *potential* advantage of the unit of account system of pricing is that it could permit the determination of a single set of common support prices for agricultural goods, applicable in each currency area of the Community. If *all* exchange rates were fixed, a decision by the Community to increase the guaranteed unit of account price by, say, 5 per cent, would result in a 5 per cent increase in the guaranteed national currency price each farmer would receive. (In practice, exchange rates between national currencies have not remained fixed, in some cases varying from hour to hour and from day to day.)

Proposition (II):

If any national currency were devalued by, say, 100 per cent against all other national currencies (so that double the initial amounts of the devaluing currency would exchange against one unit of each of the other currencies), and *if that currency were simultaneously devalued by 100 per cent in terms of the unit of account,* then the price of any commodity included in the CAP scheme would be the same in all EEC member countries, regardless of the national currency in terms of which the prices were compared.

Proposition (III):

A situation in which one national currency was devalued in terms of other national currencies, *but not in terms of units of account,* would tend to be inconsistent with the EEC's policy of common official prices for farm products, when those prices are expressed in national currencies.

In demonstrating the validity of these propositions we keep the analysis simple by assuming that there are only two countries in the Community and only one commodity covered under the CAP. Let x denote a unit of that commodity in physical terms. Call the two countries, with their respective national currency units in parentheses, Home (H) and Beyond (B). Then:

Demonstration (I′):

Suppose that the exchange rate between Home and Beyond is 2H for 1B. Suppose also that under the CAP the guaranteed price of x is one unit of account, and that the green exchange rates are such that H is valued at one unit of account while B is valued at two units of account. Thus

$$2 H = 1 B$$
$$H = 1 U.A.$$
$$B = 2 U.A.$$

Under these circumstances it is clear that the official price of x, p_x, is the same in both countries, regardless of the national currency unit in terms of which the price is expressed. Thus p_x = 1 H in Home and p_x = ½ B in Beyond, but since B = 2 H, p_x is 1 H in *both* countries, measured in terms of H. It is also the same in both countries — it is ½ B — measured in terms of B. The reader can verify that if *all* exchange rates — the green rates *and* the rate between one currency and the other — remain unchanged, and if the guaranteed unit of account price of x is raised by, say, 5 per cent, then it will be raised by 5 per cent in terms of either national currency, so that a common price will still prevail.

Demonstration (II'):
Suppose next that the situation outlined in the first two sentences of (I') initially prevails, but that H is now devalued by, say, 100 per cent in terms of B *and* in terms of units of account. It then requires 4 H to purchase 1 B and the green rate for H is such that 2 H are worth one unit of account. Thus

4 H = 1 B
  H = ½ U.A.
  B = 2 U.A.

Again it is clear that p_x is the same in both national currencies. Thus (since p_x = 1 U.A.), p_x = 2 H in Home and p_x = ½ B in Beyond. However, since 1 B = 4 H, it is 2 H in both countries. Similarly, in terms of B it is the same in both countries.

Demonstration (III'):
Finally, assume as before that the initial situation is as in the first two sentences of (I') and that H is devalued by 100 per cent in terms of B *but is not changed in value in terms of units of account*. It then requires 4 H to purchase 1 B, but the green rate for H remains such that H is valued at one unit of account. Thus

4 H = 1 B
  H = 1 U.A.
  B = 2 U.A.

In this case, p_x (measured in terms of national currencies, and given the exchange rate between those national currencies) is *not* the same in both countries. Thus (since p_x = 1 U.A.), p_x is 1 H in Home and ½ B in Beyond. Suppose for the moment that these are the actual prices obtainable in both countries (and not merely the guaranteed prices). Then, since the exchange rate between the national currencies is such that 4 H = 1 B, p_x is 1 H in Home but 2 H if exported to Beyond.

Alternatively, in terms of currency B, we can say that $p_x = \frac{1}{2}$ B in Beyond and 1 H in Home, and since 1 H = $\frac{1}{4}$ B, farmers in Beyond would obtain only $p_x = \frac{1}{4}$ B if they exported to Home, while only $\frac{1}{4}$ B would need to be paid by importers in Beyond for each unit they brought in from Home. Thus p_x would be lower in the devaluing country Home than in Beyond, regardless of the national currency in which we make the comparison.

Because of the inconsistency arising from a situation in which (i) one national currency — H — has been devalued in terms of the other national currency — B — and (ii) there has been no adjustment in the green exchange rates (the values of the two currencies in terms of units of account), farmers in Home would divert supplies away from the Home market and export to Beyond, where they obtain prices higher than the official prices in Home in terms of their own currency. This diversion of supplies away from the Home market would put upward pressure on actual prices in Home. Farmers in Beyond, on the other hand, could not compete against their counterparts in Home.

To limit the extent to which the kind of situation just outlined could occur in practice, a system was devised under the CAP whereby farmers in the devaluing country, Home, would be subject to a tax or levy on their exports to Beyond, while exports of farm products from Beyond would receive a subsidy or rebate. The levies and subsidies to which we have just referred are called *monetary compensation amounts* (MCAs).

We have remarked that under the circumstances outlined, but in the absence of MCAs, actual prices in Home (measured in H) would tend to increase above 1 H; for Home's farmers would not supply their national market unless the price they obtained there was roughly the same as that which they could get by exporting. The MCA levies, by restricting their incentive to export and thereby maintaining supplies to the national Home market, would restrain the increase in prices in Home. Similarly, under the circumstances outlined but in the absence of MCAs and intervention purchases, actual prices in Beyond (measured in B) would tend to fall towards $\frac{1}{4}$ B; however, the MCA levies on Home's exports combined with subsidies on exports from Beyond would restrict supplies being marketed in Beyond, could enable Beyond to be competitive on the export market, and would restrain the downward pressure on actual prices in Beyond.

We have used a two-country example to illustrate the complexities arising given a situation in which (i) guaranteed farm prices are fixed in units of account, (ii) exchange rates between units of account and national currencies (the green currency rates) are fixed and (iii) exchange rates between national currency units are changing. The situation is just a little more complex in the Community of nine national currencies; but the rationale behind MCAs, which have been applied by the Community on an extensive scale, remains the same.

However, in our opinion the objectives of the CAP would be pursued more rationally if MCAs were abolished entirely and (i) if official farm prices continued to be fixed in units of account and (ii) if the exchange rates between units of account and national currencies were promptly adjusted to reflect any changes in the exchange rates between national currencies. The manner in which the system would then operate is indicated in (II'), which merely illustrates Proposition (II) above. Most of the usual arguments against the scheme just suggested are, in our opinion, either erroneous or unconvincing.[3]

Suggested Reading

Directorate General for Press and Information, Commission of the European Communities *The Common Agricultural Policy,* Brussels, updated periodically.

FOOTNOTES

1. This section and that which follows on market policy draw freely on Directorate General for Press and Information, *The Common Agricultural Policy,* Brussels: Commission of the European Communities 1977.

2. S. J. Sheehy, 'Ireland and the CAP', *Community Report,* February 1978, 4.

3. Suppose that the Irish pound devalued against all other EEC national currencies and the unit of account by 100 per cent. As comparison of (I') and (II') indicates, guaranteed prices would then double in terms of Irish pounds. With Ireland a price-taker on export markets, the foreign price obtainable in other EEC countries for Irish agricultural exports would be unchanged, but in terms of Irish currency it would double. It might be argued that the resulting increase in their nominal incomes would represent an unfair gain to Irish farmers. However, as will be seen in Part Three, such an argument ignores the fact that all prices in Ireland (including the inputs used in agriculture and the goods purchased by farmers for consumption) would tend to roughly double, so short-run distributional effects aside, there would be little or no change in the real incomes of Irish farmers.

Macroeconomic Analysis

CHAPTER 9

The National Income Accounts

Macroeconomics is concerned with the determination of aggregate variables such as national output, unemployment and inflation. It gives insights into major policy issues, among them the following:

Rising prices: Why does the price level increase? Why be concerned with rising prices if wages adjust at least proportionately?

Unemployment: Why do we have unemployment? Why does the unemployment rate vary over time? Why is it lower in other EEC countries?

Stability or instability of private enterprise: Could a private enterprise economy manage by itself without recurrent bouts of inflation and unemployment? Is government intervention necessary to stabilise the economy?

Identity of National Income, Product and Expenditure

The primary task of macroeconomics is to explain what determines the size of national income and its growth and fluctuation over time. What is *loosely* termed *the national income* is a measure of the money value of *total production* of final goods and services by residents of the economy in a particular year. (Actually, national income statistics may pertain to any time period, but in Ireland complete national income data are published on an annual basis only.) Alternatively, we can describe it as a measure of the sum of *all incomes* (wages and salaries, rents, interest and profits) accruing to the factors of production as payments for their services in production during the year. As yet another alternative, we can say that it is a measure of *total expenditure* on the output of final goods and services produced by residents of the economy during the year.

Governments are interested in the size of the national income for several reasons. Given the price level, the volume of goods and services available to society as a whole affects living standards. Thus, subject to some qualifications, economic welfare (that part of individual welfare which can be brought into relation with the measuring-rod of money) is directly related to the size of the national income. Furthermore — again subject to important qualifications — employment (unemployment) tends to move in the same direction as (opposite direction to) changes in national income.

For advanced countries, official (government) national income statistics date from the late 1930s and early 1940s. This timing of public interest in national income data coincided with the commitment of governments to policies of full employment in the aftermath of the Great Depression of the 1930s; prior to then most governments played minor roles in attempting to manage their economies. Private estimates preceded official estimates of national income in Ireland. Our official estimates run from 1938 and are published annually. Earlier private estimates of Dr T. J. Kiernan and Professor George Duncan cover years between 1926 and 1938.

Appropriately defined or adjusted, national product, national income and national expenditure are identical, since they represent three different ways of calculating the same aggregate, which we denote by the symbol Y. Although the three terms may be used inter-changeably, the term national income is most often used in a generic or general sense to denote Y in all its aspects.

National Product and National Income

That national product and national income, appropriately defined, are identical, can be seen by denoting the value of the economy's output of final goods and services by Y (pounds), and by assuming that there are no net taxes (taxes less subsidies) on goods (i.e., *net taxes on expenditure*). The output valued Y (pounds) must be fully accounted for by costs of production incurred in payment of wages and salaries, rents, and interest, plus the residual between those payments and Y, profits or losses. Thus total income generated by production must equal Y: national product and national income are identical.

In reality there are taxes on expenditure. Therefore the market prices of goods diverge from their costs in terms of payments to the factors of production — their *factor costs*. Thus national product measured at market prices exceeds national income measured at factor cost. If, then, national product is measured at market prices so that it includes net taxes on expenditure, we must add those expenditure taxes to national income at factor cost in order to preserve the identity of product and income. Thus (i) national product exclusive of net expenditure taxes is identical to national income at factor cost and (ii) national product at market prices is identical to national income at factor cost plus net expenditure taxes.

National Product and National Expenditure

Consider the identity of national product and national expenditure. The reader may try to refute this as follows: 'Consider a producer of, say, widgets. Suppose his production during the year is 100 widgets priced at £x each. His total product is valued at £100x. Suppose he sells only 90 widgets. Then expenditure is only £90x; so product and expenditure are not identical.' Our only objection to this argument is that it ignores an important convention: the firm must have ended the year with 10 extra widgets in stock or inventory; its inventory must have increased by £10x, *and in national income accounting an increase in inventory is regarded as part of expenditure* — we regard the firm as spending on itself by increasing its inventory. The opposite treatment is applied if inventories are reduced. Hence national product is the same as national expenditure. We have established that

(1) national income ≡ national product ≡ national expenditure ≡ Y

Final Goods and Intermediate Goods

National income is a measure of the money value of all *final* goods and services produced by residents of the economy in a year. In this context domestic investment (increase in the economy's inventories or productive assets such as machinery and buildings) is regarded as final. Goods produced during the year but used up as inputs in the same year are not final; they are *intermediate.* Suppose, for example, that the economy produces bread using domestically grown wheat and that all the wheat is used in bread production. The bread is a final good and is therefore included in national product. The wheat is not final since it is all used as an input. If we included both the wheat and the bread in national product we would be double-counting.

Suppose that only part of the wheat is used during the year, and that some of it is allocated to warehouses, increasing the economy's wheat inventory. The wheat used in bread is not included in national product (the bread is); however, since investment is regarded as final and since an increase in inventory is investment, the increase in wheat inventory is included in national product. The central point is that in measuring national income from the *product* side we count only production of final goods and services (including investment). Similarly, in estimating national income from the *expenditure* side we count only expenditures on final goods and services (including investment).

Value Added and Transfer Payments

It follows from our definition of national income, Y, that if we measure Y from the income side — by summing payments to the factors of production — we should count only those payments made for productive activities. We should count only wages and salaries, rents, interest on capital, and profits. Alternatively, we can say that we count only those incomes representing *value added* by residents. Consider bread production again. The creation of income at each stage of production is indicated in simplified form in Table 4.

Table 4
Generation of Value Added, £ million

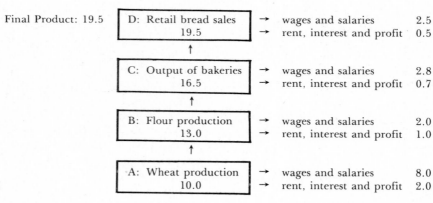

Final Product: 19.5

| D: Retail bread sales 19.5 | → wages and salaries | 2.5 |
| | → rent, interest and profit | 0.5 |

↑

| C: Output of bakeries 16.5 | → wages and salaries | 2.8 |
| | → rent, interest and profit | 0.7 |

↑

| B: Flour production 13.0 | → wages and salaries | 2.0 |
| | → rent, interest and profit | 1.0 |

↑

| A: Wheat production 10.0 | → wages and salaries | 8.0 |
| | → rent, interest and profit | 2.0 |

Final Product: 19.5   Income or Value Added: 19.5

Bread production at retail prices is £19·5 million, as indicated by box D of Table 4; this is part of national product, but boxes C, B and A are not. Income earned at any stage of production is the value added at that stage. The sum of such incomes, indicated by arrows outside the boxes, is also £19·5 million. We assume there are only four stages in production, as follows:

Suppose farmers buy no raw materials from outside agriculture. (If this assumption were relaxed we would have to go further backwards in the structure of production.) With land, labour and capital they produce wheat with a wholesale value of £10 million. This is accounted for by payments to the factors of production; profit or loss is a residual. Thus value added in agriculture is £10 million. Farmers sell their wheat for £10 million to flour mills, where £3 million is added to the value of the wheat used as an input. (We assume that wheat is the only raw material used in milling, and make similar assumptions in regard to the bakery and retail stages.) Thus income earned in milling is £3 million. Bakeries buy the flour for £13 million but sell their product to retailers for £16·5 million; value added is £3·5 million. Finally, the bread is sold to consumers for £19·5 million; value added by the retailers is £3 million.

The values added at each stage are the incomes of the factors of production; the sum of these comes to £19·5 million — the value of the final product at retail level. In calculating national product from the income side we simply sum the values added, or incomes, generated at each stage of production throughout the economy. Thus national income is national value added.

In calculating national product from the income side, only those incomes earned from production are counted. A mere *transfer payment (a transfer of income from A to B for reasons other than the provision of services in production by B) is not included.* In the example in Table 4, wages and salaries in bakeries are £2·8 million; this is part of national income since it is in payment for productive activity. But suppose that of this sum bakery workers give £10,000 as gifts to their children. That £10,000 is transfer income to the children, since it is not in payment for productive activity on their part. If we included it in national product we would be double-counting. Thus, in calculating national product via the income method, we do not include payments such as gifts, unemployment assistance or similar transfers.

Further Concepts in National Income Accounting

The provision of a service is productive (of utility) so long as it satisfies human wants. In this respect the services provided by RTE, AIB, the Bank of Ireland or the ordinary housewife are productive in the same sense as the output of Cement Roadstone or Arthur Guinness. However, in national income accounting exactly which services are regarded as productive — and are therefore included in estimating national product — is partly a matter of convention. For example, the services of a hired housekeeper are included in national income and are valued at the amount paid in cash and in kind. But the services provided by a housewife are not included — presumably due to difficulty in assessing their market values. (It follows that, other things being equal, measured national income falls when a man marries his housekeeper.)

Investment

By investment the economist usually means that part of the flow of *output* which is *not consumed*. This definition diverges from that of the plain man who speaks of investing when he buys a piece of land or an old security; the economist generally regards these as transfer payments — they are payments for the transfer of assets from one person to another. If there were no foreign trade, investment could be of only two forms: fixed investment, and investment in stocks of materials and finished goods. By *fixed investment* we mean additions to the nation's roads, buildings, machinery and equipment, etc. To avoid confusion we will describe the second form of investment — that in stocks of materials and finished goods — as *inventory investment*.

Capital is a stock of productive assets at a point in time; investment is the change in that stock over time. Thus, considerations of foreign trade aside, if the stock of fixed capital, and of inventories, were constant over time, net investment would be zero. If, however, the stock of inventories or of fixed capital increased, then the relevant category of investment, in the period under consideration, would be positive. The two kinds of investment to which we have referred — fixed investment and inventory investment — comprise what is called *domestic investment*.

Foreign Trade and National Expenditure

Foreign trade complicates the calculation of national income from the expenditure side. Suppose the economy is closed, so that there is no foreign trade. Then the identity of national product and national expenditure can be written as

(2) $Y \equiv C + I + G$, where

Y: National product

C: Consumption expenditure by resident persons on goods and services, personal consumption expenditure.

I: Private fixed investment expenditure plus private inventory investment (change in inventories in private sector), private investment.

G: Government expenditure on goods and services (including fixed and inventory investment in the public sector).

Recognising that the economy is open — that there is foreign trade — changes identity (2) in two respects. First, part of the expenditures on national product are by non-residents; these are exports of goods and services, X. Since exports are a disposal of Irish production and generate income in Ireland they are part of Irish national product.

Second, part of the expenditures by Irish residents create income abroad rather than in Ireland. For example, expenditure by Aer Lingus on a fleet of new aircraft does not in itself generate income in Ireland; it creates income abroad. Therefore expenditures on goods which are imported are not included in (Ireland's) national product. Thus by *national expenditure* in an open economy we mean expenditure by residents on *domestic output* plus expenditure by foreigners on the output of the home country. Let M_c, M_i, M_g and M_x denote the import content of C, I, G and X. Identity (2) is then transformed into

(3) $\quad Y \equiv (C-M_c) + (I-M_i) + (G-M_g) + (X-M_x)$

which says that national product is total final expenditure on domestic output.

Identity (3) can be simplified. Let M denote imports of goods and services; $M \equiv M_c + M_i + M_g + M_x$. The product-expenditure identity for an open economy then becomes

(4) $\quad Y \equiv C + I + G + (X - M)$

where all variables are as defined at (2) and

$\quad$ X: $\quad$ Exports of goods and services.
$\quad$ M: $\quad$ Imports of goods and services.

Two technical terms are often applied to $(X-M)$ in (4). Most frequently it is called the *balance of (international) payments on current account,* since it is the difference between the economy's exports and imports of goods and services. It is also called *net external investment,* which may be positive or negative. Given our definition of investment (output not consumed), it is indeed part of national investment. However, we will describe $(X-M)$ as the balance of payments on current account, and shall reserve the word 'investment' to denote domestic investment only — i.e., public and private fixed investment plus change in inventory.

Government Services

National income purports to measure total production of final goods and services *at market prices.* All government services (e.g., the Civil Service, the provision of defence, law and order) are regarded as final. However, they generally do not have market prices. For this reason the output of public administration and defence is measured in terms of its wage and salary cost. Note that it is only that part of government expenditure which is on *goods and services* that is included in the national product; transfer payments by government are not included.

Depreciation, GNP and NNP at Market Prices

National income can be measured on a gross or net basis. This leads to two concepts of national product: Gross National Product (GNP) and Net National Product (NNP). In producing the output of the economy, part of the nation's capital stock becomes worn out or damaged; there is some depreciation of the capital stock. Keeping capital intact then requires some investment to replace that part of it used up. Thus net investment equals gross investment minus depreciation. Hence GNP equals NNP at market prices plus depreciation. Thus: *Gross National Product (GNP)* measures total production of final goods and services valued at market prices, before deduction of depreciation. *Net National Product (NNP) at market prices* is GNP minus depreciation.

NNP at Factor Cost ('National Income')

Net taxes on expenditure (i.e., taxes less subsidies on goods and services) raise the market value of NNP, and of national expenditure, above the sum of incomes paid to the factors of production, called *National Income.* (Note that we are now using those two words in a specific rather than in a generic sense; that is why we have used capital letters.) However, if we deduct expenditure taxes from, and add subsidies to, NNP at market prices, we get what is called *NNP at factor cost,* which is identically equal to National Income.

We could make a similar adjustment to national expenditure at market prices (or we could add net expenditure taxes to NNP at factor cost, and to expenditure exclusive of net expenditure taxes), thereby maintaining the identity of national income, national expenditure, and national product — whether on a factor cost basis or at market prices, and whether on a gross (before deduction of depreciation) basis or on a net basis.

Other Income Aggregates

National Income or NNP at factor cost is the sum of incomes of the factors of production earned in production; it omits transfer incomes. However, the categories Private Income, Personal Income and Disposable Personal Income (what we call Disposable Income) include transfer incomes.

Private Income is the sum of incomes of residents of the community, with the exception of incomes accruing to public authorities in their entrepreneurial or business capacity, whether or not the incomes are in payment for productive activity. Private Income equals, as an approximation, NNP at factor cost, less government trading and investment income, plus transfer income from government, plus transfer income from abroad. Not all of it accrues to persons; some of it accrues to corporate bodies in the private sector.

Personal Income equals Private Income less undistributed profits of companies before tax. Not all of this is available for personal consumption expenditure and savings; some of it goes to government as taxes on incomes and wealth.

Disposable Income equals Personal Income less taxes on personal incomes and wealth; it is accounted for by personal expenditure on consumers' goods and services, plus the residual, personal savings.

The Irish National Income Accounts

What is loosely termed the national income can be calculated by the income method (summing incomes from productive activity), by the expenditure method (summing expenditures on domestically produced final goods and services) or by the output method (summing final outputs). Each method is used in Ireland. Due to incomplete information, the three methods are in practice used to supplement and cross-check each other. Estimates for Ireland by the three methods are provided in summary form in Tables 5, 6 and 7.

We make two observations in regard to the above tables. First, GNP is at *current* market prices. The word 'current' here refers to the market prices prevailing in the two years in question. This is in contrast to GNP at *constant* market prices, discussed below. Second, entry 2 for public authorities in Table 7 is for public *current* expenditure on goods and services. The word 'current' is here used in contrast to 'capital' expenditure by public authorities; it refers to expenditure by public authorities on goods and services other than capital goods. Public fixed investment is included along with private fixed investment in gross domestic fixed capital formation in Table 7.

Real GNP and Money GNP

It is necessary to distinguish between money GNP and real GNP. *Nominal* or *money* GNP, or GNP at *current market prices,* measures the value of goods and services at the prices prevailing in the year in which they are produced. *Real* GNP or GNP at *constant market prices* measures the value of goods and services using the prices of a common

Table 5
The Income Method, 1970 and 1976, £ million

Year	1970	1976
Income from Agriculture, Forestry, Fishing:		
1. Income from self-employment and other trading income	185·1	547
2. Employee remuneration	26·0	50
Non-Agricultural Income:		
3. Profits, professional earnings, interest, dividends, and income from land and buildings	248·1	523
4. Employee remuneration	818·8	2455
NNP at factor cost or National Income	1278·0	3575
5. Plus taxes on expenditure less subsidies	235·6	582
NNP at current market prices	1513·6	4157
6. Plus provision for depreciation	134·9	354
GNP at current market prices	1648·5	4511

Table 6
The Net Output Method, 1970 and 1976, £ million

Year	1970	1976
1. Agricultural	214·3	601
Non-Agricultural:		
2. Industry	457·4	1334
3. Distribution, transport, communication	240·4	682
4. Public administration and defence	84·2	283
5. Other output, and adjustments	281·7	675
NNP at factor cost	1278·0	3575
6. Plus taxes on expenditure less subsidies	235·6	582
NNP at current market prices	1513·6	4157
7. Plus provision for depreciation	134·9	354
GNP at current market prices	1648·5	4511

Table 7
The Expenditure Method, 1970 and 1976, £ million

Year	1970	1976
1. Personal expenditure on consumers' goods and services	1115·9	2912
2. Net expenditure by public authorities on current goods and services	237·4	846
3. Gross domestic fixed capital formation	361·6	1034
4. Value of physical changes in stocks	+ 34·9	+ 24
5. Exports of goods and services	627·2	2160
6. Less imports of goods and services	− 728·5	− 2465
GNP at current market prices	1648·5	4511

Source for Tables 5, 6 and 7: *National Income and Expenditure 1976,* Dublin: Stationery Office, Prl. 7191, 1978, Tables A.1, A.2, A.3. We have included the official category 'net factor income from the rest of the world' in profits, etc., in Table 5, in other output in Table 6, and in exports of goods and services in Table 7.

Table 8
Current Price Versus Constant Price GNP

Year	1970	1971	1972	1973	1974	1975	1976
GNP @ current market prices (£ million)	1648	1881	2249	2705	2968	3687	4511
GNP price index or deflator (1970 = 1)	1·00	1·09	1·24	1·42	1·52	1·89	2·25
GNP @ constant (1970) market prices (£ million)	1648	1719	1812	1907	1951	1948	2002

Source: National Income and Expenditure 1976, Table 1.

base year. Table 8 indicates that nominal GNP in Ireland increased very substantially — from £1648 million to £4511 million — between 1970 and 1976. However, most of this increase represents illusory money gains due to inflation; the table also shows that over the same period real GNP — GNP at constant 1970 market prices — increased from £1648 million to only £2002 million, or by about 21 per cent.

The Consumer Price Index and the GNP Deflator
The most frequently used measure of the rate of inflation is the percentage change in the consumer price index (CPI). A CPI is an

estimate of the cost of a 'representative' basket of consumer goods and services in a particular year relative to some base year. The estimate of the cost of the basket of goods in each year is a weighted average of the costs of the items in the basket, where the weights denote the share of each good in total consumer expenditure in the base year. Assuming that there are n goods in the basket

$$CPI = \Sigma \ p_i w_i / \Sigma \ p_i^b w_i, \text{ where } \Sigma \ w_i = 1 \text{ and } w_i = p_i^b q_i^b / \Sigma \ p_i^b q_i^b$$

(Σ is a summation sign. For example,

$$\Sigma \ p_i w_i \equiv p_1 w_1 + p_2 w_2 + \ldots + p_n w_n).$$

p_i: Price of good i.
p_i^b: Price of good i in the base year.
w_i: The weight for good i.
q_i^b: The amount of good i bought in the base year.

In distinguishing real from nominal gains in GNP over time it is necessary to deflate nominal GNP by a price index which expresses the change in the prices of all goods which make up GNP, relative to some base year. The index used is called the *GNP deflator*. It is similar to a CPI except that it includes the prices of all goods which enter GNP. For example, the prices of new machines are included in the GNP deflator but not in the CPI.

Real GNP = (Nominal GNP)/(GNP price deflator). The GNP price index or deflator in Table 8 is in 1970 prices. It indicates that prices more than doubled between 1970 and 1976. Deflating nominal GNP in each year by this price index gives the series for GNP at constant (1970) market prices.

Further Important National Income Identities

We next derive a set of national income identities based on earlier discussion. They have no behavioural content. However, they will be essential to our understanding in the chapters which follow. To understand how the levels of real national income and related variables are determined is the central objective of Part Three of this text. We shall be constructing a series of models of the economy showing how it behaves in, say, a given year. Starting with a very simple model of a closed economy without government in the next chapter, we shall relax restrictive assumptions and move in the direction of realism.

In the identities below and in the analysis of national income determination which immediately follows we shall *assume,* unless indicated to the contrary, that *all variables are in real terms* (i.e., at constant prices). This implies that either the price level remains constant or, if not, variables in nominal terms have been deflated (or inflated if prices are falling), thereby expressing them in real terms. Our interest in real rather than in nominal income is motivated by the fact that it is real income that affects living standards and, given the state of technology, the amount of employment.

A. A Simple Closed Economy without Government

Assumptions:
(i) No depreciation.
(ii) No taxes or subsidies on expenditure.
(iii) No foreign sector.
(iv) No government.

Assumptions (i) and (ii) imply that real GNP equals real national income at factor cost and also equals real national expenditure at market prices. The symbol Y denotes all three. The following identities hold in the closed economy without government

(5) Output identity: $Y \equiv C + I$
(6) Income identity: $Y \equiv C + S$

Identity (5) states that output is divided between consumption, C, and investment, I. Investment is defined as output not consumed. Identity (6) states that income is divided between consumption and saving, S. Saving is defined as income not consumed. Together (5) and (6) imply

(7) $S \equiv I$

In the simple economy, private savings are necessarily equal to private investment. That is true whether or not income is at what we shall in the next chapter call its equilibrium level. Identity (7) says nothing about what determines savings or investment. Investigation of those issues will turn out to be crucial.

B. Introduction of a Government Sector

The output-expenditure identity becomes

(8) $Y \equiv C + I + G$

where C is consumer expenditure, I is private investment expenditure and G is government expenditure on goods and services.

Further assumptions:

(v) Income earned by public authorities in their business capacity is zero. Thus all government revenue must come from taxation or borrowing.

(vi) Undistributed profits of companies are zero. Thus if companies make profits they are all distributed to shareholders. Then, private income equals personal income.

It is now necessary to distinguish between national income and disposable income, Y_d, which is that part of national income which households are free to dispose of as they wish, after they have paid income and property taxes.

(9) $Y_d \equiv Y - T$

where T denotes net tax receipts of government (i.e., tax receipts less government transfer payments to the private sector). Disposable income is divided between consumption and personal savings

(10) $Y_d \equiv C + S$

Together, (8), (9) and (10) imply

(11) $C + S \equiv Y - T$, or
$C + S \equiv C + I + G - T$, or
$S \equiv I + G - T$, or

(12) $(S - I) \equiv (G - T)$

which relates the excess of personal savings over private investment to the goverment *budget deficit*. The government budget deficit is the excess of government spending on goods and services, G, over net tax revenues, T. (If T exceeds G, the government budget is in *surplus,* if T falls short of G it is in *deficit,* while if T equals G it is *balanced.*) According to (12) personal savings no longer have to equal private investment. If the government is running a deficit, then (12) states that the private sector must be saving more than it invests. Under such circumstances the government deficit is being financed, in some ultimate sense, by household savings.

C.   An Open Economy with Government

Further assumption:

(vii) There are no transfer payments to abroad (e.g., foreign aid) and none are received from abroad.

The output-expenditure identity and the income identity now are, respectively,

(13) $Y \equiv C + I + G + (X - M)$ and
(14) $Y \equiv C + S + T$. Hence
$C + I + G + (X - M) \equiv C + S + T$

which implies, for an open economy with government,

(15) $(S - I) \equiv (G - T) + (X - M)$

We remind the reader that we have only been discussing accounting relationships without attempting to explain how the variables in those identities are determined. That is the task into which we enter in the next chapter.

Suggested Reading

National Income and Expenditure, Stationery Office, Dublin. The official Irish national accounts document, this is published annually.

O'Mahoney, David, *The Irish Economy,* 2nd edn, Cork 1967, Chapter 7.

CHAPTER 10

A Simple Model of National Income Determination

The reader should ensure himself that he is familiar with the identities toward the end of the preceding chapter. Our central task in Part Three is to explain what determines the variables in those identities, and hence to explain what determines the equilibrium level of national income. Recall from Chapter 4 the meaning of equilibrium and its stability. Given an assumption of stability, we can interpret equilibrium national income as that level of national income toward which the economy tends to converge.

In this chapter we construct a simplified model which isolates *aggregate demand,* omitting any detailed consideration of aggregate supply. Except where indicated to the contrary, a change in a macroeconomic aggregate (e.g., national income or consumption expenditure) is a change in its *real value* at *constant prices. We also assume that firms are both willing and able to supply any level of output at those prices.* These assumptions will be relaxed later. Thus the core of the present investigation is: if firms are both willing and able to supply any amount of output at the prevailing price level, what determines the equilibrium national output — equilibrium national income?

Demand must enter the picture. Under the stated assumptions we would expect firms to produce just sufficient to meet aggregate demand, or planned expenditure. If output exceeded aggregate demand, firms would find their inventories piling up; conversely, if production fell short of aggregate demand, inventories would be running down (and/or households would be unable to buy what they want; firms might post 'sold out' signs). Firms would respond to such unplanned inventory changes by altering their outputs. These considerations suggest a notion of equilibrium national income as that level of national output where aggregate demand, or planned expenditure, equals aggregate supply, so that unintended changes in inventories are zero and households' actual consumption expenditure is equal to their planned or desired consumption expenditure.

Aggregate supply is determined by firms. In deciding how much to produce, firms calculate how much investment, including inventory investment, they wish to undertake. Then, if firms miscalculate households' planned consumption expenditures, aggregate supply will almost surely differ from aggregate demand (planned expenditures, including planned changes in inventories). If firms overestimate demand it is likely that there will be unplanned inventory accumulation. If firms underestimate demand they are likely to experience unplanned inventory decumulation, as attempts are made to meet the higher than anticipated level of demand by drawing on inventories.

Thus our claim (to be demonstrated) is that the equilibrium level of national income is that level of aggregate production such that actual output equals aggregate demand (planned expenditure): there would then be no unintended accumulation or decumulation of inventories. Alternatively, we can say that in a very simple economy (one with neither government nor foreign trade) the equilibrium level of income would be given by the equality of *planned* (or *desired* or *intended*) private savings and *planned* (or *desired* or *intended*) private investment. Note that we have referred to the equality of planned private savings and planned private investment rather than to the identity of actual savings and actual investment. The reasons why we have added the adjectives 'planned' or 'intended' should become clear later in this chapter.

The Consumption and Savings Functions

Table 9, in which all variables are expressed in nominal rather than in real terms, indicates disposable income, personal consumption expenditure and personal savings in Ireland between 1970 and 1976. We see that the money values of both consumption and savings are highly correlated with the money value of disposable income: as income increases, so too do consumption and savings. It is suggested that the reader draw graphs of the relationships observed in Table 9 between nominal consumption, nominal savings and nominal income: it would be found that the graphs are approximated by upward-sloping straight lines. Qualitatively much the same kinds of relationships tend to be observed if all variables are expressed in real terms.[1]

Table 9
Income, Consumption and Savings Data, Current Prices, £ million

Year	1970	1971	1972	1973	1974	1975	1976
Personal Income	1424	1631	1952	2418	2794	3636	4365
Less Taxes on Personal Income and Wealth	143	199	230	292	338	485	669
Equals: Disposable Income	1281	1432	1722	2126	2456	3151	3696
Consumer Expenditures	1116	1256	1451	1714	2024	2392	2912
Personal Savings	165	176	271	412	432	759	784

Source: National Income and Expenditure 1976, Table A. 8.

The Consumption Function

Personal consumption expenditure is a major component of aggregate demand. What determines personal consumption expenditure? Both introspection and empirical investigation indicate that disposable income is a major determinant. In what follows we shall be discussing the determinants of aggregate personal consumption (and personal savings) in the short run — in a particular year and from year to year, rather than from, say, decade to decade. It is in this context that we shall be referring to 'the' consumption function (and to 'the' savings function).

Definition: The consumption function is the relationship between the community's planned personal consumption expenditure and its disposable income. It expresses the amount the community would attempt to spend on personal consumption if aggregate disposable income were at various hypothetical levels, other things being equal. Thus

(1) $C = f(Y_d, e)$

where C denotes the amount households in aggregate attempt to spend on consumption, in real terms, Y_d is real disposable income and e represents the other things (such as the stock of real personal wealth) upon which aggregate consumption demand depends. (The reader who is unaccustomed to functional notation should refer to the Appendix to Chapter 2.) The exact manner in which real consumption demand depends on its determinants — the explicit form of the consumption function — can be expressed as an equation. Given e, we shall assume, as a linear approximation

(2) $C = a + bY_d$

where a $>$ 0 and 0 $<$ b $<$ 1 (i.e., 'a' is greater than zero and b is between zero and one). Graphically:

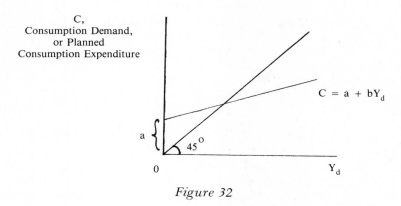

Figure 32

The 45 degree line in Figure 32, where we plot the consumption function, is the locus of points at which planned expenditure could equal output. What can we say about the form of the consumption function? First we note that the intercept 'a' is positive; if Y_d were zero, some consumption would still take place: in the virtually inconceivable case in which Y_d approached zero, consumption would, in the short run, be positive, as the community sought to maintain some consumption by running down its inventories (i.e., by dis-saving) — cattle would be slaughtered and finished food products carried forward from previous years would be consumed. Note also that b, the slope of the consumption function, $\Delta C/\Delta Y_d$, is positive but less than unity; if disposable income changes by £1 million then consumption demand changes in the same direction but by a smaller amount. This reflects an assumption for which there is a great deal of empirical support: as aggregate disposable income increases, so too does aggregate consumption, but because of increased savings, the increment in consumption falls short of the increase in income. The slope of the consumption function is of vital importance in macroeconomic analysis.

Definitions:

C/Y_d is the average propensity to consume, APC.

$\Delta C/\Delta Y_d$ is the marginal propensity to consume, MPC. It shows the amount by which planned consumption increases per unit increase in disposable income.

The Savings Function

The savings function is the relationship between the community's planned personal savings and its disposable income. Since personal savings are the residual after personal consumption has been deducted from disposable income, if we know the consumption function we know the savings function, and vice versa. Both give the same information. Thus:

Since $S \equiv Y_d - C$, and since $C = a + bY_d$, it follows that
$$S = Y_d - a - bY_d = -a + (1 - b)Y_d, \text{ or,}$$
$$(3) \quad S = -a + sY_d$$

where $s = (1 - MPC) = \Delta S/\Delta Y_d$ is the marginal propensity to save, MPS. It is the amount by which planned personal savings would increase if disposable income increased by one unit. Since an increase in disposable income is allocated to either consumption or saving, $\Delta C/\Delta Y_d + \Delta S/\Delta Y_d = 1$. Clearly, the higher the MPC, the lower the MPS, and vice versa. The savings function can be derived graphically from the consumption function, as in Figures 33a and 33b.

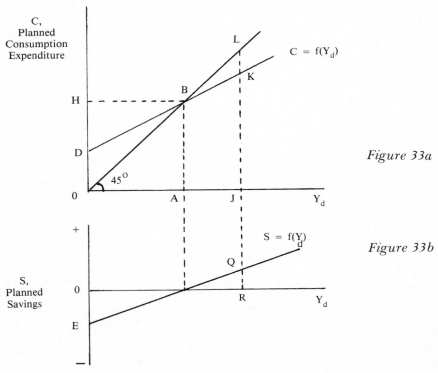

Figure 33a

Figure 33b

From the consumption function diagram, Figure 33a, we see that if $Y_d = O$, planned consumption $= OD$. Since $S \equiv Y_d - C$, this means that planned savings $= O - OD = OE$ in Figure 33b, a negative quantity. The economy would then be dis-saving, i.e., consuming its assets.

On the 45 degree line in Figure 33a, $OA = AB = BH$. So for $Y_d < OA$, $C > Y_d$, and hence $S < O$. However, at $Y_d = OA$, $C = Y_d$, so $S = O$ in Figure 33b. But for $Y_d > OA$, $C < Y_d$, so $S > O$. For example, suppose $Y_d = OJ = LJ$. At that disposable income planned consumption equals KJ. Thus planned savings equal $LJ - KJ = LK$ in Figure 33a $= QR$ in Figure 33b.

The Simplest Model

We are now ready to construct a series of models of national income determination. Each successive development will move more in the direction of realism. We start with the simplest model. We assume:

(i) There is no depreciation.

(ii) There is no government. Hence there can be no net taxes (i.e., taxes less subsidies) on expenditure.

(iii) Companies retain no earnings. Any profits are distributed to shareholders.

(iv) The economy is closed. Thus $X = M = O$.

(v) Planned investment is determined *exogenously* or *autonomously*, i.e., it is determined entirely *outside* the model, so that it does not depend on the level of national income (which is *endogenous*, i.e., it is, as we shall soon see, determined *within* the model).

Assumptions (i), (ii) and (iii) imply that real GNP, or Y, is here the same as real disposable income, Y_d.

We now wish to demonstrate that, given our earlier assumption that firms are willing and able to produce any quantity at prevailing prices, the equilibrium level of national income is determined by the level of aggregate demand (in this model, by private consumption and investment demand); alternatively, we will show that it is given by the equality of planned savings and planned investment. Turning to Figures 34a and 34b, our claim is that $Y = Y_e$ is the equilibrium level of national income.

Consider Figure 34a. Suppose first that income exceeds what we claim to be its equilibrium level, and observe what is likely to happen. Suppose that $Y = Y_1$. From the 45 degree line, $OY_1 = Y_1A$. Thus

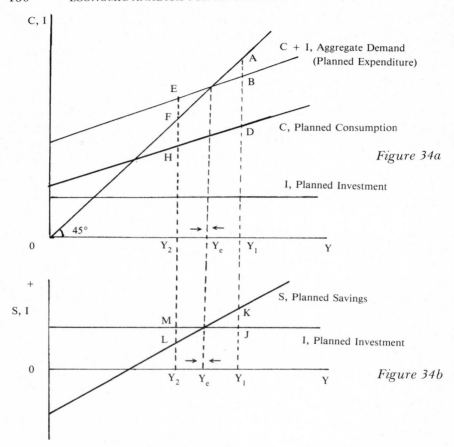

Figure 34a

Figure 34b

output is Y_1A. But planned expenditure, or aggregate demand, is Y_1B. Since actual expenditure is identical to output, it follows that actual expenditure exceeds planned expenditure. It follows that either the consumption plan or the investment plan or both will not be achieved. Suppose that the consumption plan is achieved. Then consumption is Y_1D. Since output is Y_1A, actual investment is AD, which exceeds planned investment, BD. There is, then, unplanned investment equal in volume to AB. What is this unplanned investment, and why has it occurred? It must take the form of an unanticipated accumulation of inventories (which, as indicated earlier, is counted as part of actual national expenditure). The reason for this unplanned inventory accumulation is clear: aggregate supply, Y_1A, exceeds aggregate demand (planned expenditure), Y_1B. The economy is producing too much relative to the desires of purchasers to buy the output.

The behavioural reaction of firms is also clear: in view of the build-up of inventories beyond their desired levels, retailers will reduce orders and manufacturers will cut back production. As production falls, so too will income (since firms' spending on factors to produce output is income to the factors of production). So, by definition of equilibrium, the economy is not in equilibrium if $Y > Y_e$. Income will fall towards Y_e so long as $Y > Y_e$.

Still focusing on Figure 34a, suppose next that income is initially below what we claim to be its equilibrium level. Suppose that $Y = Y_2$. From the 45 degree line we can see that output is $OY_2 = Y_2F$. But aggregate demand, or planned expenditure, is then Y_2E. Since actual expenditure is identical to output, planned expenditure then exceeds actual expenditure. So either the consumption plan or the investment plan or both will not be achieved. Suppose, as before, that the consumption plan is achieved. Then consumption is Y_2H. Actual investment, HF, must then fall short of planned investment, HE. What is happening is that there is unplanned decumulation (dis-investment) in inventories.

The reason for the unplanned run-down in inventories is clear: aggregate demand, Y_2E, exceeds aggregate supply, Y_2F, and inventories bear the brunt of this disequilibrium situation. In face of the unanticipated run-down in inventories, retailers increase their orders and manufacturers expand production. This implies that income will increase toward Y_e so long as $Y < Y_e$.

We have thus seen that if $Y > Y_e$, income will fall toward Y_e, whereas if $Y < Y_e$, income will rise toward Y_e. So, starting from any level of income, the economy converges toward Y_e. What happens when $Y = Y_e$? From the 45 degree line we see that aggregate supply then equals aggregate demand — actual output (actual expenditure) then equals planned expenditure. Thus all plans are achieved; there is no unanticipated accumulation or decumulation of inventories. Since all plans are achieved, nobody has reason to change his behaviour. The market is voluntarily absorbing exactly what producers are supplying. There would then be no change in output. Thus national income would stay at Y_e indefinitely, unless some shock causes either the consumption function or the investment function (the locus representing planned investment expenditure) to shift.

Using Figure 34a we have demonstrated: (i) The equilibrium level of national income is given by the intersection of the aggregate demand function (in the present simple model, the sum of the consumption and investment functions) and the 45 degree line. At that point aggregate demand, or planned expenditures, equal actual output. (ii) The equilibrium income is plausibly stable, so if the economy is not in equilibrium, it is likely to move towards equilibrium.

Planned Savings, Planned Investment, and Equilibrium National Income

We have explained the determination of equilibrium national income in a simple macroeconomic model with the aid of Figure 34a. We showed earlier that if we know the consumption function then we know the savings function and vice versa. Figure 34a shows the consumption and the investment functions. Figure 34b shows the same investment function and the savings function corresponding to the consumption function in Figure 34a. Since the two figures are equivalent we should be able to explain the determination of equilibrium income using Figure 34b, and the explanation should be equivalent to that already outlined. It is easy, as an equivalent explanation, to show that the equilibrium level of national income is given by the equality of planned savings and planned investment. In Figure 34b our claim is that Y_e is the equilibrium income. This claim can be verified as follows.

First, suppose that $Y > Y_e$, say $Y = Y_1$. Then planned savings exceed planned investment by an amount KJ. But actual savings are identical to actual investment. Thus either the savings plan or the investment plan will not be realised. In line with our earlier assumption in discussing Figure 34a, that the consumption plan is realised, we now correspondingly assume that the savings plan is realised; thus actual savings equal KY_1 in Figure 34b. Then, because of the identity of actual savings and actual investment, actual investment must also be KY_1 in Figure 34b. Thus actual investment exceeds planned investment by an amount KJ, which is unplanned investment. This takes the form of unplanned inventory accumulation. The reason for this is that too much is being produced relative to the level of aggregate demand. As before, output will be reduced and the system will approach Y_e.

Suppose next that $Y < Y_e$, say $Y = Y_2$, in Figure 34b. Then planned investment, MY_2, exceeds planned savings, LY_2, by an amount ML. But actual investment is identical to actual savings. Thus either the savings plan or the investment plan or both will not be realised. Assume that the savings plan is realised. Then actual and planned saving is LY_2, and by the identity of actual savings and actual investment, actual investment is also LY_2. Thus actual investment falls short of planned investment by the amount ML, which is unplanned decumulation of inventories of raw materials and finished goods. The reason for this is that too little is being produced relative to the level of aggregate demand. Because inventories are being run down below their desired levels, retailers increase their orders and manufacturers expand production. Thus output and income increase toward Y_c.

When $Y = Y_c$, planned savings equal planned investment (and, as always in this simple model, actual savings are the same as actual investment). All plans are being realised: there is no unplanned accumulation or decumulation of inventories. Nobody has reason to change his behaviour. Thus income and output stay at Y_c so long as the savings function or the investment function do not shift. Hence Y_c is the equilibrium income. We have demonstrated, for a simple closed economy without government, that the equilibrium level of national income is given by:

(i) The equality of aggregate demand, or planned expenditures, with actual output, or, equivalently, by:

(ii) The equality of planned (private) savings and planned (private) investment.

Equilibrium Conditions Versus Identities
For the simple model which we have just analysed, the *equilibrium condition* (i.e., the condition under which national income is in equilibrium) may be written in two equivalent forms, one of them corresponding to the analysis using Figure 34a, the other corresponding to that using Figure 34b. The first way of writing the equilibrium condition is

(4) $Y = C + I$

where Y is aggregate supply, C is consumption demand, or *planned* consumption expenditure, and I is *planned* investment expenditure, including planned change in inventories. Writing equation (4) as

$$Y - C = I$$

where Y is now interpreted as national income and C and I are as just defined, yields the *equivalent* equilibrium condition

(5) $S = I$

where I is *planned* investment expenditure and S is income which it is *planned* not to spend on consumption, i.e., it denotes *planned* savings.

It is essential to recognise that, for the model we have just developed, equations (4) and (5), in which C, I and S are interpreted as *planned* magnitudes, are *not true by definition* — they are *not identities.*

Towards the end of the preceding chapter we saw that at *any* level of national income it would be true, for a closed economy without government, that

(4′) $Y \equiv C + I$, and
(5′) $S \equiv I$

where C, I and S denote the *actual* values of the variables.

Equations (4) and (5) hold *only* in equilibrium; (4′) and (5′) are true *whether or not* national income is at its equilibrium level; they are identities, not theories.

Generalisation and Qualification

We have demonstrated, for a macroeconomic model in which producers are willing and able to supply any quantity at the prevailing price level, that the equilibrium level of national income is determined by (i) the level of aggregate demand, or equivalently in our simple model, by (ii) the equality of planned private savings and planned private investment. Condition (i) still holds when, by introducing government expenditure and foreign trade, we complicate aggregate demand in the direction of realism. But if we do add further complications, condition (ii) must be modified. We will need to add further qualifications when we come to place restrictions on aggregate supply.

Equilibrium Income Versus Full Employment Income

Although the matter is more complex than we pretend, we define the economy's full employment output as that level of output which, given the state of technology, and given the economy's factor endowments and the distribution of fixed capital across different sectors of the economy, corresponds to the maximum the economy is capable of producing. Thus either the capital stock or the labour force or both would be fully employed. Full employment output is more or less fixed in the short run.

The full employment level of output tends to increase if the economy's factor endowments increase. Thus if there is positive net investment in the economy, so that its capital stock is increasing, full employment output will also tend to be increasing. However, in the short run net investment can add only marginally to the existing capital stock inherited from the past. That is why we will regard full employment output as more or less given in our short run analysis. (Note that we are here on the fringe of consideration of the determinants of aggregate supply, but we defer discussion of such matters until later.)

There is nothing necessarily 'good' about being in equilibrium. Equilibrium national income is not necessarily the full employment level of national income — it is not necessarily a level of output at which all the economy's labour force and/or its capital stock are fully utilised. An economy could be in equilibrium with a great deal of capital and labour unemployed. In fact we shall see, when we bring government into the model, that one of the rationales for government intervention is to affect aggregate demand so as to drive the economy into a specific equilibrium — an equilibrium in the neighbourhood of full employment.

Effects of Shifts in the Functions

Suppose we start with the economy in equilibrium at Y_0 in Figures 35a and 35b, and, due to a campaign urging frugality, the average propensity to save, S/Y, increases. This means that, on aggregate,

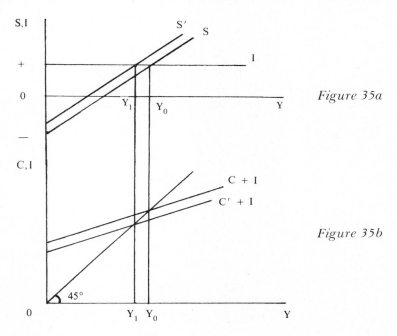

Figure 35a

Figure 35b

people are trying to save more at any level of income. The immediate effect of the attempt to save more is an upward shift in the savings function, from S to S′ in Figure 35a. If, as we assumed, planned investment is autonomous, so that it does not depend on the level of income, and if the investment function does not shift, the effect is a reduction in the equilibrium level of income from Y_0 to Y_1. Note that in this case, although the community has tried to save more, it ends up in the new equilibrium at Y_1, saving the same as at Y_0.

The upward shift in the savings function in Figure 35a is equivalent to a downward shift in the consumption function from C to C′ (neither plotted individually) in Figure 35b. Thus Figures 35a and 35b give the same information.

The Paradox of Thrift

We have seen, on the assumption that planned investment is autonomous (i.e., does not depend on the level of income) that an attempt by the community to save more will lead to no change in equilibrium savings. Suppose, however, that planned investment is not entirely autonomous, but that it increases with income. In that case the investment function — the relationship between planned investment and national income — will have a positive slope, as in Figure 36 below. There are several reasons why planned investment might be high at high levels and low at low levels of income. For example, if in the short run national income increases, greater pressures will be imposed on the existing stock of machinery and equipment, so firms might want to add to their capital stocks. Given the aggregate capital stock, it is likely that the profitability of investment will increase as

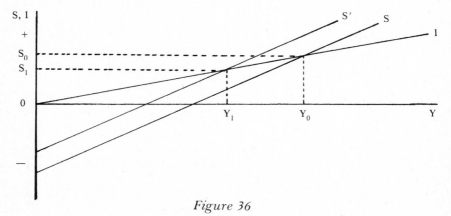

Figure 36

national income increases. Figure 36 indicates that if planned investment is an increasing function of income, and if the community's average propensity to save increases (i.e., if the savings function shifts upwards, so that S/Y at any level of Y is now greater than before) then the community will end up in a new equilibrium at Y_1, saving less than initially at Y_0. It can be seen from the diagram that aggregate savings fall from S_0 at the initial equilibrium to S_1 after the upward shift in the savings function. Thus the attempt to save more causes both realised savings and income to fall. This is known as the paradox of thrift. The paradox holds whenever planned investment is an increasing function of national income.

The Multiplier in the Simple Model

Suppose that planned investment is entirely autonomous, and that we start in equilibrium at Y_0 in Figure 37a. Since aggregate demand equals C + I, and since investment demand is assumed autonomous (the investment function has a slope of zero), the slope of C + I *is* the slope of the consumption function, the MPC, b in equation (2) above.

Consider the effect of an upward shift in the investment function. (This might have occurred because firms have become more optimistic in regard to the future.) Suppose that $\Delta I = £1$ million. Then C + I shifts up by £1 million to C + I' (where I' = I + ΔI), and the new equilibrium is at Y_1 in Figure 37a. The central point is that $\Delta Y > \Delta I$, or $\Delta Y/\Delta I > 1$; although planned investment has increased by £1 million, equilibrium income has increased by more than £1 million.

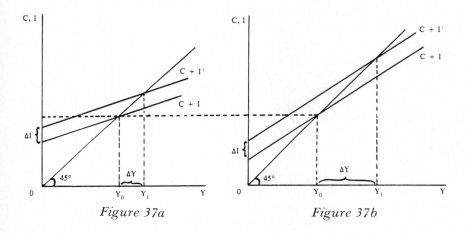

Figure 37a   Figure 37b

Turn now to Figure 37b and continue to assume that planned investment is autonomous. The slope of the aggregate demand function (the sum of the consumption and investment functions) is then the slope of the consumption function.

The main respect in which Figure 37b differs from Figure 37a is that *the implied consumption function in Figure 37b has a steeper slope —* the MPC, b, is higher. Figure 37b again indicates that $\Delta Y > \Delta I$. But in this case *the increment in income generated by a £1 million increase in planned investment is more than the increment in income in Figure 37a.*

Hence we see that (i) if planned investment increases by £1 million, equilibrium national income will increase by more than £1 million, and (ii) *the increment in equilibrium income generated by a £1 million increase in planned investment will be higher, the greater is the slope of the consumption function,* the MPC, b.

Note that we would obtain the same kinds of results as above if, instead of $\Delta I = £1$ million, there was an increase in the intercept of the consumption function, equation (2) above, so that $\Delta a = £1$ million, i.e., if the consumption function were to shift up by £1 million.

To clarify what is happening we turn to the multiplier.

Successive Rounds of Expenditure
Suppose that we start in equilibrium with an annual rate of net investment equal to £100 million, and that next the rate of investment permanently increases to £101 million. So $\Delta I = £1$ million. Assume that the overall MPC is ¾ and examine what will happen.

Since investment has increased by £1 million, the factors of production are paid an additional £1 million in wages, profits, etc. On this count, $\Delta Y = £1$ million. But there are further effects.

Because income has increased by £1 million, and because the MPC is ¾, the recipients of this £1 million spend an additional £(¾) million. This is an increment in national expenditure, so it must be matched by an equal increment in output. The producers of this output experience an increment in incomes of £(¾) million on this count.

In the *second round effects* just described, incomes have increased by £(¾) million. The recipients of this additional income will not save all of it; they will, on the assumption that their MPC is ¾, spend ¾ of it. Hence their expenditures will increase by (¾) £ (¾) million, or £(¾)² million. But this increase in expenditures is an increment in incomes somewhere in the economy, since the expenditure of one group is the income of another group.

Because incomes have increased by a further $£(\frac{3}{4})^2$ million, and because the recipients of this income are also assumed to have a MPC of $\frac{3}{4}$, those income recipients will spend $(\frac{3}{4}) £(\frac{3}{4})^2$ million $= £(\frac{3}{4})^3$ million. But as before, one group's expenditure is another group's income. The latter group therefore experiences an increase in their incomes of $£(\frac{3}{4})^3$ million. If, as we assume, their MPC is also $\frac{3}{4}$, they will spend an additional $£(\frac{3}{4})^4$ million, thereby generating an increment of $£(\frac{3}{4})^4$ million in the incomes of some other group in the economy. And so on the process continues, each increment in incomes generating further increments in expenditure, which in turn generate further increments in income.

For $\Delta I = £1$ million, we thus have (in £million):
$$\Delta Y = 1 + (\tfrac{3}{4}) + (\tfrac{3}{4})^2 + (\tfrac{3}{4})^3 + (\tfrac{3}{4})^4 + \ldots + \ldots$$
or in general,
$$(6) \quad \Delta Y = 1 + b + b^2 + b^3 + b^4 + \ldots + \ldots$$
where b is the marginal propensity to consume.

According to a theorem in the mathematics of infinite series, for any real number b such that $0 < b < 1$, the infinite series (6) converges to, or equals, $1/(1 - b)$. Since in the case at hand the number b (the MPC) is indeed between zero and unity, we have, for $\Delta I = 1$,

$$(7) \quad \Delta Y = \frac{1}{1 - b} \quad \text{or, for any arbitrary value of } \Delta I,$$

$$(8) \quad \Delta Y = \frac{1}{1 - b}\Delta I$$

Clearly, the higher b happens to be, the greater the change in national income due to a change in investment. Thus if $\Delta I = £1$ million, and if $b = \frac{3}{4}$, then $\Delta Y = £4$ million. If, on the other hand, $\Delta I = £1$ million, and if $b = \frac{1}{2}$, then $\Delta Y = £2$ million. The reason for the different results in Figures 37a and 37b should now be clear: the slope of the consumption function, the MPC, b, is closer to unity in the second diagram than in the first. The coefficient $1/(1 - b)$ above is called a national income multiplier.

Definitions: A national income *multiplier* is a coefficient relating change in equilibrium national income to changes in autonomous demand, or to policy-induced shifts in aggregate planned expenditure. *Autonomous demand* is that part of aggregate demand which does not depend on the level of national income. If all of investment demand is determined independently of national income, we say that investment demand is autonomous. In like manner, that part of planned consumption expenditure which does not depend on national income — the intercept 'a' in the consumption function (2) — is autonomous. We shall explain the meaning of policy-induced shifts in planned expenditure in the next chapter.

Writing the multiplier expression in the form $1/(1 - b)$ may suggest that when autonomous demand changes, the economy will instantly move to the new equilibrium level of national income. That in fact will not be the case, as is suggested by the multiplier expression in form (6), where the multiplier is seen to operate in a convergent lagged fashion, as income increases by successively smaller increments over time, ultimately reaching its new equilibrium level.

The Savings Leakage

The reason why the multiplier which we have just derived is a finite number (rather than infinite) is that savings are a *leakage* from the expenditure stream as the multiplier process works itself out: only part of the income earned in each round of expenditures is subsequently spent. The greater the savings leakage — the higher the marginal propensity to save — the lower the multiplier. Since the marginal propensity to save, MPS, equals 1 — MPC, we can write the multiplier derived above as

(9) $1/(1 - MPC) = 1/MPS$

which indicates that the higher the savings leakage (as represented by MPS) the lower MPC must be and, in consequence, the lower the multiplier.

We shall see later that, apart from personal savings, there are other leakages from the expenditure stream which lower the value of the multiplier. We shall demonstrate in the next chapter that if governments were to believe that the multiplier for Ireland is $1/(1 - MPC)$ they would be led to pursue nonsensical policies.

The Simple Model in Algebra

The simple model of national income determination, as developed up to now, is easily represented algebraically. Thus we have

Y = C + I, equilibrium condition.
C = a + bY, the consumption function.
I = $\bar{I}$; investment is at some autonomous planned level $\bar{I}$.

By simple substitution we obtain $Y = a + bY + \bar{I}$, which implies

$$(10) \quad Y = \frac{1}{1-b} a + \frac{1}{1-b} \bar{I}$$

which indicates that if 'a' (the autonomous element of planned consumption) or $\bar{I}$ were to increase by £1 million, the equilibrium level of income would increase by £1/(1 — b) million. Clearly, the higher the marginal propensity to consume, the larger the increase in equilibrium income generated by an increase in 'a' or in $\bar{I}$.

FOOTNOTE

1. The correlation between real consumption (or real savings) and real disposable income would be lower than that between the nominal values of the variables. But it would still be positive.

CHAPTER 11

Extensions of the Simple Model and Some Policy Implications

The main conclusion in the previous chapter was that, *assuming suppliers willing to provide any quantity at prevailing prices,* equilibrium national income is determined by the level of aggregate demand. That still holds when the simple model is extended to include government and foreign trade. Given the assumptions in regard to supply, we showed alternatively that equilibrium income in the simple model is given by the equality of planned private savings and planned private investment; however, this equilibrium condition must be modified when we extend the model to include government and foreign trade. Before proceeding, the reader should be sure that he is familiar with the identities toward the end of Chapter 9.

The Model with Government and Taxes

We continue to assume:
(i)   No depreciation.
(ii) No taxes or subsidies on expenditure (no net taxes on expenditure).
(iii) Undistributed profits of companies are zero; all company profits are distributed to shareholders. Thus private income equals personal income.
(iv) No economic relationships with the rest of the world, so $X = M = O$.

Assumptions (i) and (ii), which are made only to avoid complexity, imply that we need not distinguish between GNP and national income at factor cost; we continue to denote both by Y. Similarly assumption (iii) is made only to avoid complexity: so long as it is satisfied, we need not distinguish between company savings and personal savings; all the private sector's savings are then personal savings, S.

142

In introducing government, we assume:

(v) Income of public authorities in their business capacity is zero. Thus all the government sector's revenue must come from taxation or borrowing.

Because of assumption (ii), taxation must be raised by means other than taxes on expenditure — by income taxes, for example. That assumption is not restrictive: in practice what we call expenditure taxes — taxes on production or sale of goods and services — do exist, but their impact on the real purchasing power of consumers is similar to that of, say, income taxes. Both kinds of taxation mean that consumers can buy fewer goods with their pre-tax incomes; the impact on aggregate demand is similar. Therefore, the assumption that there are no expenditure taxes is not particularly restrictive.

The variable G in what follows denotes government (*current plus capital*) expenditure on goods and services; *it does not include transfer payments.* We can think of transfer payments by government as a form of negative taxation: they involve government giving to households rather than taking from them. We may include transfer payments in our analysis by regarding them as part of *net* tax receipts (tax receipts as commonly understood, less transfer payments by government). We use the symbol T to denote (net) tax receipts.

The existence of taxes on income implies that national income and disposable income are no longer the same. Now, disposable income equals national income less government (net) tax receipts.

As in the preceding chapter, all magnitudes are measured in real terms.

The Equilibrium Conditions

With government expenditure on goods and services in the model, national income is in equilibrium when aggregate demand (including government demand) equals actual output, i.e., when

(1) Y = C + I + G, where

Y: National product, or aggregate supply.

C: Consumer demand. We assume that consumers' expenditure plans are always realised; then C represents both actual and planned consumer expenditure.

I: Planned private investment expenditure, including planned inventory changes.

G: Planned government expenditure on goods and services. We assume that those plans are always realised.

Equation (1) is *not* an identity. It holds *only* in equilibrium, since I denotes planned private investment rather than actual private investment. (Planned investment will equal actual investment only if income is in equilibrium; otherwise there would be unplanned accumulation or decumulation of inventories.)

Parallel to the analysis of the previous chapter, the above equilibrium condition can be written in an equivalent form by interpreting Y as national income rather than as national product; then, disposable income, Y_d, is Y minus tax receipts, T:

(2) $Y_d = Y - T$

Disposable income is either consumed or saved

(3) $Y_d = C + S$

From (2) and (3)

(4) $Y = C + S + T$

Then, from (1) and (4)

$C + I + G = C + S + T$, or

(5) $S - I = G - T$

where S denotes planned personal savings and I, G and T are as already defined. Because we assume that the consumption plan is always realised, so is the savings plan. Thus S denotes both actual and planned personal savings.

Just as equation (1) is an equilibrium condition rather than an identity, so is (5), which we derived using (1); for our simple closed economy with government, income is in equilibrium only when planned personal savings less planned private investment equals the government budget deficit (or the budget surplus, if $S - I$ is negative). Otherwise actual investment would differ from planned investment, in which case income would not be in equilibrium. (Recall from Chapter 9 that (5) would be an identity if all variables were defined as their actual magnitudes.) We shall use both equilibrium conditions (1) and (5) to derive some important results in this chapter; however, we shall rely mainly on equilibrium condition (1).

We now have the conceptual base to show why modern economies rely heavily on government intervention to regulate the level of national income and employment. However, because of the number of variables now involved, graphical analysis is generally inefficient. But there are a few cases which can easily be shown graphically.

A Graphical Treatment

Consider Figure 38a. The C + I function shows aggregate demand in the absence of government: $Y = Y_e$ is equilibrium income. We now recognise that there is some maximum output which the economy is capable of producing under normal working conditions. That is Y_F, the *full employment level of output*. If Y is less than Y_F, capital and labour will be unemployed. Government may then seek to steer the economy closer to full employment by adding to aggregate demand. Suppose government finances its expenditure by borrowing. We can see from Figure 38a that if $G = \bar{G}$, and if the consumption and investment functions are unaffected, equilibrium income will increase to Y_F, the full employment level of national income. Thus *government may intervene to fill the gap which might otherwise prevail between aggregate demand and the full employment level of output.*

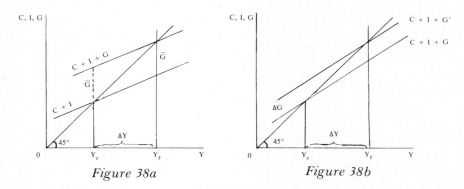

Figure 38a   Figure 38b

We note from Figure 38a that ΔY exceeds ΔG, which, since G was initially zero, is simply $\bar{G}$. This reflects the operation of the multiplier introduced in Chapter 10. Since we assume that planned private investment is autonomous, the slope of the aggregate demand function is the MPC. We infer that the higher the slope of the C + I function in Figure 38a, the larger the increase in equilibrium income induced per unit of government expenditure; equivalently, the multiplier applicable to government expenditure is higher, the higher the MPC. In the model in Figure 38a, the multiplier is $1/(1 - \text{MPC})$, as in the previous chapter: the upwards shift in the aggregate demand function by the distance $\bar{G}$ changes equilibrium income by an amount $1/(1-\text{MPC})$ times $\bar{G}$. As the MPC is less than unity, $\Delta Y > \Delta G$.

In the preceding paragraph we assumed that G was initially zero. The initial aggregate demand function might in fact be C + I + G in Figure 38b. In this case we see that if G is raised to G' (so $\Delta G = G' - G$), equilibrium income is likewise raised to Y_F. We have deliberately drawn the aggregate demand function with a steeper slope in Figure

38b, implying (on the assumption that planned private investment is autonomous) that the MPC is high. Figure 38b shows that although we start in equilibrium well below full employment, a relatively small increase in government expenditure is needed to obtain the large increase in output necessary for full employment. Suppose, for example, that the MPC is $0 \cdot 9$. Then, if $\Delta G = £1$ million, ΔY is $1/(1 - MPC)$ times ΔG, £10 million.

The Balanced Budget Multiplier

One reason why government might wish to intervene in economic activity is that the private sector, if left to itself, might not generate a full employment level of output. In the preceding exposition we assumed that the increase in government expenditure was financed by borrowing, in such a manner as not to affect the consumption or investment functions. But government often finances expenditure by increasing tax rates. Suppose, then, starting from equilibrium at Y_c in Figures 38a and 38b, that government increases its expenditure by £x million and also increases tax rates (in this case, from their initially assumed level of zero) so as to fully finance the increased expenditures. That is really a composite of two policies simultaneously: (i) an increase in G by £x million; (ii) an increase in tax rates so as to raise an extra £x million in taxation. The two policies will not exactly offset each other; the composite policy will be expansionary, given that private investment demand is autonomous. That can be seen by considering the two polices in isolation:

Suppose that the MPC is ¾. We have already seen that if government increases its expenditure by £x million, *the aggregate demand function will shift upwards by an amount £x million,* and $\Delta Y = 1/(1 - MPC)$ times x; in this example, $\Delta Y = 4x$ (in £million).

Consider next the effect of raising the extra £x million in taxation. This implies that at any level of national income, disposable income, and hence consumer expenditure, will be less than before; the consumption function would shift *downwards* in Figures 38a and 38b. The crucial question is whether the consumption function, and hence the aggregate demand function, would shift down by as much as £x million; if they did, there would be no net change in the aggregate demand function (the downward shift would offset the upward shift due to the increase in G).

Suppose that the new taxes are *lump sum,* the receipts from which do not depend on the level of national income. Thus we imagine the government raising the £x million by taxes on property or by simply assessing individuals regardless of their income or property position. At any level of national income, disposable income then falls by £x million; however, consumption expenditure at any level of national income will not fall by as much as £x million because *not all the disposable income taken from consumers would have been spent:* of that sum they would have spent only the MPC times the disposable income taken from them. Thus the consumption function in the 45 degree diagrams shifts downwards by an amount £(MPC)x. Therefore *the aggregate demand function shifts downwards by an amount smaller than £x — by £(MPC)x.* The multiplier is also applicable to this downward shift in aggregate demand. Thus $\Delta Y = -1/(1 - MPC)$ times (MPC)x, or $- MPC/(1 - MPC)$ times x. With the MPC equal to ¾, the £x million in increased taxes causes equilibrium income to fall by the amount $\Delta Y = -3x$.

Bringing the two sets of effects together:
(i) $\Delta Y = $ £4x million due to $\Delta G = $ £x million.
(ii) $\Delta Y = -$£3x million due to $\Delta T = $ £x million.

Thus $\Delta Y = $ £x million $= \Delta G = \Delta T$.

The result just obtained is an illustration of what is called the balanced budget multiplier theorem. Note that despite the nomenclature the theorem does *not* require the budget to be balanced.

Balanced Budget Multiplier Theorem: Assume a closed economy in which planned private investment is autonomous. Then, if government changes its expenditure on goods and services, and also changes (net) tax receipts by the same amount, so that there is no change in the initial budget surplus or deficit (or the budget stays balanced if it was initially balanced), $\Delta Y = \Delta G$, or $\Delta Y/\Delta G = 1$.

We shall soon see that taxes need not be lump sum (as assumed in the illustration above) for the theorem to hold.

Changes in Autonomous Demand and Policy-Induced Expenditure Shifts

In the preceding chapter we defined a multiplier as the coefficient relating a change in equilibrium national income to changes in autonomous demand or to policy-induced shifts in aggregate demand. We have not yet indicated what is meant by policy-induced shifts in demand. A policy-induced shift in demand occurs any time government policy causes a shift in the aggregate demand function. A change in government expenditure is clearly a policy-induced shift in aggregate demand. Similarly, if government changes tax rates, consumption as a function of national income will shift, leading to a shift in the aggregate demand function; this would also be policy-induced.

Algebraic Analysis

Because of the number of variables involved, the above analysis and its extensions are easier using simple algebra. We first assume that (lump-sum) tax receipts are fixed at some level $T = \overline{T}$. The model then is:

$Y = C + I + G$, equilibrium condition.

$C = a + bY_d$, consumption function.

$Y_d = Y - T$, definition of disposable income.

$T = \overline{T}$, level of lump-sum taxes.

$G = \overline{G}$, government expenditure is set at some level $\overline{G}$.

$I = \overline{I}$, planned private investment is autonomous, at the level $\overline{I}$.

By substitution, $Y = a + bY - b\overline{T} + \overline{I} + \overline{G}$, which implies

$$(6) \quad Y = \frac{1}{1 - b}(a + \overline{I} + \overline{G}) - \frac{b}{1 - b}\overline{T}$$

The parameter b in (6) is the marginal propensity to consume. From (6) we see that if 'a', $\overline{I}$ or $\overline{G}$ increase by £1 million (so that the aggregate demand function shifts up by £1 million), then equilibrium income will increase by £$1/(1 - b)$ million. If the level of lump-sum taxes $\overline{T}$ is increased by £1 million, equilibrium income will *fall* by £$b/(1 - b)$ million; alternatively, if $\overline{T}$ is reduced by £1 million, income will increase by £$b/(1 - b)$ million. Thus a £1 million increase in government expenditure is more expansionary than a £1 million reduction in tax receipts. Equation (6) also illustrates the balanced budget multiplier theorem:

Let $\Delta\overline{G} = $ £1 million and $\Delta\overline{T} = $ £1 million. Then, from (6),

$$\Delta Y = \frac{1}{1 - b}\Delta\overline{G} - \frac{b}{1 - b}\Delta\overline{T}, \text{ or}$$

$$(7) \quad \Delta Y = \frac{1}{1 - b} - \frac{b}{1 - b} = 1$$

Expression (7) is the balanced budget multiplier. It shows the amount by which equilibrium national income changes per unit change in government expenditure financed by taxation. The balanced budget multiplier for the simple closed economy model is unity.

Our understanding can be improved by noting that when government increases its expenditure on goods and services by £1 million, income initially increases by £1 million on that count; thus the *first-round effect* (see equation (6) of Chapter 10) is an increase in income by £1 million, some of which will be spent thereby generating a further increase in income, leading to a further increase in expenditure, and so on. But when government raises taxes by £1 million, the immediate effect is not a £1 million reduction in consumer expenditure; rather, households would have spent (had they not been taxed) only the MPC times the £1 million taken from them. In this case the *first-round effect* is a reduction in expenditure by an amount £b million. So the change in income generated by a £1 million increase in government expenditure is (in £million).

$$\Delta Y = 1 + b + b^2 + b^3 + b^4 + \ldots,$$ whereas the change in income generated by a £1 million increase in tax receipts is

$$\Delta Y = -b - b^2 - b^3 - b^4 \ldots$$

The sum of these two series is unity, again indicating that the balanced budget multiplier is unity.

Up to now we have assumed that government sets tax receipts at some level $T = \overline{T}$. But in reality it does not determine total tax receipts *directly*; in practice a considerable portion of tax receipts depends on both tax rates and on the level of national income (which in turn depends on tax rates). Taking these considerations into account we have, as a linear approximation, $T = t_0 + t_1 Y$, where t_0 is that part of the current year's tax receipts which do not depend on income in the current year, and t_1 is the rate of income tax (assumed for simplicity to be constant and applicable at all levels of income). Still maintaining the closed economy assumption, our model becomes

$$Y = C + I + G$$
$$C = a + bY_d$$
$$Y_d = Y - T$$
$$T = t_0 + t_1 Y$$
$$I = \overline{I}$$
$$G = \overline{G}$$

By substitution we then have

$$Y = a + b(Y - T) + \overline{I} + \overline{G} = a + bY - bt_0 - bt_1 Y + \overline{I} + \overline{G}$$

So, $Y(1 - b + bt_1) = a - bt_0 + \overline{I} + \overline{G}$, giving

$$(8) \quad Y = \frac{1}{1 - b + bt_1}(a + \overline{I} + \overline{G}) - \frac{b}{1 - b + bt_1}t_0$$

With tax receipts dependent on income, the multiplier for 'a', $\overline{I}$ and $\overline{G}$ is now less than that in (6); an increase in government expenditure at *unchanged* tax *rates* will now be less expansionary than previously, since

$$(9) \quad \frac{1}{1 - b + bt_1} < \frac{1}{1 - b}$$

The reason why the multipliers are now lower than previously is because, apart from the savings leakage as the multiplier process works itself out in successive rounds of expenditure, we have added a *second leakage*. Now, not all of the income earned at each round will be spent because, as before some of it will be saved, and because some of it will accrue to government in extra tax revenue. For example, suppose that the marginal propensity to consume is $0 \cdot 75$ and that the rate of income tax is $0 \cdot 20$; the multiplier on the left-hand side of (9) is then $2 \cdot 5$, while that on the right side is $4 \cdot 0$. Under these circumstances a £1 million increase in government expenditure financed by borrowing would generate a £4 million increase in equilibrium income if there were no taxes which depended on income, but only a £2·5 million increase in the contrary case.

With tax receipts now dependent on the level of national income, the reader may wonder whether the balanced budget multiplier theorem still applies. (It will be recalled that in illustrating the theorem we assumed lump-sum taxes.) The answer, for our simple closed economy, is yes. Suppose that government increases its expenditure by £x million and simultaneously changes tax rates in such a manner that tax receipts increase by exactly £x million at the new equilibrium. This £x million in increased tax receipts will be the net outcome of two factors: (i) Increased revenue at a given level of national income due to higher tax rates. (ii) Increased revenue induced by changes in income at given tax rates.

To demonstrate that the theorem is still valid we use equilibrium condition (5) of a few pages back, which was

(10) $S - I = G - T$, which implies

(10') $\Delta S - \Delta I = \Delta G - \Delta T$

By assumption, $\Delta G = \Delta T = $ £x million; so the right side of (10') is zero. Also by assumption of the theorem, $\Delta I = O$. Equilibrium condition (10') then implies $\Delta S = O$. But since planned savings depend on disposable income, and since there has been no change in planned savings, $\Delta Y_d = O$. By definition, $\Delta Y_d = \Delta Y - \Delta T$, so $\Delta Y =$

ΔT. And recalling that $\Delta G = \Delta T$ we conclude that $\Delta Y = \Delta G = £x$ million, or $\Delta Y / \Delta G = 1$. Hence the balanced budget multiplier theorem holds exactly for the simple closed economy, *regardless of whether taxes are lump sum*. Therefore if we start in the closed economy model at an equilibrium below full employment output, so that capital and labour are idle, increased government expenditure may drive the economy to an equilibrium in the neighbourhood of full employment even if income taxes are used to finance that expenditure.

The Model with Foreign Trade

We now bring exports (X) and imports (M) of goods and services into the picture. As before, national income is in equilibrium when aggregate demand (including now export demand) for the output of the economy equals its actual output, i.e., when

(11) $Y = C + I + G + (X - M)$

The symbols Y, C, I and G are as defined earlier in this chapter. Imports are deducted from the right side of (11) because they represent demand for foreign output rather than for that of the home economy. As before, we assume that the expenditure plans of consumers and government are realised, and we now add the further assumption that export and import plans are also realised.

Equation (11) is an equilibrium condition rather than an identity because it holds only in equilibrium; I denotes planned rather than actual private investment. (Planned investment will equal actual investment only if income is in equilibrium; otherwise there would be unplanned accumulation or decumulation of inventories.)

Parallel to the analyses in Chapter 10 and earlier in the present chapter, equilibrium condition (11) can be written in equivalent form by interpreting Y as national income rather than as national product. Then

(12) $Y = C + S + T$

Taken together, equations (11) and (12) imply that, in equilibrium,

(13) $S - I = (G - T) + (X - M)$

where all variables are at their planned magnitudes. The equilibrium condition for the present model of an open economy with government can be expressed as either equation (11) or equation (13).

What determines the levels of X and M? This is a question of great importance for an open economy like Ireland. We assume, until further notice, that *exchange rates between the home country and its main trading partners are given, and remain approximately constant.* Then, *in the short run,* we can postulate as a first approximation that export demand is determined by factors beyond our control — by the level of foreign demand. Thus we have, *for the short run,* X = $\overline{X}$; exports are at some externally determined level, $\overline{X}$. However, imports are a function of the level of our own national income. That is because, in the case of a small open economy like Ireland, imports are both a precondition for growth in national income as well as an effect of such growth. We can express the dependence of imports on national income as

(14)   M = f(Y), where $\Delta M/\Delta Y > 0$

Difficulty arises in estimating for Ireland the precise form of dependency relationship (14) because the marginal propensity to import in any year, $\Delta M/\Delta Y$, may be high or lower depending on which categories of aggregate demand vary. That can be seen as follows. Irish imports of goods and services may be broken down into four broad categories, for which unpublished research[1] suggests the following:

(i) *Capital goods* (machinery and equipment): For every £1 million increase in investment in machinery and equipment, imports of capital goods increase by close to £0·75 million. However, the import content of investment in building and construction is quite low.

(ii) *Raw materials:* It is estimated that for every £1 million increase in expenditure on consumer goods and services, imports of raw materials increase by £0·25 million; also, for every £1 million increase in inventories, imports of raw materials increase by about £0·55 million.

(iii) *Consumption goods ready for use:* The estimates here are that for every £1 million increase in expenditure on consumer goods and services, imports of consumption goods ready for use increase by about £0·35 million; however, this will be the case in a given year only if there has been no change in the volume of inventories in the previous year.

(iv) *Imports of services:* We import services when Irish tourists spend money abroad, when payments are made abroad by Irish residents to foreign transportation or insurance companies, and the like. The short-run relationship between this category of imports and changes in Irish national income appears to be less clear than for categories (i), (ii) and (iii).

In spite of the complications just raised, for ease of exposition we postulate a linear relationship between aggregate imports and national income. (In fact this has not been too poor an approximation for Ireland over the years.) Thus $M = m_0 + m_1 Y$, where m_0 is that part of imports which do not depend on national income in the current year and m_1 is the overall marginal propensity to import, $\Delta M / \Delta Y$. In order to focus on the role of imports in isolation, *we first ignore government and taxation.* Our model then becomes

$$Y = C + I + X - M$$
$$C = a + bY$$
$$I = \bar{I}$$
$$X = \bar{X}$$
$$M = m_0 + m_1 Y$$

where I and X are assumed to be at specific levels, $\bar{I}$ and $\bar{X}$. Substitution yields

$$Y - bY + m_1 Y = a + \bar{I} + \bar{X} - m_0, \text{ which implies}$$

$$(15) \quad Y = \frac{1}{1 - b + m_1} (a + \bar{I} + \bar{X} - m_0)$$

Equation (15) indicates that the multiplier is lower than it was in the simplest closed economy model:

$$\frac{1}{1 - b + m_1} < \frac{1}{1 - b}$$

Furthermore, the multiplier will be lower the higher the marginal propensity to import, m_1. The reason is that changes in import volume, induced by changes in income, are a further leakage from the successive rounds of expenditure as the multiplier works itself out.

Assume, for example, a £1 million increase in the rate of investment. Because investment has some import content, not all the £1 million will accrue as income to factors of production in Ireland; some of it will generate income abroad. Also, some of it will be saved in Ireland. The residual, after the import content and savings are deducted from the £1 million, will be spent. But some of that expenditure will be on imported consumer goods, which will create income abroad rather than in Ireland. Thus the £1 million increase in investment, and each successive round of expenditure, will generate a smaller increase in Irish national income than would be the case had there been no import leakage.

Our high overall marginal propensity to import explains why — the tax leakage aside — the multiplier is small for the open economy of Ireland. As a rough order of magnitude, $b = 0 \cdot 8$ in the case of Ireland. If we were a closed economy, and if there were no tax leakage, the multiplier would $1/(1 - 0\cdot8) = 5$. But if we now recognise that our overall marginal propensity to import is about $0\cdot6$ (still ignoring the tax leakage), our multiplier is reduced substantially to $1/(1 - 0\cdot8 + 0\cdot6) = 1\cdot25$.

We have identified three leakages from the expenditure stream — savings, taxes, and imports. The effect of each of these is to lower the value of the multiplier below what it would otherwise be. We can now include the three leakages together in an economic model.

The Model with Tax and Import Leakages

Gathering the principal equations of relevance, we have the following:

$$Y = C + I + G + X - M,$$
$$Y_d = Y - T$$
$$T = t_0 + t_1 Y$$
$$C = a + bY_d$$
$$I = \bar{I}$$
$$G = \bar{G}$$
$$X = \bar{X}$$
$$M = m_0 + m_1 Y$$

By substitution

$$Y = a + b(Y - t_0 - t_1 Y) + \bar{I} + \bar{G} + \bar{X} - m_0 - m_1 Y,$$

which implies

$$Y - bY + bt_1 Y + m_1 Y = a - bt_0 + \bar{I} + \bar{G} + \bar{X} - m_0. \text{ So}$$

$$(16) \quad Y = \frac{1}{1 - b + bt_1 + m_1}(a + \bar{I} + \bar{G} + \bar{X} - m_0) - \frac{b}{1 - b + bt_1 + m_1} t_0$$

We now see why *multipliers for Ireland must be very small.* As an approximation, $b = 0\cdot8$, $m_1 = 0\cdot6$, and the marginal net tax rate $t_1 = 0\cdot25$. Suppose government increases its expenditure by £1 million and that it finances this without affecting other components of autonomous demand. From equation (16) we calculate the multiplier for government expenditure as $1/(1\cdot0 - 0\cdot8 + 0\cdot2 + 0\cdot6) = 1$. Note that with $b = 0\cdot8$ in a closed economy with no tax receipts dependent on income, the government expenditure multiplier would be 5. Thus *recognising that we live in an open economy and that tax receipts vary with national income makes an overwhelming difference in the formation of macroeconomic policy.*

Does the balanced budget multiplier theorem still hold? Suppose that planned private investment is unaffected, that government increases its expenditure by £1 million and that tax receipts are increased by exactly £1 million so as to match the increase in expenditure: will equilibrium national income increase by £1 million as it would in a closed economy? The answer is no; income will increase by less than £1 million, and by very much less than £1 million if the marginal propensity to import is high. This is easily seen by assuming that government collects its revenue by means of lump-sum taxes; then $t_1 = 0$ in equation (16), where t_0 represents the level of the lump-sum taxes. The multiplier for an increase in G is given by the coefficient of G in equation (16); with $t_1 = 0$, $b = 0 \cdot 8$ and $m = 0 \cdot 6$, if $\Delta G = 1$, then $\Delta Y = 1/(1 - 0 \cdot 8 + 0 \cdot 6) = 1 \cdot 25$. The change (it is a reduction) in income generated by a £1 million increase in lump-sum taxes is given by the coefficient of t_0 in equation (16). Thus if $\Delta T = 1$, then $\Delta Y = -0 \cdot 8/(1 - 0 \cdot 8 + 0 \cdot 6) = -1$. Therefore, if $\Delta G = \Delta T = £1$ million, then $\Delta Y = £1 \cdot 25$ million $-$ £1 million $= £0 \cdot 25$ million. *Hence the balanced budget multiplier for the open economy of Ireland is closer to zero than it is to unity.*

Those considerations suggest that, in the open economy of Ireland, a *broadly distributed* increase in government expenditure on goods and services, financed by increased taxation, would have only a marginal impact on the level of aggregate demand. It should not be forgotten, however, that the *structure* of increases in government expenditure is important in assessing the first-round import leakage, and hence, the overall value of the multiplier. (We have not been able to deal with the structure of expenditures because of the aggregate nature of our analysis.) For example, a £1 million increase in government expenditure in recruiting police would have practically zero import leakage in the first round. But an extra £1 million spent on aircraft parts would have virtually no impact on the domestic economy in the short-run, since almost all the parts would be imported. The structure of investment expenditure by the private sector is also important in estimating the value of the multiplier applying to such expenditure. Thus, because the first-round import leakage is smaller, an increase in private investment in building and construction will have a higher multiplier than an equivalent increase in investment in machinery and equipment (which, because of the very high first-round import leakage, will typically have a negligible multiplier).

Excess Capacity and Public Policy

The multiplier analysis in this and in the preceding chapter is applicable in situations in which the economy is operating below capacity utilisation. If the economy is operating at full employment —

so that it is actually producing the maximum it is capable of producing — one form of real expenditure can be increased only if other real expenditures are reduced; if we had full employment, we could (in the short-run) produce, for example, more investment goods only by diverting labour and capital away from production of consumption goods. The theory of the multiplier, therefore, is applicable in an expansionary direction only to situations in which less than full employment prevails.

Subject to the full employment constraint on aggregate output which we have just mentioned, we have assumed throughout the last two chapters that producers are willing to supply any quantity at the prevailing price level. This assumption remains to be investigated at later stages of our macroeconomic analysis, especially when we consider the question of the real wage.

Demand Deficiency and Public Policy

Suppose that, due to a deficiency in the level of aggregate demand, the economy is producing with excess capacity, and that public policy seeks to drive the system closer to a full employment equilibrium. Since $Y = C + I + G + (X - M)$, government might do so, in the short-run, by generating an upwards shift in the consumption function, or in the investment function, or by increasing its own expenditure; alternatively, it could generate a downwards shift in the import function. The immediate effect of such shifts would be compounded by the multiplier process, even though the multiplier itself is small in an economy as open as Ireland. The principal instruments at the disposal of government in this context are fiscal policy (government policy in regard to the levels of its revenues and expenditures), *perhaps* monetary policy, and commercial policy (concerning tariffs and quotas on international trade). The consumption function could be shifted upwards by reduction in tax rates or *possibly* by reducing the cost, and increasing the availability, of credit to households. The investment function could be shifted upwards by offering various kinds of tax incentives for business investment, or *perhaps* by reducing interest rates. The import function could be shifted downwards (thereby causing the aggregate demand function to shift upwards, since imports appear with a negative sign in that function) by imposing tariffs or maximum quantity quotas on imports. (Note that we have expressed reservations in regard to the ability of the authorities to increase aggregate demand by means of monetary policy. We elaborate on this matter in detail later.)

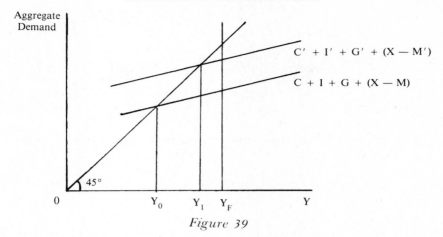

Figure 39

Suppose we start with the economy in equilibrium at Y_0 in Figure 39 and that Y_F, which exceeds Y_0, is the full employment output. *The initial aggregate demand function, $C + I + G + (X - M)$, is rather flat due to the savings, tax and import leakages.* Nevertheless, the effect of the kinds of policies which we have just discussed is an upward shift in the aggregate demand function to $C' + I' + G' + (X - M')$ and movement towards a higher equilibrium level of national income, Y_1, closer to the full employment level of income. Note that if the aggregate demand function were steeper (as it would be in a closed economy), a much smaller upward shift in the aggregate demand function would be required to get the economy to full employment output.

FOOTNOTES

1. The reference here is to research on an econometric model of the Irish economy. The public-spirited generosity of P.J. Carroll and Co. Ltd., in funding this research, is greatly appreciated.

CHAPTER 12

Determination of the Rate of Interest and the Creation of Money in a Closed Economy

For the most part we have assumed that private investment demand is autonomously determined at some level, but we did not inquire what determined that level. We now recognise that private investment demand depends on expected profits — the difference between the expected flow of returns from investment, and the initial costs of financing plus the expected flow of operating costs, associated with investment projects. Because interest is a cost of financing investment, the decision to invest depends on the interest rate. In this chapter we do not analyse in detail the relationship between the desire to invest and the rate of interest; that is reserved for analysis when we return to microeconomics. Here we need only point out that if the interest rate falls the cost of financing investment falls and therefore investment demand rises. In discussing the investment function in the preceding two chapters we implicitly assumed that the interest rate, and hence the expected profitability of investment, were given. However, if the interest rate falls, the expected profitability of investment increases, causing the investment function to shift upwards in our diagram. The immediate effect on income would be compounded by the multiplier. Similarly, if the interest rate increased, the cost of financing investment would rise, so the investment function would shift downwards causing equilibrium income to decline. These considerations suggest that we should examine the determinants of the interest rate. In the analysis which immediately follows we *assume a closed economy.* When we relax this assumption later we shall see that the implications for interest rate determination and for monetary policy may be *altered drastically in an open economy.* We continue to assume that the price level is constant.

Functions of Money and Determination of the Rate of Interest

Interest on money is the price for the services of money; alternatively, it is the cost of holding money. We normally think of interest as the cost of borrowed money. But we can also think of it as the cost of holding wealth in the form of money (which yields no financial return) rather than in assets such as real estate, machinery or bonds (which yield financial returns). A decision to hold wealth in the form of money is a decision to forgo earning interest. Thus interest is the *opportunity cost* of holding wealth in the form of money.

Functions of Money

The principal role of money is to separate the acts of buying and selling. In a pure barter economy, in which there is no money, every transaction would have to involve the exchange of goods or services on both sides of the transaction. The economist wanting a new suit might have to find a tailor wishing to listen to lectures on economics, while the tailor who wanted butter might have to find a farmer who wanted new clothes. The existence of money avoids such awkwardness, for money is a *medium of exchange*. It makes it unnecessary that there be direct coincidence of wants between parties entering trade. Money normally has three other functions. These are as a store of value, a unit of account and a standard of deferred payment.

A *store of value* is something which maintains value over time. An essential feature of a store of value is that it does not easily perish, as fresh fruit or meat would if used as media of exchange. We note that there are many other stores of value apart from money — land for example. Money is not necessarily a perfect store of value, for inflation may erode its purchasing power.

Money is a *unit of account* because it is the common denominator in which relative prices are normally expressed and in which book-keeping is maintained.

Finally, as a *standard of deferred payment* money is the measure in which repayment of loans is normally expressed. If someone buys a car on credit he does not contract to give the seller his stamp collection at some future date; rather, he agrees to pay certain sums of money, including interest.

While money performs all the above functions, its most important role is that of medium of exchange. In fact money is *anything* which is *generally* accepted as a medium of exchange. If people in general refused to accept payment in coin, banknotes or bank deposits (via cheques), such instruments would cease to be money. In practice people do accept payment in coin, banknotes or cheques; these are the principal (we shall assume the only) forms of money in modern economies. Note that money does not have to be 'backed' by anything of intrinsic worth such as gold. All that is necessary for something to be money is that people generally *believe* that if they accept it in payment, it will also be accepted in payment by others.

Liquidity

Money is a perfectly liquid asset since it can be immediately converted into goods without significant risk of loss. This is in contrast to less liquid assets such as real estate, consumer durables or bonds: if you suddenly decide to go on holidays, you cannot normally expect to finance that vacation by deciding instantly to sell your antiques while at the same time obtaining their full market values. Assets differ on a spectrum of liquidity, or ready convertability into purchasing power without loss. At one end of the spectrum stands money; toward the other end stand antiques, bonds and land.

A *bond* is a piece of paper with a face value of £x, issued by a borrower and promising to pay the bearer (perhaps the original lender) a certain sum in money over a certain period of time (say each year) until the bond is redeemed. Suppose that the government seeks to borrow £100 for twenty years. It may issue a bond with a face value of £100 to Norton, the lender. The government agrees to pay the bearer of the bond in twenty years time the sum of £100; twenty years time is then the redemption date of the bond. The government will have to pay interest. Suppose that the government agrees to pay Norton, or whoever might subsequently own the bond if Norton sells it (the bearer), a fixed sum of £15 annually for the next twenty years. This £15 is then the *interest* on the *face value* of the bond.

Perhaps Norton will wish to sell the bond in ten years time — before the redemption date. However, he may not be able to find buyers who are willing to pay the original price of the bond (£100) even though such potential buyers know that they would obtain £100 at redemption date, plus interest in the interim. Thus bonds are not perfectly liquid assets. In varying degrees the same can be said of all assets other than money — the only asset which is perfectly liquid.

The Demand for Money

We want to explain how the rate of interest is determined. Note that we said 'the' rate of interest. In reality there are many rates of interest

— those applying to short-term loans and those applying to long-term loans, as well as those applying to loans with different levels of risk of default. To facilitate exposition, when we refer to the rate of interest, we shall be referring to the rate of interest on a new gilt-edged government bond (so there is no perceived risk of default) with no fixed redemption date. Thus our rate of interest is 'pure' or riskless. All other rates of interest tend to move in phase with this central rate.

Since interest is a price, it is determined in much the same manner as any other price — by supply and demand; in the present case, by the supply of and the demand for money. As is the case with most other commodities, the demand curve for money (quantity of money demanded as a function of the price of money) slopes down from left to right, as in Figure 40 below. The lower the rate of interest the more money will borrowers seek. Also, the lower the rate of interest, the more will asset holders be willing to hold their wealth in the form of money rather than in the form of assets which yield direct financial returns. The reader may wonder why anyone might prefer money, a liquid asset, to other forms of wealth yielding direct financial returns. Broadly speaking, there are three motives for such *liquidity preference*. These are the transactions, precautionary and speculative motives.

(i) *The Transactions Motive:* One reason why people wish to hold wealth in the form of money is to facilitate current transactions. Most households receive their incomes weekly, fortnightly or monthly. Therefore they need to hold money to meet day-to-day expenses. The transactions demand of households for money depends on the payments habits of the community (in particular, whether households receive their incomes at long or short intervals) and on the level of money income. Businesses also hold money balances — normally in their bank accounts — to finance day-to-day transactions. They must hold money to meet the costs of raw materials, the wages bill, etc. The larger the turnover of the firm, the larger, other things being equal, the firm's transactions demand for money. It follows that the community's transactions demand for money is determined, broadly, by the level of national income. However, it also depends on the interest rate: if the rate of interest were to increase, people would economise on their transactions money balances, for it would have then become relatively more attractive to hold interest-bearing assets.

(ii) *The Precautionary Motive:* People hold money under the precautionary motive to guard against unforeseen contingencies. Many people hold money to provide for 'a rainy day'. The amount of money held under the precautionary motive depends on how pessimistic people are. It also depends on the level of income and on the interest rate. If the rate of interest is low, it is likely that a rich man will hold larger precautionary money balances than a poor man. But if the interest rate is high, people may be tempted to hold securities rather than money under the precautionary motive.

(iii) *The Speculative Motive:* Money may be held under the speculative motive when the prices of other assets, such as bonds, are expected to decline. If prices of assets other than money do decline, the speculator can then use his money to buy those assets more cheaply, in the prospect of holding them for a while and selling them at a profit later, if and when their prices rise.

Consider an irredeemable gilt-edged bond issued in year zero with a face value of £100 and earning an interest rate of 8 per cent. (By irredeemable we mean that the bond has no redemption date. By gilt-edged we mean that there is no perceived risk of repudiation of the fixed annual interest payments.) The bearer of such a bond is entitled to receive a *fixed* sum of £8 every year he holds the bond. If the market rate of interest remains 8 per cent — if lenders receive £8 per annum for every £100 they lend — then the market price of the bond, indefinitely, will be £100. But if the market rate of interest rises to 16 per cent in year one (after the year zero bond has been issued), the market price of a year zero bond will fall. Borrowers in year one are now offering to pay a fixed sum of £16 per annum for every £100 they borrow. The price of the year zero bond will therefore fall to £50. That is because that bond yields only £8 per annum, whereas a year one bond yields £16 per annum. People will be willing to pay only £50 per year zero bond (although it has a face value of £100) because it requires two of those bonds to yield the same income (£16) as a year one bond. Only then will they be making a return of 16 per cent on new bonds *and* on any old year zero bonds which they may buy from the original lenders. The converse would prevail if the interest rate fell to 4 per cent in year one. Borrowers would then have to pay only £4 per annum on every £100 they borrow. Someone with £200 to lend in year one could then earn a fixed return of £8 per annum. But a year zero bond would also yield £8 per annum. Therefore the market price of the year zero bond would be bid up to £200 in year one.

In the above examples we assumed that the bonds were irredeemable. That was to avoid complications which would arise in connection with the number of years remaining before redemption date. If the bonds in fact had fixed redemption dates, qualitatively much the same kind of conclusions would have emerged. Thus *the prices of bonds move inversely to the interest rate. In like manner, the price of any asset which yields income over time tends to move inversely to the rate of interest.*[1] It is these phenomena which give rise to the speculative demand for money. People will desire to hold more of their wealth in the form of money rather than in other assets if they expect the interest rate to rise.

Suppose, for example, that the current interest rate is 10 per cent, and that you hold an irredeemable bond with a face value of £100 which brings you a fixed sum of £15 per annum. (This bond was issued in a year when the interest rate was 15 per cent. How can you tell?) Suppose that you expect the interest rate to increase to 20 per cent in the near future. You may, therefore, decide to sell your bond at its current market price of £150. Having done so you now hold £150 in speculative money balances. If you are correct in your expectation of the future interest rate, the price of the bond will soon fall to £75. (Be sure that you can explain why.) You have thereby avoided losses by selling your bond while the going was good. If you sell the bond when its market price is £150, and if you are correct in your anticipations, you will shortly be able to repurchase the bond for £75, yielding a profit which exceeds the loss of interest you could have earned had you held on to the bond.

It follows that if people feel that the interest rate will soon be higher than at present (if they feel that the prices of bonds and other assets apart from money are going to fall) they will attempt to hold more of their wealth in money rather than in bonds and other assets (we shall continue to say just bonds — see note 1). Conversely, if people feel that the future interest rate will be lower than now they will attempt to hold more of their wealth in bonds rather than money.

At any point in time people have notions of 'normal' levels of the rate of interest. If the interest rate is low — say 2 per cent — they feel that it is unlikely to fall any lower and will probably soon rise. This implies that bond prices are expected to fall. People will attempt to sell bonds and hold money. Therefore at low interest rates the speculative demand for money is high. If the present interest rate is high, say 25 per cent, people feel that a higher interest rate is unlikely, and that a fall in the interest rate (a rise in bond prices) is probable. At high interest rates people therefore attempt to hold bonds rather than money. The speculative demand for money is low at high interest rates and high at low interest rates: it is a decreasing function of the rate of interest. The higher the current interest rate the greater the probability of a rise in bond prices and capital gains. The lower the current interest rate the greater the probability of a fall in bond prices and capital losses. Note that it is not the present interest rate *per se* which determines speculative demand; it is the relationship between the present and expected future rates that matters.

The Equilibrium Rate of Interest
The equilibrium interest rate is determined by supply and demand. In regard to the supply of money, we assume that it is fixed by the monetary authority. (We shall see later how this is done, as well as the limitations on the powers of the monetary authority in an open economy.) The money supply curve is SS in Figure 40. We saw that the demand for money consists of: (i) A transactions demand, which depends on national income but moves inversely to the interest rate. (ii) A precautionary demand, which is a function of income but moves inversely to the interest rate. (iii) A speculative demand, which is a decreasing function of the interest rate.

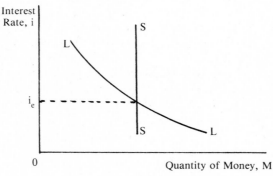

Figure 40

Let the community's demand for money *at a given level of national income* and at different interest rates be LL in Figure 40. This is the community's *liquidity preference* curve, reflecting its preference for money over other assets at different interest rates.

With the supply and demand curves for money like SS and LL in Figure 40, i_e is the equilibrium interest rate. If the authorities increased the money supply, SS would shift to the right, leading to a lower interest rate.[2] Planned private investment would increase. If we start with the system in equilibrium below full employment, the initial effect on income of the increased investment demand would be compounded by the multiplier. If (given the supply of money) the demand for money increases, the liquidity preference curve will shift to the right, implying that at any interest rate the public wishes to hold more money than previously. The interest rate will be bid upwards in consequence. Thus at a given price level (we have assumed a more or less constant price level up to now), if government expenditure is expanded, equilibrium national income will tend to increase, leading to an increase in the demand for money to facilitate a higher level of transactions and, on that count, the interest rate would rise. The rise in the interest rate would choke off some investment demand; though if the economy had initially been in equilibrium below full employment, we would expect the increase in government expenditure to exceed the reduction in investment demand induced by the rise in the interest rate, so there would be a net increase in income.

In this paragraph we relax our assumption that the price level is constant. People demand money under the transactions motive to facilitate the *money value* of their transactions; the demand for money is a function of the level of *money* income rather than *real* income. So if the price level is increasing over time, the community's demand for money curve would be shifting to the right over time. *If the money supply is held constant,* the equilibrium rate of interest would then be increasing. *By choking off some investment demand (and perhaps some consumption demand also), such increases in the rate of interest would automatically reduce aggregate demand — if the money supply is held constant.* We shall return to these considerations when we analyse inflation in the next chapter.

Interest Rates

So far we have spoken of 'the' rate of interest as though there were only one rate of interest. There are in reality many interest rates. The rate of interest on a security the redemption date of which is far into the future will *normally* be higher than that on short-term loans. The longer the life of a security, the greater the sacrifice of liquidity, and the higher the price that usually must be paid in the form of interest. A further determinant of the levels of actual interest rates is the risk associated with the securities in question. A lender will demand a higher interest rate from a borrower whose character or financial standing is doubtful than from one of repute and sound financial standing.

The central rate of interest to which we generally refer in these chapters is the long-term rate on gilt-edged government securities with no redemption date. For simplicity we ignore considerations of risk (that the borrower might repudiate either his debt or the interest payments) and we also for the most part ignore distinctions between short-term and long-term securities. Actual rates of interest will diverge from the long-term gilt-edged rate, depending on the degree of risk associated with the securities in question, and on the time which must elapse to maturity (i.e., to redemption date).

The Supply of Money

We defined money as anything that is generally accepted as a medium of exchange. In a modern economy it is of two forms:

(i) Cash or currency or legal tender. (Cash or currency is not quite identical to legal tender but the distinction is of minor importance for our purposes, so we ignore it.) In most economies cash is a liability of the central bank.

(ii) Deposits at commercial banks (those banks with whom the public normally deals). These deposits are money because transfers of bank deposits (by means of cheques) are generally accepted as media of exchange.

Central Banking
In many respects a central bank has a relationship with the commercial banks similar to that which the commercial banks have with the non-bank public. Although the precise role of central banks differs from country to country, the 'classical' (or archetypal) central bank has the following functions:

(i) It is the bankers' bank. Thus it accepts deposits — and may even demand deposits — from the commercial banks.

(ii) It is banker to the government.

(iii) It is lender of last resort. By this we mean that, upon presenta-tion of appropriate securities by the commercial banks, the central bank is normally willing to lend to those banks, but only at a price (interest rate) determined by the central bank itself. If the central bank wishes to reduce the money supply it will discourage the commercial banks from borrowing from it; it may therefore raise the interest rate at which it is willing to lend to them. (That rate of interest is called *Bank Rate,* the central bank's *Minimum Lending Rate, Discount Rate,* or *Rediscount Rate.*) The interest rate at which the central bank is willing to lend to the commercial banks may be penal, in the sense that, if the commercial banks do have to borrow from it at the interest rate charged by the central bank, they may then incur losses. Under such circumstances the commercial banks would borrow from the central bank only 'as a last resort'; hence the nomenclature 'lender of last resort'.

(iv) The central bank is the issuer of legal tender. The way it does so is simple: it buys securities and gives its own liability — cash — in exchange. In some countries the central bank may buy bonds directly from government, thereby financing government expenditure directly by the printing press. Alternatively, the central bank may buy bonds from commercial banks, insurance companies or other institutions.

(v) A central bank is usually charged by law to pursue monetary policies consistent with the overall interests of the economy.

Commercial Banking and Deposit Money

We have seen that there are two kinds of money in modern economies: cash or currency, and deposit money (commercial bank deposits). We also noted that currency, a liability of the central bank, can be created by central bank purchases of securities. Most of the central bank's liabilities are in fact reserves to the commercial banks. It is on the basis of such reserves that the commercial banks create deposit money.

The commercial banks, in conjunction with the public, create deposit money. To understand how deposit money is created, it is not vital to know how the money supply came to be what it is. The crucial question is: how can it be changed? In what follows *we can refer interchangeably to currency or cash held in commercial banks and deposits held by the commercial banks at the central bank.* (Recall that the central bank is banker to the commercial banks.) That is because *both* are liabilities of the central bank, and either one can normally be converted into the other upon request by a commercial bank. Both cash on hand and their deposits at the central bank are *reserves* to the commercial banks.

Suppose that the amount of cash in the economy is £x, and that an additional £100 is injected into the system. Perhaps someone has sold a bond to the central bank for £100, and the central bank may have paid the seller £100 in cash (or, *equivalently,* the central bank may have paid the seller by means of a cheque drawn on itself; this cheque could be 'cashed in' at the central bank, or, if it is deposited in a commercial bank, the commercial bank may deposit it in its account at the central bank — recall that such commercial bank deposits at the central bank are equivalent to cash).

Assume that the original recipient of the £100 has an account with commercial bank A, and that he places all of it on deposit. The initial impact on the balance sheet of bank A is as follows:

Bank A

Assets	Liabilities
Cash + £100	Deposits + £100

We assume that bank A is in business to maximise profits. It does so by lending, thereby earning interest. But it will not lend all of the increment in its assets: it will hold some of the additional cash as reserves — in its vaults or as deposits at the central bank — to secure against the day-to-day contingency of withdrawals by depositors. But more importantly (for reasons to be understood shortly) the central bank is likely to require commercial banks to hold a specific minimum ratio between their reserves (cash plus deposits at the central bank) and their deposit liabilities. Assume that this ratio is 20 per cent. Given that bank A can find a credit-worthy borrower, it will lend £80 of the increase in its assets, holding only £20 of the increment in assets as reserves. The change in its balance sheet then becomes:

Bank A

Assets	Liabilities
Reserves + £20 Loans + £80	Deposits + £100

The person who borrowed £80 from bank A presumably did not do so to hold it in idle cash balances — for he is paying interest on it. Suppose he borrowed the £80 to buy clothing. The retailer of clothing has an account with bank B. Assume that he deposits the whole £80. So the liabilities of bank B increase by £80. However, given the assumed required ratio of 20 per cent between reserves and deposits, bank B will hold £16 of the increase in its assets as reserves, and the remaining £64 as loans and advances. The change in bank B's balance sheet is then as follows:

Bank B

Assets	Liabilities
Reserves + £16 Loans + £64	Deposits + £80

Presumably the £64 borrowed was used to buy some commodity, say tyres. The tyre dealer banks with bank C, and deposits the whole £64. In accordance with the 20 per cent reserve ratio requirement, bank C puts £12·8 in reserve and increases its lending by £51·2. The change in its balance sheet is:

Bank C

Assets		*Liabilities*	
Reserves +	£12·8	Deposits +	£64
Loans +	£51·2		

Following the preceding reasoning, the £51·2 in loans from bank C will become deposits in some other bank, say bank D, which, in turn, will generate further loans and hence further deposits in other banks. The process of credit creation will continue by way of successive rounds, each increment in deposits being progressively smaller.

Given our implicit (stated below) and explicit assumptions, we can show that the ultimate effect of the original injection of £100 in cash will be an increase in the money supply of £500. Thus, letting ΔM denote the change in the money supply,

$$\Delta M = 100 + 80 + 64 + 51\cdot2 + \ldots , \text{ or}$$

(1) $\Delta M = [1 + (4/5) + (4/5)^2 + (4/5)^3 + \ldots](100)$

From earlier discussion in the context of multiplier theory (see equations (6) and (8) of Chapter 10) we know that (1) is the same as

(2) $\dfrac{1}{1 - (4/5)}(100)$, which equals 500.

The infinite series (1) converges to 500. Hence an injection of £100 in cash into the economy will lead to an ultimate increase of £500 in the money supply. Similarly, if the required reserve ratio were 50 per cent or ½, an injection of £100 in cash into the system would lead to an increase in the money supply of only £200. In general, if there is an injection of £x in cash into the system, the ultimate increase in the money supply will be £ (the reciprocal of the reserve ratio) (x). More formally, if l/r denotes the reserve ratio, and if x denotes an injection of cash into the system,

(3) $\Delta M = (x)/(l/r) = rx$

We have outlined the multiple expansion of deposit money in a closed economy in which there are several commercial banks. In this context the number of commercial banks is irrelevant. Thus consider a closed economy in which there is a single commercial bank — a monopoly commercial bank with many branches, and which therefore represents the consolidated commercial banking system. Suppose there is an increase in cash deposits of £100 and that the reserve ratio is 20 per cent. The money supply could then be increased by a further £400 as follows: in a relatively short period the bank could buy securities (i.e., lend) to the extent of £400 by writing cheques drawn on itself, knowing that the ultimate recipients of such cheques would deposit them with the one and only monopoly bank.

Some Qualifications

Some qualifications need to be added to our outline of the creation of money:

(i) It was assumed, when there was an injection into the system of £x in cash, that there was no permanent leakage of cash into hand-to-hand circulation. To the extent to which such leakages do in practice occur, the ultimate increase in the money supply will be less than that indicated by equation (3).

(ii) It was assumed that commercial banks kept no excess reserves. Thus, we assumed that if commercial banks were required by law to hold a ratio of *at least* 20 per cent between reserves and deposit liabilities, they would hold that ratio *exactly.* Commercial banks might in fact find it in their interest to hold excess reserves, mainly because they might not be able to find enough credit-worthy borrowers. To the extent to which they do hold excess reserves, an injection to the system of £x would lead to a smaller increase in the money supply than is suggested by equation (3).

(iii) *The above outline of the creation of money needs very substantial modification in the case of highly open economies operating under fixed exchange rates.* The reason can be seen as follows:

Suppose that the central bank buys securities from the market, thereby increasing the reserves of the commercial banks, and that those banks expand deposits in the manner already indicated. Following our earlier analysis of the supply of and the demand for money, an effect of this, in a closed economy, would be a reduction in the rate of interest. Now the Republic of Ireland is a small open economy. Until March 1979 it operated under a fixed exchange rate with the UK; also, financial assets were highly mobile between the two countries. It followed that interest rates in the Republic could not differ much from interest rates in the UK.

Suppose (under a fixed exchange rate with the UK) that interest rates in the Republic were initially in line with those of the UK. Suppose also that interest rates in the UK remained constant and that the Central Bank of Ireland pursued policies to increase the money supply here. An immediate effect would have been downward pressure on interest rates in the Republic. But given the fixed exchange rate and given the interest rate differential between the UK and Republic, this would have led to transfers of deposits from the Republic to, say, Northern Ireland. This in turn (i) would have curtailed the expansion in the money supply in the Republic and (ii) would have prevented interest rates in the Republic from diverging significantly from those in the UK. It was for these reasons that the Central Bank of Ireland could pursue independent monetary policies only within very narrow bounds.

In fact, so long as we maintained a fixed exchange rate with the UK, the scope for independent monetary policies by the Central Bank of Ireland was very limited: if the Central Bank of Ireland tried to pursue independent expansionary monetary policies (by buying bonds) the *immediate* impact would have been an increase in the reserves of the commercial banks and a multiple expansion of deposits along the lines already indicated, thereby putting downward pressure on interest rates here *vis-à-vis* the UK. Because there would then have been a tendency for interest rates in the Republic to fall below those in the UK (and for other reasons also), *there would very soon have been a tendency for deposits in the Republic to be transferred to UK banks. Indeed the resulting reduction in reserves at Irish commercial banks would have tended to nullify the increase in their reserves initially brought about by the expansionary monetary policies* on the part of the Central Bank of Ireland. Under such circumstances the net increase in the Irish money supply would have tended to zero.

When the earlier drafts of this text were written Ireland maintained a fixed exchange rate with the UK, so the two preceding paragraphs were then written in the present tense. In March 1979 Ireland joined the European Monetary System (EMS), under which Ireland entered a commitment to maintain (approximately) fixed exchange rates with the currencies of the other EEC countries, with the exception of the UK (which did not enter the EMS). At present (early in May 1979) it is too early to assess the long-term viability of the EMS, some details of which are provided in Chapter 26. The central point in the present context is that so long as Ireland remains an open economy (so that there is relatively free mobility of goods and financial assets across its frontiers) and maintains a fixed (or approximately fixed) exchange rate with any major currency (whether that be the pound sterling or the German mark), the scope for independent monetary policies by the Central Bank of Ireland will be very limited. The reasons remain those already outlined (with, say, 'continental EEC' replacing 'the UK' in the explanation above).

We will consider the Central Bank of Ireland and the monetary system of the Republic in detail later on. *Until further notice we shall ignore qualification (iii) above.*

The Instruments of Monetary Policy

In relatively closed economies central banks affect the money supply mainly (a) by directly influencing the level of commercial bank reserves (i.e., commercial bank holdings of currency, plus commercial bank deposits with the central bank), and (b) by changing the required minimum ratio of commercial bank reserves to their deposit liabilities. The principal policy instruments available to central banks in this context are:

(i) *Open Market Operations:* By this we mean purchases or sales of securities by the central bank on the open market. Suppose it wishes to increase the money supply. It may do so by buying securities on the open market (e.g., from insurance companies or from commercial banks). It pays cash or (what in essence is the same thing) cheques drawn on itself for these securities. By a direct or indirect process the reserves of the commercial banks will increase: they will end up holding more currency or their deposits at the central bank will increase. This increase in commercial bank reserves will lead to multiple expansion of deposits in the manner already indicated. If the central bank sought to reduce the money supply it could do so by selling securities. It would be paid in cash, or by cheques drawn on the commercial banks, or by direct commercial bank drawings on their deposits at the central bank. In either case the reserves of the commercial banks (their holdings of currency or their deposits at the central bank) would decrease, and a multiple contraction of deposits would occur.

(ii) *Changes in the Minimum Lending Rate (or Discount Rate, or Rediscount Rate):* If the central bank wishes to reduce the money supply it will raise the rate of interest at which it is willing to lend reserves to the commercial banks. This will discourage those banks from borrowing from the central bank, and will therefore curtail growth in the money supply. If it wishes to expand the money supply, it will lower the interest rate at which it is willing to lend to the commercial banks, thereby encouraging those banks to borrow reserves and hence to create more deposit money.

If a central bank wishes to change the money supply it will normally manipulate instruments (i) and (ii) *simultaneously.* Suppose that the central bank engages in open market sales of securities with a view to contracting the money supply. On that count the commercial banks will experience reduction in reserves, and will have to cut back their loans (and hence their deposits). However, if the interest rate at which the central bank is willing to lend to the commercial banks is relatively low, those banks might have incentive to borrow reserves from the central bank at the low interest rate, thereby generating the resources by which they could lend to their customers at a higher interest rate. *In that case, the loss in reserves generated by the open market sales could be offset by an increase in the reserves due to commercial bank borrowing from the central bank.* To prevent this happening — to make the open market sales effective — the central bank would also raise the interest rate at which it is willing to lend to the commercial banks.

(iii) *Changes in the Minimum Reserve Ratio:* Suppose that the commercial banks have £x in reserves, and that the minimum reserve ratio, as stipulated by the central bank, is 20 per cent. Assuming that the commercial banks can find a sufficient number of credit-worthy borrowers, the amount of deposit money, from equation (3), will approximate £5x. If the central bank sought reduction in the money supply it could raise the required minimum reserve ratio to, say, 25 per cent. The total amount of deposit money would then approximate £4x.

In order to comply with the new higher reserve ratio the commercial banks would have to call in loans and sell securities. They would also turn down applications for new loans. If, starting from a position in which the minimum reserve ratio was 20 per cent, the reserve ratio were increased to 25 per cent, and if the commercial banks were informed by the central bank that they must comply with the 25 per cent reserve ratio within a short period, they might have to unload large quantities of securities on the market (in exchange for cash), thereby depressing their prices. This could force the commercial banks into substantial losses. For this reason, if the reserve ratio is raised, the commercial banks may be given ample prior notice. They could then gradually adjust towards a higher reserve ratio by not issuing new loans after loans are paid off, by not buying new bonds after other bonds in their portfolios have been redeemed at redemption date, etc. We have considered the case of an increase in the minimum reserve ratio. If the central bank seeks to expand the money supply it might reduce the required minimum reserve ratio.

(iv) *Special Deposits:* The central bank might demand that the commercial banks place special deposits at the central bank and, furthermore, that such special deposits would *not* be reckoned as part of their reserves. A demand for special deposits would lead to reduction in the reserves of the commercial banks and hence to multiple contraction of their deposits.

(v) *Moral Suasion:* The central bank might make formal requests to the commercial banks, urging them to adhere to the central bank's guide-lines in regard to monetary policy. Thus the central bank might request — rather than demand — that the commercial banks maintain a specific minimum reserve ratio. Or it might seek to influence the structure of credit by urging the commercial banks to favour investors rather than consumers in their lending policies.

We have seen how central banks in closed economies could change the money supply, thereby leading to changes in the *cost* and *availability* of credit. In turn, changes in the cost and availability of credit lead to shifts in the aggregate demand function. If we start with the economy in equilibrium below full employment, the effect on real income of such a shift will be compounded by the multiplier. Thus monetary instruments, fiscal instruments or both may be manipulated to drive the economy towards full employment.

FOOTNOTES

1. For example, suppose initially that the rate of interest is x per cent and that the market value of all assets other than money, Other Assets, (such as bonds, land, housing and factories) is, say, £y. If the rate of interest rises to 2x per cent, the market will no longer be willing to pay £y for Other Assets; indeed the price of Other Assets would collapse toward £½y. This reflects the fact that market forces tend to equate the percentage yields on the current costs of all assets traded. If one asset has a higher percentage yield on its current cost than another, the market would bid up the price of that asset, thereby causing its percentage yield on current cost to fall; at the same time the market price of the low-yielding asset would tend to be bid downwards. In this manner the forces of supply and demand would tend to equate the percentage yield on current cost of the two assets.

2. If, however, the demand curve for money, LL, were infinitely elastic (perfectly flat), as it probably would be at a very low interest rate, an increase in money supply would cause no change in the rate of interest. This phenomenon is known as the 'liquidity trap'.

CHAPTER 13

Inflation in Closed and Open Economies: A Partial Analysis

We now relax the assumption that the price level remains more or less constant. By inflation, economists mean sustained — as opposed to once and for all — increase in the price level. Ireland experienced high inflation in 1970-77. This was overwhelmingly due to the fixed exchange rate we maintained between our currency and that of the UK, which was also inflating rapidly. Among the principal effects of that inflation were:

(i) Erosion in the purchasing power of persons on relatively fixed money incomes.

(ii) Redistribution of real disposable income away from individuals to government. This occurred largely because personal allowances in the tax code were not adjusted in line with inflation.

(iii) Redistribution of real wealth away from lenders in favour of borrowers. This occurred largely because *real* interest rates were in some years negative (i.e., nominal rates of interest were less than the rate of inflation). Thus lenders obtained negative real returns. Because (nominal) interest rates were often lower than the rate of inflation, many borrowers, when they repaid loans, were repaying less *in real terms* than the sum originally borrowed. The treatment of interest payments in the tax code further improved the position of borrowers.

(iv) Inflation caused difficulties in accountancy. Indeed it is not always clear what the accountancy term 'profit' means in an inflationary environment.

Note that we did not state that inflation inevitably causes an increase in aggregate unemployment. As we shall see later, if wages increase less rapidly than the rate of (general price) inflation, employment will almost certainly increase.

175

The Demand for Money and Inflation

In the preceding chapter we established that the demand for money depends on the level of *nominal* income, PY (where P is an index of the price level and Y is real national income), as well as on the rate of interest, i: if nominal income increases, so will the transactions demand for money, while if the rate of interest increases, the opportunity cost of holding money will have increased, and for that reason less money will be demanded. Thus we might write the demand for money function as

(1) $M = f(PY, i)$

The function (1) states that the demand for money, M, depends on PY and i. We established that $\Delta M/\Delta PY > 0$ and $\Delta M/\Delta i < 0$ — that the demand for money increases with nominal income but decreases as the rate of interest increases. Suppose that the price level is increasing over time, and think of i as some kind of average, or representative, nominal rate of return on *all* assets except money (on bonds, real estate, machinery, etc.) We now recognise that the function (1) is misspecified; it omits an important variable — the expected rate of inflation. In an inflationary environment there are two kinds of costs of holding money:

(i) The loss of direct financial returns which could be earned by holding wealth in the form of bonds, machinery and equipment, etc.

(ii) Loss in purchasing power of money over time: if people held their wealth in antiques, real estate or machinery they would not experience such losses, for those assets would increase in nominal value in line with inflation. The expected erosion in the purchasing power of money is represented by the expected percentage rate of inflation, which we denote by $\dot{P}$. We assume that the expected rate of inflation is approximated by the actual rate of inflation. Then, given PY and i, the higher the rate of inflation, the higher the actual and expected cost of holding money, and hence the lower the demand for money. So we now write the demand function for money as

(2) $M = f(PY, i, \dot{P})$

where $\Delta M/\Delta PY > 0$, $\Delta M/\Delta i < 0$ and $\Delta M/\Delta \dot{P} < 0$ — the demand for money increases with nominal income but decreases if either the rate of interest or the rate of inflation increase.

We assume a little more in regard to the form of (2): we assume, so long as i and $\dot{P}$ stay unchanged, that the demand for money is proportional to the level of money national income, but that the factor of proportionality between M and PY changes if either i or $\dot{P}$ changes.

Hence

(3) $\quad \dot{M} = k(i,\dot{P})PY$

where k is some number indicating the factor of proportionality between M and PY, and where $\Delta k/\Delta i < 0$ and $\Delta k/\Delta \dot{P} < 0$; the number **k (and hence M) falls if i or $\dot{P}$ increase.** The variables in parentheses after k are entered purely *to remind us that k depends on i and $\dot{P}$.* Empirical studies have been undertaken to test whether an equation like (3) closely explains the observed demand for money; it turns out that for developed economies it is a satisfactory working hypothesis for year-to-year data.

One final assumption before proceeding: we assume that the money market is always in equilibrium, i.e., that the interest rate always adjusts equating the supply of and demand for money.

Correlation Between Inflation and Monetary Expansion

We all suspect that money supply and inflation are related. Thus, in popular parlance, inflation is often described as 'too much money chasing too few goods'. However, there has been a great deal of confusion in regard to the relationship between money supply and inflation.

We start the analysis with the *identity*

(4) $\quad MV \equiv PY$

where M denotes the money supply (by assumption equal to the demand for money) while V is the income velocity of money — the ratio of nominal national product to the money supply (i.e., income velocity V is the number of times that the stock of money is turned over per year in financing the purchase of the annual flow of final output). So the left side of (4) is the purchase of national product. Moving to the right side of (4), P is an index of the average price level during the year and Y denotes the level of real national output. So the right side of (4) represents total sales of the economy's final output. As it stands, (4) is an identity — it is true by definition (of V). It states that the value of total final purchases must equal the value of total final sales. Remembering that V is by definition PY/M, (4) states that $MPY/M \equiv PY$, or $PY \equiv PY$.

A theory in applied science is a statement, or a set of related statements, in regard to the world around us, the validity of which could in principle be tested, and rejected if demonstrated as false. If a theory is true it is not true by definition. Recall equation (3) for the demand for money. This is *not* an identity; it is not true by definition.

Rather, (3) is a testable hypothesis or theory. When subjected to empirical tests it is consistent with observed experience. Also recall that we assumed that the interest rate would adjust to keep the money market in equilibrium — to equate the supply of and the demand for money. If we accept these assumptions as reasonable working hypotheses, and substitute equation (3) into the identity (4), we get

(5) $k(i,\dot{P})PY \cdot V = PY$ which implies

(6) $V = 1/k(i,\dot{P})$

Equations (5) and (6) are *not* true by definition; they are theories because equation (3), upon which they depend, is a theory. Equations (3) and (5) imply

(7) $MV(i,\dot{P}) = PY$

where V is assumed to depend in a predictable manner on i and $\dot{P}$ — it is to remind us of this dependence that we have entered the elements in parentheses after V in (7). The assumptions made in connection with (3) were that k moves in the opposite direction to changes in i and $\dot{P}$; then, from (6), V moves in the *same* direction as changes in i and $\dot{P}$. Equation (7) is the modern version of *the quantity theory of money.* Although it looks like the identity (4), equation (7) is not an identity, for the hypothesis that V depends in a stable manner on i and $\dot{P}$ is not something which is true by definition. Note that equation (6) implies that V in (7) will be constant so long as i and $\dot{P}$ remain constant. After decades of debate, the modern version of the quantity theory of money is broadly accepted by economists.

Equation (7) suggests that an increase in M will be *associated with* an increase in PY. But it does not tell us anything about *causal* forces. It is consistent with (a) an increase in M causing an increase in PY, and (b) an increase in PY causing, or inducing, an increase in M.

Case (a) could occur as follows: (i) Suppose that a closed economy is initially in equilibrium below full employment and that the central bank increases the money supply. By making credit cheaper and more available, this could increase real national income consistent with no change in P. (ii) Suppose that the economy is initially in equilibrium at full employment, so that the level of real income is approximately fixed. Equation (7) then suggests that an increase in M is likely to increase P.

Case (b) could occur as follows: (i) Suppose that an open economy is in equilibrium below full employment and that exports, and hence Y, increase. This could lead to inflows of foreign currency in payment for the increased exports, and exchange of that foreign currency into domestic money at the central bank. In that case the increase in X and Y would have caused an increase in M, without any necessary change in P. (ii) Suppose that trade unions (in, say, the construction industry) demand and obtain a higher money wage, and that this is passed on as higher prices for new housing, etc., thereby reducing the real money supply. To facilitate the existing volume of transactions the central bank may be induced to increase the money supply.

Two of the central conclusions from equation (7) are: (i) Increases in the money supply *may* cause inflation. From (7) we can see that this will generally be the case if the money supply is increased more rapidly than the growth in real income Y. (ii) Regardless of the ultimate causes of an inflationary process, inflation could not prevail for long unless the money supply were increased. From equation (7) we can see that if P is increasing, it must generally be the case that M is also increasing unless Y is decreasing. In sum, increases in the domestic money supply *may* be ultimate causes of inflation (though we shall see later that they could *not* be the ultimate causes of significant inflation in small open economies operating under fixed exchange rates with the rest of the world). If, on the other hand, increases in the money supply are *not* the *ultimate* causes of a particular inflation, expansion in the money supply must be a *permissive factor* in the inflationary process. Thus, *domestic inflation could not prevail for long if the domestic money supply were held constant.* That is *not* to say that all economies are actually *able* to control their money supplies: as we shall see later, small open economies operating under fixed exchange rates with larger trading partners may not be able to control their money supplies, and, on that count, they may not be able to control their rates of inflation (so long as they are unwilling to change their exchange rate relationships); their rates of inflation are overwhelmingly determined abroad.

Inflation in Closed Economies

Inflations are often labelled 'demand pull' and 'cost push'. Although these have not been the dominant causes of Irish inflation, we briefly review those concepts.

Demand Pull

In its simplest form demand-pull inflation prevails when aggregate demand exceeds the supply potential of the economy. In Figure 41, Y_F denotes the supply potential of the economy (the full employment level of output). By the construction of the 45 degree line we can see that the maximum real output the economy is capable of producing is $Y_F A$. However, aggregate demand exceeds this by the amount AB, called an *inflationary gap* (the excess of aggregate demand over full employment aggregate supply). The price level will therefore be pulled up.

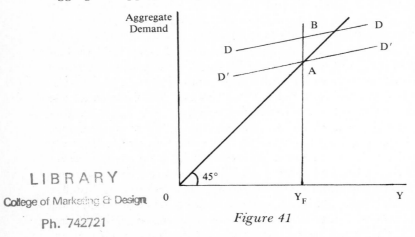

Figure 41

The inflationary gap AB could be eliminated by contractionary monetary and fiscal policies, causing a downward shift in the aggregate demand function to $D'D'$. However, it would automatically shift to $D'D'$ *if the money supply were held constant.* Thus, suppose that the (nominal) money supply is held constant and that we start with the inflationary gap AB. As the inflation proceeds, the *real* money supply will then be decreasing. Therefore the cost of money will be increasing while the availability of money for transactions purposes will, in real terms, decrease. (Alternatively, we can say that the demand curve for money — the liquidity preference curve of the preceding chapter — will be shifting upwards because it requires progressively more money to buy any given volume of output, and if the supply of money is held constant, the price of money — the rate of interest — will rise.) These will cause downward shifts in the investment function or the consumption function — or both. Hence the aggregate demand function will shift downwards. In this case, in which the nominal money supply is held constant, the inflationary gap will be eliminated automatically over time. The only way in which the aggregate demand function could remain at DD would be if the money supply were increasing in line with inflation, thereby preventing the real money supply from decreasing. Thus, if increases in the money supply are not the ultimate causes of an inflation (by, say, causing an upward shift in the investment function, thereby creating an inflationary gap), they must be regarded as permissive factors in the sense that if for any reason (such as an upward shift in the consumption function due to reductions in rates of income tax) an inflationary gap emerged, it could not prevail for long unless increases in the money supply permitted it to do so.

In the simplified exposition above we assumed that 'full employment' represented a well-defined level of output and that demand-pull inflation would not occur until after the economy had attained full employment. In reality that will not be the case, mainly because the economy generally will not attain full employment in all sectors simultaneously. Consider an economy expanding from a recession, aided, say, by successively larger doses of government expenditure over time. Ultimately, full capacity utilisation will be attained in certain sectors. But this will generally be associated with a situation in which other sectors experience excess capacity. If demand is further expanded, inflationary gaps will emerge in those sectors which have already attained full capacity utilisation. Thus demand-pull inflation will prevail before each sector has attained full capacity utilisation. Furthermore, the demand-pull inflationary pressures will become more severe the closer the economy approaches full capacity utilisation in all sectors. These considerations suggest that some slack in the economy (some excess capacity in certain sectors, as well as some unemployment) will be necessary if demand-pull inflation is to be avoided entirely.

Cost Push

Cost-push inflation is a process in which the factors of production *continuously* push up prices over time. Suppose we start with a full employment equilibrium, and that trade unions demand and obtain a higher money wage. If this cost-push pressure is to lead to an increase in the price level, it must be the case that firms react by raising output prices. But that would not in itself lead to (sustained) inflation; it would only yield a once-and-for-all increase in the price level. However, if trade unions demand and obtain a yet higher money wage (for example, to compensate for the increase in the price level) profit margins will fall unless employers raise their prices further. For cost-push inflation to proceed, it must be the case that trade unions again demand and obtain a yet higher money wage, leading to yet higher prices charged by employers, followed by further wage demands (and attainment of at least part of those demands), and so on in an upward spiral of wages and prices.

Continuous cost-push pressure by trade unions may be the initiating cause of an inflation, but if it is, *it could not prevail for long unless increases in the money supply permitted, or 'validated', such inflationary forces.* We indicated earlier that the modern version of the quantity theory of money is a satisfactory working hypothesis, namely that

(7) $MV = PY$

where V increases if either the rate of interest, i, or the *rate* of inflation, $\dot{P}$, increase. Suppose that there is initially zero inflation, that next trade unions bargain upwards the money wage, and that this is passed on by firms in the form of higher prices. It is true that V will tend to increase on this count; however, other things being equal, V would adjust to a new *constant* level if the *rate* of inflation were *constant.* But much more is likely to be happening *if the money supply, M, is held constant.* Under such circumstances we can safely ignore the possibility that V will be increasing at the same percentage rate as prices. Then equation (7) indicates that for P to increase due to cost-push pressure on a sustained basis over time, it must be the case that the level of real national income Y is decreasing. Therefore unemployment will be increasing and the bargaining power of trade unions will be weakening, thereby mitigating the cost-push pressures. It can be concluded that cost-push pressures could not prevail for long unless increases in the money supply permitted them to prevail (that is, 'validated' the cost-push pressures). If M is held constant, cost-push pressure by trade unions will lead to higher unemployment, thereby weakening that bargaining power. At some high level of unemployment trade union bargaining power would be sufficiently weakened so as to eliminate the cost-push pressure.

Mixed Cost Push and Demand Pull

For the moment we maintain the assumption of a closed economy. Neither cost-push nor demand-pull inflation are likely to prevail in isolation; in a closed economy most inflations are likely to be combinations of both. If there is a large margin of excess capacity, both demand-pull inflationary pressures and the bargaining power of trade unions will tend to be weak. But if an economy is near full capacity utilisation, demand-pull pressures will be stronger and trade unions will tend to act more aggressively in wage bargaining. But it should be clear, in either case, that if the money supply is held constant, (sustained) inflation could not prevail.

Inflation in Small Open Economies with Fixed Exchange Rates[1]

An open economy is one which depends heavily on foreign trade, and which has a high degree of capital[2] mobility across its frontiers. Ireland is a small open economy trading in a competitive international environment. From 1826 until March 1979 it maintained a fixed exchange rate with the UK. Subject to certain qualifications mainly in regard to taxes on expenditures and the composition of output, an implication of this was that our rate of inflation was largely determined by the UK's inflation rate. Our inflation was therefore largely beyond our control (given a commitment to a fixed exchange rate with the UK). Given the structure of taxation, domestic causes of high inflation can operate to a significant degree in a small open economy under a fixed exchange rate (to the extent to which they may in the long run operate significantly at all) only in those sectors of the economy which do not engage in international trade or which do not compete with imports.

It is an inescapable conclusion that so long as Ireland maintains a fixed exchange rate with *any* large country with which there is free trade we will tend to approximate that country's rate of inflation; *to deny this is to deny the existence of markets.* This follows almost as readily as the conclusion that Kildare and the rest of Ireland (which operate in a competitive environment with a fixed exchange rate between them) must experience roughly the same rate of inflation. (The reader should be able to see what would happen if Kildare's inflation rate tended to differ from that of the rest of Ireland.)

The output of an open economy, such as ours, falls into two broad categories, *tradeables* and *non-tradeables*. *Tradeables* are goods produced domestically and which enter international trade or compete against imports on the domestic market. They consist of *exportables* and *importables*.

An *exportable* is a domestically produced good some of which is exported. Since we in Ireland cannot have much effect on international prices (being small we are close to being price-takers rather than price-makers on international markets), the rate of inflation for exportables, given a fixed exchange rate with a large country, is determined mainly abroad. Even exportables retained for home consumption have their rates of inflation determined mainly abroad. That is because producers of such goods tend to withdraw supplies from the domestic market until the price obtainable here is bid up towards that obtainable on the export market. An *importable* is a domestically produced good which competes with imports on the Irish market. Given a fixed exchange rate with a large country, and given rates of taxation on expenditure, the rate of inflation for importables is also effectively determined abroad.

Non-tradeables are domestically produced goods which are neither exported nor compete with imports. To the extent that they use tradeables as inputs, their prices under a fixed exchange rate with a large country are directly subject to external influences. But to some *small* extent in the long run their prices *may* be subject to domestic demand-pull and cost-push pressures; an excess demand for non-tradeables may pull up their prices, while domestic cost-push pressure may push them up. However, the extent to which such domestic causes of inflation can operate is very much limited *partly* because a rise in the prices of non-tradeables relative to tradeables will reduce the demand for non-tradeables, tending to increase unemployment in that sector. This in turn would mitigate the internal forces generating inflation.

In the case of a small economy with a fixed exchange rate under free trade with any large country, domestic demand-pull and cost-push pressures may have different effects on the tradeables and the non-tradeables sectors. We have seen that such forces, if sustained over time, *may* cause some inflation in the non-tradeables sector. But they cannot cause much inflation in the tradeables sector — for the prices of tradeables are determined mainly outside Ireland: even in the short-run, the demand for tradeables produced in Ireland is rather price elastic.[3]

If there is *cost-push* wage pressure in the tradeables sector, and if, given output per man, trade unions obtain higher money wages, an effect will be an increase in the share of value added (national income) accruing to labour, and a decrease in the share of value added accruing to profits, etc. Real wages will increase while real profits will decline. Because they are more akin to price-takers rather than dominant price-makers, *employers in tradeables will not normally be able to mark up their prices to an appreciable extent to compensate for wage increases.*

Consider next domestic *excess demand* (demand-pull pressure) for tradeables. This may, *in the short run,* bid up the prices of tradeables, leading producers to post higher domestic prices for such goods. But the principal effect will be an increase in imports, combined, perhaps, with some fall in exports. Imports will rise partly because not all of the demand can be satisfied from domestic sources. There is also some possibility that exports will fall, as exporters temporarily divert supplies away from the export market in favour of domestic consumers. Thus *the principal effect of an excess demand for tradeables is on the balance of international payments on current account rather than on the rate of inflation.* We conclude that under a fixed exchange rate with a large country with which there is relatively free trade, excess domestic demand for tradeables in a small open economy cannot be a major cause of inflation — by which we mean sustained increases in prices over time.

It follows that so long as Ireland maintains a fixed exchange rate with a large country with which there is free trade, Ireland cannot independently generate much inflation. We cannot do so because (consideration of expenditure taxes aside) *we* can have little impact on the rate of change of prices of tradeable goods on Irish or world markets. Nevertheless, the increase in the Irish price level, relative to that of the UK in the several years before 1978, has often been cited as evidence to the contrary. The following table compares the UK's retail price index (RPI) with Ireland's consumer price index (CPI) from 1953 onwards. (Prices in the base year, 1953, are set equal to 100.) It is the similarity rather than small disparity in rates of inflation which are most demonstrative of the *a priori* theoretical considerations outlined above.

Analysis of the data indicates that a substantial part of the increase in Irish prices relative to those of the UK in the more recent years in Table 10 is accounted for by the build-up here of expenditure taxes. A key point of relevance in this context is that we export free of expenditure taxes, while imports to Ireland from the UK and other EEC countries are subject to Irish expenditure taxes. Thus increase in the Irish consumer price index due to higher taxes on expenditure does not in itself affect the competitiveness of the Irish economy. A little thought would suggest that the divergence between the Irish CPI and the UK RPI in the more recent years in Table 10 must be accounted for by:

(i) Difference in the build-up of expenditure taxes in the two countries, relative to the base year, 1953.

(ii) Possibly, differences in the method of calculating the CPI and the RPI.

Table 10
UK and Irish Inflation, 1953-1977

Year	UK (RPI)	Republic of Ireland (CPI)
1953	100	100
1955	105	103
1957	114	111
1959	118	116
1961	122	120
1963	128	128
1965	138	144
1967	147	153
1969	164	172
1971	187	203
1973	217	245
1975	312	347
1977	419	465

Source: Derived from *Statistical Abstract of Ireland, Central Bank of Ireland Quarterly Bulletin, Economic Review and Outlook, July 1978,* and *National Institute Economic Review* (UK), various issues.

(iii) Differences in the structure of output in the two countries. Consider two countries, A and B, which maintain fixed exchange rates with each other and ignore expenditure taxes. Suppose for illustration that they each produce only two goods, x and y, and that x accounts for 50 per cent of the output of A but for 75 per cent of the output of B. Finally, suppose that the price of x is increasing by 20 per cent annually in both countries and that the price of y is constant in both. Clearly country B will have the higher overall rate of inflation (because its output is more heavily biased toward the good with the high rate of annual price increase) even though the price of any given good is the same in both countries.

(iv) Differences in devaluations of the Irish and UK green pounds due to EEC agricultural arranagements. This caused the rate of increase in Irish farm prices to rise above the rate of increase in UK farm prices in the 1970s.

(v) Possibly, different rates of inflation in the non-tradeables — rather than the tradeables — sectors of the two economies.

(vi) *Increased* monopoly power of Irish manufacturers. However, because we are an open economy greatly exposed to world competition (especially from that of other EEC countries), Irish manufacturers as a group could have had little increased monopoly power on either home or foreign markets.

(vii) Increase in costs of Irish producers relative to their competitors in the UK. But if Irish costs did increase relative to those of the UK, the increase in costs of tradeable goods could be passed on in the form of higher prices only to a very limited degree.

In recent years Irish exports of goods and services were equivalent to about 55 per cent of national income at factor cost, while imports of goods and services were equivalent to about 60 per cent of national income at factor cost. Inflation in the prices of such goods — and, indeed, in the prices of exportables and importables generally — was, under a fixed exchange rate with the UK, basically that of the UK. Given the openness of the economy and given that we had a fixed exchange rate with the UK which was inflating rapidly, we inevitably had high rates of inflation in the 1970s without necessarily becoming *price non-competitive.*

Inflation, Money Wages and Unemployment
We have stated on a number of occasions that by inflation economists usually mean sustained increases in the price level. In Ireland, the most frequently cited indicator of inflation is the rate of change in the consumer price index. The rate of change in wages is *not* a reliable indicator of inflation, for wages can increase, on a sustained basis over time, consistent with a zero rate of increase in the price level (and consistent with no change in the share of profits in national income), simply because output per unit of labour (what we shall call productivity) is increasing. (Productivity tends to be increasing over time largely because of technical change and because net investment is usually positive; more and improved capital equipment enables output per unit of labour to increase.) There has been a great deal of erroneous thinking about the relationship between inflation and unemployment in the small open economy of Ireland. High inflation does not necessarily adversely affect the competitiveness of the Irish economy and thereby cause unemployment. For example, *there is little or no evidence in favour of the view that our high inflation in 1976/7 impeded our growth in those years; in fact, given the behaviour of money wages and productivity, it surely promoted economic growth in Ireland.* Some elaboration is in order.

In so far as economic growth and job creation are concerned, the crucial issue in the context of Irish inflation is not the rate of inflation itself, but rather the relationship between the rate of inflation, productivity growth, and the rate of increase in wages. As Table 5 in Chapter 9 indicates, wages and salaries (we will say just wages) are by far the dominant component of total domestic production costs, or national value added (i.e., national income). As a very close approximation, *if the rate of increase in wages, minus productivity growth, exceeds the rate of inflation* (which may be high or low and is basically determined abroad under a fixed exchange rate), *the share of profits in value added will decline.* Under such circumstances Irish goods would become *cost non-competitive.* Given the declining profits share under such circumstances, some potential exporters could not or would not compete on export markets, and some home producers could not compete against foreign suppliers on the domestic market. A short-term effect would be decreased output and employment. But there would also be a longer-term effect: because of the declining real profits share, the funds available to finance investment would be lessened, as also would the incentive of the private sector to invest. In consequence, job-creating productive capacity would be less than it would otherwise tend to be.

Thus, rather than there being any necessary trade-off between unemployment and inflation in Ireland, there *is* a trade-off between the rate of increase in real wages (i.e., in money wages relative to the price level) less productivity growth on the one hand, and employment on the other. For if wages, minus productivity growth, rise more rapidly than factor-cost prices (i.e., prices excluding their expenditure-tax component), the share of profits in value added, or national income, will fall, ultimately resulting in decreased employment. That happened in some of the earlier years of the 1970s. In the *non-tradeables* sector the pressure of wage increases was, in large measure, passed on by employers in the form of higher prices, thereby tending to maintain profit margins. In the case of *tradeables,* however, cost-push pressure could not be mainly passed on by employers in the form of higher prices so as to maintain profit margins: producers of tradeables are by and large price-takers rather than price-makers. Wage-push pressure in tradeables reduced profit margins. Given the increasing level of wage costs relative to product prices in the tradeables sector, many employers reacted by curtailing output and employment and, in some cases, by closing down entirely. Many of such employers simply could not *afford* to compete on the export market or against imports on the domestic market. Thus we *were* tending to become non-competitive in the period 1970/75. However, this was *not* because of our rate of inflation *per se,* but rather because of our high rates of *wage* increase which, given that prices of tradeables were determined by factors largely beyond our control, led to redistribution of pre-tax income away from profits towards employee remuneration in the tradeables sector of the economy.

The experience just outlined was reversed in 1976/7 — high (factor-cost) price inflation, transmitted to us via the fixed exchange rate with the UK, was well in excess of the rate of increase in wage earnings less productivity growth. Thus profit margins and improved cost competitiveness assisted our advance further into international markets and encouraged expansion of the capital stock to facilitate further growth.

Aggregate Demand and Aggregate Supply
The preceding sub-section makes it clear that there is more to the determination of equilibrium national income than consideration of aggregate demand alone, given the supply *potential* of the economy. We should now realise that an expansion in aggregate demand will not increase equilibrium national income unless firms are *willing* to increase supply. We return to the vital question of aggregate supply in the next chapter.

Irish Inflation and Fixed Exchange Rates
We have argued that so long as Ireland maintained a fixed exchange rate with the UK it tended to have the UK's inflation rate. The argument (which would be strengthened if we complicated it further by bringing international factor mobility into the analysis) was roughly as follows: (i) Ireland is a small open economy. Subject to certain qualifications in regard to agricultural products, goods moved freely between the UK and Ireland. (ii) The exchange rate between the Irish and the UK currencies was fixed. (iii) Consideration (i) implied that *in the long run and subject to qualifications stated earlier,* the prices of internationally tradeable goods in Ireland had to be roughly the same as those prevailing in the UK; for if not, international competition would tend to equate the prices of the goods in the two countries, and since the UK is the larger country *vis-à-vis* Ireland, the prices that tended to be *given* to Ireland were those of the UK. (iv) Therefore, under a fixed exchange rate with the UK, Ireland's rate of inflation had to approximate the UK's rate of inflation. (v) Due mainly to the UK's high rate of inflation Ireland had high inflation. (vi) Therefore, if we were to experience a significantly different rate of inflation from the UK in the long run, we had to end the fixed exchange rate relationship with the UK.

For the reasons just outlined, and because inflation in itself was felt to be undesirable, many people argued that Ireland should end its commitment to a fixed exchange rate with the UK. Many proposed that Ireland should attempt to maintain a fixed exchange rate with a currency such as the West German mark (because West Germany tended to inflate far more slowly than the UK). That is what we in effect committed ourselves to doing by simultaneously breaking the fixed exchange rate link with the pound sterling and joining the European Monetary System (EMS) in March 1979. It is left to the reader to reason, along the lines already surveyed, and subject to the stated qualifications, that so long as we are able to maintain a fixed exchange rate with the mark* we will in the long run tend to have West Germany's rate of inflation. Indeed, so long as we maintain a fixed exchange rate with *any* major country with which there is relatively free trade, we will tend in the long run to have that country's rate of inflation. (The reasoning amounts to little more than recognising that markets do exist; thus, by analogy, Sligo goods must have roughly the same rate of inflation as Dublin goods, so long as there is a fixed exchange rate between goods in Sligo and goods in Dublin.)

Money Supply and Inflation in Small Open Economies under Fixed Exchange Rates

We have discussed *some* of the mechanisms by which inflation is transmitted to a small open economy under a fixed exchange rate with a larger country with which it has free trade. But there are further transmission mechanisms at work, one of them being monetary in form. We shall be ready to analyse that transmission mechanism only at a later stage. Suffice it for the moment to state that, for reasons already explained, if a small open economy with fixed exchange rates has (sustained) inflation, it must be the case that its money supply is increasing over time. That is *not* to say that a small open economy under fixed exchange rates can control its money supply. However, we shall not be prepared to analyse in further detail the relationship between increases in the money supply and inflation in small open economies until we have considered exchange rate determination in a later chapter.

Postscript: Already this proviso has failed to be realised. In September 1979 the mark was revalued by about 2 per cent against most other EMS currencies; i.e., those currencies (including the Irish pound) were devalued by about 2 per cent against the mark.

Inflation and Floating Exchange Rates

Our discussion of inflation in an open economy has been entirely confined to the context of a *fixed* exchange rate relationship with *some* major country. The possibility that the exchange rate will be allowed to float — that it may vary from day to day in accordance with the free forces of market supply and demand — has not been investigated. *The conclusions of the last several pages in regard to inflation in small open economies must be substantively altered if the exchange rate is allowed to float* vis-à-vis *all major currencies.* The relationship between inflation, the money supply, and floating exchange rates is deferred until a later chapter.

Suggested Reading

McDowell, Moore, 'Ireland: The Control of Inflation in a Small Open Economy', *Studies,* Spring 1975.

FOOTNOTES

1. This section draws heavily on my papers 'The Irish Economy, 1977', *The Confederation of Irish Industry Economic Review,* No. 1, 1977; 'Money Supply and Inflation in Open Economies', *Certified Accountancy Newsletter,* September 1977; 'The Economic Environment for Growth', *Agricultural Record,* September 1977; 'The Analytical Framework: An Overview', Symposium on the Link with Sterling, *STEM, Journal of the Society of College Lecturers,* No. 1, 1978.
2. The reference to 'capital' here is to financial assets. When we refer to capital mobility across national frontiers, the reference will always be to movements of financial assets (rather than capital assets such as machinery and equipment — for such movements would be part of trade in goods).
3. Our *a priori* reasoning on this point is supported by the empirical estimates of T. O'Connell, 'Demand and Supply Functions for Irish Exports of Manufactures', *The Economic and Social Review,* July 1977.

CHAPTER 14

Aggregate Supply, Aggregate Demand and Unemployment in an Open Economy under Fixed Exchange Rates

The preceding chapter excepted, we assumed until now in Part Three that:

(i) The price level stays more or less constant.

(ii) So long as they are not fully utilising their capacities, firms are willing to supply whatever outputs may be demanded at prevailing prices.

Assumption (i) was relaxed in Chapter 13, where we saw that so long as Ireland maintains a fixed exchange rate with a large country (large in the sense that its national income is much greater than that of Ireland) with which there is free trade, Ireland's rate of inflation will approximate that country's rate of inflation. We also pointed out towards the end of Chapter 13 that expansion of aggregate demand will not increase equilibrium real income unless firms are willing to increase supply. In fact, *the equilibrium level of real national income is determined by both aggregate demand and aggregate supply* — just as, in a competitive individual market, equilibrium quantity traded is determined by demand and supply. Before proceeding, note that:

(a) When we refer to aggregate demand we shall as before be referring to demand for (planned expenditure on) domestic output, or C + I + G + X − M, where all variables are in real terms and are as defined earlier.

(b) When we refer to aggregate supply we shall be referring to the planned supply of domestic output in real terms (i.e., it indicates how much domestic firms would be willing to supply under specified conditions).

(c) From the exposition in Chapter 9 and subsequently, we know that actual expenditure on domestic output is identical to actual national output; however, it is only in equilibrium that aggregate demand equals aggregate supply.

(d) Throughout this chapter we shall be assuming that the country under analysis is small and operates under a fixed exchange rate with a large country with which there is relatively free trade.

Aggregate Supply

Consideration of aggregate supply is *crucial* for an understanding of elementary macroeconomics. Until we indicate to the contrary we suppose that the state of technology is given and that the stock of machinery and equipment is more or less constant. (Thus, for the moment we ignore the impact of fixed investment on the capital stock, and hence, on the potential of the economy to increase aggregate supply.) We also suppose that the *quality* of the labour force is constant — thus workers do not suddenly begin to work harder. *These assumptions imply that the technical conditions underlying supply are more or less constant.* Under these conditions potential aggregate output will depend on the level of employment (of the labour force).

Suppose next that the prices of final goods and services — as distinct from factors of production — are more or less given. Throughout this book we are assuming that firms seek to maximise profits.

Under the stated assumptions the output which firms plan to produce depends on the prices of the factors of production and on the technical opportunities available to firms. These technical opportunities determine how inputs may potentially be transformed into outputs. Factor prices and the technical relationships between inputs and outputs together determine how costs of production vary with output. As Table 5 of Chapter 9 indicates, wages and salaries (we will say just wages) account for the bulk of domestic production costs.

Thus, (i) given the price of output (or the relationship between price and output) and (ii) given the technical relationships between inputs and output, the output which firms plan to produce depends on (iii) the costs of the factors of production, and especially since labour is the dominant cost item, on wage rates.

If the technical conditions underlying potential supply are given, and if the prices of both products and factors are also given, then firms will produce some specific level of output (i.e., that output which maximises profits), and hence they employ some specific amount of labour. These, then, are the factors underlying aggregate supply, or the ability and *willingness* of domestic firms to supply output (and hence to vary their employment). There is little reason for believing that the aggregate supply and employment levels resulting from the profit-maximising calculations of firms will always lead to full employment.

Extending the reasoning just outlined, we can see that aggregate supply does not depend on the price level (for output) alone; nor does it depend on costs alone. The central proposition is that, other things being equal, aggregate supply depends crucially on the ratio of wage costs (the dominant component of costs) to output prices, i.e., the key consideration is the level of wage costs *relative to* the price level. Let W be the average money wage and let P be the price level; then, other things being equal, aggregate supply depends on (W/P), i.e., on the real wage. (In reality different real wage rates are paid to different groups of workers, but incorporating this in our analysis would complicate rather than illuminate.)

Suppose that we start with national income in equilibrium; then aggregate supply is equal to aggregate demand and the real wage is at some particular level. (It is at that level which induces firms to produce the level of output they are actually producing.) Suppose that the price level and the technical possibilities of production (in particular, the state of technology and the stock of fixed capital assets) are in effect constant, and that the cost to employers of hiring any given amount of labour is increased. This may have occurred because trade unions have bargained upwards the money wage, or for other reasons. The effective real wage, as seen by employers, has therefore increased. Because per unit costs have increased relative to price, firms, to avert losses, will cut back production — aggregate supply will be reduced. Thus national income will approach a new equilibrium at which aggregate supply again equals aggregate demand, but at a lower level of output and employment than previously.

It is important to note that, under the circumstances indicated, we would not expect employment to contract *simultaneously* with the rise in the real wage. Rather, we would expect employers to react with significant lags. That is because there are costs associated with the firing and hiring of labour. For these reasons if at given levels of labour productivity the real wage is increased, employers will be cautious about firing labour, for the increase in real wages may be only transitory (the price level may soon increase, thereby getting real wages down again). Given the state of labour productivity, firms tend to fire unskilled labour first if an increase in real wages is sustained over time. But they tend to be more hesitant in firing scarce skilled labour — they are likely to fear that without having to incur recruitment and other costs, they may be unable to obtain the services of skilled labour at some future date if they seek to re-employ such workers. Thus firms (which are interested in profits over time) tend to hoard labour even at a short-run loss. We have at last brought aggregate supply into the picture of macroeconomic income determination. The reader may wonder how the aggregate demand approach stands in the light of the issues just raised.

Suppose that the economy is initially in equilibrium: aggregate demand equals aggregate supply at some level of output and employment; corresponding to this there is some level of the (average) real wage. Suppose also that the system is operating well below full capacity utilisation at the initial equilibrium. Given the money wage rate, an increase in aggregate demand will induce firms to expand supply because (a) it enables them to sell more at the prevailing price level and/or (b) it increases the price level. Consider two possible sources of an expansion in aggregate demand:

(i) Export demand may increase because incomes are expanding abroad. The increase in aggregate demand abroad may cause some demand-pull inflation abroad, and because exchange rates are assumed given, it would then cause the prices of tradeable goods in Ireland to rise. Partly because non-tradeables use tradeables as inputs, the increase in the prices of tradeables would tend to induce an increase in the prices of non-tradeables. If the money wage did not increase in proportion to the price level, the real wage would have decreased, and (given the technical conditions underlying potential supply) the profitability to domestic firms of expanding output and employment would have increased. Ultimately the system would reach a new equilibrium at which aggregate demand again equals aggregate supply, at a higher level of output and employment, but at a lower real wage than previously. Note that if an expansion in aggregate demand causes prices to rise in the manner indicated, and if the money wage were simultaneously pushed up in the same proportion as the price increase, then the real wage would not have changed and firms might have little incentive to expand either output or employment.

(ii) Aggregate demand may increase because of increased real government expenditure on goods and services. In this context it is a matter of great importance whether the increase in government expenditure is on tradeables or non-tradeables. Because its immediate impact on imports and the balance of international payments is low, government expenditure on non-tradeables tends to have a more expansionary impact on national output and employment than in the case of tradeables. Suppose that all of the increased government expenditure is on tradeables (though this is unlikely in practice). To the extent to which this raises the prices of tradeables it is likely to cause some expansion in output and employment. But if it does raise the prices of tradeables, it is likely to lead (with a lag) to a rise in competing imports which will mitigate the upward pressure on the prices of tradeables and will curtail expansion of domestic output. If, on the other hand, the increased government expenditure does not raise prices, it may lead to diversion of domestic output away from the export market in favour of home sales to the government sector; in that case it might lead to no change at all in domestic output. Finally, if the technical conditions underlying supply remain more or less constant, and if increased government expenditure does raise the prices of tradeables, the effect on domestic output and employment may be zero if the money wage is increased in the same proportion as the increase in the price level; in fact, given the technical conditions underlying supply, if prices increase and if money wages are increased more rapidly than prices (so that the real wage increases), then firms will tend to reduce their production and employment, for their costs per unit would have increased relative to the price of output.

A Diagrammatic Treatment
The preceding analysis can be clarified using aggregate supply and demand diagrams like Figures 42 and 43. Except where indicated we assume:

(i) The technical possibilities underlying production are given and remain constant. In particular, the quantity and quality of the stock of fixed capital assets do not change, and the quality of the labour force is constant.

(ii) Money wage rates are given and stay constant.

(iii) The domestic economy is small and open and has a fixed exchange rate with a major economy with which there is free trade.

(iv) Foreign prices are given and stay constant.

Assumption (iii) implies that the domestic price level cannot greatly diverge from that of the larger economy with which there is free trade.

Given (i) to (iv), the level of aggregate output which domestic firms would be both *willing* and *able* to supply *if* domestic prices were at alternative levels is represented by a curve like AS in Figure 42. In the same diagram AD shows the demand for domestic output as a function of the domestic price level (given foreign prices).

At historically low levels of output, firms have excess capacity of machinery and equipment, so given the money wage rate, costs per unit may be roughly constant.[1] The aggregate supply curve AS in Figure 42 is therefore drawn flat at low levels of aggregate output (national income), implying (given the things we are assuming constant) that little or no increase in prices is necessary to induce firms to expand output. But if output is expanded towards high levels, machinery and equipment must be operated more intensively and workers may need to be put on overtime rates, so costs per unit are likely to rise; it then requires higher prices to induce firms to continue expanding production; the AS curve will slope upwards. If prices were to continue to rise (given money wage rates, etc.), suppliers would eventually provide the maximum they were technically capable of producing; no more could then be supplied from domestic sources, so the aggregate supply curve would be vertical at full capacity utilisation. (Recall that only the supply of domestic output is included in AS.)

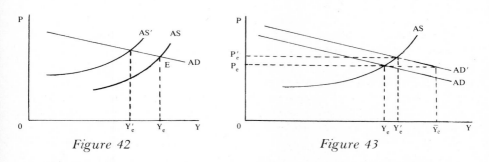

Figure 42   *Figure 43*

The *level* of the aggregate demand curve (for domestic output) reflects those components of demand which in the short-run are autonomous (or independent) of the level of national income (e.g., part of government expenditure on goods and services). Since we assume that foreign prices and the exchange rate with a large country are both given, the *slope* of the aggregate demand curve reflects the sensitivity of real net export demand (real exports less real imports) to changes in domestic prices. Because Ireland is close to being a price-taker rather than a dominant price-maker on international markets, aggregate demand is quite sensitive to changes in the domestic price level; the reader should be able to infer that at the equilibrium point E in Figure 42, demand is price elastic, reflecting relative price-taking behaviour.

Suppose that starting at point E in Figure 42 trade unions bargain the money wage upwards. Because costs have risen relative to prices, firms will be willing to supply less than before; the aggregate supply curve shifts upwards to, say, AS' in Figure 42. Inspection indicates that the price level rises by a small proportionate amount, but the main impact is on national income (and hence, though probably with lags, on employment); equilibrium real income falls from Y_c to Y_c'.

What is the effect of an expansion in aggregate demand? Suppose we start with real income in equilibrium at Y_c in Figure 43, and that there is an increase in real government expenditure on goods and services. That increase in expenditure, along with the multiplier process, causes the aggregate demand curve to shift to the right, to AD'; at the initial price level P_c, demand increases to $\bar{Y}_c$. But to induce an increase in supply, given the money wage, the price level will have to be bid upwards: the domestic price level rises slightly — to P_c' — and equilibrium real income rises to Y_c'. We add two important remarks:

(i) If, in a large neighbourhood of the initial equilibrium, there is a great deal of unemployed labour and capital equipment, and if the money wage remains constant, then the aggregate supply curve may be horizontal in a large neighbourhood of the initial equilibrium. In that case an increase in aggregate demand would enable more to be sold at the existing price level and, because of excess capacity, producers would be willing to supply more at that price level. That being the case, an increase in demand could increase equilibrium income *without* causing any increase in domestic prices. However, if we start in equilibrium near full capacity utilisation, aggregate supply can be increased only with progressively greater difficulty (by extending overtime, by bringing less efficient machines into operation, etc.) so the AS curve *must* then slope upwards. Under those circumstances an increase in aggregate demand, to the extent that it leads to any increase in domestic output, *must* be accompanied by some increase in the price level. However, under the same circumstances an increase in aggregate demand, in raising prices, would induce increased imports; it would therefore lead to a smaller increase in equilibrium national income than otherwise.

(ii) A second observation is that if the AD curve shifts to the right, and (given the technical conditions of production) if the AS curve also shifts, to the left (possibly due to minimum wage legislation or to trade unions pushing money wage rates upwards), the effect will be to reduce the expansion in output which the stimulus in aggregate demand would otherwise create. Indeed it is possible that equilibrium output and employment would actually fall under the circumstances indicated. (We leave it to the reader to demonstrate this proposition graphically. Note that it would hold even if the AS curve were horizontal.)

Money Wages, Productivity and Unemployment

We have been assuming that the technical conditions underlying supply were given. This led to the conclusion that increases in money wage rates, at given levels of employment and with a more or less given price level, would reduce national income and, in lagged response, the level of employment. These conclusions, which are correct given our assumptions, suggest that if workers through collective bargaining obtain increases in real wages, then employment must decrease. However, the assumption that the technical conditions of production remain given is not generally valid, except for very short periods.

In fact there is normally net fixed investment and this has effects on *both* aggregate demand and aggregate supply. The impact on aggregate *demand* of variations in the rate of net fixed investment should be clear. Net fixed investment affects aggregate *supply* in various ways, among them the following:

(i) At any given level of employment it means that the amount of capital equipment per worker is increasing over time. This increases the productivity of labour.

(ii) Investment is a crucial variable by means of which technical change is transmitted to the economy. New machines tend to be superior to machines of earlier vintages because they embody more recent technical designs. Thus to the extent to which new machines merely replace old machines (i.e., to the extent to which gross fixed investment is what is generally called replacement investment), output per man at each level of employment will tend to increase.

Considerations (i) and (ii) imply that output per unit of labour — what is often called labour productivity — tends to be increasing over time due to increased capital. Given money wage rates as determined by collective bargaining, the aggregate supply curve will therefore tend to be shifting to the right over time. This simply reflects the fact that corresponding to any wage-price combination, firms will be willing to supply more real output at higher levels of labour productivity. The effect of an increase in labour productivity is depicted in Figure 44, where AS is assumed to be the initial aggregate supply curve.

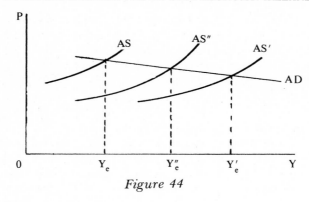

Figure 44

Given money wage rates, an increase in output per worker (which *may* be brought about by increased or improved capital per worker) means that firms are willing to increase supply at any particular price level; the aggregate supply curve shifts to the right to AS' in Figure 44 and equilibrium income increases to Y_e'. (There is also some slight downwards pressure on the price level.) But if money wage rates increase due to, say, trade union bargaining, the aggregate supply curve will not shift as far to the right as AS' in Figure 44; it may shift to, say, AS'', in which case equilibrium income would expand to Y_e'' only.

Money Wages, Inflation and Unemployment

The above exposition assumed that the price level in the larger country with which there is a fixed exchange rate stayed constant. However, the analysis is easily adapted to an inflationary environment. If inflation abroad is 20 per cent per annum, then the annual domestic rate of inflation will tend to be about 20 per cent. If the technical conditions underlying production are constant, then domestic money wage rates may increase by about 20 per cent annually without causing increased unemployment; for the real wage would then be constant. However, if technical conditions are constant and if inflation abroad is 20 per cent, then an annual increase in domestic money wage rates of more than (less than) 20 per cent represents an increase (a decrease) in the real wage, and output and employment would tend to fall (rise) on that count.

Assume next that the price level is increasing by 20 per cent and that labour productivity is increasing by 5 per cent. Money wage rates may then increase by more than 20 per cent annually — the real wage may increase — without causing any fall in the share of profits in national income and without inducing firms to reduce employment. However, if in our example the real wage increases persistently faster than 5 per cent a year, both national income and employment will surely fall.

Different Kinds of Unemployment

Demand Deficient Unemployment

The analysis up to now suggests that unemployment is due to deficiency in the level of aggregate demand and downwards rigidity, but flexibility in an upwards direction, in money wage rates. To the extent to which this analysis is *empirically* correct it implies (given the technical conditions underlying potential supply) that expansions in demand (due, say, to increased export demand or to increases in government expenditure on non-tradeables), in generating some upwards pressure on prices and downwards pressure on real wages, might quite rapidly create full employment of the labour force — provided that increases in money wage rates do not cause the aggregate supply curve to shift to the left. The kind of unemployment to which we have referred is generally termed demand deficient unemployment. In highly developed economies it tends to be that kind of unemployment which attracts much of the concern of policy-makers. We have seen that (in relatively closed economies at least) the solution is simple in principle: fiscal policy, and possibly monetary policy, can raise the level of aggregate demand, and hence the price level. Under such circumstances, if trade unions are willing to exert restraint on money wage rates, equilibrium income and employment might be substantively increased.

However, it would appear that in the case of Ireland, a highly open economy under a fixed exchange rate with a large country, only rather limited reduction in rates of unemployment could be attained by domestic policies of demand expansion alone. That is the case for three reasons:

(i) Consideration of aggregate supply for the moment aside, we have seen that multipliers for the Irish economy are very low. That is largely because of the high import leakages accompanying growth in national income in Ireland. Therefore, if exports remain constant, an increase in domestic income, in causing imports to rise, may cause balance of payments difficulties. In the next chapter we shall see what those difficulties might be. Here we simply note that the high import leakages of the Irish economy place major restrictions on the ability of policy-makers to increase income and employment via short-run policies of aggregate demand management.

(ii) An expansion in aggregate demand will not lead to any increase in equilibrium income unless supply is increased. If technical conditions and real wage rates are both constant, producers may have little incentive to increase aggregate supply if aggregate demand is increased. Given the technical conditions underlying supply, an expansion in aggregate demand in a closed economy would tend to cause real wages to fall — and employment to increase — by raising the price level. However, the extent to which Ireland can increase its price level (relative to that of countries with which it has fixed exchange rates) via domestic policies of demand expansion (thereby inducing increases in aggregate supply) is, as seen in the preceding chapter, greatly limited.

(iii) Even if the balance of payments constraint mentioned in (i) were relaxed, and even if there were moderation in trade union bargaining on the question of money wages, if money wage rates suddenly became flexible downwards we in Ireland would still encounter difficulties in *rapidly* attaining full employment. That is largely because Ireland has historically had an abundant supply of labour relative to the capital stock. Thus, given the kinds of production techniques which have been carried forward from the past, a situation in which the economy was producing its maximum potential output, so that the capital stock was fully utilised, would probably be characterised by an excess supply of labour. These considerations lead us to the phenomenon of structural unemployment.

Structural Unemployment

Structural unemployment across any region (or country) is the outcome of particular structural features of the region. In developed economies it is often the result of permanent shifts in demand away from the products in which specific regions have been specialised. Even in developed countries it can normally be effectively eliminated only in the medium-term, or in the long-run, by manpower policies (retraining and possibly resettlement of labour) and by policies concerning industrial location (for example, by fiscal incentives designed to attract new industries to the structurally depressed regions). In less developed economies it typically takes the form of a long-run overall excess in the supply of labour relative to the capital stock, given the market prices of labour and capital. Even if the capital stock were fully employed under such circumstances, there would still be unemployment or under-employment of labour. Two kinds of policy are often advocated ultimately to eliminate this kind of structural unemployment:

(i) Policies encouraging rapid accumulation of capital throughout the economy. In Ireland the Industrial Development Authority is the principal agency in this context. Since net investment in the short run can amount to only a small proportion of the existing capital stock, such policies can have significant impact in eliminating widespread structural unemployment only in the medium-term or long-run.

(ii) Subsidies to capitalists for the employment of labour, even if the capital stock is fully employed. Although the matter is more complex than we pretend, a case for wage subsidies can be argued as follows: The imbalance between the economy's labour force and capital stock is largely due to the wage rate, in the past, being high relative to the price of capital. This has encouraged firms to choose methods of production requiring large amounts of capital relative to labour (capital-intensive techniques). If the State subsidised employment of labour, the effective price of labour, as seen by firms, would be lower than the market wage. They would therefore select more labour-intensive techniques than previously in *new* projects. However, since new investment projects, in the short-run, can amount to only a small proportion of existing projects, policies of subsidising the employment of labour, if they have a significant effect in reducing widespread structural unemployment, will do so only over relatively long periods of time.

It should be clear from the above that the effective elimination of the kind of structural unemployment that is typical of underdeveloped economies can be attained only over quite long periods of time. It should also be clear that, in the absence of net emigration, its effective elimination generally implies large-scale accumulation of capital (i.e., high rates of net investment).

Frictional Unemployment

If, among that part of the labour force which is looking for jobs, unemployment is neither demand deficient nor structural, it is generally termed frictional. The existence of frictional unemployment reflects the fact that information in regard to job opportunities is not perfect. For example, in times of brisk demand for labour, new entrants to the labour market will not usually accept the first job opening that is available to them. Rather, they would generally be wise to spend some time investigating the opportunities open to them, ultimately opting for that job which is most attractive to them. Or consider the case of a university economist who has just been fired. Perhaps a post as gardener would instantly be offered to him. But he would, in general, be foolish to accept such immediate employment, for he can benefit by spending time investigating the alternatives open to him, and opting for the best offer. We have just given two examples of frictional unemployment. Because it is voluntary and transitory, frictional unemployment is not a serious social problem. The State can reduce its extent and duration by improving information on available job openings. However, it can also raise and prolong it by offering levels of unemployment compensation which are high relative to prevailing after-tax money wages.

Ireland's Long-Term Unemployment Problem

Demographic Trends[2]

The rate of unemployment is generally defined as the number unemployed as a percentage of the total labour force. Thus analysis of the rate of unemployment involves consideration of the size of the labour force and the demand by employers for its services. First of all, we should consider trends in the structure of the population and of the labour force.

The principal factors which determine the size of an economy's labour force are its population size, the age structure of that population and labour force participation rates.

The high rate of population growth in Ireland in recent years is the product of three factors. First, the birth rate has risen, from an annual average of 19.6 per 1000 inhabitants in 1926-36 to about 22 per 1000 annually since 1961. Second, the death rate has fallen, from an annual average of 14.2 per 1000 in 1926-36 to about 11.3 per 1000 since 1961. Third, net emigration, which increased from an annual average of 5.6 per 1000 in 1926-36 to over 14 per 1000 in 1951-61, fell in the 1960s, and was replaced by a small amount of net immigration in the early 1970s.

The second factor, after population size, that determines the size of an economy's labour force is the population's age-structure. Here we need to distinguish between 'dependent' age-groups (aged less than fifteen, or over sixty-four) and 'active' age-groups (those between fifteen and sixty-four, inclusive). Between 1926 and 1973, Ireland's dependency ratio—the ratio of those in the dependent age-groups to the total population—increased from 38.3 per cent to 42.4 per cent, leaving it as the EEC country with the highest proportion of its population in the dependent age-groups. Ireland's high dependency ratio is due entirely to the high proportion of the population aged less than fifteen years.

The third determinant of the size of the labour force, the participation rate — defined as the percentage of those in the active age-groups employed or recorded as seeking employment — is near normal by EEC standards.

Between 1926 and 1951 the labour force, as a percentage of the total population, was roughly constant, at about 44 per cent. But there has been a steady decline in the ratio since then; by 1973 it was about 36.3 per cent. That was mainly due to the rise in the dependency ratio. The low figure of 36.3 per cent for Ireland compares with an average of 40.6 per cent for the EEC as a whole. An implication of this is that even *if* full employment prevailed here, the Irish worker would, on average, have to support more people than his continental counterpart. The prevalence of high rates of unemployment — which have been consistently higher than in other EEC countries — makes the comparative burden on our working population heavier.

The Extent of Unemployment

One measure of unemployment in Ireland is the number on what is called the Live Register, which comprises those persons registering for certain unemployment payments under social welfare legislation. One measure of the rate of unemployment is the percentage of the labour force, insured against unemployment, who are on the Live Register. Calculated in this manner the rate of unemployment in Ireland averaged about 12 per cent in the three years 1975-77. In some respects this method of estimation overestimates the true overall rate of unemployment. But in other respects this measure, as well as the other principal official method of estimation (discussed below), leads to an underestimation of the true overall rate of unemployment. For example, thousands of school-leavers, as well as a large number of women who would work outside the home if they could find paid employment, do not appear on the Live Register; nor do they all appear in the other principal method of calculating the unemployment rate. Furthermore, apart from those who are visibly unemployed, many more are underemployed. Only some of those are on the Live Register or are covered by the other official unemployment rate statistics. Underemployment has been of particular significance on the small family farm. In 1973, the Organisation for Economic Cooperation and Development estimated that the elimination of underemployment in Irish agriculture would require a reduction of about 80,000 in the Irish agricultural labour force.[3] That full recognition of such underemployment would have a significant impact on the true effective rate of unemployment can be appreciated by noting that, on average in 1973, fewer than 67,000 persons (in and outside agricultural occupations) were recorded on the Live Register.

The Live Register is only one of two principal sources in regard to unemployment in Ireland. As it is collected weekly, it is the main indicator of short-run variations in unemployment. A second source of unemployment estimates is derived from the census of population data, and purports to measure unemployment throughout the labour force. However, the census is taken only every five years (normally). For non-census years the census results on the total labour force, total employed and total unemployed are updated by supplementing the census estimates by various statistical series (including Live Register data) and surveys. The resulting estimated unemployment rate — (total unemployed)/(total labour force) — is therefore more comprehensive than the Live Register data. The estimated unemployment rate emerging by this method is lower than that obtained from the Live Register data alone. Thus, using this second method (it is normally used in making comparisons between years), the estimated rate of unemployment averaged 8.8 per cent in 1975-77.

Precisely how we should attempt to measure unemployment in Ireland is a matter for some debate. But using either of the two commonly cited measures of the unemployment rate, rates of unemployment in Ireland have persistently tended to be far higher than those prevailing in any other EEC country.

High rates of unemployment have always been a problem of the Irish economy. However, until the 1970s emigration provided a safety valve which artificially kept down rates of unemployment, even in times of recession. Thus, in the five-year (April to April) inter-censal periods, *net* emigration from the Republic was as follows: 1951-56, 197,000; 1956-61, 212,000; 1961-66, 81,000; 1966-71, 54,000. These rates prevailed over years when total population was about 3 million.

Despite high rates of economic growth since 1958, the number of persons employed in 1977 was lower than in 1958. The number at work fell from 1.068 million in April 1958 to 1.036 million in April 1977. Between April 1958 and April 1977 employment in agriculture fell by 171,000, while that in industry increased by 67,000, and that in services increased by 72,000. Thus growth in industry and services was insufficient to absorb the natural rate of population growth and the long-term outflow of labour from agriculture.

A little reflection will indicate that the Irish economy has been, and possibly still is, characterised by a significant amount of structural unemployment of the form which typically prevails in underdeveloped countries. We observed that the labour force in Irish agriculture has been in excess supply. Furthermore, growth in capacity outside agriculture has been too slow to absorb the outflow from the land plus the natural rate of increase in the non-agricultural labour force. Thus effective elimination of our long-term structural unemployment problem will probably require rapid accumulation of our capital stock.

It is in implicit recognition of the fact that much of our unemployment has been, and for some years to come will probably continue to be, of the long-term structural type, that Irish governments, unlike their counterparts in more developed economies, have never had a short-run goal of full employment, to be attained mainly by policies of demand expansion *cum* wage moderation alone.[4]

Employment Policy in a Small Open Economy: A Dilemma

A small open economy like Ireland, under a fixed exchange rate with larger economies and with a high rate of growth in its labour force, faces severe constraints in the pursuit of full employment:

(i) Even if there were an abundant capital stock relative to the economy's labour force, the high import leakages would continue to limit the effectiveness of public policies of expanding aggregate demand. Furthermore, trade union demands for increased real wages, by affecting aggregate supply, could thwart whatever effectiveness policies of expanding demand would otherwise have.

(ii) Given the production techniques which have been carried forward from the past, it is likely, in the absence of rapid expansion in capacity via net investment, and on the assumption of low net emigration, that even if the capital stock were fully employed, we would still tend to have excess supply of labour. Hence, if emigration stays low, and if full employment is to be attained by say the mid-1980s, we shall require high annual rates of investment in the interim. Real wages are of relevance in this context also. The ability of the private sector to finance investment depends, in part, on the level of profits, and the incentive to invest depends on expectation of profits. If real wages rise at rates in excess of productivity growth, then the share of profits in national income will fall, and, on that count, private investment will tend to be low, leading to little net job creation in the long run.

Thus, from the standpoints of reducing both demand deficient unemployment and long-term structural unemployment, the behaviour of real wage rates is crucial. Note that the real wage would still be crucial if all production were provided by State enterprises.

The very openness of the economy imposes upwards pressure on real wages: if real wages here did not increase in phase with those in the UK and other EEC countries, there would be increased outflows of labour from Ireland in response to more attractive job opportunities abroad. Many workers will not offer their services to Irish firms unless the real wage obtainable is sufficiently attractive, given that they have the alternative of moving abroad. Since real wages in Ireland are likely to be increasing over time, the question arises: how can real wages here continue to increase without causing fewer jobs in both the short-run and the long-run? The answer surely is: by increases in the productivity of labour. But for rapid increase in labour productivity we are likely to need high rates of net investment, which in turn imply certain lower bounds on rates of profit. And 'adequate' profits require certain upper bounds on real wage rates. Perhaps workers would be willing to create more profits via wage restraint if they had greater personal interest in the ownership and control of business firms. Those conditions might be realised by offering workers shareholdings in the firms in which they are employed. They might then have a more long-term interest in the prosperity of Irish business. However, if moderation in real wage demands does lead to increased profits, there remains the further policy problem of designing mechanisms to ensure that a high proportion of such earnings are in fact invested in expansion of productive capacity. Thus we are in full agreement with the conclusions of J. Durkan when he states that:

> The planning problem in a society like Ireland is to devise mechanisms, within the external environment and its constraints, to increase the productive capacity and competitiveness of the economy, or, more precisely, to prevent domestic costs from increasing simply because of growth in output, and to ensure that investment made possible by curtailing domestic costs actually takes place. [5]

Suggested Reading

Development For Full Employment, (Green Paper), Prl. 7193, Stationery Office, Dublin 1978.

Development For Full Employment — The Green Paper Reviewed, Research Department, Irish Transport and General Workers' Union, Dublin 1978.

Durkan, J., 'The Irish Economy: The Recent Experience and Prospective Future Performance' in Dowling, B.R., and Durkan, J. (eds), *Irish Economic Policy: A Review of Major Issues,* Dublin 1978.

Keenan, J. G., 'Unemployment, Emigration and the Labour Force' in Dowling and Durkan.

Kennedy, Kieran A., and Foley, Anthony, 'Industrial Development' in Dowling and Durkan.

Mooney, Peter J., 'Incomes Policy' in Dowling and Durkan.

O'Hagen, John (ed.), *The Economy of Ireland,* Irish Management Institute, Dublin 1975.

Walsh, Brendan, 'Labour Market Strategies' in Dowling and Durkan.

FOOTNOTES

1. The AS curve could in fact slope downwards as output is expanded from a low level. However, it can be shown that it is very unlikely that a small open economy could be in equilibrium at a point where the AS curve has a negative slope. Strictly speaking, we should refer to *marginal* costs here, but in the interests of simplicity we do not do so.
2. This sub-section draws heavily on J. O'Hagen, 'Demographic and Labour Force Characteristics and Trends', Reading 8-A in J. O'Hagen (ed.), *The Economy of Ireland,* Dublin: Irish Management Institute 1975.
3. *Economic Survey of Ireland,* Paris: OECD 1973, 32.
4. It appears that full employment, as a goal potentially attainable over several years, was first officially analysed in National Industrial Economic Council, *Report on Full Employment,* Dublin: Stationery Office, Pr. 9188, 1967. In June 1978 the government published a Green Paper purporting to set out the basis for a programme to reach full employment by 1984. The role of investment in relaxing bottle-necks on potential output and employment was clearly recognised in that, and in other, government macroeconomic policy documents.
5. J. Durkan, 'The Irish Economy: The Recent Experience and Prospective Future Performance' in B. R. Dowling and J. Durkan (eds), *Irish Economic Policy: A Review of Major Issues,* Dublin: The Economic and Social Research Institute 1978, 54.

CHAPTER 15

The Balance of International Payments and Exchange Rate Determination

The Balance of International Payments

The balance of international payments for any year is a statement of all transactions between residents of the home country and the rest of the world in that year. This set of records, when account is taken of balancing items, must balance exactly. This does *not* mean that transactions of a given category balance. For example, the value of exports of goods may differ from the value of imports of goods. Likewise, inflows of financial capital from abroad (for example, to finance the purchase of land in Ireland or the purchase of Irish government securities) need not equal in value the outflows of financial capital from Ireland. The character and size of the balancing items in the balance of payments accounts is often of crucial importance. *The balance of trade* is the difference between the value of merchandise exports and merchandise imports. If the value of merchandise exports exceeds (falls short of) the value of merchandise imports, the balance of trade is in surplus (deficit). *The balance of payments on current account* is found by adding *net* exports of services, or so-called invisible items (such as net receipts from tourism, interest on investments held by Irish residents abroad, transportation charges, etc.) to the balance of trade. If the value of exports of goods and services exceeds (falls short of) the value of imports of goods and services, the current account is in surplus (deficit).

In the post-war years the Republic of Ireland has consistently had balance of trade deficits and net surpluses on invisibles. However, the surplus income from invisibles has usually been insufficient to offset the deficit on merchandise trade; in almost all post-war years our current account was in deficit.

The balance of payments on current account, $(X - M)$, indicates the extent to which external transactions directly contribute to aggregate demand in the economy. *The balance of payments on capital account* indicates how the current account has been financed. Since the balance of payments on capital account must equal, in absolute value, the balance of payments on current account, the balance of payments accounts balance exactly.

Suppose, for example, that in a given year we import goods and services valued £1000 million and export goods and services valued £600 million. The net debt to foreigners thereby incurred is £400 million. Some of this debt may be paid off by running down our holdings of foreign exchange (and paying foreigners those foreign monies); the residual must take the form of net borrowing from abroad.[1] Thus the current account deficit must equal (a) the reduction in Ireland's foreign exchange reserves *plus* (b) borrowing by Ireland from abroad, or, in the event that we borrow more from abroad than the current account deficit, it must equal (b') borrowing by Ireland from abroad *minus* (a') the increase in Ireland's foreign exchange reserves. If a country has a current account balance of payments deficit, its *net* claims on foreign countries are decreased, or equivalently, its net liabilities to foreigners are increased. Thus the balance of payments on capital account must offset the balance on current account, as in Table 11.

Table 11

Balance of Payments of Republic of Ireland, 1974, £ Million

Current Account		Capital Account	
Deficit on merchandise trade	537.6	Net capital inflow	347.8
Surplus on invisible items	249.9	Minus increase in foreign exchange reserves	60.1
Deficit on current account	287.7	Balance on capital account	287.7

Source: Annual Report 1976, Central Bank of Ireland, Table 50.

In Table 11 the net capital inflow, which is a form of borrowing from abroad during the year, has two components:

(i) Direct investment by foreigners in Ireland minus direct investment in foreign countries by Irish residents. This, on a net basis, typically takes the form of foreigners bringing foreign exchange into Ireland in order to finance the purchase of land, or the construction of factories, in this country.

(ii) Purchase by foreigners of securities of Irish companies or of Irish government securities, less the purchase of foreign securities by Irish residents.

The change in foreign exchange reserves is the balancing item in Table 11. These consist of changes in holdings of foreign exchange (or foreign government securities) at the Central Bank of Ireland. The table indicates that current account transactions generated a net outflow in foreign exchange of £287.7 million. But the net inflow of foreign exchange on capital account, at £347.8 million, was £60.1 million in excess of that sum. This £60.1 million was the change in the nation's foreign exchange reserves. *This balancing item is what is usually meant by the balance of payments surplus or deficit; by this criterion, if foreign exchange reserves increase (decrease), the balance of payments is said to be in surplus (deficit).*

The reader may wonder how the net inflow of £60.1 million in foreign exchange became reserves in the Central Bank. The answer is that the initial holders or recipients in Ireland of this foreign exchange either (a) sold it to the Central Bank, receiving Irish money in return, or (b) sold it to commercial banks; the commercial banks, in turn, sold it to the Central Bank, receiving Central Bank liabilities in settlement.

The change in foreign exchange reserves may be of crucial importance: if foreign exchange reserves are decreasing the nation may find it impossible to maintain fixed exchange rates with trading partners.

Determination of Exchange Rates

An exchange rate is the price of a foreign currency. *We define 'the' exchange rate as the number of units of domestic currency required to purchase one unit of foreign currency.*[2] Like any other price it is determined by supply and demand. In the exposition which follows we assume for simplicity that there are only two countries Home and Abroad. We assume that the currency of Home is the pound, while that of Abroad is the dollar. The two countries would be operating under *fixed exchange rates* if the central banks of the two countries intervene in the foreign exchange market to ensure that the supply and demand for pounds (or dollars) in that market are equated at a fixed price. They would be operating under *freely floating exchange rates* if the central banks refrained from intervention in the market for foreign exchange.

Consider the two-country example. From Home's standpoint the exchange rate is the number of pounds required to obtain a dollar. The price of a dollar is determined by the supply and demand for dollars in the foreign exchange market. The *supply* of dollars is determined by Home's exports to Abroad, and by investment in Home by residents of Abroad. The *demand* for dollars is determined by the desire of residents of Home to buy goods and services from Abroad, and by the desire of residents of Home to invest in Abroad. Figure 45 illustrates the supply and demand curves for dollars.

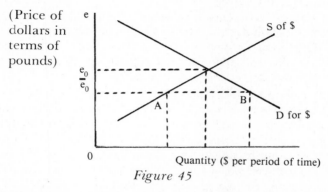

(Price of dollars in terms of pounds)

Figure 45

In discussing the slopes of the supply and demand curves, for simplicity in exposition we focus on current account variables alone. The *demand curve* slopes down from left to right, reflecting the fact that the lower the price of dollars in terms of pounds, the more anxious will residents of Home be to buy Abroad's goods. Thus if the exchange rate were low, say 1/10, a Cadillac made in Abroad and priced at $20,000 in Abroad could be bought by residents of Home for £2000. (We have ignored the impact of tariffs, transport costs, etc.) The demand for Cadillacs by Home's residents would then be high; so the demand for dollars to pay the exporters of Abroad would be high. The opposite would hold if the exchange rate were high, say 10. (One would then have to pay £10 to get $1.) The demand by Home's residents for goods made in Abroad—and hence for dollars—would then be low.

The desire of Abroad's residents to import from Home is a factor determining the *supply* of dollars. If the exchange rate were low, say

1/10, residents of Abroad would have to pay $10 to obtain £1. Their demand for Home's goods—and hence the supply of dollars in payment for them—would be low. But if the exchange rate were high, say 10, a good priced at £10 in Home could be bought by Abroad's residents for only $1. (We have again ignored the impact of tariffs, transportation charges, etc.) The demand for Home's exports would be high. But since the price of Home's exports in terms of dollars would then be lower than in our previous example, Home might or might not earn more dollars than she did before, depending on the price elasticity of Abroad's demand for Home's goods. If Home did not earn more dollars as the price of dollars increased (the price elasticity of demand for Home's exports would then be less than unity), the supply curve of dollars would have a negative slope. Although this is a possibility, we ignore it and assume that the supply curve has a positive slope. (This is equivalent to assuming that the demand for Home's exports is price elastic.)

The intersection of the supply and demand curves gives the equilibrium rate of exchange, e_0 in Figure 45. Under *freely floating exchange rates* this is the exchange rate which will tend to prevail; if the rate were higher than e_0, the supply of dollars would exceed the demand for dollars and market forces would bid the exchange rate down towards e_0; if the exchange rate were lower than e_0, the demand for dollars would exceed the supply of dollars and market forces would bid the rate up towards e_0. Thus, under a system of freely floating exchange rates, market forces will automatically tend to equate the supply and demand for foreign exchange.

Both the supply curve and the demand curve for dollars will tend to shift from time to time. For example, if GNP in Abroad rapidly rises, Abroad's imports from Home will tend to increase. This will shift to the right the supply curve for dollars, causing downwards pressure on the exchange rate. If there were a rash of strikes in Home (so that domestically produced goods become more scarce in Home), the demand by residents of Home for Abroad's goods—and hence for dollars—would tend to increase. Thus the demand curve for dollars would shift to the right, leading to upwards pressure on the exchange rate. If the exchange rate is allowed to float freely, periodic shifts in the supply and demand curves will cause the equilibrium exchange rate to fluctuate over time.

The main advantage of freely floating exchange rates is that the exchange rate will tend to an equilibrium at which the supply and demand for foreign exchange are automatically equated. There would be no need for central banks to accumulate massive holdings of foreign exchange reserves (as buffer stocks). In contrast to the case under fixed exchange rates, no country could have a balance of payments problem if rates were freely floating. However, a drawback is that it would tend to increase uncertainty. Consider, for example, a company in Home exporting to Abroad. Suppose that the company quotes its prices in terms of dollars, and that payment is made only when the goods arrive at the docks in Abroad. Unless it makes special forward provisions (which involve extra costs), the company, when it accepts an export order, will have no way of knowing how much it will be paid in terms of pounds when the goods have arrived in Abroad's docks.

Consider next the case of *fixed exchange rates.* Suppose that the free market demand and supply curves remain as in Figure 45. If the Central Bank of Home attempts to maintain a fixed exchange rate there is a danger that the rate chosen may differ from the long-run equilibrium rate. If so, it is likely that the pound will ultimately depreciate or appreciate. In this context we define a *devaluation* or *depreciation* of the pound as a rise in the price of foreign currency: in our two-country example, more pounds would have to be paid for one dollar. We define an *appreciation* or *revaluation* of the pound as a fall in the price of foreign currency.

Suppose that the Central Bank of Home seeks to maintain the exchange rate at $\dot{e}_0$ in Figure 45. (In what follows we shall abstract from the operations of the Central Bank of Abroad.) At this low rate, and in the absence of central bank intervention in the foreign exchange market, the demand for dollars exceeds the supply of dollars by the amount AB per period. There would be upwards pressure on the price of dollars. To maintain the rate $\dot{e}_0$ — to prevent a depreciation of the pound — the Central Bank of Home may resort to its foreign exchange reserves, selling AB dollars per period, in exchange for pounds. In this manner the supply of dollars would be equated to the demand for dollars at the rate $\dot{e}_0$, the Central Bank of Home being the residual supplier of AB dollars per period. But if there is no shift in the market supply and demand curves, the Central Bank of Home will not be able to maintain the exchange rate $\dot{e}_0$ indefinitely: to maintain $\dot{e}_0$ the Bank has to sell AB dollars in each time period, but no central bank has infinite reserves. Sooner or later the Bank will exhaust its holdings of foreign exchange; then it will no longer be able to supply the foreign exchange market with AB dollars per period. In the long run Home would have to devalue the pound — from $\dot{e}_0$ to e_0.

Suppose next that Home does devalue the pound to e_0, and that it wishes to keep the exchange rate fixed at e_0. The Central Bank of Home will still need foreign exchange reserves. That is because the supply and demand curves will shift reflecting seasonal factors, fluctuations in income in the two countries, etc. In the summer there may be a temporary increase in the supply of dollars, reflecting expenditures by tourists from Abroad in Home; the supply curve of dollars would shift to the right. There would then be downwards pressure on the exchange rate and the pound would tend to appreciate. To maintain the rate e_0, the Central Bank of Home would act as a residual demander for dollars, buying dollars in exchange for pounds. In the autumn there may be an increase in the demand for dollars due to seasonality in imports of goods from Abroad. The demand curve for dollars would then shift to the right putting upwards pressure on the exchange rate. The Central Bank of Home, to maintain the rate e_0, would resort to its reserves and act as residual supplier of dollars. Thus foreign exchange reserves will be needed to peg the rate at e_0.

In the above example in which Home devalued from $\dot{e}_0$ to e_0, we assumed that speculators played no role. Suppose that the long-run equilibrium rate is in the neighbourhood of e_0 but that the Central Bank of Home attempts to peg the rate at $\dot{e}_0$. In the absence of policies to be discussed below, the Central Bank of Home will ultimately have to devalue the pound. However, we now recognise that if it does not do so voluntarily, speculators will almost surely force it to do so. With the exchange rate fundamentally out of equilibrium at $\dot{e}_0$, speculators will see that there is only one direction in which it is likely to move — upwards toward e_0. Acting on these expectations they will buy dollars now at the low price, $\dot{e}_0$, with the intention of converting these dollars back into pounds at a higher price — e_0 — after the anticipated devaluation of the pound. In this manner the expectations of speculators are likely to be self-fulfilling, in the sense that the actions to which they lead precipitate the expected devaluation. That is because the increased demand for dollars by speculators will cause the demand curve for dollars to shift to the right, so the Central Bank of Home will now have to sell more than AB dollars per period in its attempt to peg the rate at $\dot{e}_0$. The Bank will therefore tend to run out of foreign exchange reserves more rapidly than would have been the case had speculators not entered the market. The Central Bank of Home might then be forced to devalue sooner than it would have done had there been no speculation against the pound.

We have seen that if a country is operating under a system of fixed (or approximately fixed) exchange rates, and if it is losing foreign exchange reserves, it may decide to *devalue*. However, there are other policy options.

Deflationary Fiscal Policies

If Home is losing reserves it may adopt deflationary fiscal policies. If these lead to reduction in national income the demand for imports will be reduced. This implies that the demand curve for foreign exchange will shift to the left, thereby curtailing the reserve loss. Deflationary fiscal policies also imply some downwards pressure on the prices of factors of production. This may make Home's goods more competitive on export markets, thereby leading to a shift to the right in the supply curve of foreign exchange. This will also curtail reserve losses.

Restrictive Monetary Policies

Home might (if it can) pursue restrictive monetary policies. *If* these are successful, interest rates will rise in Home. The higher domestic interest rates relative to those in Abroad will attract capital inflows from Abroad. These would cause shifts to the right in the supply curve of foreign exchange and would therefore curtail reserve losses. The rise in interest rates would also have a deflationary effect on aggregate demand; the demand curves for imports and foreign exchange would then shift to the left.

Restrictive Commercial Policies

Home might increase tariffs and quotas, thereby reducing the demand for imports and shifting to the left the demand curve for foreign exchange. Home might also make its exports more competitive by subsidising them. That would shift to the right the supply curve of foreign exchange.

Fixed Versus Freely Floating Exchange Rates

Compared to floating exchange rates, an advantage of a system of fixed exchange rates — if the rates really remain fixed — is that it avoids the uncertainty in regard to future exchange rates that prevails under floating rates. A disadvantage is that it may lead to a situation in which other objectives of policy — such as full employment — are un-attainable. Suppose, for example, that a country under fixed exchange rates is running out of reserves. To improve the current account balance of payments by reducing imports, government may have to depress demand — thereby increasing unemployment — by deflationary fiscal policies. Such policies, for balance of payments reasons, were adopted to a severe degree by Ireland in the mid-1950s. The need to pursue deflationary fiscal policies for balance of payments reasons would not arise if the economy were under freely floating exchange rates.

Buffer Stocks and Managed Floating

In Chapters 7 and 8 we saw that agricultural prices would fluctuate with weather and other conditions if those prices were left to the free play of market forces alone. We also saw that to peg farm prices at target levels the State could engage in intervention purchases and sales, selling from buffer stocks when prices tended to rise above target levels and buying into intervention (thereby adding to buffer stocks) at times when they tended to fall below target levels. The operation of the foreign exchange market under fixed exchange rates is similar: if under free market pressures the exchange rate tends to rise above some target (the 'fixed') level, the central bank may prevent this by selling foreign exchange, thereby pegging the rate at the target level. Similarly, if under free market pressures the exchange rate shows a tendency to fall below a target level, the central bank may intervene by buying foreign exchange, again pegging the rate at a target level.

In reality the exchange rate may be neither fixed nor freely floating; rather, the home country may engage in a *managed float* of the exchange rate. Under a managed float there is a target *range* of fluctuation of the exchange rate. To some *limited* extent, the determination of the equilibrium exchange rate under managed floating is left to the forces of market supply and demand; however, the amplitude (i.e., upper and lower bounds) of fluctuation is constrained by central bank intervention in the event that the actual exchange rate would otherwise fall outside some target range.

Under a managed float it may be decided to maintain the exchange rate within a zone of say 20 per cent of some 'central' or 'ideal' rate x. Then the central bank would sell foreign currency if, in consequence of free market forces, the exchange rate tended to rise above x + (20 per cent)x; it would buy foreign currency if the exchange rate would otherwise fall below x — (20 per cent)x. Thus a managed float is akin to a regime of rigidly fixed exchange rates if the central bank seeks to maintain a small range of fluctuation in the rate (i.e., if the acceptable upper and lower bounds of fluctuation in the rate are close to some 'ideal' rate); it is more akin to a freely floating exchange rate system if the central bank is content to permit the rate to fluctuate within a broad range of some 'central' rate.

FOOTNOTES

1. This statement ignores the operations of the International Monetary Fund.
2. The exchange rate is often defined as the amount of foreign currency required to purchase one unit of domestic currency. This is in confusing violation of convention: we define the price of a commodity such as wheat as the number of units of domestic money required to purchase, say, a bushel of wheat — *not* as the number of bushels of wheat to purchase a unit of domestic money. Hence the definition in the text: the commodity is foreign exchange; the price is the amount of domestic money required to buy a unit of foreign exchange.

CHAPTER 16

Monetary and Fiscal Policies, Inflation and Devaluation in Small Open Economies

Consider a small open economy. Monetary and fiscal policies will have different effects depending on whether the exchange rate is fixed or freely floating. (We saw at the end of the preceding chapter that managed floating of exchange rates is akin to fixed or freely floating rates, depending on the *range* of fluctuation in the exchange rate which the monetary authorities are both willing and able to permit.) *We confine most of the discussion which follows to the short-run.* Consider first the case of fixed exchange rates.

Policies under Fixed Exchange Rates

Fiscal Policy
Assume we start with the economy in equilibrium well below full capacity utilisation and that the government pursues an expansionary fiscal policy by increasing its expenditure on, say, non-tradeables. We know from elementary multiplier theory that *so long as producers are willing to supply whatever quantity may be demanded,* national income will increase by some multiple of the increase in government expenditure. However, as income increases, so too does the trans-actions demand for money. Thus the demand curve for money will shift to the right. (Recall Figure 40, Chapter 12.) If the supply of money were held constant, this would raise the interest rate, thereby choking off some of investment demand and possibly some of con-sumption demand. The rise in equilibrium income would then be less than multiplier analysis alone would predict. However, a considerable rise in the domestic rate of interest relative to that abroad could only be temporary: the higher domestic interest rate relative to that abroad

would attract capital inflows from abroad, increasing the reserves of the commercial banks, thereby *increasing the domestic money supply.* Thus the *interest rate would be bid down towards its initial level.* Under the circumstances outlined, income would increase more or less as predicted by the multiplier.

In practice (contrary to what we assumed just above) producers might not be willing to supply whatever quantity is demanded: the price level may have to be bid up slightly to induce them to expand output, though that is least likely to be the case if, as assumed, we start with plenty of excess capacity. As was indicated in Chapter 14 (in connection with Figure 42), the aggregate supply curve may be infinitely elastic (i.e., perfectly flat) around an equilibrium if there is abundant excess capacity. Under such circumstances (taking account of both aggregate supply and demand) increased government expenditure would raise income by an amount indicated by multiplier analysis. However, if we start in equilibrium below but close to full capacity utilisation, then the aggregate supply curve will be positively sloped and an increase in aggregate demand will induce some small increase in the domestic price level. The reader should know from Figure 43 that equilibrium income would then increase by less than the amount predicted by elementary multiplier analysis.

The conclusions from this subsection are:

(i) If we start with the economy in equilibrium well below full capacity utilisation, increased government expenditure on non-tradeables in a small open economy under fixed exchange rates will cause national income to increase (a) by an amount indicated by the multiplier if the aggregate supply curve is infinitely elastic or (b) by a smaller amount than in (a) if the aggregate supply curve is positively sloped. The main point is that equilibrium income increases under the specified conditions. (We shall see below that the crucial assumption yielding this conclusion is that the exchange rate *vis-à-vis* some large country is indeed fixed.) Cases (a) and (b) above are illustrated in Figure 46, where the aggregate demand curve shifts from AD to AD' corresponding to case (a), but the shift corresponding to case (b) would be from (AD) to (AD)'. (The economy would be at full capacity utilisation — sometimes called full employment — only when AS is absolutely vertical.) The diagram clearly indicates that the increase in income is smaller in case (b) than in case (a).

(ii) In the first paragraph of the present subsection we saw that the money supply in a small open economy under fixed exchange rates would *automatically* increase if there were an increase in income and

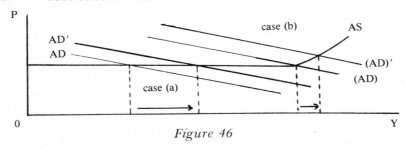

Figure 46

hence an increase in the transactions demand for money, leading to no change in the equilibrium rate of interest. From this the reader may conclude that the policy of the small country's central bank can have significant effect on *neither* the domestic money supply *nor* the equilibrium rate of interest. As we shall shortly see, this conclusion is correct — though the assumption of a fixed exchange rate is crucial.

Monetary Policy

Consider next the effects of an expansionary monetary policy in a small open economy under fixed exchange rates. Throughout this section we shall be referring to monetary policy in the form of open market operations by the small economy's central bank. Thus suppose that the central bank buys securities on the open market. The money supply therefore increases and in the first instance there is downwards pressure on the rate of interest. But this means that the domestic rate of interest falls relative to the rate of interest in the large economy, or large economies, with which the small economy has a fixed exchange rate. Domestic residents therefore prefer foreign interest-bearing assets, *so there is a capital outflow.* The capital outflow means that the demand for foreign currency increases. We know from the preceding chapter that in the absence of central bank intervention to maintain the exchange rate, the domestic currency would depreciate on the foreign exchange market. So to keep the exchange rate at its fixed level the central bank must buy domestic money with foreign exchange. Thus the central bank's holdings of foreign exchange reserves fall. In this manner *the central bank will be forced to offset the initial expansion in the money supply by a more or less equivalent contraction in the money supply.* The interest rate will then move back towards its initial level. Hence, under a fixed exchange rate with one or more relatively large countries, *monetary policy* (in the form of open market operations) *can have little or no effect on equilibrium national income.*

It is wrong to say that monetary policy has no effect at all in a small open economy under fixed exchange rates; as we have seen, an attempt to expand the money supply via open market purchases leads to *reduction in the nation's foreign exchange reserves.*

The conclusion that under the conditions specified monetary policy can have little or no effect on equilibrium income may have surprised some readers (especially those accustomed to thinking in terms of closed economies), but so long as the small economy under a fixed exchange rate remains truly open—so long as there is relatively free mobility of goods and (financial) capital across its frontiers—that conclusion is incontrovertible.

In Chapter 12 we analysed the creation of money *in a closed economy.* Given its assumptions (especially the assumption of a closed economy) that analysis was correct. However, we pointed out there that such analysis would have to be modified when we came to consider a small open economy under a fixed exchange rate. The analysis of the creation of money in Chapter 12 is *misleading or wrong* when applied to a small open economy under a fixed exchange rate. In small open economies under fixed exchange rates, attempts by the domestic central bank to control the money supply by open market operations must, other things being equal, break down. For such economies, open market operations will generally *not* lead to permanent multiple expansion (or multiple contraction) of the domestic money supply (as outlined for a closed economy in Chapter 12). At the risk of offending the reader by repetition, that is because:

(i) If the central bank buys bonds, the money supply, in the first instance, will increase, tending to cause the domestic interest rate to fall. But this will cause capital outflows, and capital outflows imply contraction of the domestic money supply. (Be sure that you can see why.) The capital outflows will continue—the domestic money supply will continue to contract—so long as the domestic rate of interest is below that abroad in countries with which the small open economy maintains fixed exchange rates. These capital outflows and the resulting monetary contraction will cause the domestic rate of interest to rise. *The capital outflows induced by the initial interest rate differentials will cease only when the domestic rate of interest has returned to its initial equilibrium level,* which must (in effect) be the same as the interest rate prevailing in the larger countries with which the small economy has fixed exchange rates.

(ii) If the small open economy under fixed exchange rates tries to reduce its money supply independently of the rest of the world via open market sales of securities, its interest rate, in the first instance, will rise.

Since its equilibrium rate of interest must be roughly in line with that abroad, a result will be capital inflows in response to the higher interest rate obtainable in the small economy, and downwards pressure on that rate of interest. *The capital inflows in response to interest rate differentials will cease only when the domestic rate of interest has returned to its initial level* — and that rate of interest must be approximately that prevailing in the larger countries with which the small open economy has fixed exchange rates.

In sum, in a small open economy under fixed exchange rates, any attempt by the central bank to control the money supply independently of the rest of the world is likely to be thwarted: in effect, its equilibrium rate of interest is that prevailing abroad (in countries with which a fixed exchange rate is maintained). If the monetary authorities cannot control the price of money — the rate of interest — they cannot control the quantity of money. Thus the analysis of the creation of money along the lines of Chapter 12 is most misleading when applied to small open economies under fixed exchange rates. Our central conclusion is that a small open economy under fixed exchange rates (if it really is open) *cannot* control its money supply independently of the rest of the world.

Policies under Freely Floating Exchange Rates
Fiscal Policy
As before, assume excess capacity and fiscal policies in the form of increased government expenditure financed by taxation or by borrowing from the non-bank public. This will cause an increase in the transactions demand for money, placing upwards pressure on the rate of interest. But any rise in the rate of interest will attract capital inflows from abroad. These capital inflows increase the supply of foreign exchange — the supply curve of foreign exchange would shift to the right. The price of foreign exchange would then decrease — the domestic currency would appreciate. But given foreign prices, this would mean that exporters (in the small economy) would be paid less in domestic money for goods sent abroad. If (as in a short-run situation) domestic factor prices stay constant, the profit margin obtainable on exports, and hence the volume of exports, will fall. The appreciation of the domestic currency also means that imports, and hence (domestically produced) importables, will be cheaper than before in terms of domestic money. If domestic factor prices stay more or less constant (as in a short-run situation), domestically produced goods which compete with imports on the home market will become

cost-non-competitive. Some domestic suppliers to the home market will therefore cut back their outputs or close down entirely. Consumer demands for such goods would be satisfied by increased imports. Imports would therefore increase in volume while, as already seen, exports would decrease in volume. The increase in government expenditure would in fact tend to be fully offset by a deficit in the current account balance of payments. *Under such circumstances there would be no net change in the level of aggregate demand.* Thus, from the standpoint of rapidly driving the economy towards full employment, fiscal policy is of little importance in a small open economy under a system of freely floating exchange rates. Note how this contrasts with what happens under fixed exchange rates.

Monetary Policy

Consider now an expansionary monetary policy, in the form of open market purchases, in a small open economy under freely floating exchange rates. As before, assume some excess capacity. The increase in the money supply will initially put downwards pressure on domestic interest rates. That will lead to capital outflows to take advantage of the relatively higher interest rates abroad. These capital outflows increase the demand for foreign currency. The demand curve for foreign exchange will therefore shift to the right, leading to a rise in the price of foreign exchange — a depreciation of the domestic currency. This means that the prices of exports, in terms of domestic money, will rise. Assuming a short-run situation in which domestic factor prices are more or less given, the profit margin obtainable on exports therefore increases; hence the volume of exports increases. The depreciation of the domestic currency also means that the prices of imports, in terms of domestic money, will increase. Therefore the prices of domestically produced goods which compete with imports on the home market also increase. Again assuming a short-run situation with rigid domestic factor prices (domestically produced) importables become more cost-competitive. The output of such goods is therefore increased, and a greater share of the home market is supplied from domestic sources. The volume of imports accordingly falls. Because of increased exports and decreased imports, the balance of payments on current account will have become more favourable, and aggregate demand will have increased. Thus, from the standpoint of driving the economy closer to full capacity utilisation in the short-run, monetary policy is of more importance under floating exchange rates than under fixed exchange rates.

Money Supply and Inflation in Small Open Economies

In our earlier discussion of inflation in Chapter 13 we stated that an inflation could not proceed for long unless the money supply were increasing. Thus, increases in the money supply might (by affecting the level of aggregate demand) be an initiating cause of inflation. Or they might be an effect of inflation. In the case of a small open economy *under fixed exchange rates,* increases in the money supply must be mainly an *effect* of inflation. From the standpoint of the small open economy under fixed exchange rates, the ultimate causes of an internal inflationary process lie outside the country. Thus expansion in the money supply in the small open economy under fixed exchange rates could not be the cause of (sustained) inflation. In fact, the supply of money in the small open economy under fixed exchange rates must react passively to the increased demand for money to finance successively higher *nominal* levels of transactions, generated by the externally determined inflation. That can be seen as follows.

Recall the quantity *theory* of money, MV = PY. Assume that the prices of tradeables are increasing by 20 per cent a year, in line with inflation abroad. If V is constant (and according to the quantity theory of money it will be approximately constant from year to year as long as both the rate of inflation and the domestic rate of interest are constant) and if Y is constant or increasing (due to economic growth), it must be the case that M is increasing. In fact the rate of increase in M must roughly equal the rate of increase in PY. Thus the central bank must passively allow the money supply to increase in line with inflation abroad.

Suppose for simplicity that there is some constant rate of inflation abroad, that the small open economy is on fixed exchange rates, and that its central bank attempts to hold the money supply constant. It is easy to see that this policy must break down. With M given, with V in the long run varying only slightly and with P increasing in line with inflation abroad, Y would be decreasing. Also, the *real* money supply would be decreasing. On this count the cost of money — the domestic rate of interest — would tend to increase. The decreases in Y — and therefore decreases in real income and imports — in each time period would lead to successively larger current account balance of payments surpluses. These earnings of foreign exchange would be converted into domestic money, thereby increasing the domestic money supply. Also, the rise in domestic interest rates would induce capital inflows. These too would increase the domestic money supply, lowering the rate of interest back towards its initial level (i.e., that level prevailing in countries with which the small economy maintains fixed exchange rates).

It might be argued that the central bank could prevent the money supply from increasing (via the channels just mentioned) by open market sales. However, it could not attain such an objective. Open market sales would lead to upwards pressure on the interest rate, inducing capital inflows. Such inflows would cause the supply curve of foreign exchange to shift to the right. Given the commitment to fixed exchange rates, the central bank would then need to buy foreign currency in exchange for domestic money. Thus the hands of central bankers in small open economies with fixed exchange rates are tied: in the face of inflation generated by forces abroad, central bankers must passively allow the domestic money supply to increase.

So long as we in Ireland remain open and maintain a fixed exchange rate with any large country with which there is free trade (a) we cannot independently control our money supply and (b) we cannot independently determine our rate of inflation. Opting for a *freely floating exchange rate* regime has some *potentially* attractive features: it is the *only* way in which *we* could determine the rate of expansion in our money supply and our rate of inflation, *independently* of what might be happening in the rest of the world.

Suppose that the Central Bank of Ireland held the money supply *constant,* that we were on a freely floating exchange rate regime with the rest of the world, and that the rest of the world was inflating by, say, 10 per cent a year. Under such circumstances the Irish pound would tend to appreciate — that is, increase in value against other currencies — by about 10 per cent a year. With foreign inflation at 10 per cent annually and the Irish pound appreciating at the same rate, the prices of Irish exportables and importables, and the prices of imports, all denominated in Irish pounds, would be constant. Thus, under the conditions specified, we would tend to have zero inflation.

The key determinant of our rate of inflation under freely floating exchange rates would be the rate of increase in our money supply (which, under a freely floating exchange rate system, would be controllable by the Central Bank of Ireland). By monetary restraint and freely floating exchange rates we could opt for a very low rate of inflation. But by rapid expansion in the money supply under a freely floating exchange rate regime we could create hyperinflation, independently of inflation in the rest of the world. (The Irish pound would then be depreciating against other currencies.)

Under a freely floating exchange rate regime there might be political pressures imposed on the Central Bank of Ireland to cause high inflation by rapid monetary expansion. Thus suppose that productivity is given, that we are on a freely floating exchange rate system, and that trade unions annually demand and obtain high money wage awards. If the Central Bank of Ireland did not increase the money supply, a consequence would be increased unemployment. It does not require much political insight to see that the Central Bank of Ireland would almost surely be pressured into averting this unemployment. How? By increasing the money supply, thereby generating high inflation (and getting real wages down) which would cause the Irish pound to depreciate on foreign exchange markets. It is because the consequences just mentioned might well be very real probabilities that we would not recommend that we independently determine our own rate of inflation by opting for freely floating exchange rates with the rest of the world.

Two final remarks, which should already be apparent:

(i) A small open economy may decide to maintain a fixed exchange rate with some large country with which there is free trade. But if it does so, it cannot independently control its rate of inflation or the rate of expansion in its money supply. Its rate of inflation will be high or low depending on whether it keeps a fixed exchange rate with a country with high or low inflation.

(ii) A small open economy may decide to control its rate of inflation, independently of what is happening in the rest of the world, by appropriate control of its money supply. But if it does so, it cannot control its exchange rate.

Devaluation as a Stabilisation Policy Instrument in a Small Open Economy

It is important to note that the analysis of the roles of monetary and fiscal policies as stabilisation devices in the earlier part of this chapter focused on short-run impact effects alone. Rigorous analysis of the long-run effects on output and employment of monetary and fiscal policies under alternative exchange rate regimes is more complex, and is accordingly left to a more advanced course in economic analysis.

Consider a small open economy under (quasi) fixed exchange rates. It is sometimes suggested that a once-and-for-all currency devaluation would improve the current account balance of payments, thereby simultaneously increasing output and employment in the small open economy. It is easy to see that such a proposition, as a statement about the long run, is likely to be erroneous; however, it does have some validity in the short run.

As before, we start with the small open economy in equilibrium below full capacity utilisation. Call the small open economy Home and call the rest of the world Abroad. Assume that a particular exchange rate prevails initially. Call Home's currency the pound and Abroad's the dollar, and suppose that the initial exchange rate is £0·5 to $1. Suppose that Home now devalues by 100 per cent to a new fixed exchange rate, so that £1 now exchanges against $1.

Since that small open economy is a price-taker in the case of tradeable goods, the dollar prices of those will remain unchanged after the devaluation; however, their prices in terms of pounds will double. If, as is likely, factor prices are more or less given in the short run, the rise in the domestic currency price of exportables will raise the profit margins of firms in the exportables sector. Such increases in the cost-competitiveness of domestic firms in the exportables sector will generate an increase in exports.

The domestic price of importables has also doubled. If domestic factor prices are given, that causes an increase in the profit margins of domestic firms in the importables sector. The increased cost-competitiveness of such firms leads to increased domestic output in substitution for imported goods. Thus imports fall in the short run.

Hence, in the short run — so long as domestic factor prices stay more or less constant — $(X - M)$, the balance of payments on current account, improves, and that increase in aggregate demand is likely to generate an increase in domestic employment. There is also a gain in the level of foreign exchange reserves in the small open economy.

In the long run, however, neither the factor market nor the non-tradeables sector can be insulated from the devaluation:

(i) If, as indeed will be the case, the prices of tradeable goods rise by 100 per cent — by the full percentage devaluation — firms in the tradeables sector will be willing to pay more for the factors of production; they will, accordingly, *bid up* factor prices. Also, since the prices of food and other tradeable goods will have increased by 100 per cent, trade unions and other organisations, on behalf of factor owners, are likely to push up factor prices so as to maintain their real incomes. These two considerations mean that in the long run factor prices are likely to adjust so as to increase by the full extent of the devaluation; in the present example they will increase by about 100 per cent.

(ii) Firms in the non-tradeables sector must pay the same prices for inputs as firms in the tradeables sector. Since the value of the output of the non-tradeables sector must equal the value of all inputs used (value added), and since the prices of inputs will have increased by the full extent of the devaluation (by 100 per cent in the present example), the prices of non-tradeables will increase by about 100 per cent in full long-run equilibrium, in response to the devaluation.

Hence we conclude: if a small open economy devalues by x per cent, *all* internal prices — those of tradeables, of non-tradeables and of the factors of production — will increase by x per cent in full long-run equilibrium. Because there would then be no change in *relative* prices, there would be no change in real wages or in real profit margins and hence, in full long-run equilibrium, there would be no change in the structure of output. Hence, other things being equal, in full long-run equilibrium, real exports and real imports, and production of tradeables and non-tradeables, will be the same as they were before the devaluation.

It follows that devaluation by a small open economy has no effect on real variables (such as real X, real M, real Y and employment) in the long run. Its only long-run effects are (a) a once-and-for-all increase in the prices of all goods and factors of production and (b) a once-and-for-all gain in the level of foreign exchange reserves. The latter gain is obtained in the short-run disequilibrium in which (X — M) is improved in response to the devaluation. But in the long run, real X and real M return to their initial levels; that is why the gain in foreign exchange reserves is a once-and-for-all phenomenon.

PART FOUR

MONEY, PUBLIC FINANCE AND COMMERCIAL POLICY IN IRELAND

CHAPTER 17

Money and Banking in Ireland

When the Irish Free State was established in 1922 the only currency of full legal tender status consisted of notes issued by the British government. British coins were legal tender for limited amounts only. The 1926 Coinage Act provided for the issue of Irish coins. About the same time the government appointed a commission of inquiry into banking, which considered whether a central bank should be established. Concluding to the contrary, it proposed the establishment of the Currency Commission to manage the issue of Irish legal tender notes. That body was established by the Currency Act of 1927. The provisions made then for the issue of the Irish pound were those which prevailed until 1971. In effect, the law provided for the issue of Irish legal tender notes in exchange for gold, British legal tender, and British government securities. The Act also specified that the value of the Irish pound should be kept equal to that of the pound sterling.

As seen in Chapter 12, a way in which control is normally exercised over commercial banks is by a requirement that those banks hold specified proportions of their assets in the form of cash or as deposits with the central bank. The Currency Act of 1927 did not impose such a requirement. One reason was that Irish commercial banks operated inside the State and in Northern Ireland. This meant that in the absence of further controls they could alter the balance of their activities between the Irish Free State and Northern Ireland independently of the monetary authorities in either, provided they had the funds to do so. In that respect the banks' activities in the Free State were similar to the regional activities of a British bank: in much the same way as a British bank could decide to expand its lending in Scotland by curbing that in other regions, so also an Irish bank could decide to lend relatively more (or less) in the Free State. Thus the position in Ireland in the 1920s and 1930s was one in which the commercial banks operated more or less independently of the official sector.

The Central Bank Act of 1942 provided for the establishment of the Central Bank of Ireland (set up in 1943) as the principal monetary authority in the State, transferred to it the duties of the Currency Commission (including the obligation to maintain the sterling link) and conferred on the Bank certain additional duties and powers. However, these fell short of those usual for a central bank: the Central Bank of Ireland did not, under the 1942 Act, acquire custody of the reserves of the commercial banks; the Bank of Ireland remained banker to the government; also, the 1942 Act gave the new Central Bank little statutory power by which it might attempt to control the volume of credit. It was not until 1971 that the Bank was given a large array of additional powers, and thereby assumed the form characterised by central banks elsewhere.

The Central Bank Act of 1942 gave the new body 'the general function and duty of taking (within the limit of the powers for the time being vested in it by law) such steps as the Board may from time to time deem appropriate and advisable towards safeguarding the integrity of the currency and ensuring that, in what pertains to the control of credit, the constant and predominant aim shall be the welfare of the people as a whole'. This section of the Act is still in force. Apart from being responsible for the issue of legal tender, the Bank was authorised to accept deposits from the government and the commercial banks. It could also act as a clearing agency for the commercial banks (an agency through which debts between commercial banks are settled) and could rediscount approved securities held by them. The last-mentioned power conferred on the Central Bank by the 1942 Act refers to the Bank in its capacity of lender of last resort: under the Act, the Bank was empowered to give sterling to the commercial banks in exchange for acceptable securities, such as Irish government Exchequer Bills. (A *bill* is a short-term bond — a paper claim representing a loan over short periods of time, paying the owner at redemption date a fixed rate of interest. A bill is discounted or rediscounted when, at some time before redemption date, it is sold for cash. The difference between the face value of the bill — the sum that will be paid to the owner at redemption date — and the amount realised if it is sold before redemption date, is the discount or rediscount rate, expressed as a percentage per annum on the face value of the bill.)

Most of the powers which the Central Bank acquired under the 1942 Act were not immediately put into effect, but were implemented only gradually after 1955. The picture which emerges, then, is that until the late 1950s the Irish banking system operated in much the same manner as it did in the years before World War II.

Commercial Bank Reserves and the Beginnings of Monetary Control, 1955-68.

During most of the period 1942-55 there was little change in the composition of the financial sector. It included eight commercial banks which were called the *Associated banks* within the terms of the Central Bank Act, 1942, and which were, together with the Post Office Savings Bank and building societies, by far the largest institutions in the deposit-taking sector. In addition, the financial sector included a few small savings banks, instalment credit companies, insurance companies and two State-owned development institutions — the Agricultural Credit Corporation (providing credit, on easy terms, for agriculture) and the Industrial Credit Company (providing credit, on easy terms, for industry).

Unlike their counterparts in other countries, the Associated banks — the principal commercial banks — did not in the period under review hold their reserves mainly in the form of Irish currency or (what is essentially the same thing) as deposits at the Central Bank of Ireland. The Irish economy had earned large amounts of sterling during World War II, when our exports helped feed the UK and when we could import little from there (because UK production was oriented to the war effort). Most of these sterling earnings became deposits in — and hence assets of — the Associated banks, which converted them into interesting-earning assets in the UK. These took the form of money on call and at short notice in London, and British government Treasury Bills, along with medium-term and long-term British government securities. Most of these assets could be readily converted into British currency, and hence (given the sterling link as in the 1927 and 1942 Acts) into the Irish pound on a one-for-one basis. Thus the commercial banks held the bulk of their reserves as external assets (in the UK) rather than as cash or Central Bank deposits in Ireland.

Deposits at the Associated banks are liabilities open to be drawn on at any time for conversion into cash or for making external payments. The Associated banks therefore had to relate their reserves — largely external assets — to their deposits in the State in determining the safe limits to which they could extend credit. Up to 1955 their reserves were so large that the only real limit to the banks' credit activities in the Republic was the number of what they considered credit-worthy borrowers and the availability of what they deemed sound investments yielding returns comparable to those available in the UK. The large current account balance of payments deficit (£35 million) in 1955, following on a succession of smaller deficits in earlier years for the first time substantially lowered the liquidity of the Associated banks.

A result was that for the first time, in 1955, the Associated banks had to resort to the rediscounting facilities of the Central Bank. Thus the Central Bank did not act as lender of last resort until 1955, when it rediscounted bills for the Associated banks. In view of the changes in the position in regard to their reserves, the Associated banks then adopted the practice of consciously relating their net external assets to their deposits in the Republic. The resulting *external assets ratio* — the ratio of Associated bank net external assets to their deposit liabilities in the Republic — has often been regarded as a reserve ratio (a ratio of reserve assets to deposit liabilities). In fact not all of the Associated banks' net external assets — which included buildings in Northern Ireland — were liquid (in the sense that they could quickly be converted into cash without undergoing substantial losses); for this reason they should not have been regarded as reserves. It is true, however, that the bulk of the more liquid assets of the Associated banks in this period were claims on the British government — they were external assets.

The Central Bank does not seem to have taken the initiative in the developments just described. The first official references to the possible policy relevance of an external assets ratio (as defined above) were in the Central Bank *Report* for 1957/58 and in the Department of Finance study *Economic Development,* also published in 1958. The latter referred to a ratio of 30 per cent between their net external assets and total domestic deposit liabilities which the Associated banks should strive to maintain. In the late 1950s and in the early 1960s, both the Department of Finance and the Central Bank came to regard an external assets ratio of 30 per cent as something *akin to* a reserve ratio for the Associated banks. Although it was felt that they should strive to maintain this ratio the Central Bank did not have the statutory power to enforce it.

The decade after 1958 saw reduction in the external assets ratio of the Associate banks and transfers of a large part of such assets to the Central Bank. One means by which that occurred was through increase in the note issue and the corresponding transfer of sterling from the Associated banks to the Central Bank.

In 1958 the Central Bank exercised its right, by virtue of the 1942 Act, to require the Associated banks to settle their clearances through the Bank. The advantage to the Bank of doing this was that its assets were augmented by the sterling the banks had to deposit with it in order to obtain their clearing balances.

The Central Bank, under the 1942 Act, could accept deposits from the government, public authorities, or any Irish bank. Originally it was not allowed pay interest on such deposits, but the Central Bank (Amendment) Act of 1964 empowered it to do so. As a result balances kept by Associated banks at the Central Bank greatly increased. They were no longer just clearing balances. They soon became reserves. As such deposits grew the inadequacy of the original 30 per cent external assets ratio, as a guide to bank liquidity, became more apparent. From the standpoint of an Associated bank a balance which it held at the Central Bank was similar to an external asset which it could convert into sterling, since both were assets which it could use to obtain Irish currency at the Central Bank. Accordingly, in 1965, the external assets ratio was amended so that balances with the Central Bank could be included with external assets in the numerator of what became known as the *Central Bank Ratio*. That was the ratio of the net external assets of the Associated banks, plus their deposits at the Central Bank less rediscounted Exchequer Bills, to the domestic deposit liabilities of the Associated banks.

Apart from the recommendations in 1958 that the Associated banks should strive to keep a 30 per cent net external assets ratio, little attempt was made by the Central Bank to influence their credit policy until 1965. Bank credit expanded very rapidly during the years 1963-65 and imports increased relative to exports. The external assets ratio fell steadily and by May 1965 stood at 17·6 per cent. In these circumstances the banks sought the advice of the Central Bank in regard to credit policy. This was a new development in Irish banking practice. The bank duly gave its advice and continued to do so in subsequent years. However, such advice was only moral suasion without effective formal backing; the Associated banks did not have to adhere to it. Until the 1970s such moral suasion was the main policy instrument which the Central Bank employed in seeking to control the volume of credit.

In formulating credit advice in the later 1960s the Central Bank focused on the Central Bank Ratio (which was a variable rather than a fixed percentage) and the total amount of new lending by the Associated banks. It also repeatedly requested that, in considering applications for credit, the Associated banks should give priority to applications of a productive nature and, within that category, to purposes directly related to the expansion of exports. Thus the Bank in effect influenced the Associated banks to ration target changes in credit in favour of productive rather than consumption or speculative uses.

The potentially adverse impact of credit expansion on our balance of international payments was a major concern of monetary policy in the later 1960s. It may be wondered why, in the period under review, the Central Bank did not use policy instruments other than moral suasion. In this context we must recall that until 1971 the Bank did not have statutory power to impose minimum reserve, or liquidity, ratios on the banks. The 1942 Act had given the Bank statutory powers to conduct open market operations. However, the openness of the economy to capital movements to and from the UK (with which we had a fixed exchange rate) would have placed great limitations on the extent to which the Central Bank of Ireland could have pursued independent interest rate and money stock policies by way of re-discount rate and open market operations. Largely for those reasons the Central Bank, in the period under review, did not engage in open market operations.

The Growth of Financial Institutions and Problems of Control

Until the 1960s the Associated banks were virtually the only sources of ordinary credit to the private sector. At the time of the Central Bank Act, 1942, these were eight in number, but following a series of amalgamations in the 1960s the Associated banks were reduced to four groups — Allied Irish Banks, the Bank of Ireland, the Northern Bank and the Ulster Bank. During the 1960s a large number of other credit providers appeared on the Irish banking scene. These are loosely called the non-Associated banks.

The non-Associated banks are composed of subsidiaries and affiliates of the Associated banks, branches of North American banks, and other banks, many of them affiliated with financial institutions abroad. The non-Associated banks, in addition to carrying on the traditional business of banking, entered fields in which the Associated banks did not operate to the same extent, or at all. All four categories of the non-Associated banks (mentioned below) tend to have assets in Ireland in excess of their liabilities in Ireland; they tend, that is, to be net external borrowers. The four categories of the non-Associated banks are as follows:

Merchant banks tend to tailor loans of large sums to the requirements of their customers. They also offer advice on mergers and take-overs, and manage portfolios on behalf of large investors. The *North American banks* also tend to deal only in relatively large sums; however, they do engage in traditional deposit-taking banking and in this respect they compete with the Associated banks. The *industrial banks* engage in instalment credit, the finance of foreign trade and company finance. The final category is termed by the Central Bank '*other banks*'; this includes banks from continental Europe as well as domestic banks.

The non-Associated banking sector expanded very rapidly in the late 1960s. At the end of 1969 the total amount of credit outstanding from the major financial institutions was in the region of £800 million. Of that sum, credit extended by the Associated banks amounted to over £600 million, while lending by the non-Associated banks amounted to about £150 million. In the two years 1968-69, non-Associated bank credit practically doubled, while during the same period credit from the Associated banks grew by little more than two-fifths.

The non-Associated banks acquire funds from the private sector and from abroad which in turn are lent to other borrowers. Although by means of 'advice' the Central Bank sought to control the activities of the Associated banks after 1965, the credit-creation activities of the non-Associated banks for some years remained exempt from the Bank's credit-creation guidelines. But, as we have seen, by 1969 the non-Associated banks were an important component of the banking system. Also, in contrast to the Associated banks, a major part of their business was and still is concerned with accepting money from abroad and re-investing it in Ireland. By the effect of their operations on the international mobility of short-term funds, they caused fluctuations in the liquidity of the Associated banks, and consequently in their ability to lend. That can be seen as follows: suppose a non-Associated bank accepted deposits from abroad. It could transform such foreign deposits into Irish currency and lend that cash in Ireland. At least some part of such loans would almost surely end up as deposits in an Associated bank, thereby increasing the liquid assets (reserves) of that bank. The reverse could occur when there was an outflow of foreign deposits from a non-Associated bank.

Until April 1969 the credit advice of the Central Bank was directed exclusively toward the Associated banks. In that year the Bank extended advice in regard to external capital flows to the non-Associated banks and in 1971 quantitative guidelines on their lending similar to those applied to the Associated banks were introduced. This became necessary because, in the words of the Central Bank, 'as the scale of their operations has grown, it has become more difficult to distinguish between them and the Associated Banks as regards the monetary effects of increases in their domestic liabilities'. [1] By 1971, then, the Central Bank was giving credit advice to all of the principal banking institutions in the private sector. However, *such advice had no effective backing in legislation.*

Given that the Central Bank had no legal power to ensure that the banks would adhere to its credit advice, it should not be surprising that its advice in the years immediately after 1965 had very limited success. For example, in reviewing the outcome of credit policy for 1970-71 the Central Bank noted that the increase in total lending by the Associated banks at £130 million was £55 million in excess of that advised. [2] Some £85 million of such lending was extended to the private sector and this was largely brought about by borrowing in excess of overdraft permissions and by an increase in the degree to which such permissions were utilised.

The difficulty of the Associated banks in quickly implementing the Central Bank's credit advice was partly due to the overdraft system of lending which then prevailed. Under that system there was typically a large volume of unutilised overdraft permissions outstanding at any one time. Thus the actual use made of permissions to borrow was largely at the discretion of bank customers and escaped attempts to control credit which—in the short run—could affect only the issuing of new permissions to borrow. The Central Bank accordingly announced, early in 1970, that the Associated banks would gradually replace the majority of existing overdrafts with negotiated term contracts subject to specific terms of reduction. Overdrafts would remain, but for strictly seasonal purposes—capable of being repaid within a year.

Centralisation of Reserves and Related Matters
We already observed that until the late 1960s the Associated banks held the bulk of their reserves in the form of external assets (in the UK) rather than in cash or Central Bank deposits in Ireland. For this reason the Associated banks held a large share of Ireland's foreign exchange reserves. Thus the Central Bank was a bankers' bank to a limited extent only. Also, Ireland departed from standard international practice in not having its central bank as the primary holder of the nations' foreign currency reserves. However, the 1960s brought substantial changes in the position of the Bank in both of these respects.

The decade after 1958 saw reduction in the external assets ratio of the Associated banks and transfers of sterling to the Central Bank. One way in which that occurred was through increase in the Irish note issue and (since Irish currency notes could be issued only in exchange for gold, British currency and British government securities) the resulting transfer of sterling from the Associated banks to the Central Bank. In 1958 the sterling assets of the Bank were increased by virtue of the requirement that the Associated banks would have to maintain clearing deposits at the Bank. In 1964 the Central Bank (Amendment) Act enabled the Bank to pay interest on deposits with it by government, local authorities and Irish banks; in consequence the Associated banks began to maintain some of their reserves as deposits at the Bank rather than in the form of liquid claims on London. The year 1964 also saw the transfer to the Bank of most of the external assets of the Post Office Savings Bank and of other (government) Departmental Funds.

In 1969 the Central Bank announced that the evolution of the banking system which it desired involved progress towards *two major objectives:* (i) Greater centralisation of external reserves. (ii) The extension of internal sources of liquidity for the banking system. The Bank accordingly improved the facilities it offered for deposits of short-term money. Among the advantages pertaining to these moves was the fact that if the Irish financial sector centralised in a Dublin money market the money at call and short notice (i.e., highly liquid short-term assets) relating to its business in the Republic which it held externally, the fund of assets so centralised could be invested in a spectrum of external assets and not just mainly in money at call and short notice in London as had previously been the case. This could increase the aggregate interest returns to the economy from external assets.

Objective (i) was attained by 1970. Until 1969 the Associated banks, as already seen, kept a large amount of their funds in London and relied largely on the London money market for their liquidity. In December 1967 their net external assets were about £130 million. In November 1968 they credited £40 million in external assets to the Central Bank in return for a *contra* credit in Irish currency. In August 1969 the Associated banks deposited about £73 million in sterling at the Central Bank in connection with the centralisation of reserves at the Bank. Part of this transfer was an increase in the banks' demand and short-term balances at the Bank. As a result, liquid external holdings of the Associated banks are now mere working balances. They now turn to the Central Bank's rediscount facilities when they run short of domestic sources of liquidity. The first admission by the Bank that it had used rediscounting at a penal rate was in its *Quarterly Bulletin* for the Spring of 1970. That was because it deemed that the banks' difficulties arose due to their failure to follow the Bank's credit advice.[3]

As a result of the changes reported above, the Central Bank became a bankers' bank in a more meaningful sense than previously. It also became the custodian of the nation's foreign exchange reserves.

The Government's Bank

Around 1970 the Central Bank of Ireland took up another function of central banks in other countries — that of banker to the government and the management of government debt. In 1969 it took over, from the Department of Finance, responsibility for the issue of three month Exchequer Bills (the principal media by which the State borrows on the short-term). From the time the State was established until the late 1960s, government accounts had been held at the Bank of Ireland, one of the Associated banks, which was also in charge of the issue of government stock. In the late 1960s the Central Bank took over the management of National Loans. In the Spring of 1970 it announced that arrangements had been made with the Bank of Ireland under which there would be a phased transfer of government accounts to the Central Bank, and provision for this was made in legislation in the following year. Thus the Central Bank of Ireland is now the government's bank.

The Central Bank Act, 1971

The Central Bank Act, 1971, contained extensive provision for the licensing and supervision of banks by the Central Bank, and made important changes in the laws governing banking. Until the 1971 Act a person engaged in the business of banking required a licence from the Revenue Commissioners, which could be obtained without any strings attached. As a result there was virtually no control over the establishment of new banks in Ireland. By the 1971 Act a person wishing to carry on banking in Ireland requires a licence from the Central Bank. The granting of the licence is discretionary. The Central Bank can impose conditions in relation to a licence. Furthermore, anyone wishing to engage in banking has to maintain a substantial deposit at the Central Bank. The overall effect is to provide tighter control than previously on the establishment of new banks and on the operation of all banking concerns. The Act also empowers the Central Bank to require bankers to maintain specified ratios between their assets and their liabilities. Specified ratios can be expressed in terms of total assets and liabilities or particular assets and liabilities, and the Bank has power to vary the specified ratios from time to time. The background to the conferral of these powers was as follows:

In its *Report* for 1968-69 the Bank noted that the Central Bank Ratio did not reflect the liquidity position of the Associated banks, and that there were two sets of circumstances which warranted a formal liquidity ratio, or liquidity ratios:

(i) The difficulty of implementing a quantitative limit on bank credit in the absence of a controlling influence on bank liquidity. The Central Bank Act, 1942, had not given the Bank the power to force the Associated banks to keep minimum ratios between liquid assets and deposit liabilities; it had to rely on moral suasion in its attempts to control the volume of credit.

(ii) The unsuitability of the Central Bank Ratio as a measure of bank liquidity, particularly in the context of the increasing availability and use of domestic assets as liquid reserves. Although the banks had begun to hold short-term Irish government stocks and bills as part of their liquid assets, none of them were reflected in the Central Bank Ratio.

The minimum liquidity ratios now enforced by the Central Bank apply to both the Associated and the non-Associated banks. There are two liquidity ratios, but before explaining what they are, some definitions are in order.

Primary Liquid Assets comprise the sum of a bank's holdings of notes and coin and its balances at the Central Bank.

Secondary Liquid Assets comprise the sum of a bank's holdings of Irish government securities, including Exchequer Bills.

Relevant Resources are the sum of a bank's current and deposit accounts and net external liability, less balances with and lending to all other commercial banks within the State.

The Primary Liquidity Ratio is the ratio of Primary Liquid Assets to Relevant Resources. At present the minimum for this ratio permitted by the Central Bank is 13 per cent for Associated Banks, North American Banks, and Merchant Banks, and 10 per cent for Industrial Banks and Other Banks.

The *Secondary Liquidity Ratio* is the ratio of Secondary Liquid Assets to Relevant Resources. At present the minimum for this ratio prescribed by the Central Bank is 30 per cent for Associated Banks and 10 per cent for all other commercial banks.

By varying these ratios the Central Bank could seek to affect the volume of credit in Ireland. The objective of the two ratios differs. The main purpose of the Primary Liquidity Ratio is to ensure that the banks are able to meet their customers' day-to-day demands for cash. The Secondary Liquidity Ratio, on the other hand, is a means of guaranteeing demand for government securities.

Apart from requiring the commercial banks to maintain those two liquidity ratios, the Central Bank (by virtue of its powers under the 1971 Act) has from time to time announced steps to curb the inflow of foreign funds into the banking system, thereby controlling further expansion of credit. For example, in June 1977 the Bank announced that the banks would have to deposit with the Central Bank 50 per cent of any increased foreign capital inflow and that such special deposits at the Bank might not attract commercial rates of interest. In making regulations of this kind, inflows to finance industrial projects have been exempted from the special deposits requirement.

The 1971 Act enabled the Irish pound to be issued in exchange for currencies other than sterling. Under the Currency Act, 1927, and the Central Bank Act, 1942, the Irish pound had to be maintained at a one-to-one exchange rate with the pound sterling. This effective statutory requirement to value the Irish pound in terms of sterling was also terminated by the 1971 Act. In March 1979 we formally broke the 'link with sterling' when we joined EMS.

Conclusion

In the few years 1965-72 the Central Bank moved from a position of being little more than the issuer of legal tender in a monetary system in which private financial institutions operated largely independently of the official sector to an institution which began to conduct, in greater or lesser degree, all of the main functions generally attributed to a central bank, namely, government's bank, bankers' bank, issuer of legal tender (and insofar as is possible in an open economy under fixed exchange rates, controller of the money supply) and lender of last resort. This change in status of the Central Bank brought with it a package of additional policy instruments for possible use by the central authorities.

Despite these institutional changes and additional powers, the analysis of the preceding chapter on the role of monetary policy in a small open economy under a fixed exchange rate with a large country still substantively holds. Until March 1979 we maintained a fixed exchange rate with the UK—though after 1971 we were no longer required to do so by statute. So long as we kept that fixed exchange rate, and in the absence of rigid controls on international capital movements, the structure of interest rates in the Republic had to move closely with that of the UK. However, it seems that there was some narrow band around UK interest rates within which Irish rates could fluctuate in response to domestic monetary conditions without inducing major capital movements. The Central Bank could pursue independent interest rate policies only subject to the constraints of that band. For that and other reasons the Central Bank of Ireland, under a fixed exchange rate, can have little long-term effect on the domestic money supply. Note that it was not the sterling link *per se* which limited our ability to pursue independent interest rate and monetary policies. In the long run the limiting factor was and is a fixed exchange rate — regardless of the large country with which we maintain a fixed exchange rate. It follows from Chapter 16 that if we do want to add substantially to the potency of monetary policy in Ireland, we must allow our exchange rate to float freely against all major currencies. But we also saw in Chapter 16 that the potency of fiscal policy would be diminished. For the reasons just mentioned it is mainly by influencing the *structure* of credit — discouraging credit to finance consumption or speculation, and discriminating in favour of investors — that the Central Bank, under a fixed exchange rate, is most likely to be in a position to promote the economic growth of the nation. Finally, it should be clear from Chapter 16 that the principal role of monetary policy under fixed exchange rates is in affecting the level of the economy's foreign exchange reserves.

Suggested Reading

Central Bank of Ireland, *Annual Reports* and *Quarterly Bulletins.*

Gibson, N. J., 'The Banking System', Chapter 7 in Gibson, N. and Spencer, J. (eds), *Economic Activity in Ireland: A Study of Two Open Economies,* Dublin 1977.

O'Donoghue, Martin, 'Monetary Policy', Chapter 4 in Bristow, J. and Tait, A. (eds.), *Economic Policy in Ireland,* Dublin 1968.

O'Mahony, David, *The Irish Economy,* 2nd ed, Cork 1967, Chapter 4.

FOOTNOTES

1. Central Bank of Ireland, *Report 1970-71,* 40.
2. *Ibid.,* 43.
3. Central Bank of Ireland, *Quarterly Bulletin,* Spring 1970, 78.

CHAPTER 18

Public Finance in Ireland

In most economies fiscal policy plays a role in promoting growth and, in the short run, in stabilising income and employment. We have examined the theory underlying short-run fiscal policy. This chapter is descriptive.

The Public Sector
The public sector in Ireland consists of central government, local authorities and agencies or enterprises commonly called semi-state bodies.

Semi-state bodies engage in three kinds of activity: they provide public utilities (as in the case of the ESB, CIE and Aer Lingus), they engage in manufacturing and trade (Comhlucht Siúicre Eireann is an example) or they engage in other activities which it is felt are best left to the public sector — the Industrial Development Authority (IDA) is an example. Some of them are financed entirely by central government; others are largely or entirely self-financing.

Local authorities (such as county councils and Dublin Corporation) engage locally in activities such as construction of housing, construction and repair of subsidiary roads, provision of water and sewage facilities, rubbish disposal, and to some extent in provision of education and health services. Grants and loans from central government are their main sources of finance.

Central government provides social security, defence, and law and order. It also transfers large sums in grants to local authorities and semi-state bodies. Its expenditure is financed mainly by taxation and borrowing. Virtually all of the State's receipts are paid into a fund called *the Exchequer* — the State money box. Also, almost all of the money required by the State to make payments is withdrawn from the Exchequer.

The Budget
The annual Budget is a statement of central government's expenditure programmes. It also indicates how it is intended to finance those expenditures.

The *Current Budget* is concerned with central government current revenues and expenditures. Current revenues consist of receipts from taxation and from provision by central government of services such as those of the Department of Posts and Telegraphs, plus miscellaneous current receipts. Current expenditures are outlays on activities other than the creation of capital assets. They consist largely of wage and salary payments to the Civil Service, the army and the police, and transfer payments such as interest on money borrowed by central government and unemployment assistance. In Ireland the budget is said to be *balanced* if current revenue is equal to current expenditure — note that this convention diverges from that of other countries.

The *Capital Budget* includes all expenditures financed by the Exchequer other than those which are part of the Current Budget. What is called the *Public Capital Programme* accounts for almost the entire Capital Budget on the expenditure side. Much of expenditure under the Capital Budget is financed by Exchequer borrowing. However, the Public Capital Programme also includes items financed from internal resources of semi-state bodies and from borrowing on the market by those bodies, as well as some capital expenditures financed by local authorities. The Public Capital Programme plays an important role in the country's investment and, consequently, in its long-term growth. It accounts for about one-half of national fixed investment.

Principal Classes of Central Government Revenue and Expenditure

Table 12 outlines the principal classes of central government current expenditure.

Most of the entries in Table 12 are self explanatory. Service of Public Debt refers mainly to interest on monies borrowed by central government. Other entries pertain to remuneration of public servants, or to expenditures on goods and services or in the form of transfer payments, by the respective government departments. Public services remuneration comprises the pay of civil servants, national and secondary school teachers, the defence forces, police, and the Exchequer contribution to the pay of health board employees and vocational teachers. The only other item in Table 12 needing comment is 'Payments relating to Own Resources of EEC'. Under EEC arrangements receipts from customs duties under the Common External Tariff of the EEC and from agricultural levies constitute 'Own Resources' and

Table 12

Current Government Expenditure, 1977, £ Million

Service of Public Debt	403·3
Social Services	840·1
Social Welfare, Health	584·3
Education	255·8
Economic Services	217·4
Agriculture, Forestry, Fisheries	121·1
Industry and Energy	38·5
Tourism, Transport and Power	57·8
General Services	294·8
Post Office	88·9
Defence and Justice	152·1
Public Service Pensions	53·8
Payments relating to Own Resources of EEC	24·7
Other Current Expenditure	178·1
Total	1958·4

Source: Pre-Budget Tables 1978, Dublin: Stationery Office, Prl. 6874.

are payable by Member States to the EEC. Government current expenditure increased at a rapid rate in recent years. In 1972 it came to 20 per cent of GNP; the figure for 1977 was 36 per cent of GNP. Table 13 indicates how the expenditure in Table 12 was financed. It shows that the most important taxes in Ireland are Income Tax, Customs and Excise Duties, and Value Added Tax.

Before Ireland joined the EEC there was a wider variety of duties than at present imposed on imported goods. Although all had the effect of raising revenue, some were introduced to protect Irish industry from foreign competition; others were introduced primarily to raise revenue. However, now that we are in the EEC we have little control over the structure of our *customs duties.* That is because all Member States of the EEC are expected to maintain free trade between each other, while applying a Common External Tariff against non-EEC countries. Thus the structure of our customs duties is similar to that of other EEC countries. Apart from raising revenue for the EEC

Table 13

Central Government Current Receipts, 1977, £ Million

TAX REVENUE	
Customs and Excise	477·3
Estate, Etc., Duties	6·7
Capital Taxes	10·2
Stamp Duties	24·6
Income Tax	521·9
Corporation Tax	77·7
Value Added Tax	321·2
Agricultural Levies	9·4
Motor Vehicle Duties	32·7
Sub-Total (Total Tax Revenue)	1481.7
NON-TAX CURRENT REVENUE	
Post and Telegraphs	121·5
Surplus Income of Central Bank	23·5
Other Current Revenue	130·2
Sub-Total (Total Non-Tax Current Revenue)	275·2
Total Current Revenue	1756·9
Plus Current Budget Deficit	201·5
Equals Total Current Expenditure	1958·4

Source: Estimates of Receipts and Expenditure for the Year Ending 31 December, 1978, Dublin: Stationery Office, Prl. 6842.

under the 'Own Resources' system, an objective of the customs duties at present in force in Ireland is to protect goods made in the EEC from non-EEC competition.

Excise duties are imposed on a smaller variety of goods than in the case of customs duties. The raising of revenue is the main objective of these duties. They are directed toward 'old reliables'—tobacco, beer, spirits and hydrocarbon oils, the principal reason being that those commodities are price inelastic.

In different countries death duties are imposed in two general forms—estate duty or inheritance tax. The amount of estate duty due is generally arrived at by aggregating the values of properties passing at death and applying rates of duty to the aggregate value of such property. Inheritance tax is an acquisitions tax — a tax on receipt of assets. The emphasis is not on the deceased but on the beneficiaries. The rate of tax is determined for each beneficiary by his relationship to the deceased and by the value of the property received by him. In Ireland estate duties were abolished in 1975. They were replaced by the Capital Acquisitions Tax — a tax on gifts and inheritances. The entry in Table 13 of £6.7 million for receipts from *Estate, Etc., Duties* in 1977 is largely due to lags in payment of those taxes.

Three *capital taxes* were in force in Ireland at the time of the 1978 Budget. These were the Capital Acquisitions Tax to which we have just referred, the Wealth Tax, and the Capital Gains Tax. Each of these was introduced by legislation of 1975. The Wealth Tax was abolished as from April 1978. A capital gains tax is on the increase in the value of an asset between the dates at which it is bought and later sold. Various kinds of capital gain — such as the increase in the value of a principal private residence — are exempt from the tax. In 1977 *Stamp Duties* yielded more revenue than capital taxes. These are duties from stamping documents such as deeds, which are invalid without stamps.

More than one-third of tax revenue is raised by *Income Tax.* The amount of income tax payable was estimated, until 1974, by application of a Standard Tax Rate to a tax base known as Taxable Income. In 1973 and in the immediately preceding years this standard rate was 35 per cent of Taxable Income. The Sur-Tax system, which involved application of many tax rates depending on income, was a separate tax structure. The income tax code was revised in 1974 when both Sur-Tax and the Standard Tax Rate were abolished, being replaced by the present system involving several tax rates, with higher rates applied to higher bands of taxable income.

Until recently company profits were subject to Income Tax and Corporation Profits Tax. Income tax on companies, along with the Corporation Profits Tax, were abolished in 1976, and replaced by a single company profits tax, called *Corporation Tax.* Company profits are taxed at different rates depending partly on the amount of profits being assessed for tax.

Before 1972 sales taxation comprised two taxes, the retail *Turnover Tax* which was a general tax on sales, and the *Wholesale Tax* which applied to a limited range of goods only. These taxes, which had been introduced in the 1960s, were abolished in 1972 and transformed into the *Value Added Tax,* which is levied at different rates on different categories of goods and services. The principal objective in this shift to value added taxes was to bring Ireland's tax system more into line with those of the EEC, which Ireland was about to enter. The meaning of value added taxes is simple. In the course of production and distribution, goods pass through several stages before reaching the consumer. At each stage value is added — it comprises the payments to factors of production in the form of wages, rent, interest and profit. This is the 'value added' which is taxable under a value added tax. Each taxpayer arrives at his liability by first taking the full amount charged by him for taxable goods sold or taxable services rendered and applying the rate of value added tax appropriate thereto. From the resultant sum he deducts the value added tax already paid on goods and services he has bought. The difference is the tax payable to the Revenue Commissioners.

Agricultural Levies are special charges on import of food from non-EEC countries. The final item under Tax Revenue in Table 13 — *Motor Vehicle Duties* — consists of driving licence fees and taxes levied on vehicles.

The items needing comment under Non-Tax Current Revenue in Table 13 are *Surplus Income of the Central Bank* and *Other Current Revenue.* The surplus income of the Central Bank is akin to the distributed profits of a private company, with the Exchequer as sole shareholder. Interest from the Bank's holdings of British and US government securities has been the principal source of this income. The final revenue item in Table 13 — Other Current Revenue — includes interest from loans by the Exchequer to semi-state bodies and fees for services provided by central government, such as broadcasting licence fees and the issue of passports.

The Public Capital Programme

Expenditure under the Capital Budget came to £691 million in 1977. Some £658·5 million was under the Public Capital Programme; the residual £32·5 million was under 'other' Capital Budget expenditure. Table 14 summarises the Programme in 1977.

The table indicates that *Building and Construction* is by far the largest component of the Public Capital Programme. Within that category expenditure under Housing is by far the largest single element (£100 million in 1977). It includes construction of local authority dwellings, provision of grants by local authorities for erection and reconstruction of housing, and loans by local authorities for house purchase. Building and Construction also includes provision of new

Table 14
Public Capital Programme, 1977, £ million

Building and Construction	2/3·5
Ports, Harbours and Airports	4·4
Tourism	2·7
Agriculture and Lands	31·9
Loan Finance for Agriculture	84·9
Forestry and Fisheries	10·8
Energy	70·8
Telephones	50·5
Transport	27·0
Industry	120·3
Loan Finance for Industry	37·3
Miscellaneous (RTE, etc.)	4·4
Total	658·5

Source: *Public Capital Programme 1978*, Dublin: Stationery Office, Prl. 6875.

sanitary facilities and construction and improvement of educational buildings and hospitals. Expenditure on *Ports, Harbours and Airports* mainly consists of investment connected with improvement of facilities at those locations. Grants administered by Bord Fáilte related to construction and improvement of holiday accommodation are included under *Tourism*.

Capital expenditure on *Agriculture* includes cattle disease eradication schemes, subsidies to encourage farmers to use more fertilizers, grants for drainage schemes, and grants for construction, repair and conversion of farm buildings and for provision of piped water systems. The allocation under *Lands* includes the cost of lands sold to the Land Commission under the EEC scheme designed to encourage people to leave farming. *Loan Finance for Agriculture* relates to loans made by the Agricultural Credit Corporation (ACC). The ACC gives loans to farmers for the purchase of livestock, land purchase and improvement, erection of farm buildings and dwellings and the purchase of farm machinery, seeds and fertilizers. The ACC also makes loans to processing firms such as creameries, meat factories and grain millers. The allocation under *Forestry* includes the cost of acquiring and preparing land for forest development. Expenditure under *Fisheries* is largely on provision of grants and loans to fishermen for fishing vessels and equipment as well as providing for facilities such as ice plants.

Investment by the ESB is the principal item under *Energy*. Also included is capital expenditure by Bord na Móna on expansion of peat moss production and development of bogs for electricity generation. The allocation under *Telephones* is on installation of new telephones, enlargement of exchanges, extension of automatic working to new areas, etc. Included under *Transport* are capital expenditures by the publicly owned air companies, by CIE, and by Irish Shipping and the British and Irish Steampacket Company.

Capital expenditure under *Industry* in the Public Capital Programme relates to a variety of projects in the semi-state and private sectors. It provides for capacity expansion in semi-state bodies such as Irish Steel Holdings, Nitrigin Éireann, Gaeltarra Éireann and Comhlucht Siúicre Éireann. However, the bulk of the expenditure under Industry is on allocations to the IDA and the Shannon Free Airport Development Company (SFADCO).

The IDA has the following functions under the Industrial Development Act, 1969: (i) to act as a body having national responsibility for the furtherance of industrial development; (ii) to provide and administer such grants and other financial facilities for industry as it may be authorised by the Oireachtas to provide and to administer; (iii) to develop, construct, maintain and administer industrial estates and factory buildings (other than at Shannon Customs Free Airport), and (iv) to foster regional industrial development.

The Exchequer provides almost all of the IDA's funding: in 1976 capital expenditure by the IDA came to £53·7 million; £51 million of this came from the Exchequer. Grants to encourage native and foreign firms to invest in industrial projects are the dominant component of the IDA's capital expenditure; in 1976 some £45·9 million of its total capital expenditure was absorbed by such grants. SFADCO, which has functions in the area around Shannon similar to those of the IDA in the country at large, is also financed mainly by the Exchequer. Its allocation under Industry in the Public Capital Programme has been mainly on factory construction at Shannon and elsewhere in the Limerick-Clare-North Tipperary region and on provision of housing at Shannon.

Loan Finance for Industry has two main components — credit facilities to industry provided by the Industrial Credit Company, and financial assistance rendered by Fóir Teoranta to what are considered viable firms in temporary difficulties.

Public Sector Borrowing

When the Exchequer's current revenue falls short of its current expenditure, the resulting Current Budget deficit must be met by borrowing. We have seen that in 1977 the Current Budget deficit came to £201·5 million. The bulk of Capital Budget expenditures must also be met by borrowing—though not all of this is by the Exchequer. In 1977 the total Exchequer Borrowing Requirement came to £545 million. Since £201·5 million of this pertained to the Current Budget deficit, the remaining £343·5 million represents the contribution of borrowing by the Exchequer in financing the Capital Budget, which came, in 1977, to a total of £691 million. The remaining £347·5 million (£691 million minus £343·5 million) required to finance the Capital Budget had to come from other sources. These were largely (i) the internal resources of semi-state bodies and local authorities, and (ii) borrowing from sources other than the Exchequer by semi-state bodies and local authorities.

In Ireland what is officially called the *National Debt* represents the total debt of the Exchequer outstanding on monies which it has borrowed from all sources, both in Ireland and abroad. Thus, as officially defined in this country, the National Debt does not include that part of the debt of semi-state bodies or of local authorities which is owed by them to sources other than the Exchequer. (The debt of semi-state bodies and local authorities reflecting loans to them from the Exchequer is indirectly reflected in the official National Debt, since the Exchequer generally has to borrow in order to lend to them.) It will be clear, when account is taken of the debt of semi-state bodies and local authorities other than that due to the Exchequer, that the total public sector debt is well in excess of what is officially termed the *National Debt*.

In effect, the National Debt represents the sum of all past Current Budget deficits plus the sum of all past Exchequer borrowings to finance capital expenditure, less all repayments of such indebtedness by the Exchequer. Substantial sums in interest payments must be made each year in servicing this debt.

The Debt has risen rapidly in recent years reflecting both extensive borrowing by the Exchequer to finance capital programmes and Current Budget deficits in the 1970s. As a percentage of GNP the Debt increased from about 66 per cent in 1971 to about 90 per cent in 1977. By international standards these debt ratios are very high. Corresponding to the rapid rise in the Debt, both in absolute terms and as a percentage of GNP, there has been substantial increase in the cost of servicing the Debt — in paying interest to holders of the Debt and in making provision for repayment. The cost of servicing the National Debt (£403 million in 1977, from Table 12) is a charge on the Current Budget. The bulk of these charges consist of interest payments. From Table 13 we see that these charges came to over 75 per cent of receipts from income tax in 1977.

The Exchequer borrows from a large variety of sources in Ireland, including the Central Bank, commercial banks, insurance companies and the public. The commercial banks are in fact obliged to lend a considerable proportion of their assets to the Exchequer: recall the Secondary Liquidity Ratio which they must maintain. One consequence of the rapid increase in the government's annual borrowing requirement in recent years is that it has not been able to raise all the money at home and has had to borrow abroad: that part of our National Debt held abroad increased from £90 million at the end of 1970 to £1039 million at the end of 1977.

The servicing of the Debt involves not only the stream of service charges on the Current Budget but may also involve frictions in the economy associated with raising taxes and redistribution of income in the community. Increased taxation, needed to finance debt service charges, may lead to some loss of real output because of its disincentive effects on economic activity, even though the redistribution of income from taxpayers to recipients of interest is a domestic transfer payment as far as that part of the Debt which is held in Ireland is concerned. However, service of externally held Debt entails direct loss of real resources, because payment of interest abroad involves a foreign exchange cost, and in the long run that foreign exchange is obtained by exporting more or importing less. Thus the liability of having to pay interest abroad involves loss of potential consumption in Ireland.

Given that a large national debt may have implications of the forms just discussed, it may be wondered why the Debt was accumulated in the first place. The principal reasons are twofold:

(i) The bulk of the Public Capital Programme has been financed by borrowing rather than from current revenue. A rationale for this is that a large part of this expediture is on the creation of assets which provide flows of goods and services over time. In principle such increased production should, directly or indirectly, create the means by which the Exchequer can repay the debt incurred in creating the assets in question. But in recent years the Exchequer has generally had to borrow to repay loans.

(ii) Until the early 1970s Irish governments sought to balance the

Current Budget. If a deficit appeared in the out-turn, this was unplanned, reflecting underestimation of expenditure or over-estimation of revenue. In 1972, for the first time, the government budgeted for a Current Budget deficit. The objective was to stimulate the level of aggregate demand. We know from earlier discussion of the balanced budget multiplier that an increase in government current expenditure matched by an equal increase in tax revenue would generally have negligible effect on the economy. But to the extent that increased tax revenue falls short of increased government expenditures, the Current Budget will tend to be more expansionary. The departure in 1972 from the tradition of balancing the Current Budget was maintained in subsequent years: government sought to boost aggregate demand by planning Current Budget deficits. Hence the National Debt increased much more rapidly in the 1970s than would otherwise have been the case. However, the resulting increase in Debt service charges brought difficulties in public finance.

Classification of Taxes and Principals of Taxation

The classification of taxes is an arid subject. That most frequently made is between *direct and indirect taxes.* It is not always clear what is meant by this distinction. Before elaborating we need to explain the meaning of the *incidence* of taxation. The problem of the incidence of a tax is generally conceived as the problem of who ultimately pays it. For example, if a tax is imposed on a good, and if sellers mark up the price to fully reflect the tax, the incidence of the tax is seen to be on the buyer — assuming that he does not demand and obtain a higher wage to maintain his purchasing power.

The criterion generally employed in determining whether a tax is direct or indirect is whether the incidence is mainly on the person upon whom the tax is legally imposed. By this criterion a direct tax is borne entirely or mainly by the person upon whom it is legally imposed, while an indirect tax is imposed on one person, but paid wholly or partly by another. In short, an indirect tax is often conceived as one which can be shifted or passed on; a direct tax is one that cannot. The distinction is less clear than might be supposed. Nor is it uniform in common usage. For example, an income tax is generally regarded as a direct tax; however, the United States Supreme Court in 1868 held it to be indirect when they wished to declare it constitutionally valid.[1] But this was just the tactics of lawyers in a tight corner. Taxes on income or property are generally regarded as direct, while those on production or sale of goods and services—what we called expenditure taxes in earlier chapters—are normally classified as indirect.

There is also a distinction between *specific* and *ad valorem* taxes on goods. A specific tax is based on some physical measure such as weight or volume, for example, a tax of £x per gallon of whiskey. An *ad valorem* tax is based on a unit of value, for example, a tax of 20 per cent of the value of a certain commodity.

Four famous maxims or canons of taxation were enunciated by Adam Smith in *The Wealth of Nations*. These were (i) that taxation should be 'equal', by which he meant proportional to income; (ii) that taxes should not be uncertain or arbitrary; (iii) that the State should not exact payment in a manner inconvenient to the taxpayer, and (iv) that taxes should be economical to collect.

Most people agree with the second to fourth maxims. However, the first has been unacceptable to most in the twentieth century. Historically there have been two principal approaches to the extent to which different individuals should be assessed for payment of taxation. These may be referred to as *the benefit approach* and *the ability-to-pay approach*.

Writers in the seventeenth and eighteenth centuries tended to adopt the benefit approach; for this reason they were inclined to favour *proportional taxation*—taxation levied at rates proportional to one's income or wealth. Individuals were seen to benefit from the services provided by the State—such as the provision of defence or law and order—roughly in proportion to their income or wealth. For that reason it was argued that they should pay in proportion to their income or wealth. Thus in 1677 Sir William Petty wrote that 'it is generally allowed by all that men should contribute to the public charge but according to the share and interest they have in the public peace; that is, according to their estates and riches'.[2] A similar view reappeared a century later in Smith's *Wealth of Nations*.

Reflecting advances in marginal utility theory and changes in social philosophy, the ability-to-pay view became dominant in the late nineteenth century and remained so into the present century. Combined with the law of diminishing marginal utility as applied to income and wealth, and along with interpersonal comparisons of utility, the ability-to-pay philosophy was put forward as a rationale for *progressive taxation*—tax structures taking a higher *percentage* of their income or wealth from the rich than from the poor.

Two versions of the ability-to-pay approach can be distinguished. The first is that tax shares should be imposed in a 'just' and 'equitable' manner, somehow in accordance with the ability to pay of taxpayers. According to the second version, taxes should be imposed so as to minimise the total sacrifice involved; this is attained by equating marginal sacrifices of utility across all taxpayers.

Considerations of 'justice' aside, the notion that the ability-to-pay approach implies progressive taxation is based on the law of diminishing marginal utility and interpersonal comparisons of utility. The argument runs along the lines that for any individual the increment in total utility decreases as income increases; furthermore, it is asserted that the marginal utility of income is lower for the rich than for the poor. *If* this reasoning is correct, then in order to minimise total sacrifice entailed by taxation — to equate the marginal sacrifices of all taxpayers — high income must be taxed at higher percentage rates than low incomes. The assumption that one can legitimately make inter-personal comparisons of utility is crucial in this reasoning. It is not clear that one can logically make such comparisons. Nevertheless this is the kind of reasoning generally put forward as a rationale for progressive taxation.

The Irish income tax structure is progressive: a higher percentage of their incomes is taken from persons with high incomes than from those on low incomes. However, some indirect taxes in Ireland are *regressive*; they absorb a higher percentage of the incomes of those with low incomes than in the case of persons with high incomes. Taxes on cigarettes are probably in the regressive category.

Suggested Reading

Bristow, J. A., 'Public Finance and Fiscal Policy', Chapter 6 in Gibson, Norman, and Spencer, John (eds), *Economic Activity in Ireland: A Study of Two Open Economies,* Dublin 1977.

Budget, Stationery Office, Dublin, published annually.

FOOTNOTES

1. H. Dalton, *Public Finance,* 5th edn, London: Routledge 1929, 34.
2. William Petty, 'A Treatise of Taxes and Contributions', 1677, in C. Hull, (ed), *The Economic Writings of Sir William Petty,* Cambridge University Press 1899, Chapter 15, 91.

contrast, were years of crises and stagnation, resulting in exceptionally high emigration. In retrospect we can see that this was almost inevitable, given the emphasis on import substitution rather than export promotion, given official attitudes towards borrowing from abroad, and given our high propensity to import.

In discussing exchange rate determination in Chapter 15 we noted that a country under fixed exchange rates might pursue deflationary fiscal policies if it wished to maintain the exchange value of its currency. Deflationary fiscal policies would lead to reduction in GNP and in the volume of imports, and would hopefully arrest losses in foreign exchange reserves, thereby enabling the currency to maintain its international exchange value. To maintain the exchange value of the Irish pound, Irish governments adopted such deflationary fiscal policies in the 1950s. Due to this and other factors, growth in those years was slow.

Failure to sufficiently reorientate Irish industry and to promote adequately services such as tourism, towards export markets, after possibilities of growth via import substitution based on the small domestic market had tapered off, were major policy deficiencies of the late 1940s and early 1950s. Imports have averaged close to 50 per cent of national income at factor cost since the war. Despite import substitution, the ratio of imports to national income had increased between the 1930s and the 1950s. Owing to the high and increasing average propensity to import, and given our foreign exchange reserves in the absence of considerable foreign borrowing, increased import demand in the 1950s, necessary for, as well as generated by, growth in income, had to lead to balance of payments crises (as in 1951, 1955 and 1956) unless exports of goods and services increased sufficiently fast. Given a fixed exchange rate with the UK, fear of weak balance of payments positions, largely reflecting the lack of export orientation in our industrialisation drive, inevitably restrained the extent to which Irish governments could have pursued expansionary fiscal policies in the 1950s.

Economic Expansion

An era of outward-looking expansionary policies since the late 1950s saw reversal of the strategy of tariff and quota protection. Having established an industrial base through import substitution, the State now began to prepare industry for conditions of free trade, by way of phased tariff reductions, outright grants for the rationalisation of existing industry, and other measures. Above all, policy became overwhelmingly export oriented. More grants were made available to finance the cost of new export-geared industrial activities. A campaign was stepped up abroad to attract foreign industrialists to Ireland; these were to export the bulk of their production. Tax exemption on company profits from new or increased industrial exports had been introduced in 1956; a variant of this is still in effect. Owing to the improved performance of manufactured exports, the balance of payments on current account became less of a constraint on expansionary domestic policies, while changes in official attitudes towards foreign borrowing — both in the form of direct investment in Ireland by foreign industrialists and by way of borrowing by the State in foreign capital markets — also eased the balance of payments constraint on domestic expansion. A Free Trade Agreement was signed with the UK, effective July 1966, under which Ireland agreed to remove, over a ten-year period, all tariff and quota protection against the UK, in exchange for the immediate removal of all remaining duties on Irish industrial exports to the UK and concessions affecting Irish agricultural exports. And at the beginning of 1973, Ireland entered the freer trade environment of the EEC.

The period since the late 1950s saw, in summary:

(i) Greater realisation that economic growth would be contingent on growth of exports. Industrial development policy became much more export oriented and tourism was greatly encouraged. Fiscal incentives played major roles in those longer-term policies.

(ii) Change in official attitudes towards borrowing in the form of ownership by foreigners of industry in Ireland, or by the Irish public sector raising funds on foreign capital markets. The Control of Manufacturers Acts were amended in 1958, exempting from the operation of the Acts new export-oriented foreign-owned industry, and the remaining limitations imposed by the Acts were removed in 1964. In the mid 1960s taboos on State borrowing on foreign capital markets were cast aside.

(iii) Expansionary fiscal policies replacing those of demand deflation. *Because of the high marginal propensity to import and balance of payments constraints, such stimulation of demand, given a fixed exchange rate with the UK, would not have been possible in the absence of the changes in (i) and (ii).*

(iv) Movement towards free trade.

Due largely to the changes in (i), (ii) and (iii) — but also assisted by general expansion in world trade — Ireland experienced rapid industrial growth in the 1960s. A corollary was that emigration fell and the 1971 *Census of Population* showed that 1961-71 was the first intercensal decade since 1831-41 in which the population of (what is now) the Republic of Ireland increased.

The Role of Fiscal Policy in the Short Run, 1960-70

In order to assess just how expansionary fiscal policy was in the 1960s, we ideally need a model of the economy to compare what actually happened in any year with what would have happened in that year had there been no changes in discretionary fiscal policy instruments in that year. Such a model has been constructed elsewhere[1] and has been employed to assess, over the period 1960-70, the year-to-year effects of discretionary fiscal policy changes on two key variables: the level of real GNP and the balance of payments on current account. As the model was used to assess only *short-run* effects of fiscal policy, exports in a given year were *assumed* to be unaffected by fiscal policy changes in that year (or in previous years). Analysis with the model led to the following conclusions:

(i) Fiscal policy in the eleven years 1960-70 was, in contrast to the 1950s, quite expansionary. Real GNP increased by about 55 per cent — an average annual growth rate of 4 per cent. This is in contrast to an average annual growth rate of about 1 per cent in 1950-58. *With exports regarded as unaffected, in the short-run, by changes in fiscal policy instruments,* it was estimated that the average annual effect on real GNP of discretionary fiscal changes was an increase in real GNP of $1 \cdot 9$ per cent, that is, of the overall annual growth rate of 4 per cent, an average annual growth rate of $1 \cdot 9$ per cent can be attributed to the short-run effects of fiscal policy changes. Thus, the cumulative short-run effects on real GNP of discretionary fiscal changes account for close to one-half of the overall growth in the economy in the eleven years from 1960.

(ii) The short-run trade-off between increase in real GNP and the current account balance of payments was very unfavourable. On average, a one million pound increase in *real* GNP brought about by discretionary budget changes, was attained at a cost of an increase in the nominal current account balance of payments deficit of about a million pounds. Therefore, in the absence of foreign borrowing considerably in excess of that which actually occurred, *the expansionary fiscal policies would have foundered on balance of payments constraints had exports not been increasing rapidly.*

Current Budgets, Balanced and Unbalanced

The year-to-year role of budgetary policy, as seen by successive Ministers for Finance, has undergone some changes. Over the greater part of the post-war period it was regarded as axiomatic that the Current Budget should not show a deficit. The reasons for these views are not clear; indeed, there are reasons for feeling that Ministers for Finance did not understand the impact of the Current Budget on aggregate demand. Thus in the course of introducing the 1952 Current Budget in the Dáil the Minister for Finance stated that 'we may take it as common ground on all sides of the House that the current Budget must be balanced',[10] while on the same occasion in 1953 we find the view that 'the simple rule of health — that current expenses should be met out of current revenue — retains all its old validity'.[11] In introducing the deflationary Budget of 1957 the Minister informed the Dáil that 'the principle of the balanced Budget has been fully accepted by every Minister for Finance who has sat in these benches. This year I am resolved that it will be put fully into practice.'[12]

We know from basic theory that (i) at a given level of government current expenditure, budgeting for a surplus tends to be deflationary, while budgeting for a deficit tends to be expansionary, and (ii) a balanced budget at high levels of revenue and expenditure is more expansionary than a balanced budget at low levels of revenue and expenditure. It is not clear that these propositions have always been understood in forming Irish budgetary policy. For example, in his 1961 Budget speech the Minister for Finance remarked that 'the measures taken in 1957 to bring revenue and expenditure into line and to revive economic activity could not be fully effective at once'.[13] Here the Minister seemed to be suggesting that the deflationary policies of 1957 were expansionary. The 1966 Budget statement appears to have been the first to recognise that planned Current Budget deficits may be desirable on economic grounds. However, it was not until 1972 that the first of such Current Budget deficits was planned.

Budgetary policy affects the economy in two principal ways: (i) it affects aggregate demand, via both the Current Budget and the Public Capital Programme, and (ii) by expanding capacity under the Public Capital Programme, it increases the supply potential of the economy. Until the 1970s Ministers for Finance tended to view budgetary policy mainly under impact (ii). In the 1970s, however, the impact of budgetary policy on aggregate demand received more recognition, as governments planned Current Budget deficits to boost domestic demand in the short run.

We know from the analysis of Chapter 11 that the simple balanced budget multiplier for a closed economy is unity. However, we also saw that in the open economy of Ireland balanced budget multipliers have certainly been well below unity. But in contrast to the Current Budget (which, until the 1970s, tended to be balanced) the Public Capital Programme has been financed largely by borrowing, both at home and abroad. Thus, given the different methods of financing, the multiplier effect of public capital expenditure has probably been higher than that of current expenditure financed mainly by taxation. (Note also that a large part of the Programme — especially Building and Construction — has been on non-tradeables.) It would appear, therefore, that it was mainly through the Public Capital Programme rather than the Current Budget that fiscal policy was most deflationary in the 1950s and most expansionary since then.

Fiscal Policy, Freer Trade and Exports

A fundamental structural problem of the economy has been the fact that the industrial sector, and services, failed to expand sufficiently fast to absorb the natural increase in population, and the long-term outflow of labour from agriculture. Also, despite the build-up of tariffs and quotas, the ratio of imports to GNP increased between the 1930s and the 1950s. The high ratio between imports and national income, combined with the fact that opportunities for import substitution based on the small domestic market had tapered off by the early 1950s, meant that further growth would be contingent on export performance. Owing largely to delays in recognising this fact, the decade of the 1950s saw unusually high emigration. The emphasis then shifted, away from tariffs and quotas, towards fiscal incentives geared to trade liberalisation and export growth.

State aid to private industry in the 1930s and 1940s was confined to tariff and quota protection and provision of credit facilities. Policy in those years contained no direct subsidy to manufacturing industry. In 1949 the IDA was set up to promote the establishment of new industrial enterprises. The next step, which did not attain much immediate importance, was the formation in 1952 of An Foras Tionscal to administer a scheme of grants for the establishment of industries in designated underdeveloped areas in the west of the country. The grants scheme introduced by the 1952 Underdeveloped Areas Act was designed to compensate industrialists for disadvantages inherent in the location of their factories in the western counties; it envisaged that only where a competitive disadvantage attached to a location would the question of State aid be favourably considered. The two major locational disadvantages contemplated at that time were transport costs and labour training costs. While it was intended that grants would help to compensate for such competitive disadvantages, it was still recognised that tariff protection against external competition would continue to be the major form of help. Córas Tráchtála — the Irish Export Board — was also set up in 1952 to promote exports.

The Industrial Grants Act, 1956, which empowered the IDA to give grants for new industrial projects located outside the underdeveloped areas, had two broad objectives: to arrest the rising trend in emigration through expansion of industrial employment, and improvement of the balance of payments position through both import substitution and increased industrial exports. The year 1956 also saw the introduction of a scheme of tax exemption of company profits from new or increased industrial exports.

In 1958, the first *Programme for Economic Expansion*[14] — a five-year plan covering the years 1959 to 1963 — in reviewing government policy for promoting industrial development, highlighted two facets of it which had come to demand greater emphasis than in the past. The Programme document emphasised the view that further industrial growth would have to be based largely on export markets rather than import substitution and stated that, while the development of industry under Irish ownership would continue to be fostered, foreign investment would be welcome where it was likely to result in increased industrial exports. In line with this policy, the industrial tax concessions introduced in 1956 were extended; also, new industries manufacturing mainly for export were exempted from the restrictions imposed by the Control of Manufactures Acts, and increased financial resources were made available to the Industrial Credit Company to give greater credit assistance to industry.

The Industrial Grants Act, 1959, provided that industrial grants could be given towards the establishment of projects located outside the underdeveloped areas where there were sound reasons why they should not be located in the West, or where they would be of exceptional national importance because of their size or export potential. It also transferred the administration of those grants from the IDA to An Foras Tionscal, which was already administering grants in the underdeveloped areas, thereby enabling the IDA to concentrate on promotion. (Subsequently, by legislation of 1969, An Foras Tionscal and the former IDA were merged into the new IDA.) The Act provided, for the first time outside the underdeveloped areas, that an existing concern embarking on an extension of its productive capacity could qualify for a grant in the same way as if it were a completely new enterprise.

The development of the Shannon Industrial Estate is also worthy of note. Shannon Airport had been customs-free since 1947, when legislation was enacted to enable the establishment at the airport of manufacturing, processing and warehousing. But no progress was made with the development of the area as an industrial centre until 1957/59, when SFADCO was set up and further legislation was enacted to provide the company with the necessary powers and finance, from State sources, to develop an industrial estate at the airport.

In 1963 a report of the Committee on Industrial Organisation (CIO) suggested that decentralisation of industry should be fostered through the promotion of a small number of industrial development centres. The Industrial Grants (Amendment) Act, 1966, empowered An Foras Tionscal to establish and administer such industrial estates. The development of two industrial estates — at Waterford and Galway — was initiated in 1966.

The Threat of Free Trade

A desire to encourage exports was not the only motivation behind fiscal incentives in the 1960s. There was also a need to prepare existing Irish industry for conditions of freer trade. Following the UK, Ireland applied to join the EEC in 1961 (but did not, along with the UK, actually become a member until 1973). The government thereafter remained committed to a policy of phased trade liberalisation. In June 1961 the government accordingly appointed the CIO to appraise the measures which might have to be taken to adapt Irish industry to conditions of freer trade.

Studies of twenty-six industries, employing 87,000 persons, were carried out by the survey teams appointed by the CIO. At the same time the Department of Agriculture conducted a survey of four agricultural processing industries employing 15,500 persons. Among the problems which were common to most industries and to which the CIO and Department of Agriculture survey reports[15] drew attention were: small scale of production units; under-utilisation of plant and high costs resulting from short production runs; lack of specialisation; obsolete equipment and poor export marketing. Most of these factors were largely attributable to the small size of the domestic market and the high level of protection given to Irish industry. The CIO made various proposals with a view to limiting redundancies in Irish industry in an environment of freer trade, among them that interest-free loans should be provided towards the financing of re-equipment within the existing spheres of firm activity. This recommendation was implemented by the government, with the addition of an alternative to the re-equipment loans, in the form of a 25 per cent re-equipment grant, which was in fact more widely availed of by industry than the loans.

Fiscal Incentives, 1978[16]

Fiscal and other incentives administered by the IDA in 1978 were provided under the headings of: new manufacturing or service industries or major expansions of existing ones; re-equipment of existing manufacturing industries; new or existing small industries (defined as manufacturing firms with up to fifty employees and fixed assets of up to £300,000); enterprise development (providing IDA assistance for loans raised towards working capital).

New Industries or Major Expansions

Financial incentives offered by the Revenue Commissioners and the IDA to new Irish or foreign-owned projects include:

(i) Complete exemption from taxation on export-generated profits in the remaining years up to 1990.

(ii) Non-repayable cash grants towards the cost of fixed assets, defined as site, site development, buildings, new machinery, and equipment (other than road vehicles and office equipment). Grants operate on a dual system. For acceptable projects where the investment does not exceed £1 million, or the investment per job created is not over £15,000, grants may be negotiated up to maxima of 50 per cent of eligible costs in the so-called Designated Areas (mainly the western part of the country) and 35 per cent of eligible costs in the rest of the country. For other projects, grant levels are determined on a cost-per-job basis.

(iii) Non-repayable cash grants towards approved capital costs of research and development facilities, negotiable up to 35 per cent of eligible costs.

(iv) Training grants towards the costs of wages, travel and subsistence of workers being trained in Ireland or at parent companies abroad.

(v) Grants towards factory rent reduction.

(vi) Loan guarantees and interest subsidies.

(vii) IDA equity participation (joint ownership) where desired and possible.

Re-equipment/Modernisation of Existing Industries

Re-equipment grants are available towards the cost of modernisation of plant and machinery in existing industries. The grants are payable up to maxima of 35 per cent of eligible costs in the Designated Areas and 25 per cent elsewhere.

Small Industries

Under the Small Industries Programme of the IDA capital grants are available to new and existing small manufacturing firms up to maxima of 60 per cent of fixed asset costs in the Designated Areas and 45 per cent in the rest of the country. Training grants are also provided under the Programme.

Other Incentives

The so-called tax holiday — exemption from taxation of export-generated profits — and the various schemes administered by the IDA are not the only fiscal incentives affecting investment in manufacturing industry. The treatment of depreciation in the tax code also affects investment. Taxes on profits are assessed after a deduction has been made from gross profits for depreciation of assets such as plant and machinery and buildings. Such assets actually depreciate over several years. However, the provisions for 'free depreciation' in the tax code enable the entire cost of investment in buildings and in plant and machinery to be deducted straight away (in the year of investment) for tax purposes. These provisions are equivalent to an interest-free loan to investors, the Revenue Commissioners foregoing tax revenue in the year of investment but recouping by increased tax receipts in subsequent years. (Tax receipts are increased in subsequent years because depreciation allowances for assets written off for tax purposes in the year of investment are zero in later years.)

Fiscal Policy and Growth

The most outstanding feature of Ireland's progress in the 1960s was its rate of industrial expansion. Average annual real growth in the industrial sector in 1960-69 was 7 per cent, while real industrial exports increased by over 200 per cent in the ten years. From the beginning of the 1960s to 31 March 1970, 595 *new* industrial projects were set up with the aid of grant incentives. Over 400 of these were foreign owned. Almost all of the new projects were export oriented. It is difficult to know how much of the increase in industrial activity over the decade was due to fiscal incentives (in contrast to labour availability, market accessibility, etc.). In 1967 the *Survey of Grant-aided Industry* concluded that 'it seems clear that State financial inducements, in the form of export profits tax relief and grants, have attracted more foreign industrialists to Ireland than any one of the inherent attractions offered by the country'.[17]

In regard to the role of grant-aided new industry in manufactured exports, a more recent study[18] reports that in the years 1973 and 1974 such firms exported on average 70 per cent of their output and accounted for between 62 per cent and 69 per cent of all exports of manufactures. It would appear, therefore, that the longer-run impact on exports of the fiscal incentives has been considerable. In the absence of fiscal incentives, much of the grant-aided foreign industry would probably have located elsewhere.

As previously stated, real GNP growth in Ireland in 1960-70 was at an average annual rate of about 4 per cent. That contrasts with an average annual rate of 1 per cent in 1950-58. The sub-section above on fiscal policy in the short-run, 1960-70, reported that a macroeconomic model of the economy estimated that the average short-run effect of discretionary fiscal changes in the 1960s was an average annual increase in real GNP of 1·9 per cent, or close to one-half of the average annual growth in the economy in the decade. It seems unlikely that fiscal changes in a given year significantly affected exports in the same year: that was why, in the short-run model, they were regarded as unaffected by fiscal policy. However, it should now be clear that in the case of Ireland, industrial exports cannot plausibly be regarded as unaffected in an analysis of the impact of fiscal policy *on long-term growth*. Rapidly rising exports have been both a source of growth (via their effects on aggregate demand) and (under a fixed exchange rate) a condition for growth (by relaxing balance of payments constraints on domestic expansion), and they in turn were strongly affected by fiscal policy — by tax relief for export-generated profits and by the new industry grants in particular. Although the model used to estimate the short-run effects of fiscal policy may in some respects over-estimate the cumulative short-run effects on real income, its treatment of exports as unaffected by fiscal policy leads to under-estimates of the longer-term impact of fiscal policy on economic growth. It appears, therefore, that a very considerable part of real GNP growth in Ireland since the late 1950s can be attributed to changes in a rather diverse set of fiscal instruments since that decade.

'Productive' and 'Redistributive' Investment

In the past, much emphasis has been placed on the distinction between 'productive' and 'redistributive' investment. By the definition of the Capital Investment Advisory Committee, 1958, investment is 'productive' to the extent that it provides 'a continuing flow of new goods and services which over a period of time can be sold, without subsidy of any kind at competitive prices'. However, 'to the extent that an investment expenditure does not provide a flow of goods and services capable of being sold at competitive prices it is redistributive'.[19]

In the long run an economy grows because (i) the supply potential of the economy is increased due to investment, population growth, technical advances, etc., and because (ii) the level of aggregate demand is increased. It is supply potential rather than aggregate demand that exerts the ultimate upper-bound constraint on the growth rate. But in the short run, aggregate demand is often at a level below productive capacity. On such occasions expansionary fiscal policies, boosting the level of aggregate demand, are generally desirable.

In varying degrees all fixed investment affects both capacity (i.e, potential supply) and aggregate demand. However, the capacity effect tends to be greatest with 'productive' investment, and lowest with 'redistributive' investment. The impact on aggregate demand, on the other hand, tends to be strongest in the case of 'redistributive' investment. That is because in Ireland, projects which are primarily of a 'productive' character tend to have a high import content (think of investment in machinery and equipment), while the import content of 'redistributive' investment (think of subsidised housing or public works) tends to be low. Hence the multipliers attached to the latter exceed those applying to the former type of investment. It follows that by increasing potential supply, 'productive' investment is vital for long-term growth, while (important social considerations aside) 'redistributive' investment is most desirable as a means of rectifying a short-run deficiency in aggregate demand. These considerations suggest need for policies of changing *the composition* of aggregate demand at times of balance of payments crisis combined with high unemployment, rather than conscious reduction in the level of demand.

Suggested Reading

Dowling, Brendan R., and Kennedy, Kieran A., *Economic Growth in Ireland: The Experience since 1947,* Dublin 1976.

Industrial Development Authority, *Report,* published annually.

McAleese, Dermot, *A Profile of Grant-Aided Industry in Ireland,* Industrial Development Authority 1977.

Meenan, James, *The Irish Economy Since 1922,* Liverpool 1970.

FOOTNOTES

1. Much of what follows draws on my papers 'Fiscal Policy and Growth in an Open Economy: The Case of Ireland', *Public Finance/Finances Publiques,* No. 2, 1974, and 'Fiscal Policy: A Long View', *Administration,* Summer 1975.
2. Mary C. Bromage, *De Valera,* London: Hutchinson 1956, 117.
3. Dáil Éireann, *Parliamentary Debates,* 8 May 1946, 2363-4.
4. *Ibid.,* 2 April 1952, 1155.
5. *Ibid.,* 4 May 1955, 690-1.
6. Meenan, 151.
7. T.K. Whitaker *et al,* Economic Development, Dublin: Stationery Office, Pr. 4803, 1958, 232.
8. Dáil Éireann, *Parliamentary Debates,* 2 April 1952, 1115.
9. See my 'Estimation of the Short-Run Effects of Fiscal Policy in Ireland, 1960-70', *The Economic and Social Review,* April 1975, and Brendan R. Dowling, 'Budget Deficits and Fiscal Policy' in Dowling and Durkan (eds), *Irish Economic Policy: A Review of Major Issues,* Dublin: The Economic and Social Research Institute 1978.
10. Dáil Éireann, *Parliamentary Debates,* 2 April 1952, 1136.
11. *Ibid.,* 6 May 1953, 1201.
12. *Ibid.,* 8 May 1957.
13. *Budget 1961,* Dublin: Stationery Office.
14. *Programme for Economic Expansion,* Dublin: Stationery Office, Pr. 4796.
15. See Committee on Industrial Organisation, *Final Report,* Dublin: Stationery Office, Pr. 8082. The report on dairy products indicates extreme inertia in that industry. When creameries were first set up, the distance which could conveniently be travelled by horse transportation regulated their location. About four miles was usually the limit for a farmer to travel to a creamery. But modern transporation has made an anachronism of the four-mile limit. In 1962, there were 599 creameries in Ireland; 461 of these were in Munster. In Munster over 80 per cent of all creameries were located within six miles of the premises nearest to them. Thus the survey team which investigated that industry in 1962 concluded that 'these figures . . . convey a strong impression that the horizontal organisation of the industry as it is today is almost completely out of touch with modern conditions'. See Department of Agriculture, *Report of the Survey Team established by the Minister for Agriculture in the Dairy Products Industry,* Dublin: Stationery Office, Pr. 6960, Chapter 7 and Appendix 8.

16. The details in the next several paragraphs are drawn from Industrial Development Authority, *Annual Report 1977,* Appendix B.

17. C. Carolan and C. McGrath, *Survey of Grant-Aided Industry,* Dublin: Stationery Office, Prl. 117, 60.

18. Dermot McAleese, *A Profile of Grant-Aided Industry in Ireland,* Industrial Development Authority, Publications Series Paper 5, 1977.

19. Capital Investment Advisory Committee, *Third Report,* reprinted in Basil Chubb and Patrick Lynch (eds), *Economic Development and Planning,* Dublin: Institute of Public Administration 1969.

PART FIVE

MICROECOMONIC ANALYSIS

CHAPTER 20

The Theory of Demand

In Part Two we saw that in a perfectly competitive market the equilibrium price is determined by the intersection of the supply and demand curves. We assumed that demand curves slope downwards. In this chapter we attempt an explanation of the demand curve in terms of the structure of consumers' tastes and their budgets, leaving further analysis of supply until later chapters. Here we focus on two central questions in demand theory:

(i) How must a consumer with given tastes, a fixed money income and facing given market prices, allocate his expenditure between goods in order to maximise satisfaction?

(ii) Why do demand curves usually slope downwards? Can we be sure that they will *always* slope downwards?

Marginal Utility Theory

The theory of demand, like the science of economics itself, is of relatively recent origin. Until the publication in 1871 of W.S. Jevons's *Theory of Political Economy* most economists adhered to some cost of production theory of value. They believed that the exchange value (i.e., the price) of a good was determined by its costs of production, particularly its subjective cost in terms of the necessary labour time embodied in its production. Cost of production is a major determinant of supply. On the role of demand and utility they had little to say. By utility we mean the satisfaction which consumers derive from possession of a good. The early economists did agree that there is some connection between the demand for a good and its utility: they felt that without utility a good would not be demanded at all. But they saw little direct relationship between utility and price. What they believed, in sum, was that, possessing utility, the price of a good is determined by its cost of production.

The Paradox of Value
Because he did not understand the role of utility in price determination, Adam Smith was led to his famous 'paradox of value'

279

when he wrote that goods 'which have the greatest value in use have frequently little or no value in exchange; and . . . those which have the greatest value in exchange have frequently little or no value in use. Nothing is more useful than water, but . . . scarcely anything can be had in exchange for it. A diamond, on the contrary, has scarcely any value in use; but a very great quantity of other goods may frequently be had in exchange for it'.[1] No cost of production theory could rigorously explain why the price of diamonds is high and that of water low, even zero. However, by his distinction between total utility and marginal utility, Jevons resolved the paradox of value.

Total Utility and Marginal Utility
The total utility of n units of good x to a consumer is the total satisfaction from possession on n units of that good. The marginal utility of x, when n units of x have been purchased, is the change in total utility due to the possession of n instead of (n — 1) units of x.

The Law of Diminishing Marginal Utility
The marginal utility theorists went beyond total utility by invoking the law of diminishing marginal utility. According to this hypothesis, the more one has of any good x per period of time, the smaller is the increase in total utility due to the possession of a further unit of x, the amount possessed of all other goods remaining constant. Alternatively, the law states that total utility increases at a diminishing rate as one obtains more of a good. The relationship between total utility and marginal utility can be seen in Figures 47a and 47b. Note that q represents quantity *per period of time.*

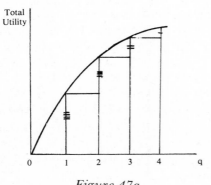

Figure 47a

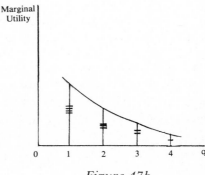

Figure 47b

The Paradox of Value Resolved

Marginal utility analysis quickly resolves the paradox of value. Because they are very scarce relative to demand, diamonds have high marginal utility. Consumers are therefore willing to pay a high price for them. Water, because it is abundant, has a low marginal utility and hence a low — even zero — price. *Given supply,* the determinant of price is thus seen to be marginal utility rather than total utility.

The Consumer's Allocation Problem

Using marginal utility theory we now consider the consumer's allocation problem. To maximise satisfaction or utility a consumer, with given tastes, a fixed money income, and facing given market prices, must allocate expenditure between various goods in such a manner that the last unit of expenditure on each brings to the consumer the same increase in total utility (yields the same marginal utility). This is equivalent to saying that the consumer must spend his money in such a manner that for all goods purchased, marginal utilities are proportional to prices.

Suppose, for simplicity, that a consumer buys only two goods, x and y. To maximise satisfaction he must allocate his expenditure so that

(1) $MU_x/p_x = MU_y/p_y$

If the consumer allocated his expenditure in any other manner he would not be maximising utility. If, when he had spent all his money on the two goods, $MU_x/p_x > MU_y/p_y$, he could have increased his utility by buying more x and less y. Define a unit of x as that amount of x which costs £1, and define a unit of y as that amount of y which costs £1. Thus $p_x = p_y$. But $MU_x > MU_y$: the last £1 spent on x yields a greater increase in utility than the last £1 spent on y. The rational consumer must therefore transfer expenditures from y to x. As he buys less y and more x, MU_x will fall and MU_y will rise (because of the law of diminishing marginal utility). Eventually a point will be reached at which $MU_x = MU_y$. The consumer can then no longer gain by transfering expenditures from y to x. Hence, allocation in accordance with condition (1) is necessary for utility maximisation.

If the consumer spends his money on N goods, then in order to maximise satisfaction he must allocate his expenditure among those goods in such a manner that

(2) $MU_1/p_1 = MU_2/p_2 = \ldots = MU_N/p_N$

— marginal utilities, for all goods bought, must be proportional to their prices. The pattern of behaviour implicit in conditions (1) and (2) is called the *equimarginal* principle of consumer's behaviour.

The Consumer's Demand Curve

We now turn to the second question in demand theory posed at the beginning of the chapter. It is often stated that demand curves slope downwards because of the law of diminishing marginal utility. Given tastes and money income, and given the prices of all goods except that in which we are directly interested, if the law of diminishing marginal utility as applied to goods were the *only* factor determining the slope of a demand curve, then all demand curves must slope downwards. Consider the reasoning behind such a conclusion.

The equimarginal principle showed how a rational consumer with given tastes, a fixed money income and facing given market prices for all goods, would allocate his expenditure between N goods. He would act in accordance with the principle in condition (2). Now examine the adjustment in the consumer's purchase plan for some good n as its price (p_n) varies.

The set of ratios in condition (2) must equal some number. Let this number be k (k for constant). Then, $MU_n/p_n = k$, or

(3) $p_n = MU_n/k$

which implies a unique relationship between the price the consumer is willing to pay for good n and its marginal utility to him. Thus its seems that the price the consumer is willing to pay for good n can be derived directly from the MU curve of good n. If it can be derived from the law of diminishing marginal utility, the individual's demand curve must slope downwards. If, given money income and the prices of all other goods, diminishing marginal utility as applied to goods were the only factor determining the shape of individual demand curves, then every individual's demand curve for any good would slope downwards. Since a market demand curve for any good is the horizontal sum of the individual demand curves for that good, the market demand curve, derived from marginal utility theory, would slope downwards. Marginal utility analysis thus suggests that *all* demand curves must always slope downwards.

Some Problems

The above analysis is defective on a number of counts. First, we assumed that utility, and hence marginal utility, is *cardinally measurable* — just as height and distance are cardinally measurable (i.e., we assumed that we could *quantitatively* compare the difference in total utility obtainable from, say, six units and seven units of a good, just as we could quantitatively compare the average height of six-year-old and seven-year-old children). Many have objected to marginal utility analysis on the grounds that utility is not cardinally measurable. Secondly, marginal utility analysis led to the conclusion that demand curves must always slope downwards. In a more refined analysis that conclusion is not necessarily true. Indifference curve analysis helps to provide more rigorous solutions to the two questions posed at the beginning of this chapter.

Indifference Curve Analysis

In indifference curve analysis we do not assume that utility is *cardinally* measurable. But we do assume that the consumer makes his purchases in accordance with a scale of preferences, by which he is able to *rank* all conceivable bundles of goods in order of importance to him. This implies that he is able to indicate the bundles of goods between which he is indifferent. But instead of making statements of the form 'the consumer obtains 100 units of utility from purchase plan A and 100 units of utility from purchase plan B, but only 50 units of utility from purchase plan C' (the *cardinal* utility approach), in indifference curve analysis we need only make statements of the form 'the consumer is indifferent between A and B and prefers either to C, but it is not necessary and it may not be possible to know *by how much* he prefers B to C' (the *ordinal* utility approach). In what follows we assume for simplicity that there are only two goods, x and y, entering the consumer's purchase plan.

Indifference Curves
The indifference curve owes its origin to the Irish economist Francis Ysidro Edgeworth (1845-1926).[2] An indifference curve shows the combinations of two goods between which an individual is indifferent (i.e., yield the consumer the same *level* of satisfaction). The curve IC_1 in Figure 48 shows combinations of goods x and y between which the consumer is indifferent. We assume that more goods are preferred to less (the assumption of non-satiety). It is obvious, in Figure 48, that bundle C will be preferred to bundle B (or A): if the consumer had bundle C he would have more of both goods than if he had bundle B. There are several combinations of goods which would yield the consumer the same satisfaction as commodity bundle C. These all lie on the indifference curve of bundle C, IC_2.

The consumer is indifferent between all combinations of x and y which lie on IC_2. But every point on IC_2 is preferred to any point on IC_1. However, we cannot, or need not, say *by how much* (by how many units of utility) the consumer prefers a bundle on IC_2 to a bundle on IC_1; we merely say that the utility of bundles on IC_2 exceeds that of bundles on IC_1.

The locus IC_3 in Figure 48 represents yet another level of consumer satisfaction. All commodity bundles on this locus are equally attractive to the consumer. But every point on IC_3 is preferred to any point on a lower indifference curve. The higher the indifference curve, the greater the level of utility or satisfaction.

On the assumption that he can rank all conceivable bundles of goods according to preference or indifference (this is called the axiom of completeness) the rational consumer has infinitely many indifference curves. These indicate all commodity bundles between which he indifferent, the commodity bundles which he prefers to any given bundle, and the bundles which give less satisfaction than any given commodity bundle. The whole series of indifference curves is the consumer's *indifference map*. An indifference map is a graphical depiction of a consumer's *preferences* among goods.

The higher the indifference curve, the higher the level of utility, but utility is constant along a given indifferent curve. Thus in indifference curve analysis we need attach only *ordinal* rather than cardinal significance to the utility of one bundle of goods as compared to another. We can say that the utility on one bundle is greater than (less than or equal to) that of another; this is merely *ranking* bundles in *order* of preference and indifference — it does not require any assumption of *cardinally measurable* utility.

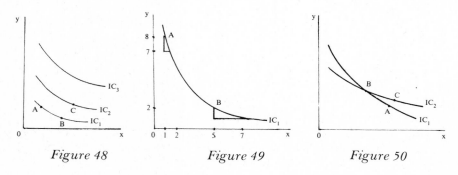

Figure 48   Figure 49   Figure 50

Properties of Indifference Curves
Three properties of indifference curves are as follows:

(i) Indifference curves slope downwards. (*Any* other shape would be inconsistent with the assumption that more goods are preferred to less.)

(ii) Indifference curves are strictly convex, reflecting the diminishing marginal rate of substitution of good x for good y (DMRS$_{xy}$). (DMRS$_{xy}$, explained below, which implies strict convexity of indifference curves, is *an assumption* concerning consumer tastes rather than something which is necessarily true.) The MRS$_{xy}$ is the rate at which the consumer is willing to substitute x for y consistent with feeling no better or worse off (i.e., while staying on the same indifference curve). The MRS$_{xy}$ is approximately or precisely equal to the slope of an indifference curve (we ignore the negative sign of slope). For example, consider the indifference curve in Figure 49, and suppose that initially the consumer has commodity bundle A. We can see that he is willing to give up 1 unit of y for an extra ½ unit of x: he is made no better or worse off by making such a substitution, for he has remained on the same indifference curve. But note that in the neighbourhood of point A the absolute value of the slope of the indifference curve (approximated by $\Delta y / \Delta x$) equals 2, approximately. If the consumer could substitute in infinitesimally small amounts, then the absolute value of the slope of the indifference curve would exactly equal the consumer's MRS$_{xy}$.

Note also that as the consumer obtains more x, the absolute value of the slope of the indifference curve diminishes. This reflects *D*MRS$_{xy}$. If, for example, the consumer has a lot of y but little x (as at point A in Figure 49), it is likely that for a unit reduction in his holdings of y he will accept a small increase in holdings of x. However, as his holdings of y are reduced and those of x are increased, it is likely that the consumer will require progressively larger increments in his holdings of x to offset reduction in his holdings of y. If, as at point B in Figure 49, he has 5 units of x but only 2 units of y, he will be willing to sacrfice an additional unit of y only if he obtains an additional 2·25 units of x.

We assume that the consumer's MRS$_{xy}$, as represented by the absolute value of the slope of an indifference curve, will always diminish as one moves down an indifference curve. If that is the case indifference curves must be strictly convex.

(iii) Indifference curves cannot intersect. Suppose that they can intersect, as in Figure 50. That is contradictory. Bundle C is preferred to bundle A, since C contains more of both x and y than does A. The consumer is indifferent between A and B, since they both lie on the same indifference curve (IC$_1$). He is also indifferent betwen C and B, since they too lie on the same indifference curve (IC$_2$). The consumer is, therefore, indifferent between A, B, and C. But C is preferred to A. Thus an assumption that indifference curves can intersect is contradictory.

The Consumer's Allocation Problem

Indifference-curve analysis can aid us in answering the first question posed at the beginning of this chapter — how will a consumer with given tastes, with a fixed money income, and given market prices, allocate his expenditure among goods if he is to maximise satisfaction? For simplicity we assume that he spends all his income on two goods, x and y.

If the consumer spent all his money income on good y, he could buy an amount of that good equal to his money income divided by the price of good y. Let that amount be OA in Figure 51. Thus OA = (money income)/p_y. If he spent all his money income on good x, he could buy an amount of that good equal to his money income divided by the price of good x. Let that amount be OA' in Figure 51. Thus OA' = (money income)/p_x. The consumer could buy, with his fixed money income, any of the combinations of x and y on the locus AA'. That is called the consumer's *budget constraint* — it is the constraint imposed on the consumer's purchases by this fixed money income, given market prices. Ignoring the negative sign, the slope of the budget constraint is the price ratio. Thus, slope of AA' = OA/OA' = (money income/p_y) ÷ (money income/p_x) = p_x/p_y.

Given market prices, the level of the budget constraint is determined by the level of money income. If the consumer obtains an increase in money income while prices are unchanged, his budget constraint will shift upwards, perhaps to BB' in Figure 51. If his money income is reduced, while prices stay constant, his budget constraint will shift downwards, perhaps to CC' in Figure 51.

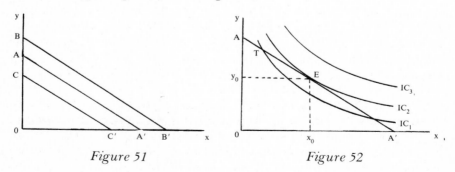

Figure 51   Figure 52

We now superimpose the consumer's budget constraint on his indifference map, as in Figure 52. The indifference map depicts the consumer's preferences, which we assume given. The consumer has a fixed money income and faces given prices for x and y. The corresponding budget constraint is AA′. The consumer's problem is to get to the highest indifference curve consistent with that budget constraint.

In Figure 52 the consumer could not get to IC_3, which lies above his budget constraint. He could attain IC_1 by buying bundle T, but he would not be maximising satsifaction. It is clear that given his budget constraint, the highest indifference curve which the consumer can attain is IC_2. He can reach IC_2 if he buys bundle E, given by the tangency of an indifference curve to his budget constraint.

The tangency of an indifference curve to the budget constraint gives the highest level of satisfaction attainable by a consumer with given tastes, with a fixed money income, and facing given market prices. The slope of an indifference curve is the MRS_{xy}. The slope of the budget constraint (again ignoring the negative sign) is p_x/p_y. Thus, at point E, $MRS_{xy} = p_x/p_y$. Hence, if a consumer with given tastes, a fixed money income, and facing given market prices is to maximise satisfaction obtainable from a fixed money income, he must allocate his expenditure in such a manner that, for *any* two goods x and y bought,

(4) $MRS_{xy} = p_x/p_y$

Condition (4) is the indifference-curve-theory version of the equimarginal principle, stated earlier as condition (2).

Changes in Consumer Equilibrium

The consumer is in equilibrium at point E in Figure 52. Buying bundle E (x_0 of x and y_0 of y) he has no incentive to change his purchase plan, for he is obtaining maximum satisfaction consistent with his tastes, his money income and market prices. The conditions underlying equilibrium may change. In what follows we assume that the consumer's tastes or preferences remain constant — that his indifference map remains unchanged.

Suppose that all prices change by some proportion but that money income changes in the same proportion, and in the same direction, as the changes in prices. This will cause no change in the rational consumer's behaviour. Suppose, for example, that prices and money income double. The budget constraint was initially $p_x x + p_y y =$ money income, where p_x, p_y and money income are initially given. After the changes in prices and money income, the budget constraint becomes $2p_x x + 2p_y y = 2$ (money income), which is identical to the initial budget constraint. The consumer's behaviour will not change because neither of the factors underlying that behaviour—his tastes or the budget constraint—will have changed.

Assuming tastes to be constant, there are three general ways in which the conditions underlying consumer equilibrium may change:

(i) (a) Absolute prices might remain constant but the money income of the consumer might change. (b) Relative prices (the price of one good relative to others) and money income might stay constant, but absolute prices might change. Although (a) and (b) would cause no change in the slope of the budget constraint (which reflects relative prices), they would cause that constraint to shift upwards or downwards. Because real income would have changed, the consumer would be made better or worse off. The adjustment in his purchase plan due to a change of type (i)—a change in real income without change in relative prices—is called *the income effect*.

(ii) Money income might be constant but relative prices might change in such a manner that the consumer is made no better or worse off—he remains on the same indifference curve. A change of this kind could occur if, for example, a tax were imposed on y and if a subsidy were granted on x. Although, in this case, the consumer remains on a particular indifference curve, he will substitute the good which has become relatively cheaper for that which has become relatively dearer. The adjustment in the consumer's purchase plan due to a change in relative prices which causes no change in attainable utility is called *the substitution effect*.

(iii) Money income might stay constant but relative prices might change so that the consumer is made better or worse off. For example, the price of one good might change while prices of all other goods stay constant. The adjustment in the consumer's purchase plan due to such a change is called *the price effect*.

The Income Effect

We start the analysis with the consumer in equilibrium at point E in Figure 53. Suppose that the consumer's money income is increased, while both absolute and relative prices stay constant. The consumer's budget constraint shifts upwards to BB′. The rational consumer will try to get to the highest indifference curve consistent with this new budget constraint: he will buy bundle E′.

If the consumer obtains a further increment in income the budget constraint will again shift upwards, to CC′ in Figure 53. The bundle which the rational consumer will buy is then E″.

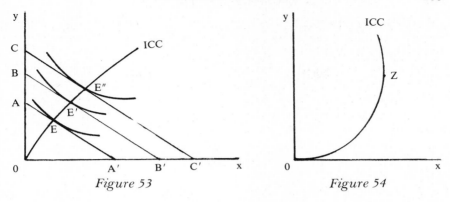

Figure 53   Figure 54

There is an infinity of possible tangency points between successively higher budget constraints and successively higher indifference curves. If we could plot all of these points we would obtain the smooth curve ICC in Figure 53. This is called an *income consumption curve.* It shows how much of x and y the rational consumer would buy at different levels of money income, given his tastes and market prices.

Note that both x and y in Figure 53 are 'normal' goods — higher income increases purchases of both. The income effect for both is positive. Alternatively, we can say that the income elasticity of demand for both is positive.

Recall from Chapter 5 that the income elasticity of demand for some goods is negative — all else remaining constant, an increase in money income leads to reduction in purchases. A good is *inferior* if increased money income reduces purchases of that good. In Figure 54 good x is inferior beyond point Z — purchases of x are reduced after income rises beyond a certain level. The term *inferior good pertains to the direction of the income effect:* a good is inferior if the income effect is negative.

The Substitution Effect

The substitution effect pertains to the adjustment in the consumer's purchase plan when a change in relative prices just enables the consumer to remain on the same indifference curve as initially. However, he will substitute the good which becomes relatively cheaper for that which is made relatively more expensive.

We start with the consumer in equilibrium at E in Figure 55. Suppose that a tax is imposed on y. Since his money income is unchanged the consumer can now buy less y than before. Instead of being able to buy OA units of y he can buy only OB units. Suppose that a subsidy is simultaneously granted on good x. If the consumer is to remain on the same indifference curve as initially, the subsidy on x must be sufficiently large so as to enable the consumer to buy OB' units of x. Supposed a subsidy of that amount is granted. The consumer's new budget constraint is BB'. By adjusting his purchase plan—from E to E'—he can remain on IC_1. The substitution effect is the movement along the indifference curve from E to E'.

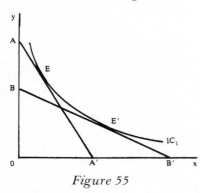

Figure 55

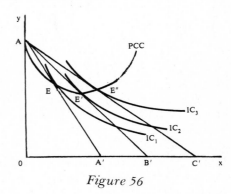

Figure 56

The Price Effect

The price effect is concerned with the adjustment in the consumer's purchase plan due to a change in relative prices which leaves the consumer better or worse off. Suppose, given his money income, tastes and the price of good y, that the price of x changes. Relative prices will then have changed. The price effect analysis focuses on the relationship between quantity demanded of x and variations in its price. It is, therefore, concerned with the individual's demand curve for good x.

We start with the consumer in equilibrium buying bundle E in Figure 56. If p_x is now reduced, the consumer will be able to purchase, with his given money income, more of x—an amount OB'. Since p_y has not changed, the consumer can still buy OA of y. The locus AB' is the consumer's new budget constraint. The rational consumer will move to the highest indifference curve consistent with that budget constraint—he will buy bundle E' in Figure 56.

If p_x fell further, the consumer's budget constraint would fan further out along the x axis—to a point like C'. AC' would then be the budget constraint, so the consumer would buy bundle E".

There is an infinity of budget constraints corresponding to different possible prices of good x. With each of these budget constraints the rational consumer will buy that commodity bundle indicated by the tangency of the budget constraint to an indifferent curve. The curve PCC, called a *price consumption curve*, is the locus of tangency points between successive budget constraints and successively higher indifference curves as p_x is reduced. It shows the amount of x (and y) bought as p_x varies.

The observant reader will notice that, in the present case, a reduction in p_x increases purchases of x. Therefore, the demand curve for x must slope downwards.

Our immediate concern is the relationship between p_x and quantity of x demanded. To see how changes in real income, *due to price changes,* affect the slope of the demand curve, we next show that the price effect is a combination of income and substitution effects.

The Price Effect Is a Combination of Income and Substitution Effects

There are two forces affecting the consumer's purchases of x when p_x is reduced, all else remaining constant. In reality both operate simultaneously. However, we consider the two forces separately:

(i) If p_x is reduced, while all other prices (p_y in the present example) and money income remain constant, the consumer experiences an increase in real income. Increased real income, taken in isolation, causes an upwards shift of the budget constraint. The price effect thus involves an income effect. If x is 'normal', this income effect will increase purchases of x. However, if x is inferior, the income effect of a price reduction will tend to reduce purchases of x.

(ii) If p_x is reduced, all other prices and the consumer's money income remaining constant, then relative prices have changed. Good x is now relatively cheaper and y relatively dearer than before. The consumer will therefore substitute x for y. Thus the price effect involves a substitution effect. *Since indifference curves are assumed strictly convex, the substitution effect, by itself, always increases purchases of the good the price of which has fallen.*

Shown graphically in Figure 57, the price effect (the movement from A to B) is a combination of an income effect (a movement up an income consumption curve to a higher budget constraint and to a higher indifference curve) and a substitution effect (a movement along a given indifference curve).

When p_x is reduced, all else remaining constant, the consumer experiences an increase in real income. The income effect, treated in isolation, is represented by an upwards shift of the budget constraint. The consumer moves along his ICC to point C in Figure 57. Note that the income effect on good x is here positive—by itself, it increases purchases of x by an amount $(x_1 - x_0)$.

Having examined the income effect in isolation, we now turn to the substitution effect. The income effect has brought the consumer to point C on IC_2 in Figure 57. The substitution effect is a movement along IC_2. If we now recall that relative prices have changed, the consumer's budget constraint, FF', will pivot to the right—to EG. Note that EG is tangent to the same indifference curve (IC_2) as FF'. The substitution effect, in isolation, causes the consumer to move along IC_2 from C to B. The substitution effect of the price change increases purchases of x by an amount $(x_2 - x_1)$.

The movement from A to B (the price effect) is a combination of movement from A to C (the income effect) and from C to B (the substitution effect). The income effect increased purchases of x by an amount $(x_1 - x_0)$. The substitution effect increased purchases by $(x_2 - x_1)$. The total increase in purchases of x due to the price reduction is $(x_2 - x_0)$. So for the price variation considered, the demand curve for x must slope downwards.

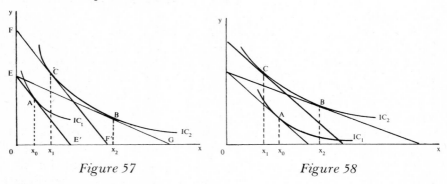

Figure 57   *Figure 58*

Inferior Goods

If x is an inferior good we cannot be sure that a reduction in its price will increase quantity demanded. The negative income effect of the price change, by itself, would reduce purchases. Whether or not the price effect increases purchases hinges on the relative sizes of the negative income effect and the substitution effect. If the substitution effect is strong enough to offset the negative income effect, the demand curve will slope downwards in the normal way, implying that reduction in price increases quantity demanded.

Figure 58 depicts the price effect for an inferior good. The income effect (the movement from A to C), by itself, would reduce purchases from x_0 to x_1. The substitution effect (the movement from C to B), by itself, would increase purchases, from x_1 to x_2. However, the full price effect increases purchases because the substitution effect $(x_2 - x_1)$ is strong enough to more than offset the negative income effect $(x_1 - x_0)$. Hence, although x is inferior, the demand curve slopes downwards.

Giffen Goods

Some goods might be so inferior that the negative income effect of a price reduction (which, by itself, reduces purchases) would more than offset the substitute effect of the price reduction (which, by itself, increases purchases). A price reduction would then *reduce* purchases. Such goods are called *Giffen goods.* A Giffen good is one for which the negative income effect of a price reduction is so strong that it dominates the substitution effect, causing the demand curve to slope *upwards* rather than downwards, for some range of price variation.

A Giffen good is an inferior good, but not all inferior goods are Giffen. The term *Giffen good pertains only to the price effect. An inferior good is Giffen if and only if it is so inferior that the negative income effect of a price change is so strong that it more than offsets the substitution effect, leading to a perverse price effect, a demand curve which slopes upwards.* Although they must be rare, there is no logical reason why Giffen goods cannot exist.

The Demand Curve Once More

We have just examined the relationship between quantity demanded by an individual of any good x and its price. We assumed that the consumer had given tastes and a fixed money income, and that the prices of all goods, other than that under analysis, remained constant. We conclude:

(i) Individual demand curves generally slope downwards because: (a) Both the income and substitution effects of a price reduction may increase purchases, or (b) if the income effect is negative, the substitution effect will usually be strong enough to offset the negative income effect.

(ii) If for an individual a good is Giffen over certain ranges of price variation, the individual's demand curve for that good will slope upwards over those ranges of price variation.

A market demand curve for a good is the sideways sum of the individual demand curves. The market demand curve will generally slope downwards for reasons (a) and (b) in (i) above. A market demand curve may, for some ranges of price variation, slope upwards for reason (ii) above.

We now see why the statement that 'demand curves must slope downwards because of the law of diminishing marginal utility' is wrong. The central reason for the inadequacy of the marginal utility approach to demand curves is that it cannot adequately handle the income effect of price changes. We have at last provided a rigorous solution to question (2), posed at the beginning of the chapter.

FOOTNOTES

1. Adam Smith, *The Wealth of Nations,* Indianapolis: The Bobbs-Merrill Company 1961, 29, 30.
2. Born at Edgeworthstown House, Co. Longford, studied at TCD, Professor at Oxford and first editor of *The Economic Journal.* His *Mathematical Psychics* (1881) is one of the great works of economics. Oddly enough, although Edgeworth invented the indifference curve he believed in cardinally measurable utility.

CHAPTER 21

The Firm, Production and Costs

Chapter 4 outlined the theory of price determination by supply and demand in perfectly competitive markets. In Chapter 20 we left supply in the background and examined the factors behind demand curves. This chapter leaves demand in the background and investigates production, costs and supply. In the chapters which immediately follow we shall bring together what is relevant in our detailed treatment of supply and demand, to consider determination of price and output in different market structures.

Profit Maximisation

Economic theory usually assumes that firms seek maximum profits. Economists do not believe that profit maximisation is the sole objective of all firms. Why then do they make that assumption? First, all theory must simplify to attain general conclusions. Second, experience suggests strongly that the assumption of profit maximisation yields predictions which are broadly consistent with reality. Third, if the assumption of profit maximisation be rejected, it is not clear what should take its place, consistent with being able to make predictions which are both general and empirically plausible. For these reasons we assume that firms maximise profit.

Cost and Profit

Profit is the difference between revenue and cost. We define the cost of a factor of production to a firm as *that payment necessary to keep the factor in employment with the firm.* This definition draws on the notion of opportunity cost. Thus, as an approximation, firm A must pay for the services of a factor just as much as that factor could earn in its most lucrative alternative employment, with, say, firm B. Suppose firm B were just willing to pay the factor £x per period; if all markets are competitive and in equilibrium, that must be because, in some sense to be defined later, the factor would 'produce' £x of output for firm B. Therefore, if the factor is currently employed by firm A, A must pay the factor £x to maintain its services; if A offered less than £x, the factor would transfer to B. Sometimes the economist's notions of factor costs are implicit rather than explicit; sometimes they diverge from, sometimes they correspond to, the accountant's measures of costs.

Consider *the cost of hiring labour*. This is an explicit cost; labour services are hired at some wage rate (which includes employer's contribution to social insurance) and it might reasonably be assumed that this is the amount labour would earn in its best alternative employment. The economist's measure of labour costs is similar to the accountant's. However, in the case of *capital costs* economists diverge from the conventions of accountants: instead of looking at the historical cost to a firm of, say, a machine, economists regard the implicit (economic) cost of the machine's services per period as what someone else would be we willing to pay for its use. Thus the (economic) cost of a machine-hour in any use is the rental rate for that machine in its most lucrative alternative use: by continuing to use the machine itself, the firm is implicitly foregoing the rental rate someone else would be willing to pay for its use. The economic *cost of using land* is similar to capital cost. It is an implicit or an explicit rental cost, depending on whether the firm owns the land.

Turning to the *costs of entrepreneurial services* (the services of the owner of the firm, which include risk-taking), note that much of what accountants call 'profit' is regarded as a cost of production by economists. Profit is a payment to the owner of a firm, and that part of the payment — called *'normal profit'* — necessary to keep the owner in a particular business is a cost to that business. To an economist, economic or 'supernormal' profit is entrepreneurial income in excess of 'normal profit'.

Thus we define economic profit — profit in the sense of the economist rather than the accountant — from the sale of goods as the difference between revenues from sale and the opportunity costs of the factors (including entrepreneurial services) used in their production. It follows that although an accountant might say that a firm is making a profit, an economist would say that (economic) profit is negative — that the firm is making a loss — if profit in the accountant's sense were less than 'normal profit'.

The Production Function

Suppose a firm can increase or decrease the amount used of all inputs. How must it use inputs if it is to minimise the cost of producing any given level of output? The answer has two aspects—a technical aspect and a financial aspect. The central concept on the technical side, which we consider first, is the production function.

A production function shows the *maximum* levels of output obtainable from alternative combinations of inputs, and the extent to which one input can be substituted for another in the production of a given output. It indicates how inputs may be transformed into outputs consistent with technical efficiency.

Suppose, for purposes of illustration, that only two inputs—labour and capital—are used to produce a certain good. The production function, representing the relationship between technically efficient input use and output, might be

(1) $q = f(x,y) = 2xy$

where q represents quantity produced, and x and y are the amounts used of labour and capital, respectively. Knowing the production function (1), we could plot the relationship between the amounts of inputs used and the resulting output on a three-dimensional diagram. However, it is easier to regard q as a parameter. We might, for example, think of setting quantity produced at ten units, in which case (1) would become

(2) $10 = 2xy$

We could now find the combinations of x and y satisfying (2). In doing so we would be finding the combinations of labour and capital use which could produce ten units of output in a technically efficient manner. Looking at (2) we see that:

If x = 1; y = 5   *If* x = 5; y = 1
     x = 2; y = 2½   x = 6; y = $^5/_6$,
     x = 3; y = 1⅔   and so on.

There are infinitely many combinations of x and y which satisfy (2). If we could plot them all we would get a smooth curve like I_{10} in Figure 59.

Isoquants
The curve I_{10} in Figure 59 is called an equal product curve, or more briefly, an *isoquant*. Total product along this curve is constant at ten units. Formally, if two inputs, x and y, are used in the production of a given good, an isoquant is the locus of combinations of x and y which produce the same level of output in a technically efficient manner.

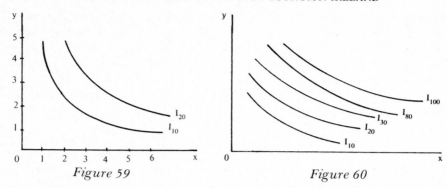

Figure 59   Figure 60

To trace the input combinations which produce twenty units, set q = 20, in which case (1) becomes

(3) $20 = 2xy$

Now find the combinations of x and y which are solutions to (3). Thus:

If x = 2; y = 5   *If* x = 10; y = 1
    x = 4; y = 2½   x = 12; y = $^5/_6$,
    x = 6; y = 1⅔   and so on.

Plotting these values in Figure 59 gives isoquant I_{20}. We could likewise set q = 30 in (1) and plot the input combinations which yield thirty units of output. There is an infinity of levels, q_1, q_2, q_3, . . . , at which we could set q. For any of these we could plot the corresponding isoquant. If we did so for many levels of q we would obtain an *isoquant map,* like that in Figure 60. An isoquant map is merely a (partial) graph of the production function.

Properties of Isoquants

The isoquants in Figure 60 are downward sloping, strictly convex, and non-intersecting. The reasons are as follows:

(i) The isoquants slope downwards reflecting an assumption that if less of one input is used, more of the other must be used to keep output constant. The slope of an isoquant is the marginal rate of technical substitution of one input for another (of x for y), $MRTS_{xy}$. It is the rate at which x can be substituted for y (using the inputs in a technically efficient manner, and keeping output constant).

(ii) The isoquants are strictly convex, reflecting an assumption of *diminishing* $MRTS_{xy}$. It is assumed that as production is made more x-intensive, it becomes progressively more difficult to substitute x for y (more difficult in the sense that each unit increment in x can be offset by only progressively smaller reductions in y) if output is kept constant. For example, both labour and capital are required to produce 100 pairs of shoes. Starting at some particular capital/labour ratio, if the production process is made more labour intensive, it will become progressively more difficult to substitute labour for machinery and tools if output is kept constant.

(iii) Isoquants cannot intersect. An isoquant shows *technically efficient* input combinations yielding a given output. Thus, corresponding to any level of input x, an isoquant shows the *minimum* level of input y that will yield a specific level of output. To assume that isoquants could intersect implies a logical contradiction.

Marginal Physical Products and MRTS

We define the marginal physical product (MPP) on the nth unit used of input x as the change in total physical product due to using n instead of (n-1) units of x, the state of technology and the amount used of all other inputs remaining constant. The slope of an isoquant at any point is approximated by $\Delta y / \Delta x$, where Δx is small. If use of input x changes by a small amount, then the resulting change in output is approximated by $(MPP_x)(\Delta x)$. If use of input y changes by a small amount, the change in output will be $(MPP_y)(\Delta y)$. It follows, if x is varied by a small amount, Δx, and if y is also varied by a small amount, Δy, then the change in output is approximately $\Delta q = (MPP_x)\Delta x + (MPP_y)\Delta y$. Because output is constant along an isoquant, $\Delta q = 0$. Hence, along an isoquant,

(4) $(MPP_x)\Delta x + (MPP_y)\Delta y = 0$, or, rearranging terms,

(5) $\Delta y / \Delta x (= MRTS_{xy}) = - MPP_x / MPP_y$

Thus the slope of an isoquant ($MRTS_{xy}$) is the negative of the ratio of the marginal physical products of the two inputs.

Isocost Curves

We now turn to financial aspects of production. If the firm could buy as much as it might wish of all inputs—of just x and y in the present case—it could buy various combinations of those inputs for any particular cost outlay. Suppose, for example, that it decides to spend £1000 on inputs. With £1000 it could buy, say, OA of x if it bought only input x (see Figure 61). If it spent the whole £1000 on y it could buy OB of y. Alternatively, it could buy, for £1000, any of the combinations of x and y given by locus AB—so long as the cost outlay and the prices of inputs remain constant. The locus AB in Figure 61 is called an isocost curve: it shows the amounts of two inputs which the firm could obtain for a given cost outlay (£1000). We know that slope AB = OB/OA. OB is the amount of y which could be obtained if the whole £1000 were spent on y: OB = $1000/p_y$. Similarly OA = $1000/p_x$. Hence

(6) Slope AB = $-(1000/p_y)/(1000/p_x)$ = $-p_x/p_y$

The higher the isocost curve, the higher the cost outlay. Assuming that per unit costs of x and y are constant, CD in Figure 61 is the isocost curve for an outlay of £1500. Conversely, the lower the isocost curve, the lower the cost outlay. GH is the isocost curve for £500. There is an infinity of isocost curves, each pertaining to a different cost outlay. The slope of each is $-p_x/p_y$.

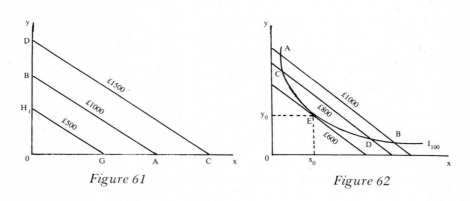

Figure 61   Figure 62

Cost Minimisation

Assuming that the firm can vary in either direction all inputs—in the present case just x and y—all we need do to find the input levels which achieve a given output at minimum cost is bring together the technical data, as represented by the production function (isoquant map), and the financial data, as represented by the map of isocost curves.

Suppose that the firm seeks to produce 100 units at minimum cost. I_{100} in Figure 62 is the relevant isoquant. We see that using input combinations A or B the firm could produce 100 units—for both points lie on I_{100}. But it would be doing so at a cost outlay of £1000, as indicated by the isocost curve through A and B. Factor combinations C or D, which lie on the isocost curve of £800, could also produce 100 units. But £800 is not the lowest possible cost for production of 100 units: there are many lower isocost curves (only one of which is shown in the diagram) which either intersect or touch I_{100}. Therefore, there are many factor combinations costing less than £800 which can produce the 100 units. The lowest isocost curve which at least touches I_{100} is that which is tangent to I_{100}. Using combination E the firm can spend £600 on inputs to produce the 100 units. But it could not produce 100 units by spending less than £600, because the isocost curves for outlays less than £600 lie entirely below I_{100}. The tangency solution E is therefore the input combination which minimises the production cost of 100 units. When two curves are tangent, their slopes are equal. At E, the slope of I_{100}, $-MPP_x/MPP_y$, equals the slope of the isocost curve, $-p_x/p_y$; thus, at E,

(7) $MPP_x/MPP_y = p_x/p_y$

Note that (7) does not hold at any other point on I_{100}. At any point other than E (e.g., at A or D), $MPP_x/MPP_y \neq p_x/p_y$. To minimise the cost of producing any given level of output when it can vary all inputs, the firm must employ those inputs in such a manner that condition (7) holds. Cross-multiplying we see that, at E,

(8) $MPP_x/p_x = MPP_y/p_y$

We have shown that point E (x_0 of x, y_0 of y) is the cost-minimising input combination for production of 100 units. Generalisation indicates that the tangency of an isocost curve to whatever isoquant is relevant is the cost-minimising input combination for *any* level of output. Thus if a firm is to produce any level of output at minimum cost it must use inputs such that condition (8) holds—the marginal physical products of the (variable) inputs must be proportional to their prices (their per unit implicit or explicit costs).

We have been discussing production using only two inputs, x and y, both of them variable in either direction. Nevertheless, condition (8) is perfectly general: if a firm uses any number (N) of inputs, and *if each of those inputs can be increased or decreased*, then, to minimise the cost of producing any given output, it must use those inputs in such a manner that

(9) $MPP_1/p_1 = MPP_2/p_2 = \ldots = MPP_N/p_N$

The principle in (8) and (9) is the *equimarginal principle* of factor employment.

The Expansion Path

(A): All Inputs Variable

If the firm wishes to produce 54 units at minimum cost, if input prices are given and if all inputs are variable in either direction, then it will use input combination E_1 in Figure 63. If it wishes to produce 87 or 101 units it will use input combinations E_2 and E_3 respectively. The points along OE are tangencies between successively higher isoquants and higher isocost curves: they are the cost-minimising input combinations of successively higher output levels. There is an infinity of isoquants, each denoting different output levels. There is also an infinity of isocost curves, each implying different minimum cost outlays. OE in Figure 63 is called an expansion path. It is the locus of cost-minimising input combinations as the firm expands output from zero to progressively higher levels. Each point on the expansion path shows two things:

(i) A certain level of output as given by the isoquant through the point.

(ii) The minimum cost associated with the output in question, given by the isocost curve tangent to the isoquant at the point.

Point E_4, for example, represents the level of output indicated by the isoquant through that point. At E_4, $x = 5$, $y = 7$. Suppose $q = 126$ at E_4. That point also implies a certain minimum cost outlay, as given by the isocost curve tangent to I_{126} at E_4. Suppose $p_x = 1$ and $p_y = 2$. It is easy to calculate the value of the isocost curve tangent to I_{126} at E_4; total cost $= p_x x + p_y y$. Thus, the minimum cost of producing 126 units is $(1)(5) + (2)(7) = 19$. Similarly, we could read off from the expansion path the minimum cost of producing any other level of output, given that both (i.e., all) factors are variable to the firm.

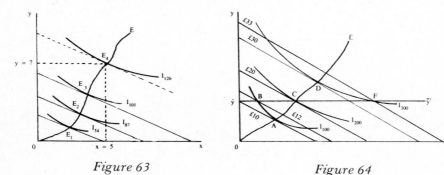

Figure 63   Figure 64

(B): Some Inputs Fixed, Some Variable

Not all factors are necessarily variable in a given period. Suppose that the firm has a fixed amount of y (say capital equipment) denoted by ȳ in Figure 64, but that it can expand or reduce its employment of x (say labour). OE would be its expansion path if both (all) factors were variable. However, with y fixed at ȳ, the firm can efficiently expand output only by moving along ȳȳ'. We could call ȳȳ' the expansion path given y = ȳ; however, to avoid confusion with the case where all factors are variable we call ȳȳ' a *factor limitation locus*.

We see from point A in Figure 64 that if *both* factors were variable the minimum cost of producing 100 units would be £10; but with y = ȳ the minimum cost of that quantity, as given by point B, is £12. It can be inferred from the diagram that with both factors variable, the minimum cost of producing *any* output less than 200 units would be lower than the minimum cost at which the same output could be produced if y = ȳ. The diagram also shows that there is one (but only one) output, i.e., q = 200 at point C, at which the minimum cost of production when y = ȳ is the same as when both x and y are variable. However, for outputs exceeding 200 units the minimum cost is lower when both factors are variable than when y is fixed at ȳ. For example, when both factors are variable the minimum cost of 300 units is £30, as at D; but point F shows that the minimum cost of 300 units when y = ȳ is £33.

It should be clear that with both factors variable we can read off the minimum cost of any output by moving along OE; with y = ȳ we read the minimum cost of any attainable output by moving along ȳȳ'.

The principal inferences from Figure 64 are quite general: if a firm employing several factors can vary its employment of some factors but cannot vary that of others, the minimum cost at which it could produce any particular output will generally be higher than would be the case if all factors were variable; however, there may be some specific level of output at which minimum cost is the same in either case (as at point C in Figure 64).

The Short Run and the Long Run

In the preceding exposition which for simplicity assumed only two factors of production (thereby enabling us to use graphical methods) we saw how to find the minimum cost of producing different levels of output (i) when both factors were variable and (ii) when one factor was fixed and one was variable. Whether or not all factors are variable depends on the period under analysis. It is unlikely that the firm will be able to vary the services of machines, warehouses, etc., (capital equipment) available to it in a given day. But within two years it probably could. Within short periods the amount of physical capital available to the firm is likely to be fixed; over long periods it is variable.

The *short run* is defined as a period in which the firm can vary only some inputs, the amount available to it of other inputs being fixed. Those factors which it can vary are called *variable inputs*. Those which are fixed are called *fixed inputs*. The *long run* is defined as a period of time in which the firm can vary the amount used of *all* inputs.

It follows that there are two types of costs in the short run—fixed costs and variable costs. *Variable costs* are those incurred due to hire or purchase of factors which can be varied in amount. In the short run, labour costs, the cost of raw materials and that of fuel, transport and power are normally variable. *Fixed costs* are those which do not vary with output. They are incurred, in the short run, even if output falls to zero. Suppose that a firm faces a trade recession. Although sales fall its fixed costs do not change. It still has to meet overheads like rent, insurance, depreciation and maintenance costs. For a plant of a given size, these costs must be incurred regardless of output. Since the scale of a firm's operations can be varied (it can go out of business or grow very large) in the long run, long run costs are all variable. Fixed costs do not normally exist in the long run.

It should now be clear that the locus OE in Figures 63 and 64 above—what we called the firm's expansion path—pertained to the long run; it traced the minimum cost of producing various levels of output when both (all) factors were variable. The factor-limitation locus, $\bar{y}\bar{y}'$ in Figure 64, pertained to a short-run situation; it traced the minimum cost of producing higher outputs when (at least) one factor was fixed and (at least) one was variable.

If a firm used many inputs to produce some good, there would exist an expansion path analogous to OE in Figures 63 and 64 if all factors were variable (a long-run situation); if many inputs were fixed and some were variable in the production of some good, there would exist a factor-limitation locus analogous to $\bar{y}\bar{y}'$ in Figure 64.

Returns to Scale

The phrase 'returns to scale' refers to the response in output to a *simultaneous proportionate change* in the amount used of *all* inputs. Returns to scale are long-run phenomena, since all inputs cannot be varied in the short run. Returns to scale are *increasing* if a simultaneous proportionate change in all inputs yields a greater proportionate change in output. If a 100 per cent increase in all inputs yields a 200 per cent increase in output, returns to scale are increasing. If a simultaneous proportionate change in all inputs yields a smaller proportionate change in output, returns to scale are *decreasing.* If a simultaneous proportionate change in all inputs yields an equiproportionate change in output, returns to scale are *constant.*

Inspection of the isoquant map indicates returns to scale. If isoquants are plotted *so that they represent equal increments in output,* and if they remain *equidistant,* returns to scale are constant (see Figure 65a). What do we mean by equidistant? Draw any ray from the origin through the isoquant map. If, *moving along any such ray,* the isoquants are equidistant, constant returns to scale prevail. The isoquant map in Figure 65a has constant returns to scale. If the distance between the isoquants progressively increases, as in Figure 65b, decreasing returns to scale prevail. If the distance between isoquants decreases, as in Figure 65c, returns to scale are increasing.

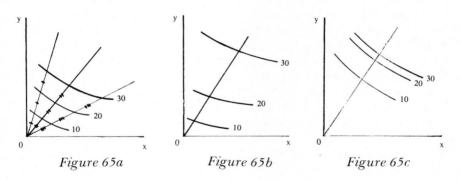

Figure 65a   Figure 65b   Figure 65c

Derivation of Long-Run Cost Curves

There is no reason why the firm's production function must always have increasing, constant or decreasing returns to scale over all outputs. It is more likely that as the firm expands from a low level it will experience increasing returns to scale, that it will then enter a phase of constant returns, and that for high outputs (perhaps not observed) returns to scale would decrease. In the analysis which follows we assume that the firm's production function at first has increasing returns to scale, that a phase of constant returns is then entered, and that for very high outputs returns to scale would be decreasing.[1]

Some of the causes of increasing returns to scale are:

(i) There may be unavoidable excess capacity at low outputs because *certain factors are indivisible.* For example, if CIE wished to double services on given railway routes, it is unlikely that it would need to double the size or number of railway tunnels. Nor would it need to double its rolling stock on the routes. Managerial input is also indivisible. If output is low it is unlikely, in order to double output, that the number of managers would need to be doubled.

(ii) *Both men and machines can be made more specialised as the scale of operations increases.* Instead of performing several tasks, each man or machine can become more efficient on a smaller number of tasks.

A phase of constant returns to scale may be reached if all net technical advantages of further expansion are exhausted.

If output is very high, returns to scale might decrease because *managerial efficiency and communications within the firm, are likely to break down if the firm grows beyond a certain size*; that is one reason why we might not observe firms growing beyond certain sizes.

Assume that returns to scale are increasing, constant, and decreasing, depending on the scale of operations. Then, plotting isoquants for equal increments in output, the firm's isoquant map would be like that in Figure 66. Assume also that input prices are given. The isocost map then consists of a series of parallel lines, as in Figure 66. We can now construct the firm's expansion path, OE. Each point on OE shows two things: (a) a certain level of output and (b) the minimum cost of producing that output when all factors are variable. If we read off (a) and

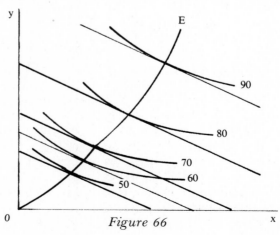

Figure 66

(b) from the expansion path, and plot them on different axes, we obtain a long run total cost (LRTC) curve like that in Figure 67a. The firm's LRTC curve shows the minimum cost of producing each output level when all factors are variable.

Given input prices, the shape of the LRTC curve is determined by the production function. In Figure 67a the LRTC curve at first increases at a diminishing rate due to increasing returns to scale. When the phase of constant returns to scale is entered (from $q = d$ to $q = e$) total costs increase at a constant rate. If the firm continues to expand output it will experience decreasing returns to scale (which prevail for q in excess of $q = e$) and total costs will increase at an increasing rate.

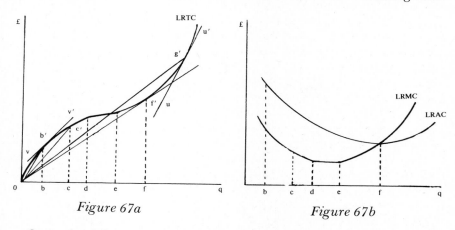

Figure 67a   *Figure 67b*

Once the LRTC curve is known it is easy to derive the long-run average cost (LRAC) curve since $LRAC = (LRTC)/q$. This is drawn in Figure 67b. The LRAC of any level of output is the slope of the ray from the origin to the LRTC curve at the output in question. For example, the LRAC of b units is bb'/Ob. But bb'/Ob is slope Ob'. Similarly, the LRAC of c units is slope Oc', while that of f units is slope Of'. Note that the slopes of the rays from the origin to the LRTC curve are diminishing as output is expanded from 0 to f units, so LRAC is falling over such output ranges. Beyond f' the slopes of successive rays from the origin to the LRTC curve are increasing, so LRAC is rising over outputs beyond f units. An inference is that the LRAC curve attains its minimum when f units are produced.

Having derived long-run average costs from the LRTC curve we now derive the long-run marginal cost (LRMC) curve. The marginal cost (MC) of the nth unit is the change in total cost due to producing n instead of (n-1) units. The LRMC of any unit is $\Delta(LRTC)/\Delta q$, where $\Delta q = 1$; it is approximated by the slope of the total cost curve. The LRMC curve can, therefore, be derived directly from the LRTC curve. For outputs below $q = d$ in Figure 67a, the *slope* of the LRTC curve is falling. Therefore the LRMC curve is also falling, as in Figure 67b. Between $q = d$ and $q = e$ in Figure 67a the slope of the LRTC curve is constant, so LRMC is constant over the same output ranges. Beyond $q = e$ the slope of the LRTC curve is rising, so LRMC is rising over those output ranges.

What is the relationship between the LRAC and the LRMC curves? In Figure 67a we see, for all output levels below f units, that the slope of the LRTC curve is less than the slope of the ray from the origin to the LRTC curve at the same output (e.g., slope vv' < Ob'). Therefore, between 0 and f, LRMC < LRAC. At f the slope of the LRTC curve is equal to the slope of the ray from the origin to the LRTC curve. Therefore, at f, LRMC = LRAC. But for any output beyond f units, the slope of the LRTC curve exceeds the slope of the ray from the origin to the LRTC curve (e.g., slope uu' > slope Og'). That is why, in Figure 67b, LRMC > LRAC for $q > f$.

There is an alternative explanation of the relationship between the LRAC and the LRMC curves. LRMC was defined as $\Delta(LRTC)$ when $\Delta q = 1$. If $\Delta(LRTC)$ due to producing an additional unit is less than the LRAC previously established, then LRAC is being pulled down. Hence so long as LRMC < LRAC, LRAC must be declining. That is true whether or not LRMC itself is falling, constant or rising. If $\Delta(LRTC)$ due to producing an additional unit is greater than the LRAC previously established, then LRAC is being pulled up. So long as LRMC > LRAC, LRAC must be rising. That is true regardless of whether LRMC is falling, constant or rising. Hence, (a) if LRMC < LRAC, LRAC is falling and (b) if LRMC > LRAC, LRAC is rising.

It follows that the LRMC curve cuts the LRAC curve at its minimum point. Note that the statement 'if LRMC is falling, then LRAC is falling, and if LRMC is rising, then LRAC is rising' is incorrect.

Given the prices of inputs, the shapes of the LRMC and LRAC curves were determined by the production function. The reason why both were *U*-shaped was because we assumed that the production function has increasing and decreasing returns to scale.

At this stage the informed reader might ask: why do many empirical studies suggest that the LRAC is *L*-shaped (rather than *U*-shaped, as we assumed). The following considerations are relevant:

(i) Some firms may curtail expansion if rising unit costs are threatened. If that is the case a rising LRAC curve will not be observed in empirical studies.

(ii) A profit-maximising firm might have a very lengthy plateau of constant long-run average costs. It might find that its profit-maximising output is along that plateau. For such firms, even though the LRAC curve would ultimately increase *if* output were expanded indefinitely, we would not observe such rising long-run average costs.

(iii) The state of technology — and hence the firm's production function — changes over time. Empirical studies of cost and output over time — over, say, a decade — record the effects of changing technology. However, we assumed that the firm had a *given* production function: we assumed that the state of technology was constant. The analysis of the last several pages applies to circumstances in which (a) all factors are variable and (b) the firm's production function is given.

Having considered long-run cost structures we now turn to the short run.

The Short-Run Cost Structure of the Firm

The short run was defined as a period in which some factors are fixed, some variable. Assume that the firm has a plant of a given size — a fixed number of machines, a fixed amount of warehouse space, etc. Associated with a plant of fixed size the firm must incur certain overheads which do not vary with output. Whether the firm produces much or little, short-run overhead costs are fixed. Such costs were earlier defined as fixed costs. Variable costs are those which vary with output. Costs incurred on unskilled labour, raw materials and on purchase of fuel and power are usually variable.

The short-run cost structure of the firm is derived from its factor limitation locus (recall Figure 64) and financial data. However, we do not outline the derivation here. We merely consider the type of cost structure we would expect in the short run. Having done so we shall examine some relationships between short-run and long-run costs.

Short-run total costs (SRC) at any level of output in a plant of a given size is the sum of total fixed cost (TFC) and total variable cost (TVC):

In the short run, $C = TFC + TVC$
Therefore, $C/q = TFC/q + TVC/q$
i.e., $AC = AFC + AVC$

— average (total) cost is average fixed cost plus average variable cost. To construct the firm's AC curve it is necessary to consider AFC and AVC. Since TFC is a constant, the AFC curve ($= TFC/q$) must be a rectangular hyperbola, as in Figure 68. Discussion of the shape of the AVC curve is less straightforward. It is reasonable to assume that it is U-shaped, as in Figure 68. We now justify that assumption.

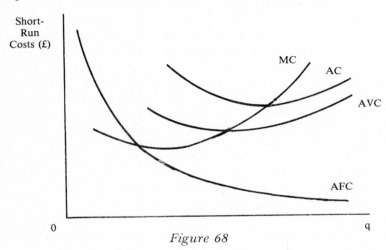

Figure 68

Rising average productivity of variable factors is the main reason why AVC is likely to fall. It is probable that the average product of labour will rise as output is expanded from a low level. Suppose that a clothing firm has available a cutting room, a machine and finishing room with ten sewing machines, and a general office in which packing, correspondence, and general secretarial work are conducted. If only one man is at work in the factory he must act as cutter, machinist, finisher, packer, typist and telephone operator. He might produce five garments per week. However, if a second worker is employed, production will almost certainly rise above ten garments per week — the marginal product on the second unit of labour is likely to exceed that on the first, thereby pulling up the average product of labour. For *economies of the division of labour* can occur:

(i) Each worker can become more expert on a smaller range of tasks.

(ii) There is saving in time lost in passing from one kind of work to another.

Such considerations make it probable that the average product of labour will continue to rise until the firm has at least one cutter, several machinists and finishers, and someone to attend to packing and office work. However, if the price of labour is given, rising average productivity of labour implies declining labour cost per unit. Other things being equal, AVC will fall due to rising labour productivity entailed by economies of the division of labour.

The AVC curve will eventually rise because of the law of diminishing returns which states that, *given the state of technology, as equal increments of one or more variable factors are combined with one or more fixed factors, total output will tend to increase, but, after a certain point at least, at a diminishing rate.* If successively more workers are hired in a plant of a fixed size, declining marginal productivity of labour will eventually set in. The law of diminishing returns is axiomatic. It is obvious, if successively more machinists are set to work on ten machines, that a point will ultimately be reached at which the marginal product of machinists will start to decline. Since the marginal product of labour will ultimately decline so also will the average product decline. Given the price of labour, labour cost per unit will therefore rise. Other things being equal, AVC will rise because of declining average productivity of the variable factors entailed by the law of diminishing returns. Thus, the AVC curve is *U*-shaped because:

(i) AVC will decline with economies of the division of labour.

(ii) AVC will rise because of the law of diminishing returns.

It is now simple to construct the short run AC curve. Since AC = AFC + AVC, we need only add the AFC and AVC curves vertically, as in Figure 68. Note that the difference between AC and AVC is AFC. The AC and AVC curves converge as output increases, reflecting the fact that the difference between these curves — AFC — is decreasing. Note also that the minimum point of the AC curve lies to the right of minimum AVC. That is because AFC continues to fall after AVC has started to rise.

The SRAC curve, like the LRAC curve, is *U*-shaped — but for different reasons. The LRAC curve is *U*-shaped because of economies and diseconomies of scale. The SRAC curve is *U*-shaped because:

(i) The SRAC curve declines since (a) AFC falls as overheads are spread over larger outputs, and (b) AVC falls due to rising average productivity of the variable factors.

(ii) The SRAC curve rises due to the law of diminishing returns.

There is a further cost of relevance in the short run — short-run marginal cost, SRMC. SRMC bears no relation to AFC. On the basis of reasoning similar to that in our discussion of LRAC and LRMC, we conclude that if AVC is declining, SRMC < AVC, and if AVC is rising, SRMC > AVC. Similarly, if AC is declining, SRMC < AC, and if AC is rising SRMC > AC. It follows that the short-run MC curve cuts the AVC and AC curves at their minima.

Relationships between the LRAC and SRAC Curves

When we speak of a short-run average cost curve we are referring to the relationship between AC and output in a plant of a given size. Since plant size is fixed in the short run, the firm in the short run is confined to a given SRAC curve. In the long run it can vary its plant size, thereby moving from one SRAC curve to another.

Suppose, in Figure 69, that the profit-maximising firm seeks to produce output A. In the long run it will build a plant (plant 1) which enables A units to be produced at minimum possible cost, $£C_1$. $SRAC_1$ shows AC in plant 1. If it wants to produce B units it can do so in the short run only at an AC of $£C_2$, because of the law of diminishing returns. In the long run it can add to its capital stock and construct plant 2 — that plant which permits production of B units at minimum possible AC, $£C_1$. $SRAC_2$ is then the appropriate AC curve. If, with plant 2, the firm wishes to produce D units, it can do so, in the short run, only at an AC of $£C_3$. But in the long run it can adjust the scale of its plant to that (plant 3) which produces D units at minimum possible AC, $£C_1$. $SRAC_3$ is the AC curve for plant 3. The pattern of reasoning should be clear: if a firm wishes to produce any output at minimum AC it will, in the long run, construct that scale of plant which enables it to do so. If, in Figure 69, it wishes to produce E units, plant 4 is appropriate.

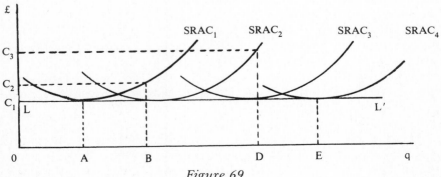

Figure 69

The firm's LRAC curve shows the minimum possible cost of producing *any* output when all factors are variable. But in moving from one plant size to another — from one SRAC curve to another — that is precisely what we have been tracing in Figure 69. If plant size were continuously variable the curve LL′ would be the firm's LRAC curve.

In the above analysis we implicitly assumed that the firm experienced no net economies or diseconomies of scale: we assumed that if all factors were variable, LRAC would be constant as the firm expanded plant size. If economies of scale prevail, then the higher the output, the lower the unit cost that can be attained by expanding plant size. In Figure 70, for example, the minimum possible unit cost of producing A units is £C_1. The cheapest way of producing B units is by constructing plant 2, in which unit cost is £C_2. If the profit-maximising firm wishes to produce quantity D, it will build plant 3, which produces that output at a unit cost £C_3. Within the range OD, larger plants can bring about expansions in output at lower unit cost.

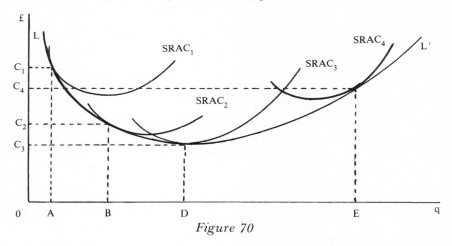

Figure 70

If diseconomies of scale prevail, larger outputs can be produced only at rising unit costs. In Figure 70, plant 4 can produce E units at the minimum possible unit cost of producing that level of output, namely, £C_4. The reason why the minima of the SRAC curves are increasing as output is expanded beyond q = D is because of diseconomies of scale (i.e., decreasing returns to scale).

If plant size were continuously variable, the LRAC curve LL′ in Figure 70 would trace the minimum possible cost of producing *any* output. It first slopes downwards due to economies of scale. Eventually it slopes upwards due to diseconomies of scale.

What, then, is the relationship between the firm's LRAC and SRAC curves? The answer is that the LRAC curve is the envelope of the SRAC curves for plants of different sizes. The reader can think of the LRAC curve as the nest of adjustment possibilities, through time, of the firm's SRAC curves as it moves from plants of small to progressively larger sizes at a given state of technical knowledge.

FOOTNOTE

1. The fact that returns to scale may change from increasing to constant to decreasing as output is expanded causes possible problems for our definition of returns to scale. Suppose, for example, that isoquants representing equal increments in output are progressively closer together as output is increased from zero to, say, 1000 units (increasing returns to scale prevail) and become equidistant over the output range 1000 to 1100 units. Our definition, unqualified, would imply that there were increasing returns to scale over the output ranges 1000 to 1100 units — which is something we do *not* wish to imply. However, if we interpret 1000 units as the new origin, our definition is quite satisfactory. Likewise, if isoquants representing equal increments in output become progressively further apart as output is expanded beyond 1100 units, we regard 1100 as the new origin, and say, consistent with our definition, that returns to scale are decreasing beyond q = 1100.

CHAPTER 22

Equilibrium of the Firm and Industry under Perfect Competition

In this and the next chapter we consider price and output determination in markets which are (a) perfectly competitive (b) monopolistic (c) imperfectly competitive and (d) oligopolistic. Chapter 21 analysed cost structures. Before we consider firm and industry equilibrium in different market structures we must examine the pattern of demand which the firm faces. Then we will bring together cost (supply) considerations and demand considerations.

In this chapter we confine ourselves to equilibrium in perfectly competitive markets. First, we clarify the meaning of equilibrium in the context at hand. A firm is in equilibrium in a given time period (short run or long run) if it has no incentive to change its policies within that time period. We assume that technology is constant. A perfectly competitive *firm* is in *short-run equilibrium* if, given prices and plant size, it is producing that output which maximises profits; it is in *long-run equilibrium* if, given prices, it is operating in that plant size, and producing that output, which maximise profits. The *industry* is in (full) *equilibrium* if there is no tendency towards change in the output of the industry. Two conditions are necessary for industry equilibrium under perfect competition:

(i) Each firm in the industry must be in long-run equilibrium.

(ii) There must be no tendency towards change in the number of firms in the industry. If, for example, each firm were in long-run equilibrium — condition (i) — making economic profits, more firms would be attracted to the industry. Entry would change the industry's output. Thus, each firm must be earning only normal profits in long-run equilibrium for industry equilibrium under perfect competition.

Demand in Perfectly Competitive Markets

We saw in Chapter 4 that there are large numbers of traders in perfectly competitive markets. Equilibrium price and quantity are determined by market supply and demand. Each firm is a price-taker; it cannot, by its own actions, influence price. In Figure 71a, P_0 and Q_0 are equilibrium price and quantity of a particular good. The individual firm is one of a large number of suppliers; its output is an infinitesimally small part of total supply. It will not affect market price by variation in its own output; locus dd' in Figure 71b is therefore the demand curve which *the individual firm* faces in a perfectly competitive goods market. Locus dd' is also its average revenue (AR) curve. A firm's AR curve *is* its demand curve. For example, if it sells 100 units at £6 each, total revenue (TR) is £600; AR is TR/q = £600/100 = £6; so price and AR are the same.

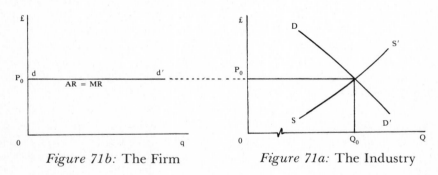

Figure 71b: The Firm   Figure 71a: The Industry

We define marginal revenue (MR) on the Nth unit sold as the change in TR due to selling N instead of $(N - 1)$ units. If price (AR) is constant, as in the case of a perfectly competitive firm, then MR = AR. Suppose, as before, that a firm can sell 100 units at price £6. Then TR = £600. If the firm operates in a perfectly competitive market it can sell 101 units at price £6 (AR = £6), and TR = £606. Then MR = ΔTR = £(606 − 600) = £6 = AR; for the perfectly competitive firm, AR = MR, as in Figure 71b.

Short-Run Equilibrium of the Perfectly Competitive Firm

There are very many firms in a perfectly competitive industry. Nevertheless, we often refer to *'the'* firm in what follows. When we do so we shall be assuming that this firm is in relevant ways representative of all firms in the industry. We also assume that each firm is a price-taker in the factor market; thus we assume that the firm regards the (explicit and implicit) prices of inputs as data beyond its control. Hence the firm, by expanding output, will not bid up factor prices against itself; however, expansion of the industry may bid up factor prices.

There are two constraints on industry output in the short run: (i) Each firm has plant of fixed size. (ii) The number of firms in the industry is fixed.

In Figure 72a, SS' is the short-run supply curve of the perfectly competitive industry. Given the market demand curve DD', equilibrium price and quantity are P_0 and Q_0 respectively. The individual firm accepts that price as a datum. That is why the demand curve which the firm faces is $AR_0 = MR_0$ in Figure 72b. The firm's short-run cost structure is shown in the same diagram.

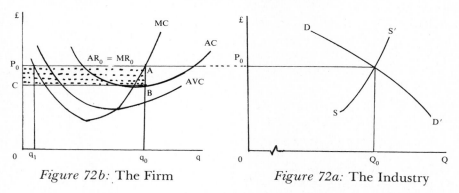

Figure 72b: The Firm   *Figure 72a:* The Industry

How much will the firm produce? If it produces anything, it must produce a quantity for which MC = MR. That is a necessary condition for profit maximisation. Now MC = MR at both q_0 and q_1. Which of these is the profit-maximising output? The answer is given by the second-order condition for profit maximisation, which states that *the MC curve must cut the MR curve from below,* as at q_0. Quantity q_0 is the firm's profit-maximising output. Given price P_0, the firm is in equilibrium-producing q_0; it has then no incentive to change its policies, as it is maximising profits.

Why is the firm in equilibrium at q_0, the output level at which the MC curve cuts the MR curve from below? Consider what would happen if output were at any other level. It is clear that the firm would not produce q_1 (or any output less than q_1); if it did so, its sales price would not cover even variable cost per unit (AVC). Nor would it produce any other quantity below q_0. If output were less than q_0 (but greater than q_1), MR > MC. Hence the firm, by expanding output, could add more to TR than to TC. The firm would expand output to q_0. But it would not go beyond q_0. By producing more than q_0 it would be adding more to its costs than to its revenues, since MC > MR for q > q_0. Thus, q_0 — the output at which the MC curve cuts the MR curve from below — is the profit-maximising output.

The Short-Run Supply Curve of the Perfectly Competitive Firm

We have seen why the perfectly competitive firm, in the short run, would supply quantity q_0 at price P_0. If we could tell how much it would supply at every other price, we would know the firm's short-run supply curve. To find this we examine in Figure 73 how much the firm would produce at various hypothetical prices. Suppose, in Figure 73a, that the price of the firm's product were P_1. The corresponding AR = MR curve is the horizontal line $AR_1 = MR_1$. It is obvious that in this case the firm will produce nothing, because price is insufficient to cover unit variable costs of any possible quantity. The firm will not produce if P < AVC. Thus, short-run supply from the firm will be zero when P < P_2.

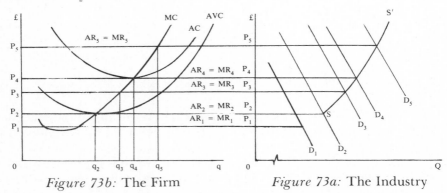

Figure 73b: The Firm   *Figure 73a:* The Industry

Let price now rise above P_2, to P_3. Note that P_3 < AC, so the firm will incur losses if it produces at price P_3. Note also that at P_3 the firm *can* cover unit variable costs. We know that if it does produce it will supply q_3 units, since that is the output at which the MC curve cuts the MR curve from below.

Will the firm have incentive to produce q_3 units? If output were zero the firm would incur losses: fixed costs are incurred in the short run regardless of output. If price were P_3, the firm, by producing q_3, could cover variable costs per unit. But since, at q_3, AR > AVC, it would also contribute *something* towards meeting fixed costs. By producing q_3 the firm would incur smaller losses than if output were zero. We conclude that the firm will produce q_3 at price P_3. This situation often prevails in the short run. Consider a firm during trade recession. Price has fallen, so that the firm cannot cover its full costs at any level of output. The firm faces a choice of remaining in production or temporarily closing down. If it closes down its fixed costs must be met either by borrowing or by drawing on funds accumulated in the past. If price, though less than AC, exceeds AVC, then the firm can, by staying in production, cover all variable costs and *part* of its fixed costs. In such cases it would incur smaller short-run losses by producing than by not producing. The firm will produce to where MC = MR so long as price exceeds AVC. Thus, if price were P_4 or P_5 the firm would produce q_4 or q_5, respectively.

We have examined how much the firm would produce at various prices in the short run: so long as price exceeds AVC, it will produce to where MC meets MR from below. As price rises the firm expands along its MC curve until MC = MR. It follows that *the firm's short-run supply curve is that part of its MC curve which lies above its AVC curve.* The short-run supply curve of a perfectly competitive *industry* is the horizontal sum of the short-run supply curves of the firms in the industry.[1] The short-run industry supply curve SS' in Figure 73a is thus the horizontal sum of the marginal cost curves of the firms in the industry, for MC > AVC.

Normal Profits and Economic Profits

We noticed that the perfectly competitive firm could, in short-run equilibrium, be earning economic profits (as at price P_5 in Figure 73b), making losses (as at P_3) or just breaking even (as at P_4). We define economic profit as the difference between costs and revenues. But recall from Chapter 21 what we mean by costs. A firm's costs are those payments it must incur to maintain factor supplies. There are four kinds of factors — land, labour, capital and enterprise. The firm's total costs include payments to each. Rent must be paid for land, wages must be paid to labour, and an implicit or explicit rental must be paid for capital. Otherwise the factors will not be supplied to the firm. The *supply price* to the firm of any factor is the minimum price that factor must be paid if it is to be supplied to the firm.

Normal profit is the supply price of enterprise. Normal profits in any industry are the minimum profits an entrepreneur must receive if he is to have incentive to stay in the industry in the long run. They are payments to the factor *enterprise.* Since they are the supply price of a factor they are costs of production. *Normal profits are therefore included in the firm's AC curve.* Economic or 'supernormal' profits are returns to enterprise in excess of normal profits. In Figure 72b the firm is in short-run equilibrium earning economic profits represented by the shaded area P_0ABC. However, we shall soon see that in the long run these will be competed away. In long-run competitive equilibrium each firm earns zero economic profits. That does not mean that the firm earns zero profits in the long run: the perfectly competitive firm in long-run equilibrium earns normal profits; otherwise it would leave the industry.

Long-Run Equilibrium of the Firm and Industry Equilibrium

In the long run the firm can adjust plant size to produce any output at minimum possible cost. The conditions for long-run equilibrium of the firm are: (i) The firm must be able to cover all costs of production. This condition is satisfied if its AR is at least as great as its long-run average cost (AC_L). Thus, in the long run, $AR \geqslant AC_L$. If, in the long run, the firm cannot cover its full production costs, it will go out of business. (ii) Assuming condition (i) satisfied, the firm in the long run will produce that level of output at which its long-run marginal cost (MC_L) curve cuts its MR curve from below. The perfectly competitive firm's long-run supply curve is that part of its MC_L curve which lies above its AC_L curve.

The long-run analysis of perfectly competitive markets is complicated. The *long-run* supply curve of the perfectly competitive *industry* is *not* the sideways sum of the long-run supply curves of the individual firms. (We clarify this assertion in the next few pages.) Two types of adjustment in plant availability can occur in perfectly competitive markets in the long run. Suppose that because of an increase in demand each firm earns supernormal profits in the short run. In the long run each can adjust its plant size. But because of supernormal profits, and because there is freedom of entry, new firms will be attracted to the industry in the long run. The resulting increase in supply will force price down. Entry will continue until supernormal profits are no longer available — until price (AR) has been forced down to AC_L.

In the long run, therefore, the industry will be in equilibrium when each firm is producing an output at which (i) its MC_L curve cuts its MR curve from below, and (ii) AC_L = AR. Condition (i) implies that each firm is in long-run equilibrium. Condition (ii) implies that there will be no tendency towards entry to, or exit from, the industry. If AC_L = AR, each firm in the industry is earning only normal profits, supernormal profits then being zero.

External Economies and Diseconomies

External economies occur if an increase in the size of an industry reduces unit costs of the firms in the industry. These economies are external to the individual firm — they occur because of growth of the industry as a whole rather than growth of any particular firm. A firm experiences external economies if its cost curves *shift down* because of expansion in the output of the industry. For example, it is possible that the price of steel to each firm in an industry using steel as an input will be reduced if expansion of that industry enables the steel industry to avail of economies of scale. That would not be due to the expansion of any particular firm in the steel-using industry; it would be *due to growth of the steel-using industry as a whole*. That is why such economies are considered external to the individual firm — they are not caused by its own growth. Note that the lower price of steel would cause the AC curves of firms in the steel-using industry to shift down, implying that each can now produce any given output at lower unit costs.

External diseconomies occur if an increase in the size of an industry increases per unit costs of the firms in the industry. For example, each firm in an industry experiences external diseconomies if expansion in the size of the industry bids up the price of skilled labour. Due to forces external to itself, the individual firm must then pay more for skilled labour. The firm could then produce a given output only at higher unit costs. External diseconomies cause *upward shifts* in the average cost curves of the firms in the industry.

If (net) external diseconomies prevail in an industry, its long-run supply curve *slopes upwards;* it is an *increasing-cost* industry. If external economies prevail, the industry's supply curve *slopes downwards;* it is a *decreasing-cost* industry. If neither external economies nor external diseconomies prevail, the industry is a *constant-cost* industry; its long-run supply curve is *horizontal.*

Industry Equilibrium in an Increasing-Cost Industry

We now consider a perfectly competitive industry's adjustment towards full equilibrium. We begin with the industry in equilibrium and then allow demand to change and examine adjustment towards a new industry equilibrium.

With price P_0 in Figure 74a, the industry is in equilibrium since: (i) The typical firm is in long-run equilibrium. It has adjusted plant size to produce q_0 at minimum possible cost. It is operating that plant up to the point at which the short-run marginal cost curve, MC_s, cuts the MR curve, MR_0, from below. (ii) The typical firm, in a plant of optimum size, is earning only normal profits ($AC_s = AR_0$); therefore the number of firms in the industry shows no tendency to change.

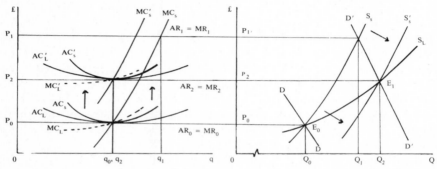

Figure 74b: The Firm   *Figure 74a:* The Industry

Suppose that the industry demand curve shifts to $D'D'$. In the short run price rises to P_1. The typical firm's AR and MR curve is now given by $AR_1 = MR_1$. The firm expands along its MC_s curve and produces q_1. Note that since $AR_1 > AC_s$ at q_1, the firm earns supernormal profits. In the long run more firms therefore enter the industry. As more firms enter, the short-run industry supply curve S_s shifts to the right. This causes price to fall and eliminates some of the supernormal profits.

However, there is another force reducing supernormal profits. If, as we assume here, external diseconomies prevail, expansion in the size of the industry causes the cost curves of each firm to shift upwards, as in Figure 74b. Entry to the industry will cease only when the typical firm is no longer earning supernormal profits. Such a situation prevails when price has fallen to P_2 in Figure 74a. The industry is then in equilibrium since its output shows no tendency to change. Entry has caused price to fall from P_1 to P_2. But it has also caused the AC curves of the representative firm to shift up, because of external diseconomies.

Locus S_L is the long-run supply curve of the perfectly competitive industry. *It is the horizontal sum of the minima of each firm's long-run average cost curve.* The reason why, in this case, it slopes upwards is because external diseconomies cause each firm's LRAC curve — and hence its minimum — to shift up as the industry expands. Point E_0 might be the horizontal sum of the minima of each firm's LRAC curve when there are 1000 firms in the industry; E_1 might be the sum of the minima of each firm's LRAC curve when the industry has expanded to 2000 firms. The reason why E_1 lies above E_0 is because each firm's LRAC curve shifted up as the industry expanded.

An observation before proceeding: In Figure 74b we drew AC_L' so that its minimum is at the same q as that of AC_L. Alert readers ask whether that is inevitable; the answer is no. External diseconomies cause upward shifts in the firm's AC curves, but that may be directly upwards or upwards to the right or left, depending on the precise form of the external diseconomies. (A similar observation applies to the situation with external economies, discussed below.)

Industry Equilibrium in a Decreasing-Cost Industry

We now consider adjustment towards industry equilibrium in a decreasing-cost industry — when expansion in the size of the industry yields external economies to all firms in the industry. As before, we start with the industry in equilibrium at price P_0, and consider the adjustment after an increase in demand.

The curve S_S in Figure 75a is the industry's short-run supply curve — it shows the amounts supplied at various prices, given the supply potential of the industry in the short run. DD is the market demand curve. Equilibrium price and quantity are P_0 and Q_0 respectively. The representative firm's AR = MR curve is $AR_0 = MR_0$ in Figure 75b.

At price P_0 in Figure 75b the typical firm is in long-run equilibrium — it has adjusted to optimum plant size and has no incentive to change its output from q_0. Since the firm is making no economic profits ($AC_L = AR_0$), the industry is also in equilibrium.

Suppose that demand increases to $D'D'$ in Figure 75a. In the short run price rises to P_1, a datum to the representative firm. Its AR = MR curve is $AR_1 = MR_1$ in Figure 75b. In the short run it expands along its MC curve until $MC_S = MR_1$, producing q_1. Note that it is earning supernormal profits per unit, given by the distance between AC_S and AR_1 at q_1. Therefore, in the long run firms enter the industry, causing

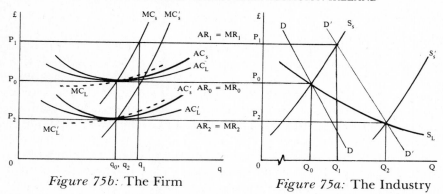

Figure 75b: The Firm   *Figure 75a:* The Industry

S_s to shift to the right, which forces price down. If, as we assume, expansion in the size of the industry causes external economies, the cost curves of the typical firm shift downwards.

Entry continues until the firm no longer earns supernormal profits. Throughout this adjustment process, the industry's short-run supply curve continues shifting to the right, causing price to fall, while simultaneously, the AC curves of the typical firm continue to shift downwards, due to external economies.

Eventually a situation at which the typical firm is no longer earning supernormal profits is reached. The industry has then reached a new equilibrium. Such a situation is attained in Figures 75a and 75b when price has fallen to P_2 and industry output has increased to Q_2. The firm's AR and MR curves are now $AR_2 = MR_2$. Its cost curves — AC_s' AC_L', MC_s' and MC_L' — have shifted downwards because of external economies. When, at price P_2, the firm is producing q_2, the industry has reached a new equilibrium. The firm then has no incentive to change output or plant size. And since with price P_2 and quantity q_2 the firm is only breaking even, there is no tendency for the number of firms in the industry to change.

Locus S_L in Figure 75a is the industry's long-run supply curve. It is the horizontal sum of the minima of the LRAC curves of the firms in the industry. It slopes downwards because external economies cause each firm's LRAC curve — and hence its minimum — to shift down as the industry expands. The long-run supply curve of a perfectly competitive industry slopes downwards if external economies prevail.[2]

We have examined adjustment towards industry equilibrium in increasing and in decreasing cost industries. It is left to the reader to trace the adjustment in constant-cost industries and to show that the long-run industry supply curve is then a horizontal line (i.e., it is infinitely elastic).

Perfect Competition, Efficiency and Income Distribution

We mentioned earlier that few if any actual markets satisfy *all* the requirements of perfect competition. But there are several reasons why analysis of perfect competition is worthwhile. Actual markets often approximate the requirements of perfect competition. Knowledge of perfectly competitive markets gives insights into the workings of such similar markets; that was shown in Chapters 6 to 8 where we considered some applications of supply and demand analysis. Furthermore, perfect competition is a *desideratum* which yields criteria by which we may judge actual market structures.

Resource Allocation

If we assume (i) that marginal cost to the firm (MPC — marginal private cost, or, more simply, MC) corresponds to marginal social cost (MSC) and (ii) that market price is a measure of marginal social value (MSV), than a necessary condition for an optimal allocation of resources from the point of view of society is that each firm produce up to the point at which MC = price. We now elaborate on that statement.

We define the MSC of the Nth unit of a good as the change in total cost, *no matter by whom in society it is incurred,* due to producing N instead of $(N - 1)$ units of that good. For example, if production of an additional unit of a good involves emission of smoke which pollutes the atmosphere, then the MSC of that unit equals the expenditure incurred by the firm to produce that additional unit (MPC) *plus* the monetary value of the damage done to all persons in the community by the air pollution.

We can think of the MSV of the Nth unit of a good as the change in welfare of society due to consumption of the Nth unit of that good. It is reasonable to assume that the price an individual is just willing to pay for a good is a measure of the relative subjective value of that good to him. If that individual's consumption does not interfere with the welfare of others, it seems reasonable to regard price as in some sense a measure of marginal social value.

A necessary condition for an optimal allocation of resources is that each firm produce up to a point at which MSC = MSV. That can be seen by considering the implications for the welfare of society if MSC $\gtrless$ MSV. If, when a firm is producing a given level of output, MSC < MSV, then the cost incurred by society in the production of an additional unit would be less than the increase in welfare of society due to consumption of that additional unit. The social interest therefore requires that the firm expand production so long as MSC < MSV. However, if, when a firm is producing a given level of output, MSC > MSV, the cost incurred by society in the production of the last unit would exceed the increase in welfare of society due to consumption of the last unit. The social interest requires that the firm contract output so long as MSC > MSV. Thus a necessary condition for an optimal allocation of resources from society's point of view is that each firm produce an output for which MSC = MSV.

Is this requirement for optimality attained in perfectly competitive markets? Both in the short run and in the long run, the perfectly competitive firm produces an output for which MC equals price. Given assumptions (i) and (ii) above, it follows that the perfectly competitive firm produces an output for which MSC = MSV. We can accordingly state that if assumptions (i) and (ii) are valid, a necessary condition for an optimal allocation of resources would be attained in perfectly competitive markets. Given those assumptions, perfectly competitive markets satisfy one of the requirements for overall economic efficiency.

Income Distribution

We noticed that the perfectly competitive firm could be in short-run equilibrium earning supernormal profits. But supernormal profits could not prevail for long. We saw that if the representative firm earns supernormal profits in the short run, these will be competed away in the long run by entry to the industry. When the industry is in full equilibrium each firm is earning only normal profits. Thus the pattern of income distribution emerging from perfectly competitive markets might tend to be more egalitarian than that emerging from market forms in which the individual firm can continue to make supernormal profits in the long run. However, note that *as economists* we cannot say that there is anything 'good' or 'bad' about the pattern of income distribution emerging from any particular market structure.

<hr />

FOOTNOTES

1. For simplicity we assume that as the industry expands its output in the short run, it does not bid factor prices upwards.
2. The presence of external economies in a given industry would often imply unexhausted increasing returns to scale in some firm supplying inputs to the given industry. As will be made clear in Chapter 23, this implies that the industry supplying the input in question could not be perfectly competitive.

Industrial Organisation, and Economic Law in Ireland

We now turn to goods markets which substantively deviate from perfect competition. Towards the end of the chapter we review legal attitudes in Ireland concerning market structure. We shall see that although openness implies that much of the tradeable goods sector approximates perfect competition in relevant ways (recall Chapters 6 to 8), there may be significant departures from perfect competition in certain sectors, especially in non-tradeable goods. In such cases the state may be a monopoly producer, or legislation seeks to foster competition.

Pure Monopoly

A pure monopolist is the sole seller of a good which has no close substitutes. Pure monopoly and perfect competition are extremes on a spectrum of market structures. Actual goods markets lie between them, some approximating pure monopoly; others closer to perfect competition.

Demand Under Pure Monopoly

Because there is only one firm in the industry under pure monopoly, there is no distinction between firm and industry. The monopolist's demand curve is the industry demand curve. As such it slopes downwards. DD′ in Figure 76 is the monopolist's demand curve; its AR curve. To sell more the monopolist must reduce price; the monopolist is a price-maker. That is why, under monopoly, MR < AR, as in Figure 76. Note how this contrasts with the perfectly competitive firm.

Suppose, for example, that the monopolist can sell 10 units at £6 each (TR = £60, AR = £6). If he wishes to sell 11 units he must

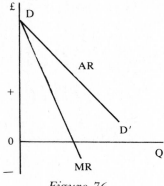

Figure 76

reduce price, say to £5·95, since he faces the industry demand curve. TR is now £(11)(5·95) = £65·45, and AR = £5·95. The corresponding MR (=ΔTR) is £5·45. Because he must reduce price to sell an eleventh unit, MR (£5·45) < AR (£5·95).

The monopolist's MR can become negative. Suppose the firm could sell 20 units at £3 each (TR = £60, AR = £3). To sell 21 units it must reduce price, say, to £2·8. Its TR is then £(2·8)(21) = £58·8, and AR = £2·8. But MR = ΔTR = £(58·8 − 60) = − £1·2; MR has become negative (implying that demand is inelastic at low prices).

The Sources of Monopoly

The central reasons why monopoly exists is that other firms find it unprofitable or impossible to enter the industry. Thus, the persistence of monopoly over time is due to *barriers on entry* to an industry. Such barriers *may* enable the monopolist to earn supernormal profits in the long run. Conspiracies, intimidation and brute force aside, there are two principal kinds of barriers; *technical barriers* and *legal barriers.*

The prevalence of increasing returns to scale in a single firm is a major *technical barrier* on entry and hence an important source of monopoly power. If economies of scale in a single firm prevail over all relevant ranges of industry output, then total supply can be produced most cheaply by a single firm. Such a firm is called a natural monopolist. Public utilities are frequently natural monopolies: a large town or average-sized city is usually best served by a single gas company, a single supplier of electricity, and a single sewage-disposal authority. Competition in such markets may imply wasteful duplication of resources: a natural monopoly can normally supply any level of output at lower unit cost than a large number of competing firms.

Another technical basis of monopoly is unique knowledge of a low-cost production technique. The problem of a monopolist fearing entry is then to keep this technique to himself alone. That may be difficult unless the technology is protected by a patent (see below). Sole ownership of essential resources (e.g., mineral deposits), prohibitive transport costs or absolute cost advantages due to entrepreneurial efficiency may be other technical sources of monopoly.

Entry to an industry is often limited by *legal* controls. Patent rights are important in this context. A patent gives the inventor of a new process the exclusive right to use that process for a number of years. Patent rights thus encourage innovation. But they also restrict entry of potential competitors to an industry. High tariff protection of a small domestic market, or the provision of a licence giving a single firm exclusive rights to supply the domestic market, may be further legal sources of monopoly. Finally, the State may form a monopoly in some good if it reserves to itself the provision of that good to the domestic market. (Note, however, that State monopolies are often industries which, because of increasing returns to scale, would tend to be monopolies in the absence of State ownership; this consideration, along with the fact that they might be in a position to earn supernormal profits indefinitely, may be one of the reasons for the nationalisation of such industries.) In what follows in this chapter we shall confine ourselves to the private sector of the economy.

Price and Output Under Monopoly

Assuming that the firm can cover its *variable* costs, the monopolist, in the short run, will produce that level of output at which its short run MC curve cuts its MR curve from below. In the long run it can adjust the size of its plant so as to produce any level of output at minimum cost. Assuming that the firm can cover its *total* costs, the monopolist, in the long run, will produce that output at which its long run MC curve cuts its MR curve from below.

The pattern of demand which the monopolist faces is shown by the curve AR in Figure 77a. The AR and MR curves both slope downwards for reasons already indicated. The firm's long-run cost structure is also shown in the same diagram.

The profit-maximising monopolist in Figure 77a will produce Q_0 — the quantity given by the intersection of its MC_L and MR curves. It will charge the highest price consistent with that quantity, p_0. If quantity

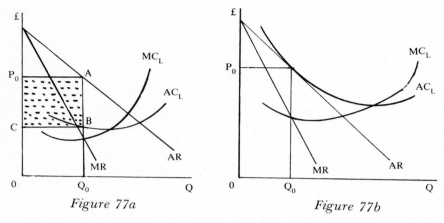

Figure 77a   Figure 77b

were less than Q_0, MR > MC: the firm could add more to its total revenue than to its total costs by expanding output. It will therefore expand up to Q_0 at least. If it produced beyond Q_0, MC > MR: the firm would be adding more to costs than to revenues. Thus, price p_0 and quantity Q_0 are the profit-maximising price and quantity under monopoly. Charging p_0 and producing Q_0, the firm is in long-run equilibrium because it has no incentive to change the size of its plant or its output. The industry is in full equilibrium because the firm is in long-run equilibrium, and because the firm *is* the industry.

The firm in Figure 77a is earning supernormal profits given by the rectangle p_0ABC. If it remains a monopolist it can earn such supernormal profits indefinitely; they will not be competed away by entry to the industry. However, there is no reason why a monopolist *must* earn supernormal profits in the long run, even if it tries to do so. A monopolist could not earn supernormal profits if its demand and long-run cost conditions were as depicted in Figure 77b. At best such a firm could only break even.

Non-existence of Supply Curves Under Monopoly

In Chapter 4 we stated that it is only in perfectly competitive markets that price is determined by the intersection of supply and demand curves. That is mainly because a supply curve does not normally exist in market structures other than perfect competition. Recall our definition of a supply curve in Chapter 4 — a supply curve shows the various alternative quantities of a good which producers will supply at various alternative prices, other things being equal. Consider now the monopolist whose MC curve is depicted in Figure 78. We see that,

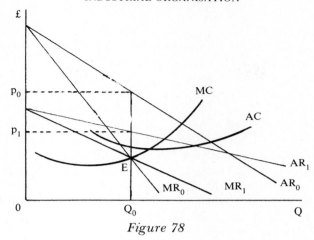

Figure 78

whether its demand curve is AR_0 or AR_1, the firm will supply the same
output, Q_0. That is because the firm's MC curve intersects MR_0 and
MR_1 at the same point, E. The two patterns of demand imply two
different prices, p_0 and p_1; nevertheless, quantity supplied in either
case is the same, Q_0. There are, in fact, an infinity of possible demand
patterns for which MR can cut MC at E. Each of those demand
patterns implies a different equilibrium price. Hence we conclude that
a monopolist may supply Q_0 at any one of an infinity of possible prices;
it will do so as long as the MR curve intersects the MC curve at point E.
There is thus no definite relationship between price and quantity
supplied under monopoly; hence a supply curve does not exist under
monopoly. It is wrong, therefore, to state that the equilibrium price
under monopoly is determined by the supply and demand curves. For
the supply curve does not then exist.[1]

Some Issues in Assessing Monopoly

Resource Allocation
From the standpoint of society, the profit-maximising monopolist
misallocates resources *if* (i) private costs coincide with social costs and
(ii) market price can correctly be regarded as a measure of marginal
social value. The monopolist produces an output for which MC =
MR. But since MR is less than price (i.e., AR), the monopolist, when
in equilibrium, produces an output for which MC < P. Hence, if
provisos (i) and (ii) are satisfied, MSC < MSV in monopoly

equilibrium. Recall from Chapter 22 that a necessary condition for an optimal allocation of resources throughout the economy is that each firm produce an output for which MSC = MSV. Thus, in the absence of government regulation, monopoly equilibrium yields a smaller output than the public interest requires.

We also noted in Chapter 22 that so long as provisos (i) and (ii) above are satisfied, MSC = MSV under perfect competition. This may *appear* to imply that, for the maximisation of social welfare, monopolistic markets must be dismembered and made perfectly competitive. However, as we shall shortly illustrate, the latter conclusion does not follow at all; *if* the source of monopoly is increasing returns to scale, it may be impossible, on any sustained basis, to transform (e.g., by legislation) a monopolistic industry into a perfectly competitive one, and indeed it *may* be downright foolish to attempt to introduce even a moderate degree of competition to a monopolistic industry. The argument is that (a) for technical reasons, it may be impossible to have perfect competition in an industry; (b) for technical reasons, monopoly may be inevitable, but if unregulated, this will involve misallocation of resources as already explained, and (c) given that monopoly may sometimes have to be accepted as a fact of life, the only way in which government may ensure a sensible allocation of resources may have to involve *regulation* of monopoly — sometimes involving subsidisation of private-sector monopolies, or nationalising them and perhaps operating them at commercial losses. Our reasoning under (a), (b) and (c) above will be clarified shortly.

'Excess Capacity', Price and Output

We know that the individual firm in industry equilibrium under perfect competition produces as much as possible, and charges the lowest possible price, consistent with the firm breaking even. Since such a firm would tend to be operating at minimum AC_L, this implies, in a sense, that the individual firm under perfect competition would tend to be fully utilising its capacity. It is extremely unlikely that it would be in the interests of a profit-maximising monopolist to produce at the minimum point of its AC_L curve; it would do so only if the MR curve *happened* to intersect the MC curve at that minimum point. It is sometimes said that if a situation like that depicted in Figure 77b arises, the monopolist must be operating with excess capacity because it is producing an output below that corresponding to minimum AC_L. However, we cannot see anything of substance in such reasoning because: (i) Given the size of the market as represented by the monopolist's demand (i.e., AR) curve, it is not clear how the industry depicted in Figure 77b could possibly be made perfectly competitive. (ii) If the monopolist in Figure 77b did produce at minimum AC_L, he would not only be making losses, but also, *too much* would be produced from the standpoint of efficient resource allocation: since MC would then exceed AR, i.e., price, we would have, given the assumptions of coincidence of private cost with social cost, and of market price with marginal social value, MSC > MSV.

Except when a situation like that depicted in Figure 77b arises, the unregulated profit-maximising monopolist charges a price in excess of average cost. On the basis of such considerations it is often said that the price charged will be higher, and quantity produced will be lower, under monopoly than would be the case if there were a large number of competing firms in the industry. Such conclusions are not necessarily correct: they overlook the importance of increasing returns to scale as a source of monopoly. If a monopolist experiences increasing returns to scale over all ranges of output, it could produce *any* level of output at lower unit cost than a large number of competing firms. Under such circumstances it is possible that price will be lower under monopoly than in a more competitive environment. Furthermore, under the conditions specified, an attempt to dismember the monopolist, and to introduce something like perfect competition to the industry, would surely break down: increasing returns to scale accruing to any single firm over all ranges of industry output are inconsistent with perfect competition. Thus *technology* may decree that perfect competition is unattainable. These propositions are illustrated in Figure 79.

The existence of increasing returns to scale over all ranges of industry output is clearly the source of monopoly for the firm depicted in Figure 79. The monopolist, if unregulated, would produce Q_m and charge price p_m. Suppose that the monopolist were dismembered and that several competing firms were introduced in its place. It is reasonable to assume that the technology available to those competing firms would be the same as that of the monopolist. Suppose, shortly after the monopolist was broken up, that each of the competing firms was producing a small proportion of the previous industry output, say q_c. The average cost of the competing firms would then be very high; in the case depicted in Figure 79 it would exceed the price consumers are willing to pay for the good. Some of the competing firms would therefore leave the industry. A greater share of market demand would then accrue to those remaining. Suppose that there were only two

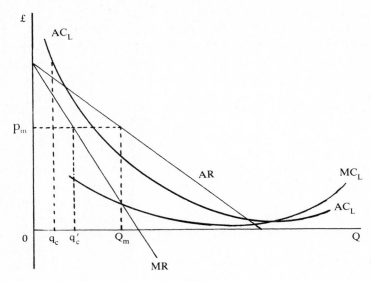

Figure 79

remaining competitors, each producing q'_c. Clearly, average cost in each of the competing firms would exceed the AC_L which would prevail under monopoly equilibrium. Furthermore, because of increasing returns to scale, if one of the competing firms expanded its output, it could produce at lower AC_L than its rival. The increased industry output would also mean that price would have fallen. Hence the firm expanding output would drive its sole remaining rival out of business and would itself become a monopolist.

We have shown: (i) If increasing returns to scale are the source of monopoly, price may be lower, and industry output higher, under unregulated monopoly than in a (short-run) situation involving competition. (ii) An attempt to break up a monopoly and to introduce something like perfect competition in its place would, if increasing returns to scale were the source of the monopoly, tend to break down. Competition among firms, each with increasing returns to scale over relevant ranges of industry output, would tend to restore the initial monopolistic market structure. Indeed, increasing returns to scale over all ranges of industry output are inconsistent with perfect competition (except in some very transitory sense).

We emphasise that the above remarks pertain to situations in which increasing returns to scale are the source of monopoly; they will frequently be invalid if legal controls (e.g., patents or tariff protection) are the sources of monopoly. For example, if tariff protection in the domestic market is the source of monopoly, it will usually be possible to attain a lower equilibrium price by removing the tariff.

Income Distribution

We have seen that except when situations like that in Figure 77b arise, an unregulated monopolist earns supernormal profits in the long run. That could not occur under perfect competition. When the industry is in equilibrium under perfect competition, the typical firm is earning only normal profits. Thus unregulated monopolistic markets may tend to exacerbate income inequality.

Regulation of Monopoly: Some Extensions

The preceding analysis suggests two objectives of public policy in regulation of monopoly:

(i) To induce the monopolist to produce more than he would if exempt from regulation. Without regulation the monopolist would produce to where MC = MR. At that output, MC < P. Therefore (if two assumptions stated toward the end of Chapter 22 are satisfied) MSC < MSV. The objective of regulation may be to improve resource allocation by removing the divergence of MSC from MSV.

(ii) A second objective of regulation may be to reduce supernormal profits.

Marginal Cost Pricing and Profits

Government may try to improve resource allocation by requiring the monopolist to produce that output at which its marginal cost curve cuts its AR curve from below; then MC = P. However, there is no guarantee that this would eliminate supernormal profits. Furthermore, if increasing returns to scale are the source of the monopoly, government may need to subsidise the firm if it is required to produce to where MC = P. Figures 80a and 80b clarify these points.

In Figure 80a the monopolist, unregulated, would produce Q_0 and charge p_0. If the firm were required to produce Q_1 it could obtain only the lower equilibrium price p_1. Marginal cost would then equal price, but some supernormal profits would remain. These are shown by the rectangle p_1ABC. (Of course the government could require the monopolist to supply the even larger output at which AC = AR,

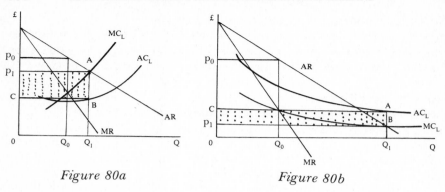

Figure 80a   *Figure 80b*

thereby eliminating the supernormal profits; but since marginal cost
would then exceed price, this would involve misallocation of resources
— the monopolist would then be producing too much.) Government
could eliminate the supernormal profits attained at Q_1 by imposing a
lump-sum tax per period equal in value to the rectangle p_1ABC. Such
a lump-sum tax would in effect be a charge per period for a *licence* or
franchise permitting the firm to produce the good under
consideration. Since, by definition of lump sum, the tax would not
vary with output, it would in effect be a fixed cost. Precisely because it
would not vary with output, it would not affect MC_L. The MC_L curve
would remain as in Figure 80a, while the AC_L curve would shift
upwards; if the lump-sum tax were p_1ABC per period, the
supernormal profits would be eliminated entirely, while the point at
which MC_L intersects AR would remain unchanged. Under the
circumstances indicated the monopolist would be producing output
Q_1, at which MC = P, earning only normal profits.

   That it may be necessary to subsidise a monopolist who is required to
produce to where MC = P is evident from Figure 80b. In this case the
monopolist, unregulated, would produce Q_0 at price p_0. Government
could eliminate the supernormal profits then being earned by
requiring the monopolist to produce an output for which AC = AR,
but we see from the diagram that the monopolist would still be
producing too little, since under such circumstances, MC_L < P. Suppose that the government required the monopolist to produce Q_1; then
$MC_L = p_1$. However, since $MC_L < AC_L$, the monopolist would be
making losses, as represented by the shaded rectangle $CABp_1$. To give
the monopolist incentive to stay in production supplying the regulated
quantity Q_1 per period, it would be necessary for government to offer
the firm a subsidy of $CABp_1$ per period.

State Ownership

Rather than regulate private monopolies the State may nationalise them. The objectives of State monopolies in different countries have varied. Some of them are constrained to produce an output at which average cost, or even marginal cost, equals price; others seek to maximise profits like firms in the private sector. In the latter case the primary objective may be the raising of government revenue.

Imperfect Competition

The words 'imperfect competition' are used in two senses by different authors. Sometimes they refer to *any* market structure other than perfect competition. However, we define imperfect competition as a market structure in which there is a *large number* of firms selling goods which are *close* though not perfect *substitutes* in the minds of buyers. Although the firms might sell goods which are physically very similar, product differentiation in the form of trade marks, brand names, colour and packaging, renders different sellers' products non-homogeneous in the minds of buyers. Competitive advertising is a key characteristic of imperfect competition: each firm attempts to convince buyers that its product is both significantly different and better than that of rivals. To some extent, most actual goods markets are imperfectly competitive.

Imperfectly competitive markets, being intermediate between perfect competition and monopoly, have characteristics of each of those extremes. The imperfectly competitive firm may earn large supernormal profits in the short run. But in the long run more firms would be attracted into the industry until supernormal profits are competed away. The analysis, in that context, resembles that of perfect competition in the long run. However, each firm in an imperfectly competitive industry has some monopoly power. Since, in the minds of at least some buyers, the products of no two firms in the industry are identical, each firm, in a sense, has a monopoly of its own product (e.g., of its brand name). If one firm raises price just a little, it will not lose *all* its sales.

Brand names and competitive advertising are not the only reasons why consumers discriminate between the product of one supplier and that of another. Some importance may be attached to transportation costs. A further reason why buyers might become attached to a particular supplier is because of goodwill. This might arise due to the reputation of a given seller, due to personal acquaintance with him, or merely because of habit or custom.

Because each firm under imperfect competition has some monopoly power, the demand curve for the product of any particular firm slopes downwards, reflecting the fact that in the absence of increased advertising, the firm must reduce price of a given product if it wishes to expand sales. It follows that at any level of output of the individual firm under imperfect competition, MR < AR, as in Figure 76.

The imperfectly competitive firm can manipulate three variables to influence its sales: (i) It can change the *price* of its product. (ii) It can change the form of its *product*. The firm changes the form of its product if it changes the size, colour, design, or packaging of its 'product'. (iii) It can change *advertising* outlay.

In the analysis which follows we assume that each firm keeps the form of its product, and the level of its advertising outlay, constant. We speak throughout in terms of a representative firm. This implies an assumption that all firms in the industry have similar cost structures and that the pattern of demand which each firm faces is similar for all firms in the industry. These assumptions are made for analytical simplicity only. We also assume that the industry is a constant-cost industry—that there are no external economies or diseconomies.

Equilibrium of the Firm and Industry Under Imperfect Competition

In the short run the representative firm under imperfect competition may be in equilibrium earning supernormal profits. The pattern of demand which it faces is given by AR_0 and MR_0 in Figure 81a. The short-run cost structure of the firm is depicted by the MC_s and AC_s curves in the same diagram.

The profit-maximising firm in Figure 81a will produce that output

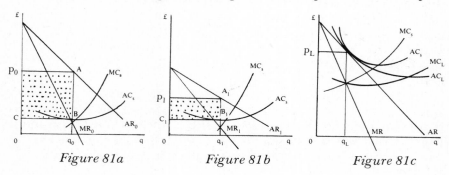

Figure 81a   *Figure 81b*   *Figure 81c*

at which the MC_s curve cuts the MR_0 curve from below. Thus the firm is in short-run equilibrium producing q_0, charging p_0. Note that the firm is earning large supernormal profits indicated by rectangle p_0ABC.

Because the representative firm in Figure 81a is earning super-normal profits new firms enter the industry. That reduces the share of the market held by any one firm. The representative firm's demand (AR) and MR curves therefore shift to the left, as in Figure 81b. That is because the firm can now sell less than initially at any given price, as there are more firms in the industry. Producing q_1 and charging p_1, the firm still earns supernormal profits at its new short-run equilibrium, shown by rectangle $p_1A_1B_1C_1$ in Figure 81b. Although profits of the representative firm have been reduced, the industry has not yet attained equilibrium. Because the firm still makes supernormal profits, even more firms enter the industry. The AR and MR curves of the typical firm therefore continue to shift to the left. As they do so the firm moves from one short-run equilibrium to another.

The adjustment towards industry equilibrium will be complete only when the firm is in long-run equilibrium earning zero economic profits. Such a situation is depicted in Figure 81c where the representative firm is in equilibrium producing q_L, charging p_L. The industry is in equilibrium because: (i) The representative firm has no incentive to change its price-quantity combination or the size of its plant. (ii) Since the representative firm is in long-run equilibrium earning only normal profits, there is no tendency towards change in the number of firms in the industry.

Resource Allocation

Like monopoly, and for one of the same reasons, imperfectly competitive markets tend to misallocate resources. Both in the short run and long run the representative firm produces an output for which MC = MR. But MR < price. Therefore MC < price. If (i) MC and MSC coincide and (ii) price is a measure of MSV, then imperfectly competitive firms produce outputs for which MSC < MSV. *On this count* imperfectly competitive markets lead to a smaller level of production than the social interest requires.

Income Distribution: Supernormal Profits

We saw that the imperfectly competitive firm could, in the short run, earn supernormal profits. In the long run these would be competed away by entry to the industry. Imperfect competition is in this respect similar to perfect competition, unlike monopoly.

Competitive Advertising

Although it is a central characteristic of imperfectly competitive markets, we treated advertising outlay in the foregoing analysis as though it were non-existent. The case against competitive advertising has at least two aspects, one that of the moralist, the other more closely related to economic analysis. (However, note that strictly speaking there is no 'economic case' for or against anything — recall the neutrality of economics from Chapter 1.)

The moral argument against competitive advertising is that it involves a breach of the privacy of the consumer's mind. It is psychological seduction which creates in the consumer wants which did not previously exist. The consumer is told what he 'must' have and is convinced of new needs by forces largely independent of his mind. For example, the manufacturers of well-known brands of toiletries have long been attempting to convince us that in order to have 'personality', or to be 'desirable', we must use a particular firm's toiletries. If many people were not fooled by such sales tactics, the associated selling expenses would have been fruitless. Such tactics create new wants which, it can be argued, imply reduction in consumer welfare.

Perhaps want-creation through competitive advertising has gone beyond the bounds of the public interest. In developed countries we have reached a stage in which, in a given firm, 'goods' are being made to satisfy what the firm might describe as 'urgent human needs', while simultaneously, the marketing unit of the same firm, by means of its sales tactics, is 'manufacturing' the needs. By the engineering of synthetic demand for products through advertising, scarce resources may be drawn away from vital social uses (housing for the poor, the aged or the infirm, hospitals, schools, pollution control, etc.), so as to produce products of little or no social urgency.

A less emotive argument against competitive advertising is that since firms must, in the long run, cover full costs (production costs plus selling costs) if they are to stay in an industry, competitive advertising forces prices up against consumers. Firms in imperfectly competitive markets advertise their products as being superior to those of their rivals. Suppose that no advertising exists to begin with. Firm A now advertises, attempting to convince the public that its product is superior to that of firms B, C, D. . . . If B, C, D . . . do not follow suit, firm A will invade their markets. To protect themselves against declining sales, B, C, D . . . must advertise also, thereby diminishing A's share of the total market. In response A might advertise further, in which case B, C, D . . . , to protect their own interests, do likewise.

But sales of the industry (e.g., toothpaste, automobiles, or headache 'cures') may not have increased at all. If that is the case, unit costs must have risen due to competitive advertising. The argument that advertising in imperfectly competitive markets forces up prices which consumers must pay has substantive validity. *For this reason an increasing number of intelligent people are openly averse to brand names which are heavily advertised; they usually cost more than the (perhaps) physically identical variant which is not backed by massive advertising outlays.* Rather than buy the best-known (by virtue of advertising 'gimmickry' and other indoctrination) brands of, say, aspirin, the consumer may be advised to buy less-known brands — perhaps by asking his friend the chemistry student to make aspirin for him at an economic cost of not many pence.

There are, however, some arguments in favour of product-differentiation and advertising. If, for example, there were only a single variant of each good, the range of consumer choice would be greatly limited. With product-differentiation in imperfectly competitive markets, the consumer is faced with more variants of a good between which to make a choice. Some advertising, furthermore, is more informative than competitive; it makes consumers aware of products of which they would otherwise be ignorant.

Oligopoly

Neither the supply-and-demand framework of perfect competition, the simple monopoly model, nor the model of imperfect competition, is appropriate for analysing markets in which there are only a few sellers. An oligopolistic industry is one in which there are only a few sellers. There is no simple, generally applicable, model of oligopoly. Rather, several models have been proposed to explain certain aspects of observed oligopoly behaviour. We defer consideration of such models to a more advanced course and confine ourselves to some general remarks:

(i) Because they are few, firms in an oligopolistic industry are likely to be conscious of their interdependence. Suppose, for example, that oligopolist A is considering a price increase. Whether it deems it in its interest to do so depends on what *conjectures* or guesses it makes in regard to the reactions of its rivals. On the one hand it may feel that if it raises price, this will act as a signal for a general price increase throughout the industry, in which case A would be a 'price-leader'. On the other hand it may feel that its rivals will *not* follow suit if it raises price, in which case it could lose all or most of its sales. Similarly, in regard to the effects of a price reduction by firm A, A would consider whether its rivals are likely to follow suit: if its rivals do follow suit it may be initiating a price war, making all firms (including A itself) worse off; but if its rivals do not follow the price reduction, or do so only with a substantive lag, then A might gain by cutting prices.

(ii) Sporadic episodes of cut-throat competition aside, firms in an oligopolistic industry may *collude*; they may make explicit or tacit agreements limiting forms which competition within the industry may take (i.e., establishing 'rules of the game') or restricting entry to the industry. Collusion may take many forms. It may be a tacit agreement among firms (indicated by nods at 'the Club') not to pursue price competition. They may enter market-sharing agreements. If, for example, there are only three firms in the industry it may be agreed that firm A will be assigned the southern part of the country as 'zone of influence' and will not compete elsewhere, while the north and midlands may be similarly allocated to firms B and C respectively. There is also the possibility that the firms in an oligopolistic industry agree to act *like* a monopolist. In that case maximum-output quotas would be agreed by each firm. Total industry output could then be restricted to that which a monopolist would produce, and price could thereby be raised to that which a profit-maximising monopolist would charge. The latter kind of collusion would maximise the profits of the oligopolists as a group. The collusion in recent years by the members of the Organisation of Petroleum Exporting Countries (OPEC) is an example along those lines which immediately comes to mind.

Economic Law and Competition Policy in Ireland

Ireland is a small open economy in a free-trading environment within the EEC. Because Irish producers of tradeable goods are price-takers, or are close to being price-takers (in the sense that they can generally exert little control over the prices of their outputs), many markets in Ireland are, for most purposes, adequately analysed using the supply-and-demand framework of perfect competition. That remains true even though there may be only one or two domestic producers in some industries producing tradeable goods; to the extent to which these firms face external competition by way of imports or potential imports, their ability to raise price by restricting output is severely limited. Thus free trade enforces a high degree of competition on the tradeable goods sectors of the Irish economy. However, in the non-tradeable goods sectors (which include many service industries as well as other activities) there is greater scope for oligopolistic or monopolistic policies.

Irish markets have not always been as competitive as in the 1970s. The Irish economy was surrounded by a wall of tariff and quota protection from the early thirties to the early sixties. This meant that scope for oligopolistic and monopolistic trading practices was greater than it is today. For example, we noted in Chapter 19 that, referring to the textile, clothing and footwear industries in his 1952 Budget speech, the Minister for Finance remarked that 'the Government some time ago reinforced the protection of these industries by increases in tariffs and reductions in quotas. The home market is now virtually reserved to the Irish manufacturer'. However, legislation of 1953 for the first time ever in the Republic enabled the government to veto or regulate oligopolistic and monopolistic trading practices.

Regulation of Market Structure: Restrictive Practices[2]

Until 1953 there was no law in Ireland specifically designed to enable government to investigate or curb restrictive business practices. Thus (subject to qualifications imposed by price-control legislation) price-fixing and market-sharing agreements were immune from legal attack.

Public policy, from the early 1930s onwards, provided an environment favourable to business restrictions. In its industrialisation drive the government followed a protectionist policy which excluded or severely limited imports of various goods. Cement was produced after 1936 by a single firm operating under government licence, protected from import competition but subject to control of prices and profits. Tyres were produced by a single licensed company, protected by a tariff and import licensing. Other goods were produced under protection of tariffs, quantitative restriction of imports and preferential taxation. Where imports were subject to quantitative restrictions, government usually allocated them by quotas to individual firms—in many cases just a few firms. Thus 'sheltered from foreign competition and often with potential market shares limited by allocation of imported supplies, Irish producers and traders enjoyed opportunities to control domestic markets by agreement'.[3] During World War II efforts by government to deal with shortages fostered creation of trade associations to develop schemes for allocation of supplies. Traders became accustomed to a situation in which trade in particular categories of goods was confined to those previously engaged in dealing in them and in which new entrants to particular industries were discouraged. After the end of the war many firms sought to maintain their protected status by adopting private restrictions to replace governmental ones.

Control of prices, initiated by the Prices Act, 1937, had been exercised under emergency powers during the war and was extended to the post-war years. In 1952 the Minister for Industry and Commerce stated that although he desired to end emergency price control, 'there is no point in getting rid of . . . government price controls, if combinations of traders are immediately going to get together to impose their own controls'.[4]

Collusion among firms resulted in complaints to government, most of them coming from firms which had been subjected to exclusion or discrimination. These complaints concerned: (i) Discrimination against new firms in an industry and against firms not recognised by trade associations, e.g., by refusal to sell inputs to them. (ii) Exclusive dealership rights. (iii) Limitation on the number of wholesalers. (iv) Collusion in regard to minimum prices (retail price maintenance) enforced by boycotts.[5]

In 1952, the government sponsored the bill which led to the Restrictive Trade Practices Act, 1953. Although the bill was based on the assumption that restrictive agreements among firms must be viewed with suspicion, the resulting legislation did not include any *general* prohibition of restrictive trade practices. Implicit in this was the view that some forms of collusion among firms were acceptable, or even desirable; thus a specific restrictive practice in a particular industry was to be assessed in accordance with the details of the specific case. These views were embodied in the 1953 Act, which set up the Fair Trade Commission, the functions and duties of which were practically the same as those of the more recent Restrictive Practices Commission, discussed below.

The general content of legislation in regard to restrictive trading practices has not changed much since 1953. The law seeks to strengthen the tendency (since the 1960s) towards fairly competitive markets; its primary purpose has been to encourage what is described as free but fair competition in supply and distribution. It does not outlaw any restrictive trade practice *in general*; rather, it establishes media of public scrutiny to prevent specific abuses in specific trades or industries. Thus a certain form of restrictive practice may be outlawed in one trade or industry, but legal in others. Two agencies, the *Examiner of Restrictive Practices* and the *Restrictive Practices Commission* (formerly the Fair Trade Commission) act as overseers, and if an unfair trading practice is established, it may be reported to the Minister for Industry and Commerce, who may make an Order outlawing that practice in a particular trade or industry.

The Restrictive Practices Act, 1972, (which consolidated Acts of 1953 and 1959) is the principal legislation of relevance to market structure. It regards it as the duty of the Restrictive Practices Commission and the Examiner to ensure that fair-trading conditions apply in domestic markets. Guidelines on what are deemed unfair practices include: measures by individuals or groups which 'unjustly' enhance prices or restrain 'fair' competition or 'unjustly' eliminate competitors or 'unjustly' create territorial divisions of markets among certain suppliers to the exclusion of other suppliers, or which 'in any other respect operate against the common good or are not in accordance with the principles of social justice'. The usefulness of these guidelines in assessing the substantive character of unfair practice is small, for each category of practice is defined as unfair when it is unreasonable, unjust, without just cause or reason or contrary to the public interest.

The Examiner has powers to investigate any aspect of fair trading guidelines, and as a result of his investigations he may recommend that the Commission hold an Enquiry. The Commission is empowered to conduct enquiries into the supply and distribution of goods and services, and to determine whether restraint of competition is involved. The Commission's report following an enquiry states whether the Minister for Industry and Commerce should make an Order, and if so, what form the Order should take.

Neither the Commission nor the Examiner have any power to make binding decisions: it is up to the Minister to decide what to do when he gets a report from the Commission. On the basis of a report the Minister may issue an Order which, when confirmed by the Oireachtas, has legal force. Such Orders typically prohibit specific restrictive or 'unfair' practices by suppliers in some specific industry. No restrictive practice is unlawful unless a confirmed ministerial Order makes it so. No *general* standards of market conduct are imposed by law, but to disobey a confirmed Order is unlawful, offenders being liable to fines and/or imprisonment.

EEC Regulations
EEC regulations on competition are also applicable to Ireland. Articles 85 and 86 of the Treaty of Rome indicate that the objectives of the EEC's competition policy are to maintain and promote competition, to

ensure that competition is 'fair', and to unify the EEC market. Article 86 deals with dominant market positions relating to monopolies, oligopolies, mergers and take-overs. It does not prohibit dominant market positions as such; rather it prohibits abuses of them.

Patents

Privileges associated with patent rights have been important sources of monopoly. Viewed in this context monopoly rather than very competitive markets may be an engine of economic progress. Dynamic rather than static efficiency is the issue at hand here. Because of their tendency to earn zero economic profits, competitive firms would not have the means to finance research and development (R and D) on the scale experienced in the past three centuries, and even if they could borrow to finance such expenditures they might have little incentive to do so if they could not obtain exclusive monopoly rights to their technical innovations. On the other hand, a monopoly earning supernormal profits can finance R and D from its own internal funds; also, if patent laws are in force, a firm may have definite incentive to do so in the knowledge that the law will give it (for some years at least) exclusive rights to its innovation.

Irish law on patents is set out in the Patents Acts, 1964 and 1966. The term of each patent is sixteen years from the date of the patent; there is also a provision under which the patent may be extended. The owner of a patent has exclusive power to use in the State the invention for which the patent is granted.

Price Control

The Prices Act, 1958, repealed the Prices Act, 1937. The 1958 Act is the main legislation in this area, though its powers were increased by the Prices (Amendment) Acts 1965 and 1972.

Even in 1958 government policy recognised that where competition was active there was no need for price control. Thus the 1958 Act empowers the government to regulate prices of certain goods and services when, after an investigation, it believes that such prices are excessive because of restrictive practices.

The 1965 Act provided that, whenever the government believed it desirable to maintain stability of the price *level,* it may by Order authorise the Minister for Industry and Commerce (i) to require firms to notify the Minister of any proposed price increase and (ii) to fix by Order maximum prices. The term of such Orders was confined to six months (though they could be, and were, renewed). However, the 1972 Act gave them indefinite duration.

The National Prices Commission (NPC) was established in 1971. It has been active in considering applications for price increases, and advising the Minister thereon. Since late 1975 it has limited the range of its activities so that it could concentrate on applications for price increases from the larger firms and give more attention to prices and charges in services, such as those provided by the professions. These priorities make good sense: the elimination of tariff barriers between Ireland and the UK in 1975 led to increased competition from UK manufacturers which further reduced the extent to which Irish producers of tradeable goods could independently raise prices. For these and other reasons, most firms were exempted from detailed price control after 1975.

The procedure underlying price control in recent years has been roughly as follows: If a firm, subject to price control, notifies the Minister for Industry and Commerce of a proposed price increase, the firm is required to give details of the reasons which have given rise to that proposal. The case is passed on to the NPC who, after consideration and/or investigation, make a recommendation on the proposal to the Minister, who may accept, reject or vary the NPC's recommendation. However, almost always the Minister has accepted the NPC's recommendation, whereupon the recommendation may be implemented. In the overwhelming majority of cases, the length of time which has elapsed between submission of an application and approval of a price increase has been less than two months. Any person who commits an offence under the Prices Acts is liable to fines and/or imprisonment.

Price Control and Inflation

It would appear that price control has had little effect on the overall rate of inflation in Ireland. Its main impact seems to have been to *delay* price increases in those sectors of the economy where competition has been weak, and thereby, in the face of rising input prices, to restrain profits in such sectors. The legislation on price control has complemented that on restrictive trade practices. Thus a member of the Restrictive Practices Commission has written that

> the area of strict control and examination of claimed price increases has been limited by the [National Prices] Commission. All the time, however, the Commission have stressed the importance of competition as a major factor in price control, and this stress on competition as the ultimate long-term solution appears to have increased over the years . . . Exemption from control is

either total or partial for many firms where competition is felt to be sufficient. . . . Exemption has not been, and is unlikely to be, extended to those areas where there is a single firm, or a few firms, or a dominant firm in an industry, or to industries which are sheltered from external competition by the nature of their products or by high transportation costs.[6]

Suggested Reading

Edwards, Corwin, *Trade Regulations Overseas,* New York 1966, 479-540.

McMahon, Bryan M.E., *Report on Irish Economic Law,* Studies, Competition — Approximation of Legislation Series No. 20, Commission of the European Communities, Brussels 1977.

Nunan, Donal, 'Control of Monopoly and of Restrictive Practices in Ireland', mimeograph, Department of Economics, University College Cork circa 1975.

FOOTNOTES

1. The equilibrium price in any market is determined by supply and demand forces. The central point in the present context is that it is only in perfectly competitive markets that price is determined by the intersection of a supply curve and the demand curve, since a definite supply curve does not exist in other market structures.

2. This section draws heavily on Corwin Edwards, *Trade Regulations Overseas,* Dobbs Ferry, New York: Oceana Press 1966, 479-540, and Bryan McMahon, *Report on Irish Economic Law,* Studies, Competition — Approximation of Legislation Series No. 20, Brussels: Commission of the European Communities 1977.

3. Edwards, 480.

4. Quoted *ibid.*

5. *Ibid.,* 481.

6. Patrick M. Lyons, 'Recent Experience of Price Control in Ireland', Dublin: Restrictive Practices Commission 1975, unpublished or of limited circulation only, 47.

CHAPTER 24

The Factor Market and Distribution Theory

In the immediately preceding chapters we investigated the determination of prices and outputs of goods traded in different kinds of product markets. We now consider how factor prices and the amount of each factor hired by profit-maximising firms are determined. Those are the topics of distribution theory.

Each of the productive factors falls into one of four categories — land, labour, capital and enterprise. The returns to these are rent, wages, interest and profit, respectively. Each of the factors has a supply price. The supply price of a factor is the *minimum* return the factor must obtain if it is to be kept in supply. The market price of a factor may differ from its supply price (the factor may earn a surplus above its supply price).

Marginal Productivity

Marginal productivity provides the key to factor pricing. We have seen that a necessary condition for profit maximisation is that each good be produced such that MC = MR. Alternatively, from the standpoint of the factor market we can say that to maximise profits, the firm must seek to hire each *input* up to a point at which its marginal revenue product equals its marginal cost (marginal factor cost). Throughout this chapter we assume that whatever factor is under consideration is the *only* variable factor. This keeps the analysis simple without affecting the qualitative results.

The *marginal physical product* on the Nth unit of factor x used (MPP_x) is the change in total physical output due to using N instead of $(N-1)$ units of factor x, the amounts used of all other factors and the state of technology remaining constant. MPP_x may increase at first as successively higher levels of x are combined with one or more fixed factors; in that case a more 'appropriate' mix of fixed and variable factors is being approached. After a certain point MPP_x will decline as progressively more of x is used, due to the law of diminishing returns. Thus the relationship between MPP_x and employment of x will typically be as in Figure 82a.

349

The *marginal revenue product* on the Nth unit of x (MRP_x) is the change in the firm's receipts from employing N instead of $(N-1)$ units of x, the amounts of other factors and the state of technology being constant.

If perfect competition prevails in the product market the price of output is fixed and $MRP_x = (MPP_x)(\text{price of output})$. We can thus derive the firm's MRP_x curve from its MPP_x curve. The shape of the MRP_x curve in Figure 82b is a mirror image of the MPP_x curve.

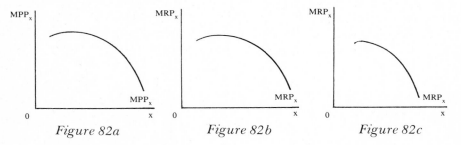

Figure 82a   Figure 82b   Figure 82c

If the firm sells in an imperfectly competitive or monopolistic market, $MRP_x \neq (MPP_x)(\text{price of output})$. Output price is no longer constant—the firm must lower price to expand sales. The MRP_x curve for a firm which is not a perfect competitor in the product market is illustrated in Figure 82c; it slopes down more rapidly than the MRP_x curve of the perfectly competitive seller in Figure 82b.

Pricing in Perfectly Competitive Factor Markets

In a perfectly competitive factor market there are large numbers of buyers and sellers of a factor. No individual can affect a factor's price—he must accept it as a datum. In Part Two we showed that in perfectly competitive markets equilibrium price is determined by intersection of supply and demand curves; factor markets are not exceptions. In the exposition in this section we assume that the commodity is labour service of a particular kind, in which case the price in question is the wage rate for that kind of labour. However, we should *bear in mind throughout, that the analysis is general; the commodity, the services of which we shall be analysing, could be land or capital.* Although the fundamentals of the present analysis are applicable to the pricing of services of land and capital (as well to those of labour), we shall later recognise that land and capital have features which merit more detailed analysis.

Wage Determination in Perfectly Competitive Labour Markets

S_L and D_L in Figure 83a are the supply and demand curves for a homogeneous type of labour (perhaps unskilled agricultural labour). The equilibrium price is W_0 and the amount of labour hired is N_0 (N for number of labour hours).

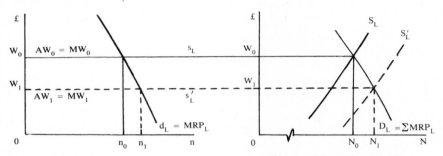

Figure 83b: The Firm   *Figure 83a:* The Market

If, as we assume, the factor market is perfectly competitive, each firm must accept W_0 as a datum determined by overall market conditions. The firm is such a small part of the buyer's market for labour that it can hire any amount of it at the established price, W_0. The unbroken line s_L in Figure 83b is therefore the supply curve of labour to the firm.

Define the marginal wage (MW) as the change in the firm's total wage bill due to employing N instead of $N-1$ units of labour. If the firm can hire any amount of labour at a fixed price, W_0, then the marginal wage equals the average wage. Thus s_L in Figure 83b is the firm's average wage and marginal wage curve.

We saw in Figure 83a how the equilibrium wage and the overall employment level are determined in perfectly competitive labour markets. The individual firm pays a wage W_0. How much labour will it employ?[1]

The profit-maximising firm will employ labour up to the point at which the MRP_L equals the MW. Thus the firm in Figure 83b will employ n_0 units of labour. If $n < n_0$, $MRP_L > MW$. The firm, by expanding employment, would add more to its total revenue than to its total costs. If $n > n_0$, $MRP_L < MW$; the firm would be adding more to its total costs than to its total revenue by increasing employment. Thus n_0 is the firm's optimal employment level.

The downward-sloping part of the MRP_L curve shows how much labour the firm would hire at any price of labour; it is *the firm's demand curve for labour.* (Generalising, we can say that MRP_x is the firm's demand curve for any factor x.) The market demand for labour is the sum of the demands by all buyers of labour. The curve D_L in Figure 83a is therefore the horizontal sum of the demand curves for labour of the individual firms.

Suppose now that the market supply of labour were to increase. The curve S_L in Figure 83a would shift to the right, perhaps to S_L'. If the pattern of demand for labour remained unchanged, employment would rise to N_1 and the equilibrium wage would fall to W_1. The firm, moving down its MRP_L curve, would expand its employment to n_1.

Non-competing Groups

The above analysis established that the price of labour services in perfectly competitive markets is determined by the intersection of the supply and demand curves. Perhaps our analysis was of the market for unskilled agricultural labour. The forces of competition yielded a wage W_0. All units of labour in the category under discussion received the same wage, W_0.

Competition does tend to equalise the wages of any given category of workers. Yet high wage differentials prevail between different kinds of labour. That is largely because the labour market is divided into non-competing groups. Competition (and hence a tendency toward wage equalisation) may indeed prevail among agricultural labourers. But there is little direct competition between that type of labour and, for example, civil engineers. The two groups are non-competing. If they could compete effectively, labourers would become civil engineers. This would bring down the wages of civil engineers and raise the wages of agricultural labourers. If competition between the two groups prevailed, the wages of the two groups would tend to be equated. The labour market is divided into non-competing groups because of trade union restrictions on entry to a trade, inequality of opportunity, differences in ability, custom, immobility, or merely because many people are ignorant of the opportunities open to them.

Wage Determination under Monopsony

Perfect competitive and monopsonistic factor markets are extreme opposites. A monopsonist is the sole buyer of a commodity, in the present context, a factor of production. As such, he can influence the price of the factor. Suppose that the factor is a particular type of labour. Assume, furthermore, that there is perfect competition on the seller's side of the labour market. (Note that the analysis may be generalised to cases in which the factor is land or capital.) Consider now how the wage and amount of labour employed are determined under monopsony.

In the discussion of perfectly competitive factor markets we saw that the supply curve of labour to the firm is a horizontal line. Thus, in perfectly competitive labour markets, $MW = AW$. That equality does not hold under monopsony. Since the monopsonist is the only buyer of the type of labour under discussion, he bids up the price of labour as he hires more. Hence $MW > AW$. For example, if the monopsonist could hire ten units of labour at a weekly wage of £100, the total wage bill $(TWB) = £1000$ and $AW = £100$. Assume that in order to hire eleven men he must offer a wage of £120. For eleven men, $TWB = £1320$ and $AW = £120$. But $MW = \Delta(TWB) = £320$. Since £320 > £120, $MW > AW$.

Let AW_m and MW_m in Figure 84 be the AW and MW curves of the monopsonist. They slope upwards and are unequal for the reasons indicated above. The curve MRP_L is the MRP curve for the type of labour under discussion. The firm will employ labour to the point at which $MRP_L = MW$. The corresponding employment level is N_0. (If $N < N_0$, $MRP_L > MW$; if $N > N_0$, $MRP_L < MW$.) At the equilibrium level of employment N_0, the firm pays a wage W_0. Note that the wage each worker obtains, W_0, is less than the marginal wage. Thus, under monopsony, labour receives a wage less than its MRP. Such a situation is sometimes termed 'monopsonistic exploitation'.

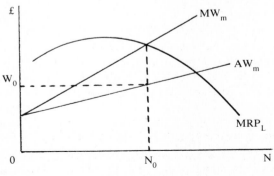

Figure 84

Collective Bargaining

So far we have set aside collective bargaining. This can take many forms. In what follows we assume that a trade union demands and obtains a higher wage, without any stipulation in regard to numbers employed. Assume that the union is willing to supply as much labour as is required at the agreed wage, and examine the effect on employment in perfectly competitive, and in monopsonistic, factor markets.

Perfect Competition in the Factor Market

Figures 85a and 85b depict the pattern of wages and employment in a perfectly competitive factor market. Prior to demands for a higher wage, the equilibrium wage is W_0 and employment is N_0. Suppose now that a trade union demands and obtains a wage W_1, and agrees to supply as much labour as is required at that price. The curve S_L in Figure 85a is now irrelevant. The horizontal line S_L' is the new supply curve of labour to *both* the industry and the firm. Figure 85a shows that equilibrium employment falls to N_1; some unemployment results.

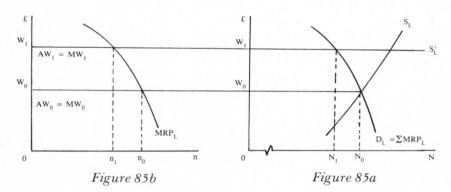

Figure 85b   Figure 85a

Monopsony

The levels of employment and wage rates prior to collective bargaining with the monopsonist are shown in Figure 86 as N_0 and W_0, respectively. Suppose now that a trade union demands and obtains a wage W_1 and agrees to supply as much labour as is required at that price. Since the union has agreed to supply any amount of labour at wage rate W_1, the firm's AW and MW curves are the same: it no longer bids up the price of labour as it increases employment. Thus the supply curve of labour to the firm is $S_L = AW_1 = MW_1$. The profit-maximising firm employs labour up to the point at which $MRP_L = MW$. The monopsonist's MW curve in Figure 86 is now MW_1. Thus the monopsonist will employ labour up to point E. Hence we conclude that a rise in wages — due to a very specific form of trade union activity — has led to an increase in employment from N_0 to N_1.

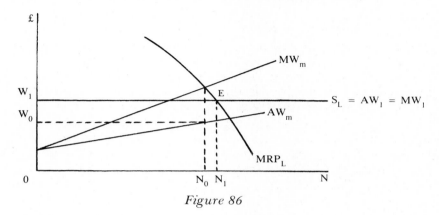

Figure 86

Conclusion on the Labour Market

We have seen how wage rates are determined in perfectly competitive and monopsonistic factor markets. We have considered the effects of one form of collective bargaining. Most factor markets are intermediate between the perfectly competitive and monopsonistic extremes. To the extent that actual labour markets are highly competitive, they approximate the characteristics of the perfectly competitive (labour market) model discussed above. Labour markets in which there are only a few firms hiring a particular type of labour tend to be closer to the monopsonistic model rather than the perfectly competitive one. Finally, trade unions must recognise the constraints imposed on their actions by different kinds of factor markets.

Generalisation and Extension

The manner in which the price of labour services in different kinds of factor markets is determined in accordance with the marginal productivity theory of distribution should now be clear: the profit-maximising firm seeks to employ any particular category of labour up to a point at which MRP_L equals the marginal cost of that labour to the firm (MW). The marginal productivity theory can be generalised to explain the price and amount employed of *any* simple factor — not only labour — which is variable in supply to the firm. Thus in the long run the firm will employ land, or a particular kind of capital equipment, up to a point at which the factor's MRP equals its marginal cost.

Some factors of production have their own peculiarities. This is true of the factor land, the return to which is rent.

Rent: Conventional and Economic

When we use the word 'rent' in the everyday sense, we mean a payment made for the use of some commodity. For example, when we refer to the rent of land or the rent of a dwelling, we normally mean the payments made for the use of those commodities. In this chapter we refer to payments of this form — rent in the everyday sense of the word — as *conventional rent,* as distinct from *economic rent.* Conventional rent and economic rent may be different types of payment. *Economic rent is defined as the surplus earnings over and above the supply price (or transfer earnings) of any factor of production.* The *supply price* of a factor in any employment X is the minimum payment that factor must receive if it is to be kept in supply to use X. If a factor of production in any employment X does not receive its supply price it will, in the long run, transfer to some other employment.

Assume, for example, that I am motivated solely by monetary returns. Suppose, furthermore, that my most lucrative employment is as a mechanic earning £100 a week, and that my second most lucrative employment is as a labourer earning £75 a week. As long as I am offered at least £75 I will supply myself as a mechanic. My supply price as a mechanic is £75. However, if I expect to earn only £70 as a mechanic I will transfer to being a labourer. A weekly wage of £75 is the minimum that will prevent me from transferring to being a labourer. If I earn £100 per week as a mechanic, £25 of this is a surplus above my supply price. I am then earning a species of economic rent to the extent of £25.

The Rent of Land

A much-debated question in the history of economics is whether the earnings of land are an economic rent. We consider those earnings from the standpoints of (i) the economy as a whole, (ii) a particular industry and (iii) an individual. But first we should clarify what we mean by the factor land.

By the factor land we mean land *in its virgin state,* as originally supplied by nature. Thus if someone rents land upon which there are farm buildings, or which has been improved by clearing or fertilizers, part of the payment made is for the services of *capital* rather than of land *per se*. We conceptually isolate and exclude from consideration such payments for capital services in discussing the rent of land in what follows.

(i) Rent and the Supply of Land to the Economy

Consider an island of uniform grassland. Let this island be inhabited solely by tenant farmers, who have no contact with the outside world except when paying rents to proprietors who reside abroad. Assume that land is wanted only to grow food, and that conditions close to perfect competition prevail among landlords and tenants. Note that we are making these assumptions purely for simplicity in exposition.

SS' in Figure 87 represents the fixed supply of land in the island community. Regardless of the level of rent, the supply of land to the community cannot be increased. If the island population is low, the demand for food, and hence the demand for land, will be low. Let D_1 be the demand curve for land when population is very low. Since the supply and demand curves fail to intersect in the positive quadrant the rent of land must be zero. The community is so small that it does not want to farm the whole island. And since there is perfect competition among landlords no farmer need pay rent. If a landlord tries to extract rent from a tenant, that tenant can move to some other piece of land.

Suppose now that population increases while technology in agriculture stays constant. This will raise both the demand for food and its price. The demand curve for land will therefore shift to the right —

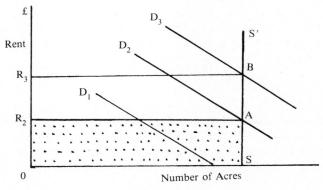

Figure 87

perhaps to D_2. Note that the supply and demand curves now intersect in the positive quadrant. A positive price — rent $£R_2$ — is now charged per acre. Competition among tenants will bid price up to that level. The aggregate level of rent payments is shown by the shaded rectangle $OSAR_2$. If population growth continues, the demand for food and its price will also continue to increase. Perhaps the demand curve for land will shift out to D_3 in Figure 87. This pattern of demand yields a rent per acre of $£R_3$. Total rent payments are then given by the rectangle $OSBR_3$.

Do high rents cause high prices or do high prices cause high rents? The general view among the public is that high rents cause high prices. The reason why rents in our island community increased was because the demand for food and the price of food increased. Thus high prices cause high land rents rather than vice versa.

In our discussion of the earnings of the factor land we have used the term rent to denote payments for the use of land. Thus we have been investigating the determinants of the level of conventional rent in the community. But does land, from the standpoint of the economy as a whole, earn any economic rent?

Economic rent was defined as the surplus earnings above the supply price of a factor of production. The aggregate amount of land is fixed in supply. *From the standpoint of the economy as a whole, the supply price of land is zero.* In Figure 87 we see that the supply of land is fixed regardless of the level of rents. The transfer earnings of land are zero — if it is not utilised its earnings will be zero. Thus, whatever land does earn is a surplus above its supply price. Hence, from the standpoint of the economy as a whole, conventional rents on land are also economic rents.

Since the economic rent on any factor constitutes a surplus above the supply price of that factor, it follows that *a lump-sum tax could be imposed on economic rent without causing any change in the amount supplied of the factor in question. Thus a lump-sum tax could be imposed on the earnings of land without causing any change in the overall supply of land.*

(ii) Rent and the Supply of Land to an Industry

Relax the assumption that land is uniform in quality and has only one use. The demand for any particular acre then depends on its fertility in different potential uses and on its location. From the standpoint of any particular industry, not all of the earnings of land are economic rents. Suppose that industry A is willing to pay £1000 a year for the use of a certain acre of land, and that the land could earn £800 annually in its second most lucrative use, in industry B. Competition will drive the land into industry A, because industry A can pay the highest conventional rent (£1000). The land will be supplied to industry A so long as it is paid at least £800 annually. The supply price of the land to industry A is £800. If any less were paid by industry A it would go to industry B, which will pay £800. The transfer earnings of the land in industry A are £800. Thus, the economic rent of the land in industry A is £200. Assuming that the earnings of the land in industry B would not be taxed, £200 is the maximum lump-sum tax which could be imposed on the land in industry A without causing the land to transfer to industry B.

(iii) Rent and the Supply of Land to an Individual Firm

From the standpoint of the individual producer the economic rent of land is usually zero. Suppose that perfect competition prevails, and that the market rental of some acre of land is £80. This means that several producers, after they have payed all the other factors of production used in conjunction with the land, could just afford to pay a (conventional) rent of £80. If the land is let to one of those producers, say X, he must pay the market rent, £80. If he refuses to pay £80 he will not get the land. The supply price of the land to producer X is £80. Thus although the conventional rent is £80, the economic rent — the surplus earnings of the land over and above its transfer earnings — is zero from the standpoint of an individual producer X.

On Lump-Sum Taxation of Land Values

We have seen that since the supply price of land to the economy is zero,[2] lump-sum taxes could be imposed on all land valuations without affecting the *overall* supply of that factor. Note that in this respect land differs substantively from the other factors of production. Taxation of labour income affects the supply of effort. If all of the earnings of capital were taxed firms would not invest. And if all of the earnings of enterprise (including normal profits) were taxed, potential entrepreneurs would not undertake the risks of loss associated with production.

   These considerations suggest that lump-sum taxation of land may be the most efficient, or one of the most efficient, means of taxation, in the sense that it may not adversely affect the *overall supply, or the allocation,* of resources. That inference is correct provided the scheme of lump-sum taxes is carefully designed. Note that under a system of lump-sum land taxes it would generally be essential to assess land for taxation *regardless of the uses to which the land was put*; otherwise the allocation of land between industries would tend to be adversely affected.

Suppose that each acre of land were assessed for payment in annual taxation a sum equal to (up to 100 per cent of) the earnings of the land in its most lucrative possible use. Land would then flow into those uses in which it produced most (if it had not been initially allocated to those uses). The supply of effort would not be affected; firms and employees would still seek to maximise the returns on labour, capital and enterprise used in conjunction with the land.

Of course the above scheme of lump-sum land taxation is extreme; we are merely trying to highlight a fundamental point. Not all of us would like to see land *always* allocated in such a manner that the output of measurable goods and services is maximised; most of us appreciate scenic parkland to which we have free access. However, the State could exempt allocations of land to certain uses from payment of the tax if (on non-commercial grounds) that were deemed in the public interest.

Other Forms of Economic Rent

Land is not the only factor which earns economic rent. *Rent of ability* is a form of economic rent accruing to persons who have some ability inelastic in supply. For example, if a professional footballer can earn £50,000 annually playing soccer, while his most lucrative alternative is in an occupation earning £10,000 a year, his rent of ability as a footballer is £40,000 annually. *Quasi-rent* is a return above the supply prices of factors of production inelastic in supply in the short run but elastic in the long run. If supernormal profits are earned by a perfectly competitive firm in the short run, those earnings are a species of quasi-rent. They are a surplus above the supply price of the factor enterprise (normal profit) and will be competed away by entry of firms to the industry in the long run.

The supernormal profits of a monopolist are economic rents — they may be earned in the long run as well as in the short run. As noted in Chapter 23, the imposition of a lump-sum tax on supernormal profits does not change the monopolist's output. In general, we can tell whether any earning is an economic rent by using the test of a lump-sum tax: *if imposition of a lump-sum tax on an earning causes no change in supply, then that tax has been imposed on an economic rent.*

Capital and Interest

To the economist, monetary claims such as banknotes, securities or equities are not capital. To the economist, capital consists of productive assets such as railways, aircraft and equipment, ships, roads, machines and factories. Capital is the only factor deliberately made by man for productive use. Investment means addition to the capital stock. The economist, therefore, does not regard purchase of securities as investment, for these are not, in themselves, productive assets. (However, note that there is some departure from this nomenclature in the context of the balance of international payments.)

The Demand for Capital Services

Just as the demand for labour or land is a demand for the services of those factors, the demand for capital is a demand for capital services. The profit-maximising firm seeks to employ the services of any type of capital asset up to a point at which the marginal revenue product of those services equals their marginal cost. We assume that the marginal cost of capital services to the firm is constant (so that marginal and average costs of capital services are the same). The cost to the firm of the services of a capital good is the *rental price* of capital. If the firm does not own the capital assets it uses, it must pay an explicit rental; if it owns a capital good which it uses internally it is implicitly foregoing the rental it could obtain if it made the services of the capital good available to somebody else. In either case the rental price is the economic cost of capital services to the firm. The capital rental is a composite of two, and possibly three, elements — a pure (risk-free) interest charge, depreciation, and possibly a risk premium. For the moment we ignore risk. Suppose a firm employs a new capital good which costs £1000, and that the interest rate obtainable on loans to government is 5 per cent. By employing the capital good for, say, one year, the firm is forgoing £50 in interest which it could have earned had it loaned the £1000 at a risk-free interest rate of 5 per cent. So interest (although in this case it is implicit rather than explicit) is a component of the cost of the services of a capital good. In addition, the capital good will be worth less than £1000 in real terms — say it will be worth £900 — at the end of the year, due to depreciation. That £100 in depreciation is also part of the cost of the services of the capital good.

If the firm does not own some of the capital which it employs, it is renting it. It is easy to see, considerations of risk aside, that the rental which the firm has to pay tends to be a composite of an interest charge and a charge for depreciation of the asset over the term of the rental.

Although we have regarded the economic cost of using a capital good as the rental value of the capital asset, businessmen do not usually think of the matter in the same terms. Businessmen focus on the *stock* of capital assets, and on changes in the stock of such assets, rather than on the *services* of capital assets. Note, however, the following:

(i) We showed that a firm seeks to employ the services of a capital good in any time period up to a point at which the MRP of those services equals their marginal costs. However, focusing on the stock of capital assets, we can say that a firm seeks to expand its capital stock (ii) up to a point at which the rate of return over cost on a marginal unit of capital equals the rate of interest, or (iii) up to a point at which the present value of a marginal unit of capital equals its cost. It can be shown that under certain conditions the three approaches are equivalent, in the sense that they lead to precisely the same decisions. In what follows we focus on approaches (ii) and (iii).

Present Value
Suppose that you have £1 million available and that if you invested that sum in a new machine you would expect a sum of returns, over the next ten years, of £1·5 million. Whether or not you should rationally invest depends on the rate of interest. That is true whether one is contemplating using one's own funds or borrowing to finance the proposed project. The fact is that 'time is money'; the present value of £100 in three years time is less than £100 now. (All variables are in real terms.)

The *present value* of £100 in three years time is that sum X which when compounded over three years will yield £100. Suppose that the rate of interest, i, is constant. Then,

$X(1 + i)$ is the nominal value of £X invested now at the end of one year.

$X(1 + i)^2$ . . . . two years.

$X(1 + i)^3$ . . . . three years.

Suppose $X(1 + i)^3 = 100$. Then $X = 100/(1 + i)^3 < 100$. X is the present value of £100 in three years time.

The Two Approaches
There are two main approaches which firms take in the decision to invest:

The first involves computing the rate of return which the asset under consideration is expected to earn, and comparing that to the interest rate which must be paid to finance the purchase (or, in the case of internally generated funds, the interest foregone by not lending).

The second approach involves computing the present value of the asset and comparing that with the cost of the asset.

Suppose that we are contemplating investment in a capital asset which is expected to last N years. Then, the rate of return, r, is the unknown in the following equation:

$$(1) \quad C = \frac{R_1}{(1 + r)} + \frac{R_2}{(1 + r)^2} + \ldots + \frac{R_N}{(1 + r)^N}$$

C here denotes the cost of the asset, while $R_1 \ldots R_N$ represent the expected flow of (after tax) revenues in excess of expected operating (i.e., non-capital) costs associated with the asset. R_N includes the scrap value of the asset. Assume that the rate of interest, i, is expected to remain constant. Then, whether investment in an additional machine (or piece of equipment) will be made depends on whether r exceeds i.

Suppose that for a marginal 'machine', $r > i$. Then the firm will invest in a marginal machine. Indeed, it will continue to invest in further machines up to the point at which $r = i$. Diminishing returns to capital equipment imply that there will be some finite volume of investment for which $r = i$. Clearly, the lower the rate of interest, i, the lower the rate of return required to justify further investment. We have thus established an inverse relationship between the rate of interest and the volume of planned private investment.

Consider now the second approach which a firm might adopt in appraising a potential investment.

The present value of a potential new capital asset equals the additional (after tax) revenues it is expected to generate in the future minus an estimate of the additional operating costs it will incur (excluding depreciation), all discounted by the rate of interest prevailing in each time period. If the rate of interest, i, is expected to remain constant, we have, for present value (PV)

$$(2) \quad PV = \frac{R_1}{(1 + i)} + \frac{R_2}{(1 + i)^2} + \ldots + \frac{R_N}{(1 + i)^N}$$

Under this approach, the firm will rationally plan to invest in an additional asset if the present value of that asset exceeds the cost of the asset. Indeed it will seek to invest in additional machines up to the point at which the present value of a marginal machine exactly equals the cost of the machine. In the event that the firm cannot raise all the finance which it desires, it will seek to invest in those projects with highest PV, so long as PV > C.

Normally, if the interest rate is constant over time, we can expect the two alternative approaches to the investment decision to yield identical results (in terms of projects selected or rejected). It has been demonstrated elsewhere in the literature that when the two decision rules do yield different results, the present-value criterion is superior to the rate-of-return criterion.

As we should expect, the present-value approach establishes an inverse relationship between the volume of investment and the rate of interest. From (2) we can see that if i increases, PV will decrease. That implies that investment projects which would be chosen at low i (because PV > C) will no longer be justified commercially (since, with high i, PV < C).

Profits: The Return to Enterprise

'Normal' profit is the supply price of enterprise. It is the minimum return an entrepreneur must expect to receive if he is to have incentive to risk his capital by investment in any industry. Normal profit, since it is a cost of a factor of production, is a cost of production.

Suppose, by way of illustration, that I am thinking of opening a small shop up the road. £30,000 of my capital would be tied up by doing so. Suppose that I own the land, provide my own capital, and employ myself, for fifty hours per week, behind the counter. I will not find it worth my while to open the store unless I earn an acceptable return on my land, capital and labour, *plus* some return for bearing the risks of enterprise.

Assume that I could earn £500 a year by renting the land at its market value, that if I purchased £30,000 worth of gilt-edged securities I could obtain annual interest returns of £2500, and that I could earn £8100 a year in wages working for someone else. The sum of these payments amounts to £11,100.

If the annual income I expect to receive as a shopkeeper is only £11,100, then, assuming that I am motivated solely by financial considerations, I will not become a shopkeeper. For I can earn £11,100 annually without shouldering the non-insurable risks and uncertainties inherent in enterprise. Perhaps, if I open shop, sales will be below my expectations, and I will incur losses.

In deciding whether to open a shop, I will, therefore, demand some premium for risk bearing. Perhaps I will open the shop only if I can expect an annual income of at least £13,000. If that is the case, £1900 is the minimum return which will entice me to shoulder the non-insurable risks and uncertainties I will face as a businessman. This £1900 is my supply price as an entrepreneur. It is my level of normal profit. My services as a shopkeeper will not be offered unless I expect to receive that sum. Normal profit is, therefore, a cost of production.

Suppose, however, that I am the only shopkeeper in my locality. Owing to absence of competition I might now expect to earn £15,000 annually. Let us continue to assume that of this sum, £500, £2500 and £8100 are the market returns to my land, capital and labour respectively. If that is the case the remaining £3900 is profit. My supply price as an entrepreneur is £1900, so some £1900 of the £3900 is my normal profit and is a cost of production. The residual £2000 is a surplus above normal profit; it is supernormal profit. As such it is economic rent, which can be taxed in lump-sum manner without affecting my incentives.

FOOTNOTES

1. We assume throughout that the average revenue product of labour is at least as great as the average wage at some level of employment.
2. The reader may argue that land is not quite fixed in supply, as the experience of the industrious Dutch in filling in the sea indicates. However, reclaimed land has more of the character of capital than of 'land', as we defined land above.

CHAPTER 25

Overview of the Market Mechanism, and Income Distribution in the Republic of Ireland

The Market Mechanism

In Part Two, Chapter 3, we opened our discussion of microeconomics by stating the allocation problem of every economy. This problem has three aspects: (i) Society has to decide *what* goods will be produced. (ii) Decisions must be made in regard to *how* goods will be produced. (iii) Society must establish some procedure to decide *for whom* goods will be produced.

We indicated that society's allocation problem could, in principle, be solved by centralised planning without use of market prices. A central planning bureau could lay down quantity commands for all goods as well as directions on choice of technique in their production. It could then distribute the goods among society in accordance with the government's ethical priorities.

A private-enterprise economy relies on a system of markets and prices to solve its allocation problem. In such an economy prices serve as *signals* which allocate flows of goods among competing consumers and flows of resources into different uses. Since the pricing of the factors of production determines the pattern of income distribution, it also determines for whom goods are produced. It is useful to refer to Figure 88 to see how the price mechanism solves society's allocation problem. The upper half of Figure 88 refers to the goods market; the lower half to the factor market.

In the factor market, firms demand land, labour and capital to carry on production. The prices of these factors — land rents, wages and capital rentals — are determined by supply and demand. Factors will not flow to firms which cannot pay those market prices. Thus,

366

factor prices act as a means of allocating resources among competing firms. Since firms are assumed to seek maximum profits, each firm, in the long run, will employ each factor which it hires up to a point at which the factor's marginal revenue product equals marginal factor cost. Since firms minimise the cost of producing any level of output of any good, each will select a choice of technique, in the production of any good, such that for all variable factors used, marginal physical products are proportional to factor prices. *Thus the profit motive acting through a mechanism of factor markets determines how goods shall be produced.* Since factor prices — and hence the pattern of income distribution — are determined in the factor market, *the question for whom goods shall be produced is also solved in the factor market.*

Figure 88

Turn now to the upper half of Figure 88. The holders of factors have earned incomes in the factor market. As consumers, they now spend their money by demanding goods from firms. Being motivated by utility maximisation, each consumer allocates his expenditure among goods in such a manner that, for every two goods x and y purchased, $MRS_{xy} = p_x/p_y$. Given the pattern of demand, profit-maximising firms produce up to a point at which $MC = MR$. Given the pattern of demand, *the market thus determines what goods — and how much of each good — shall be produced.*

It should be noted that the lower and upper halves of Figure 88 are not independent. This should not be surprising, for we know that national *income,* national *output,* and *expenditure* on the economy's output are identically the same.

Hence, we see that the price mechanism solves society's allocation problem. Although each individual is assumed to pursue his own interests, the totality of individual actions determines (i) What goods shall be produced? (ii) For whom shall goods be produced? (iii) How shall goods be produced?

Note that we have not been justifying the price mechanism from a political standpoint. We do not believe that the pattern of income distribution emerging in the factor market is necessarily an equitable one. All we have been saying is that the market mechanism — in the absence of any controlling organisation such as a planning bureau — provides one way of solving society's allocation problem.

Efficiency in Resource Allocation and Market Failure

As economists, we cannot say whether the pattern of income distribution generated by the market mechanism is 'good' or 'bad'; that is a question for the moralist. The question of income distribution aside, most economists believe that highly competitive market systems tend to allocate society's resources in an efficient manner; but they do not believe that this is always the case. In the latter event the State may intervene to improve resource allocation. As a first approximation we can say that the market mechanism works efficiently to the extent that:

(i) Marginal private costs coincide with marginal social costs,

(ii) Market price coincides with marginal social value and,

(iii) Each good is produced to a point at which marginal social cost equals marginal social value.

We saw in Chapter 22 that if conditions (i) and (ii) are satisfied, then condition (iii) would be satisfied in perfectly competitive markets; that is the central reason why perfect competition is regarded as an ideal of efficiency. Of course conditions (i), (ii) or (iii) may not be satisfied in practice, in which case the market system is said to have *failed,* meaning that from the standpoint of society, the market system would be supplying the wrong amounts of at least some goods:

(i′) If a firm pollutes the environment, and if it is not charged for the cost imposed on society by that pollution, then marginal private cost is less than marginal social cost.

(ii′) Market price is regarded as a measure of the marginal social value of a good because it indicates how much consumers are willing to pay for the marginal unit of that good supplied. But if an individual's consumption of a good affects the welfare of others, there is no presumption that price paid measures marginal social value.

(iii') *If* conditions (i) and (ii) were satisfied, condition (iii) would be satisfied *exactly* only if markets were perfectly competitive; in other forms of market structure marginal social cost would be less than marginal social value.

The circumstances mentioned in (i'), (ii') and (iii') are three sources of market failure. A fourth source is in the case of *public goods*. A public good is a good such that any one individual's consumption of its services does not detract from the amount available for consumption by others. Examples include the security provided by national defence and national storm-warning systems. In general, the market mechanism cannot enforce payment for public goods since there is no way to prevent a person from enjoying the services of the good if he refuses to pay for it. But government can enforce payment by all via the tax system. The market mechanism would not supply such goods, the social benefit of which may be considerable, or if it did it would supply too few of them.

The market fails in the case of public goods and when conditions (i) to (iii) break down. Hence resource allocation may be improved by State intervention. The State may also intervene to affect income distribution. A survey of some aspects of income distribution in Ireland is provided below.

Partial Equilibrium Analysis and General Equilibrium Analysis

The method adopted in the microeconomics sections has been that of partial equilibrium analysis. That is, analysis of individual markets in isolation, on the assumption that conditions in all other markets remain unchanged. When we examined the determination of price and output in a particular market we did so on the assumption that demand and supply in all other markets remained unchanged. Hence we assumed that the prices of all goods other than that in which we were directly interested, and the money incomes of consumers, remained constant.

There are, however, complex interactions between markets. In a sense, all prices are interdependent. So too are the levels of production of all commodities. For example, suppose that there is an increase in demand for shipping. This will spark off a chain of reactions in other industries. As more ships are built the demand for steel, timber, and other inputs to shipbuilding will increase. More steel production will increase demand for coking coal. Since inputs must be transported to shipyards, the increased demand for shipping implies an increased demand for transport. It is probable, indeed, that the increased demand for shipping will lead, indirectly, to increased demand for the services of water transportation. The higher output of transportation industries will increase demand for oil — and so on.

The study of interdependence among markets is the realm of general equilibrium analysis, which is deferred for a later course.

Income Distribution in the Republic of Ireland[1]

In discussions of the distribution of income, reference is often made to summary measures of concentration. Such concentration is often depicted graphically by a Lorenz curve, which graphs the cumulative per cent of total income against the cumulative per cent of income units (individuals or households). By way of example, two Lorenz curves are shown in Figure 89. They depict the distribution of personal income before tax in the UK and West Germany in 1964.[2] The so-called Gini coefficient is the most frequently adopted summary measure of concentration in the distribution of income. It is used for two main purposes: (i) to compare two distributions, either in a given country at different times or between countries, and (ii) to provide a summary measure of inequality. The Gini coefficient expresses the area of the bow-shaped section between the Lorenz curve and the diagonal of equality, as a proportion of the total area under the diagonal. It can vary from 0 (perfect equality) to 1 (perfect inequality).

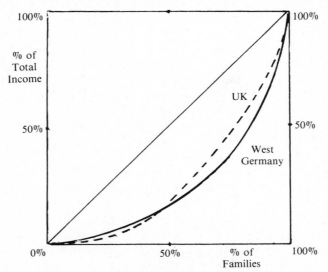

Figure 89: Lorenz Curves; UK and West Germany, 1964

Summary statistics of concentration, such as the Gini coefficient, must be treated with caution. If Lorenz curves for two distributions do not intersect, 'then we can say unambiguously that the distribution closer to the diagonal is less unequal than the other, subject only to the condition that we are ranking the distributions independently of the average levels of income'.[3] But there is added complexity if the curves intersect. Note that the Gini coefficient for a given population would be unchanged if there were a transfer of income shares (between, for example, the very rich and the very poor) which left the area below the Lorenz curves for that population unchanged. (The two Lorenz curves would then intersect.) Similarly two populations may have different Lorenz curves; yet the Gini coefficients may be the same.

It can be seen from Figure 89 that the Lorenz curves for the UK and West Germany in 1964 intersect. The share of the bottom 40 per cent of income units is highest in Germany. Nevertheless the Gini coefficient has a lower value for the UK ($0 \cdot 40$ in contrast to $0 \cdot 47$ for West Germany). This example highlights two points concerning use of summary measures of inequality. First, summary measures are not necessarily purely statistical; they may embody value judgements concerning 'deservedness' of different income groups. For that reason not everyone would agree that inequality had fallen just because the Gini coefficient had fallen. Second, Lorenz curves play a role in determining whether alternative summary measures of inequality yield the same conclusions. Hence 'if we are concerned solely with comparing two distributions of income (and the ranking is being made independently of the average income levels) then the first step should be to draw the Lorenz curves'.[4]

In the formation of social policy we need Lorenz curves for different groups in the population and for different regions (i) before direct taxes and transfer payments, and (ii) after direct taxes and transfer payments. Lorenz curves of type (i) would highlight to policy-makers the kinds of social policies that are desirable, while those of type (ii) would be useful in assessing the effects of such policies. A small amount of data is available by which we can derive some tentative information on the pattern of income distribution in Ireland in the second half of the 1960s. However, *the quality of the data is such that only limited confidence can be attached to the estimates below.*

To construct Lorenz curves for the urban sector (including towns and villages) we can use data on the average weekly incomes of a sample of 4759 urban households published in the *Household Budget Inquiry, 1965-66.*[5] In designing this sample the Central Statistics

Office attempted to make it representative of the population of urban households. The *Inquiry* suggested a 10 per cent understatement of average incomes by the households surveyed. However, if the understatement applied to each income group it would not affect estimates of relative income levels. But understatement by categories such as the self-employed may yield some bias in the estimates. Manipulation of the *Inquiry* data gives the estimates in Table 18.

Table 18

Percentage of Households	Percentage of Household Income		
	(a) Before Direct Taxes or Transfer Payments	(b) After Transfer Payments	(c) After Direct Taxes and Transfer Payments
6·3	0·17	0·85	0·92
8·0	1·05	2·15	2·30
7·2	2·39	3·02	3·16
19·6	11·52	12·04	12·53
18·7	15·96	15·93	16·37
12·6	14·03	13·74	13·97
8·5	11·66	11·29	11·35
10·8	18·99	18·19	18·05
4·3	9·89	9·37	9·13
4·0	14·34	13·41	12·22
100	100	100	100

The Lorenz curves for these estimates are drawn in Figure 90. The Gini coefficients are approximately as follows: for (a) 0·39; for (b) 0·36; for (c) 0·33.

The similarity in the values of Gini coefficients (b) and (c) above to their counterparts in the UK in 1967 is noteworthy. The UK data to which we refer were drawn from a large sample of income tax returns. The relevant income unit was the nuclear family (man, wife and dependent children) — which could differ from the household. Furthermore, the UK data cover both urban and non-urban families. Finally, the UK data were for incomes inclusive of transfer payments. Manipulation of this data[6] gives a Gini coefficient of 0·37 for family income before tax (remarkably similar to the Irish urban household figure (b) of 0·36) and of 0·34 for family income after direct taxation

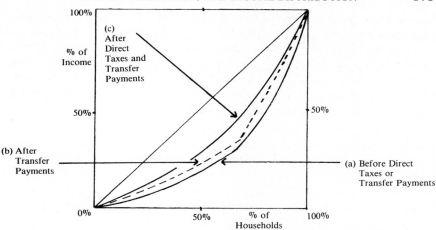

Figure 90: Lorenz Curves, Urban Households, Ireland, 1965-66.

(remarkably similar to the Irish urban household figure (c) of 0·33).

Confidence intervals for the non-urban distribution of income are far broader than those of the urban sector. That is due to the quality of available data. For agriculture it appears that the only data pertaining to years *circa* 1965-66 (the years to which the above figures pertain) to which we can meaningfully refer are those in Table IX of the *Farm Management Survey, 1966-1967.*[7] That table presents, within a sample of 1138 family farms, the distribution of family farm income per head of family labour, classified by size of farm (the sum of all family holdings). Furthermore, it pertains only to those farms having at least one full family labour unit. Thus it can be interpreted as pertaining, more closely than any other relevant statistics, to full-time farmers. However, with a view to estimating the pattern of income distribution in the population of full-time family farms, the 1966-67 data were adjusted in various ways.[8] Considerable inequality in income distribution was suggested: the bottom 40 per cent of family farms obtained about 12 per cent of total family farm income. Correspondingly, the Gini coefficient is high — approximately 0·44. But in view of the limited data and the resulting method of derivation, these estimates are tentative.

How does the pattern of income distribution in Ireland compare with that in other countries? In this context we note that international comparisons are difficult to make with confidence. As one authority was written, 'the data for one country are collected from tax returns and do not cover the whole population; those for another are based on special surveys which do not achieve a 100 per cent response; a third country relies on data from a census of population where certain types of income are likely to be under-reported.'[9] Furthermore, the definition of income unit may differ from country to country. Despite these limitations some comparative estimates are presented in Table 19. While efforts have been made to ensure comparability, there remain important differences in classification. The income unit is, in general, the nuclear family — husband, wife, and dependent children — but in France and the Republic of Ireland it is the household, while in Sweden the incomes of husband and wife are not combined. Furthermore, because of the limitations of the Irish family farm estimates reported above, the Irish estimates are restricted to households in urban areas.

Table 19
Income Distribution in Europe, North America, and Japan; Share in Total Personal Income Before Tax

Country	Year	Top 20%	Bottom 40%
Canada	1965	40·2	20·0
Norway	1963	40·5	16·6
Republic of Ireland	1965-66	42·0	17·5
U.S.A.	1966	44·0	15·0
Sweden	1963	44·0	14·0
U.K.	1964	44·2	15·3
Japan	1962	46·0	14·3
Netherlands	1962	48·4	14·0
West Germany	1964	52·9	15·4
France	1962	53·7	9·5

Source: A.B. Atkinson, *The Economics of Inequality,* Oxford: OUP 1975; estimates for Ireland derived from *Household Budget Inquiry, 1965-66,* Dublin: Stationery Office Prl. 226, 1969.

We can infer that the top 20 per cent of urban households in Ireland appear to command a smaller share of total urban income, even before tax, than the top 20 per cent of income units (urban and rural) in most of the other countries tabulated, while the bottom 40 per cent of Irish urban households appear to fare relatively well, even before tax, in contrast with the bottom 40 per cent of income units elsewhere.

Suggested Reading

Atkinson, A.B., *The Economics of Inequality,* Oxford 1975.

Geary, Patrick T., 'Wages and Prices, Expenditure and Savings and the Distribution of Income and Wealth', Chapter 5 in Gibson, N. J., and Spencer, J. (eds), *Economic Activity in Ireland,* Dublin 1977.

Nolan, Brian, 'The Personal Distribution of Income in the Republic of Ireland', *Journal of the Statistical and Social Inquiry Society of Ireland,* 1977/78.

FOOTNOTES

1. This section draws directly from D. Norton, 'Income Distribution in the Republic of Ireland: A Note', *Social Studies,* Spring 1976. After this chapter had been prepared an excellent paper by Brian Nolan (1978) came to my attention. Nolan's paper, cited as suggested reading, is more up-to-date and more comprehensive than the material reviewed in the present section. Anyone interested in income distribution is urged to refer to it.

2. Figure 89 has been reproduced from A.B. Atkinson, *The Economics of Inequality,* Oxford: Oxford University Press 1975, 46.

3. Atkinson, 47.

4. *Ibid.*

5. Central Statistics Office, *Household Budget Inquiry, 1965-66,* Dublin: Stationery Office, Prl. 266, August 1969, 50-51.

6. Central Statistics Office, *National Income and Expenditure 1969,* London: HMSO, Table 23.

7. J. Gughan, J.F. Heavey, B.C. Hickey, *Farm Management Survey 1966-67,* Dublin: An Foras Talúntais, September 1969.

8. For details see my paper cited in note 1, above.

9. Atkinson, 25.

PART SIX

INTERNATIONAL ECONOMICS: SOME EXTENSIONS

CHAPTER 26

The Gains from International Trade, and International Monetary Systems

The Theory of Comparative Costs

Two of the central questions in the theory of international trade are:
 (i) Do countries gain by international trade?
 (ii) If countries do gain by trade, what determines which goods a country produces and exports, and which goods it imports?

The answers to these questions are analytically the same as those to:
 (i′) Do individuals gain by trade?
 (ii′) If individuals do gain by trade, what determines the production and consumption mix of each individual?

Thus, although we shall be specifically focusing on countries, the analysis which follows is equally applicable to individuals who both produce and consume.

For simplicity we assume that there are only two goods, X and Y. However, the spirit of the analysis can be generalised to the case of any number of goods. Our analysis is in terms of only two countries, A and B; however, these are regarded as merely a microcosm of a world of many countries.

Production, Consumption and Economic Welfare in a Closed Economy

Consider an economy which does not trade with the rest of the world. The production possibility frontier (the transformation frontier) of this economy is the locus TT′ in Figure 91. (Recall Figure 1, Chapter 1). It shows the maximum amount of one good which the economy is capable of producing, given the amount produced of the other good.

We have drawn the production possibility curve as a concave (i.e., bow-shaped) locus, reflecting *an assumption* of diminishing returns in productive transformation. We can 'justify' that assumption as follows: Suppose good Y is food and good X is non-food. It is likely, if the nation tries to become more specialised in non-food, that the production of more non-food will require sacrifice of progressively more food products. That is because some factors of production are relatively *specific* to food production; others are more suited to non-food production. As progressively more non-food is produced, factors of production most suited to food, but not particularly suited to non-food, must be drawn out of food production and allocated to non-food production. In that case the *opportunity cost* of non-food (in terms of food foregone) will be increasing as more non-food is produced; there will be diminishing returns in productive transformation (via reallocation of factors of production) of good Y into good X. Under such circumstances the production possibility or transformation curve will be concave, as drawn.

The slope of the transformation curve is the marginal rate of transformation of Y into X, MRT_{yx}. It is the opportunity cost of X in terms of Y. On the assumption that the economy is operating on TT′ rather than below it, it indicates how much of Y must be foregone per unit increase in the amount of X produced: it measures the marginal cost of X in terms of Y. Thus (ignoring the negative sign of slope)

$$MRT_{yx} = MC_x/MC_y$$

The production opportunities of society are represented by the area bounded by TT′ in Figure 91. How much will the closed economy seek to consume? (Note that, in this closed economy model, a decision on the amounts to produce *is* a decision on the amounts to consume.) The answer depends on society's preferences between Y and X. These are represented by a map of *social indifference curves* in Figure 91.

The indifference curves in Figure 91 are analagous to those of an

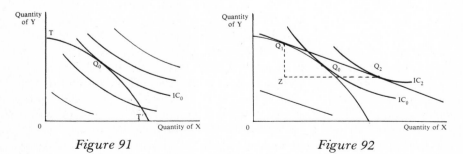

Figure 91   *Figure 92*

individual; except that now they pertain to society. As before, they are drawn strictly convex; also, the higher the indifference curve, the more preferred the position. We assume that the closed economy's objective is to allocate resources in such a manner that, given its production opportunities, it gets to the highest social indifference curve attainable. The economy will therefore produce the combination of Y and X indicated by the point Q_0 in the diagram; social welfare is then being maximised. Thus, for maximisation of social welfare, that combination of goods will be produced so that

$$MRS_{xy} = MRT_{yx}$$

where MRS_{xy} is society's marginal rate of substitution of X for Y and MRT_{yx} is its marginal rate of transformation of Y into X.

Production, Consumption and Economic Welfare in an Open Economy

We now drop the assumption that the economy is closed. What will be produced and what will be consumed then depends on trading opportunities. We assume that the economy can export and import at fixed prices; it is a price-taker. Relative prices, p_x/p_y, are given by the slope of the parallel straight lines in Figure 92.

Will the open economy produce Q_0, as it did in the absence of trading opportunities? The answer is no: to maximise welfare (to get to the highest indifference curve attainable), the economy should produce Q_1, i.e., it should produce that output given by the tangency of a price ratio locus and the transformation frontier. At the optimum point for production

$$MRT_{yx} = (MC_x/MC_y) = p_x/p_y$$

At the given international price ratio, p_x/p_y, the economy, producing Q_1, can consume Q_2; it can get to Q_2 by exporting Q_1Z of Y in exchange for Q_2Z of X. At Q_2, $MRS_{xy} = p_x/p_y$, as in ordinary consumption theory. Note that trade increases the nation's welfare. Without trade the nation could at best attain only the difference level IC_0; after trade it can get to the higher indifference curve IC_2.

In the absence of international trade the economy could not separate its production decision from its consumption decision. But with trade the two decisions are separated. The optimum production point is found first, by equating $MRT_{yx}(= MC_x/MC_y)$ to p_x/p_y. The optimum consumption point, Q_2, is then found by trading, moving down the price ratio line until $MRS_{xy} = p_x/p_y$, Taken together, the optimum production and consumption decisions are represented by

$$MRT_{yx} (= MC_x/MC_y) = p_x/p_y = MRS_{xy}$$

We have not discussed what determines the international price ratio, p_x/p_y. This is determined by supply and demand internationally.[1]

Two Open Economies

We have seen how a country may gain by trade. We now wish to show that the country which we have just considered did not increase its welfare at the expense of the other countries with which it traded. For purposes of illustration we assume that there are only two countries, A and B, but bear in mind that these are only a microcosm of a world of many countries.

The transformation loci in Figures 93a and 93b are such that country A is more suited to the production of Y and country B is more suited to the production of X. In the absence of international trade the two countries would produce Q_a and Q_b. Note that $MRT^A_{yx} \neq MRT^B_{yx}$,

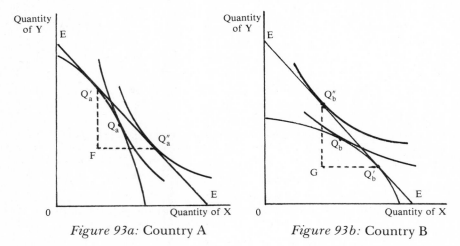

Figure 93a: Country A   *Figure 93b:* Country B

i.e., the comparative or opportunity costs in A differ from those in B. The introduction of trade establishes some price ratio, p_x/p_y, as is represented by the slope of the price ratio locus EE in the two diagrams; since we assume that there is unrestricted free trade between the two countries, and since we ignore transport costs, this is the same for both countries. To maximise its welfare under trade, A produces Q'_a but consumes Q''_a. It exports Q'_aF of Y to B in exchange for $Q_a''F$ of X. Country B produces Q_b' but consumes Q_b''. It exports $Q_b'G$ of X in exchange for $Q_b''G$ of Y. Since both countries move to higher indifference curves after trade, both countries are better off under free trade than under national self-sufficiency.

When will two countries gain from free trade? The answer is that two countries, A and B, can gain from free trade so long as $MRT_{yx}^A \neq MRT_{yx}^B$ before trade. Since $MRT_{yx} = MC_x/MC_y$, we can say that A and B can gain from trade so long as the opportunity costs, or *comparative* cost ratios, in the absence of trade differ between the two countries. Note that *nowhere* in the above exposition did we need to examine *absolute* costs in A or absolute costs in B; it was only the comparative or opportunity-cost ratios, rather than absolute costs, that mattered. For these reasons the theory just outlined is called *the theory of comparative costs*. With the opening of trade both A and B move towards greater specialisation in the good in which they have a comparative advantage. Thus, before trade in the example in Figures 93a and 93b, $(MC_x/MC_y)^A > (MC_x/MC_y)^B$; country A has a comparative advantage in the production of Y and B has a comparative advantage in the production of X. Hence under free trade A moves toward specialisation in Y while B moves towards specialisation in X.

We leave it to the reader to show that if it so happened that $MRT_{yx}^A = MRT_{yx}^B$ in the absence of trade, then the two countries would *not* gain by specialisation and trade between each other.

The Terms of Trade

Gains from international trade accrued to both countries in the above illustration of the theory of comparative costs. However, one country may gain more than the other (though both gain). The division of the gains depends on the terms upon which trade takes place. What are called *the terms of trade* are defined as the amount of domestic goods which must be exported in order to obtain one unit of foreign goods. If (as in Figures 93a and 93b) country B is exporting good X and importing good Y, and if p_x increases while p_y stays constant, then B's terms of trade are said to have improved (but they would have moved unfavourably for country A).

The terms of trade, then, depend on relative prices, p_x/p_y. This price ratio emerging from international trade must lie between MRT_{yx}^A and MRT_{yx}^B in the absence of trade; otherwise one of the countries would not have incentive to engage in international trade. The reader should be able to see that, within the above interval, the closer p_x/p_y

under free trade is to MRT_{yx}^B before trade, and the further p_x/p_y under free trade is from MRT_{yx}^A before trade, the greater the gain from trade accruing to A and the smaller the gain accruing to B.

Generalisation

The theory of comparative costs can be generalised to a world of any number of goods and any number of countries. Thus the theory suggests that free trade is in the interests of all countries, in the sense that total world production can be increased, and that each country can be made better off by improved international allocation of resources, under free trade than under national economic independence. Thus the theory provides a rationale for free-trading areas such as the EEC. It also provides a rationale for the General Agreement on Tariffs and Trade (GATT). Under this agreement, member countries of GATT meet from time to time to negotiate reductions in tariffs. GATT has accelerated the movement towards freer world trade, away from the international protectionism of the 1930s.

Free Trade and Protection

The theory of comparative costs suggests that unrestricted trade is in the interests of the world as a whole because it enables total world production to be higher than it would otherwise be. Hence free trade would make it *possible* for every household in the world to consume more of *all* goods than would be the case if every nation pursued self-sufficiency. However, there are a few cases in which it might be in the interests of an individual country to interfere with the mechanism of free trade:

(i) Suppose that a country faces a price-inelastic demand curve for its exports. For example, we saw in Chapter 7 that it is in Brazil's interests to limit its coffee exports, thereby maximising its foreign exchange receipts. However, we also pointed out in Chapter 7 that *world* production would be higher if production of goods price inelastic on world markets were not restricted. Thus it would be *possible* for other countries as a group to compensate a country exporting a good price inelastic in demand for *not* restricting its exports, and yet for *all* countries to be better off.

(ii) The most common argument in favour of restrictions on international trade is the so-called *infant industry argument* for protection. The argument is that an underdeveloped economy, if exposed to free trade in manufactured goods, could not develop certain industries, the technology of which is subject to increasing returns to scale, unless those industries were given an opportunity to grow under protection; it is argued furthermore that if those industries are given an opportunity to grow in the domestic market under protection, then they will ultimately be able to survive in a free-trade environment. For example, when the Irish Free State introduced tariff protection in the late 1920s, the country was producing few manufactured goods except alcoholic beverages, simply because potential domestic industry could not withstand the competition of established industry in Britain. To give domestic Irish industry a chance to grow, tariffs were required. Many of the industries in Ireland which were given tariff protection in the 1930s have proved themselves viable in the freer trade environment of the EEC in the 1970s. However, a problem with the infant industry argument for (temporary) protection is that many infants do not grow up; for example, some of the industries in Ireland which were developed from the 1930s to the late 1950s under the shield of tariff and quota protection collapsed under freer trade in the 1970s.

(iii) Questions of efficiency in resource allocation aside, there may be social and political reasons for interfering with the free flow of goods in international trade. Considerations of defence are of particular relevance here. For example, a country may seek to protect domestic agriculture (thereby maintaining incomes in agriculture higher than they would otherwise be, and curtailing the outflow of labour from agriculture into the industry or services sectors) just in case food supplies are cut off in times of war.

(iv) Tariffs and quotas may be placed on imports in order to protect the exchange rate at times of balance-of-payments difficulties — recall the discussion towards the end of Chapter 15. However, if tariff or quota protection is required to maintain the exchange rate over sustained periods of time, it may be in the interests of the country in question to remove such protection and allow the domestic currency to float.

International Monetary Systems

International monetary arrangements have changed on several occasions in the twentieth century. Before World War I the principal countries of the world maintained a system of fixed exchange rates with each other by means of the gold standard. That system was abandoned in the 1930s, when exchange rates were largely determined by the market forces of supply and demand. From the post-World-War-II years to 1971, most countries of the world maintained relatively fixed exchange rates with each other under the so-called Bretton Woods System. However, that system broke down in 1973. Since then some countries have been operating under regimes of floating exchange rates; others have sought to maintain fixed exchange rates with the currencies of certain major economies.

The Gold Standard

The gold standard was a fixed exchange rate system. The way in which it operated was quite simple. Each country declared itself willing to exchange its currency for a certain weight in gold. Since each country valued its currency in terms of the common denominator gold, one country's money exchanged at a fixed rate against the money of another country. For example, in 1914 the pound sterling was convertible into $0·257$ standard ounces of gold. The US dollar, on the other hand, was convertible into $0·053$ standard ounces of gold. This meant that the pound was convertible into $4·86$ times more gold than the dollar; thus the exchange rate between the dollar and sterling was $4·86$ dollars for one pound.

The gold standard was self-regulating in the sense that balance-of-payments surpluses or deficits tended to be eliminated automatically by means of international movements in gold stocks and induced changes in domestic money supplies and price levels. Suppose that country A had a balance-of-payments surplus and that country B had a deficit. Since gold was the standard means of international settlement, gold would flow into the surplus country A. The deficit country B, on the other hand, would be making payments of gold to foreigners, so gold would flow out of country B. Under the gold standard the domestic money supply of each country was linked directly to gold; the bulk of the reserves of the banking system consisted of gold. Hence the money supply would expand in the country (A) with the balance-of-payments surplus, and contract in the country (B) with the deficit. From the quantity theory of money we know that prices (and/or real income) in A would rise, while prices (and/or real income) in B would fall. Since exchange rates were fixed, these changes would cause A's imports to increase and its exports to fall, while B's imports would fall and its exports would increase. Thus both countries would automatically move towards balance-of-payments equilibrium.

The gold standard would have worked smoothly so long as prices were perfectly flexible downwards. Suppose a country had a deficit. It would then tend to lose gold; however, if prices were sufficiently flexible in a downwards direction, such losses of gold would soon be arrested via the mechanism described above. However, if prices adjusted slowly, a deficit country might lose all of its gold holdings, in which case it would be knocked off the gold standard. Problems like these arose in the early 1930s, when certain key countries abandoned the gold standard.

The 1930s were years of experimentation. Many countries allowed their currencies to float: others sought to maintain fixed exchange rates with certain key currencies. The world was experiencing the Great Depression in those years. In the hope of protecting employment by increasing exports and reducing imports, many countries introduced or increased tariffs and quotas on imports, subsidised exports, and devalued their currencies. These actions led to retaliation by other countries. A result of the increased restrictions and uncertainty in regard to exchange rates was a collapse in the volume of world trade.

The Bretton Woods System

With a view to averting the international economic chaos experienced in the 1930s, several of the leading nations of the world came together to negotiate at the village of Bretton Woods, New Hampshire, USA, in 1944. The central objective was to design for the post-war world a system of exchange rates which would encourage the free flow of international trade. The agreements reached at Bretton Woods formed the basis of the international monetary system which prevailed until 1971. Under this system countries agreed to maintain fixed exchange rates with each other; however, devaluation (revaluation) would be considered acceptable if at an existing exchange rate a country's balance of payments was in fundamental disequilibrium, i.e., if it showed a persistent tendency to be in deficit (surplus).

Central features of the Bretton Woods system were twofold: (i) US dollars held by central banks were made directly convertible into gold at a fixed price (of $35 an ounce) by the US government. (ii) National currency authorities declared a fixed exchange rate between their own currency and the US dollar. The rates at which national currencies were pegged to the dollar could be changed in the event of fundamental disequilibrium in the balance of payments. In order to maintain exchange rates against the dollar at fixed levels, the central banks of each country had to be willing and able to buy their own currency with foreign exchange (along the lines outlined in Chapter

15). Thus accumulation of foreign exchange reserves was a key factor in enabling each country to maintain its declared fixed exchange rate with the US dollar.

The International Monetary Fund (IMF) was established under the Bretton Wood's agreements. Among its tasks were (i) to ensure that countries maintained fixed exchange rates except at times of fundamental disequilibrium in their balance of payments, and (ii) to make short-term loans of foreign exchange — out of funds subscribed by member nations — to enable the central banks of countries in temporary (rather than fundamental) balance-of-payments difficulties to defend their fixed exchange rates. The IMF still exists today, although the Bretton Woods system has collapsed.

The provision of adequate levels of foreign exchange reserves to iron out short-term fluctuations in international receipts and payments was a central problem of the Bretton Woods system. If exchange rates were free rather than pegged, fluctuations in both current and capital account payments would cause exchange rates to fluctuate. Therefore inventories of foreign exchange were required if exchange rates were to be pegged. However, the rapid growth in international transactions in the post-war years meant that the absolute values of short-run balance of payments surpluses and deficits tended to increase over time. This implied an increase in the demand for foreign exchange reserves. But how were these reserves to be provided?

The keystone of the Bretton Woods system was gold: countries were supposed to maintain fixed exchange rates with the US dollar, which, in turn, was expressed in terms of, and was convertible into, gold. Thus gold was the ultimate means of international settlement, and hence one reserve asset, under the Bretton Woods system. The use of gold as a reserve asset caused two serious problems. First, the world's supply of monetary gold did not expand fast enough to provide adequate reserves to finance rapidly expanding levels of world trade. That was largely because, despite generalised inflation, the dollar price of gold (i.e., the rate at which the dollar was convertible into gold by the US government) was held fixed at $35 an ounce. Secondly, given that the supply of monetary gold did not increase sufficiently fast to ensure adequate levels of international reserves, the only way (in the absence of changes in the Bretton Woods system) in which those reserves could be increased in the face of growing international transactions was by countries the currencies of which were generally acceptable as means of international settlement — mainly the US and the UK — running balance-of-payments deficits; in this way the foreign exchange holdings of the rest of the world were increased. But as the US pumped more reserves into the world economy by running balance-of-payments deficits, it was inevitably destroying the attractiveness of the dollar as a reserve currency. Thus the Bretton Woods system, immediately based on the dollar but actually based on gold, contained the germs of its own destruction. In the earlier years of the system the nations of the world were happy to make and to accept international payments in US dollars because (since the dollar was convertible into gold at $35 an ounce) the dollar was in effect 'as good as gold'. But US deficits, increasing foreign exchange reserves and hence increasing the means of international settlement, inevitably undermined confidence in the dollar: the longer the US deficits continued, the less able was the US to ensure convertibility of the dollar into gold. For this reason the US lost more and more of its gold stocks as the 1960s progressed; doubting the ability of the US authorities to maintain convertibility of the dollar into gold, more net earners of dollars began to demand payment for their dollar holdings in the form of gold.

The desire to provide an additional reserve asset not tied to the currency of any particular country led to the introduction in 1969 of so-called Special Drawing Rights (SDRs) at the IMF. Each member country of the IMF was assigned a quota of SDRs that was dominated in terms of a fixed gold value (hence SDRs were referred to as 'paper gold') which it could use to buy an equivalent amount of foreign exchange from other member countries. SDRs could and have been used to finance balance-of-payments deficits. They have, furthermore, outlived the Bretton Woods system which they were initially designed to assist.

The Collapse of the Bretton Woods System

Gold, US dollars and the pound sterling were the principal reserve assets of the nations of the world under the Bretton Woods system. However, the balance-of-payments deficits of the UK and the USA, which in the short run facilitated the operation of the system by increasing foreign exchange reserves in the world economy, inevitably undermined it. They increased the means for speculation against the pound and the dollar. At first it was the pound that tended to be under pressure. In the 1950s and 1960s holders of sterling had reasons for believing that the UK might not be able to maintain convertibility at a fixed exchange rate between the pound and the currencies of countries such as the US, Switzerland and West Germany. This led to speculative rushes to sell sterling before its anticipated devaluation. However, such speculation only exacerbated the forces making it necessary for the UK to devalue against the dollar. When sterling was forced into devaluation (as in 1949 and in 1967) many countries with strong trading links with the UK also devalued against the dollar.

The other principal reserve currency, the US dollar, was tending to become weaker in the 1960s. In those years the US experienced growing balance-of-payments deficits, partly related to Vietnam War expenditure. People therefore rushed to buy gold because they believed that an inevitable devaluation of the dollar would take the form of a rise in its gold price.

In the late 1960s pressure to buy gold could not be resisted, and the major economies of the world were forced to stop pegging the free market price of gold at $35 an ounce. From 1968 onwards there were two prices of gold. One was the official price at which monetary authorities settled debts between each other by transferring gold. The other was the free market price, determined by the forces of supply and demand independently of intervention by central banks. The free market price quickly rose far above the official US price of $35 an ounce.

Once the free market price of gold was allowed to be determined independently of the official price, speculation in favour of gold against the dollar shifted in favour of those currencies which were clearly undervalued relative to the dollar. The task of central banks to maintain fixed exchange rates in the face of such speculation became more difficult.

The core of the Bretton Woods system came to an end in the autumn of 1971 when the US announced suspension of the convertibility of the dollar into gold. However, speculation against the dollar (in favour of 'strong' currencies such as the German mark) had already become so severe that some countries had already allowed their currencies to appreciate against the dollar by floating upwards. The suspension of convertibility of the dollar into gold accentuated such speculative rushes, in response to which several other countries decided to join Germany and the Netherlands in allowing their exchange rates to float.

The Smithsonian agreements of December 1971 sought to restore the world to fixed exchange rates. Under these agreements the US devalued the dollar by raising its official gold price by 7.9 per cent while at the same time the currencies of some countries which had persistent balance-of-payments surpluses were revalued against the dollar. A regime of fixed exchange rates with a nominal gold base was thereby renewed, but since the free market price of gold remained substantially above the official price, central banks were generally unwilling to use gold to settle debts among themselves. Thus immediately after the Smithsonian agreements the world was on a *de facto* dollar standard. Central banks held some of their reserves in the form of dollars, which were no longer convertible into gold.

The Present International Monetary System

The devaluation of the dollar in December 1971 did not end speculation against that currency. In the first few months of 1973 there were massive speculative flows from the US to Europe and Japan. In February 1973 the US indicated intent to devalue again. This exacerbated speculative flows out of the dollar. The currency chaos of early 1973 led to abandonment of the system of fixed exchange rates. Since then the world has been on a *managed* floating system: although exchange rates have been floating, there has been a good deal of central bank intervention in foreign exchange markets. The principal objectives of such intervention have been to limit the amplitude of exchange rate fluctuation and, in the case of *groups* of countries wanting fixed exchange rates with each other (such as those of 'the Snake'—see below), to maintain approximately fixed exchange rates *within* the groups. Thus central banks still hold reserves in the form of gold, foreign currencies and SDRs, to influence exchange rates.

The Snake, and the Goal of Monetary Union in the EEC

The Bretton Woods system did not quite seek to maintain *precisely* fixed exchange rates; rather, each central bank was expected to maintain the exchange rate of its national currency within a band of ±1 per cent of a fixed rate against the US dollar. However, the Smithsonian agreements widened the band within which each nation's exchange rate could fluctuate to ±2.25 per cent of a fixed rate against the dollar. (Thus the Smithsonian agreements sought to restore the economies of the world to a regime of *approximately* fixed exchange rates.)

By 1970 the member countries of the EEC recognised that further integration of the Community, once the industrial customs union had been achieved and once the Common Agricultural Policy had been initiated, involved progress towards monetary integration of member countries. An ultimate goal of many EEC policiticians was full economic and monetary union by 1980. A report to that effect (the Werner

Report of October 1970) was endorsed by the EEC Council of Ministers in February 1971. Economic and monetary union would imply a supranational central bank, a single EEC currency or *irrevocably* fixed exchange rates between the currencies of EEC member countries, a central fiscal authority and the virtual elimination of national central banks.

In 1972, as a first stage in the evolution toward monetary union, the EEC nations sought to narrow the margins of fluctuation in the exchange rates between member countries: their currencies were to vary against each other by no more than ±1·25 per cent, but the whole Community band could move within the wider band of ±2·25 per cent against the dollar as provided for in the Smithsonian agreements. Those EEC exchange rate arrangements initiated in 1972 were called *the Snake*. In anticipation of their entry to the EEC, the UK, Ireland and Denmark joined the Snake in May 1972; however, speculation against sterling forced the UK to withdraw some weeks later. (Because it then opted to maintain its fixed exchange rate with sterling, Ireland also withdrew from the Snake in the summer of 1972.)

In 1973, when the system of approximately fixed exchange rates against the US dollar was finally abandoned, five of the member countries of the EEC decided to continue the attempt to stabilise their currencies against each other, but to float against the dollar: thus after 1973 the Snake was a *joint float* of some EEC currencies against outside currencies, especially the dollar. The monetary authorities of a number of EEC countries continued to intervene in exchange markets to keep the exchange margins of 'Snake' countries relative to each other within narrow limits. However, the UK stayed outside the amended Snake system and allowed sterling to float against all major currencies. As Ireland remained tied to sterling, we floated in unison with the UK currency against the currencies of the rest of the world.

As an attempt to maintain approximately fixed exchange rates between the currencies of EEC member countries, the Snake was not an unqualified success. As already indicated, UK and Irish membership of the Snake (actually prior to their entry to the EEC) was very brief. France withdrew from the Snake in January 1974 and returned in 1975 but withdrew again in 1976. And Italy was an even more occasional member of the Snake system than was France.

A number of considerations have made it difficult or impossible, and may continue to make it difficult, for the countries of the EEC to maintain (approximately) fixed exchange rates with each other and thereby to progress towards monetary union:

(i) We saw in Chapter 16 that, other things being equal, monetary expansion by the central bank of a small open economy under fixed exchange rates results in losses in that country's foreign exchange reserves. (We also saw that such reserve losses, by their effects on the domestic money supply, tend to offset the initial monetary expansion.) The effect is similar under (nearly) fixed exchange rates if the central bank of a single EEC country increases the domestic money supply more rapidly than that of other EEC countries. Hence for a Snake-type fixed exchange rate system to be viable there must be co-ordination of monetary policies between member countries. In practice there was insufficient co-ordination in the Snake system: some countries sought to expand their money supplies more rapidly than some of their partners in the Snake. The ensuing reserve losses induced speculation against the currencies of the countries pursuing the more expansionary monetary policies; such speculation exacerbated the losses of foreign exchange reserves, thereby leading to decisions to devalue the currencies in question *vis-à-vis* other Snake currencies.

(ii) In the short run, and at given levels of labour productivity, cost-push wage pressure in one EEC country may exceed that in another EEC country with which there is a fixed exchange rate. However (because of free trade and fixed exchange rates), the rate of inflation of tradeable goods would tend to be the same in both countries. Profits, output and employment would therefore tend to fall in the country with the higher cost-push wage pressure. The increased unemployment would in itself tend to abate the cost-push pressure on the real wage. However, such an adjustment mechanism (via unemployment) may be politically unpopular; the country in which money wage rates are increasing most rapidly might seek to get real wages down by wilfully forcing prices up — by devaluation of the domestic currency.

(iii) In the long run under (approximately) fixed exchange rates within a multi-national Community in which both goods and factors of production are mobile, prices of tradeable goods would tend to increase at roughly the same rate in all member countries, and factor prices (especially money wages rates) would also tend to increase at the same rate across member countries. However, suppose that labour productivity is increasing more slowly in one of the countries than in the others. With money wages and prices in the low-productivity growth country increasing at about the same rates as in the high-productivity growth countries, real profit margins in the low-productivity growth country will be falling over time, leading to reductions in output and employment in that country and inducing outflows of the excess supply of labour to the high-productivity growth countries. Such emigration might be politically unpopular in the low-productivity growth country. To avert declining real profit margins and declining employment, the low-productivity growth country might be tempted to maintain its competitiveness by means of a sequence of devaluations. However, the political necessity for such devaluations, which are inconsistent with monetary union, could be averted if countries in the Community were willing to assist in raising productivity growth in member countries which would otherwise lag behind. They could do so by aiding the (otherwise) lagging countries to increase their capital stocks by means of resource transfers to those countries. To some small extent such resource transfers are made in the EEC through the European Regional Fund, which is designed to assist lagging regions (countries) of the Community. (Ireland negotiated resource transfers over and above the very limited amounts provided to it by the European Regional Fund, in arranging for its membership of the European Monetary System in mid-March 1979.)

EMS, 1979

We have seen that the Snake arrangements brought little progress towards monetary union in the EEC. That was largely because individual countries were not willing to pursue policies consistent with the maintenance of (approximately) fixed exchange rates between EEC member countries: rather than handle their macroeconomic problems by way of internal policies, some of them found it politically more palatable to devalue their currency or to let it depreciate in the context of a floating rate against their EEC partners. However, the EEC's second scheme to lock the currencies of member countries, after about nine months of negotiation, finally came into existence in March 1979. This new system, which replaced the Snake arrangements, is called the European Monetary System (EMS). In some respects the EMS is merely a reform of the old Snake; in others it appears to be much more. Partly due to limited information at the time of writing, it is too early to assess the prospects of the EMS in restoring monetary stability to the EEC and in making concrete progress towards monetary union; however, some details are as follows:[2]

Under the EMS, France rejoined the five surviving members of the old Snake (Germany, Belgium, the Netherlands, Luxembourg and Denmark) in a system of nearly-fixed exchange rates (fluctuation limited to ±2·25 per cent of central rates). Ireland finally broke the so-called 'sterling link' — the fixed exchange rate we had kept with the pound sterling — and joined the EMS on the same terms in regard to exchange rate margins as France. A looser arrangement was made for Italy, permitting fluctuation of ±6 per cent around the new central rates fixed between the lira and the other currencies in EMS. But the UK did not join the EMS. Thus no limits on fluctuation were set for the ninth EEC member, though its monetary authorities did promise to maintain 'stable' exchange rates against the eight EMS currencies.

However, the EMS is not just a set of currencies with nearly-fixed exchange rates between them. Each of the eight members of the EMS also has a fixed 'central rate' against a new international currency unit, the European Currency Unit (ECU). The ECU is the old EEC unit of account (recall from Chapter 8) under a new name and with a new role. It is a weighted average of national EEC currency units (including the pound sterling). The ECU is also:

(i) The currency in which international debts and credits between EMS members will be settled. Thus it represents a concrete development towards a common EEC currency. Suppose that the Central Bank of Ireland borrows marks from the Bundesbank to support the púnt on exchange markets. That debt will be expressed in ECUs.

(ii) It is also intended that the ECU will be an international reserve asset. At latest information it is intended that members of the EMS will gain ECUs in return for the 20 per cent of their gold and US dollar reserves which they have agreed to deposit with the European Monetary Co-operation Fund (which might be regarded as the beginnings of an EEC Central Bank).

Along the lines outlined earlier in the context of the Snake, the success of the EMS in launching the EEC towards full monetary union will be contingent on the willingness of the EMS member countries to pursue appropriate policies.

FOOTNOTES

1. For details see Jack Hirshleifer, *Price Theory and Applications,* New Jersey: Prentice Hall 1976, 179-81, upon which the present exposition is based.
2. These are drawn from *The Economist,* 17 March 1979, 74-5.

Index